# WEST'S LAW SCHOOL
# ADVISORY BOARD

# CORPORATE FINANCE

## IN A NUTSHELL

### SECOND EDITION

By

Jeffrey J. Haas
Professor of Law
New York Law School

**WEST**®

A Thomson Reuters business

Mat #40828827

*Nutshell Series, In a Nutshell* and the Nutshell Logo are trademarks registered in the U.S. Patent and Trademark Office.

© 2004 West, a Thomson business
© 2011 Thomson Reuters

    610 Opperman Drive
    St. Paul, MN 55123
    1–800–313–9378

Printed in the United States of America

**ISBN:** 978–0–314–90878–0

*To Samantha and Peter, my amazing
children whom I love dearly!*

# PREFACE

This book is designed for those interested in learning the fundamentals of corporate finance from both a business and legal point of view. In particular, it is targeted towards lawyers without a finance background who find themselves engaged in transactional work. It is also designed to assist law students who are taking a corporate finance, corporations, mergers and acquisitions or related course.

Corporate finance is unique in that it is an amalgam of substantive disciplines. Those with even a tangential familiarity with it are likely aware of the crucial role that mathematics and accounting play. Indeed, it is the math and accounting aspects of a corporate finance course that frequently frighten law students away from taking it. Accordingly, Part I makes a serious attempt to explain these concepts in a straight-forward, plain English manner.

Corporate finance, however, is much more than math and accounting, as Parts II through IV make clear. Under the umbrella of corporate finance falls a whole host of other disciplines. Especially important is economics, particularly macroeconomics. Changes in fiscal and monetary policy at the national level directly impact economic growth and the interest rate environment, while indirectly affecting corporate growth and earnings. Corporations attempt to navigate the economic landscape and the concomitant risk it carries by engaging in various risk reduction strategies, especially the use of derivative instruments.

The law also plays a large role in corporate finance. Securities laws, both Federal and state, regulate, influence and guide companies raising capital through the sale of their common stock, preferred stock and debt securities. Corporate law, particularly Delaware corporate law, also affects the ability of companies to raise capital due to its strong influence on internal corporate governance and control. Finally, the law of mergers and acquisitions plays a significant role as companies increase or decrease their size through mergers, acquisitions and divestitures.

While this book is entitled Corporate Finance, much of what it contains applies to business entities other than corporations. All businesses, regardless of their form, need capital to survive and grow. While the capital structure of these other entities may differ from that of the corporation, the ways in which they pursue and, ultimately, raise capital are similar.

I endeavor to put the most current and accurate information available in this book. Accordingly, I welcome any suggestions or comments that could improve on its contents. Please feel free to contact me with those suggestions or comments.

JEFFREY J. HAAS

New York, New York
E-mail: jeffrey.haas@nyls.edu

# ACKNOWLEDGEMENTS

*Second Edition (2011)*

I received a great deal of support and encouragement from my lovely wife, Alicja, my parents, Mike and Nancy, my brothers, Steve and Greg, and from my colleagues at New York Law School, particularly Rick Matasar, Grace Lee and Cathy Jenkins. Substantive assistance and support were given by Larry Mitchell, Larry Cunningham, Robert Campbell, Brent Friedman and Ron Sarubbi. Lastly, my research assistants—Trina Obi ('11), Kristin Olsen ('11), Jacklyn Swerz ('11), Jon Nowakowski ('10), Armen Khajetoorian ('10), Nick Koumoulis ('10) and Linda Hoffman ('10)—provided dedicated and much appreciated support.

*First Edition (2004)*

Many provided significant assistance in the preparation of this book. I would like to thank my colleagues at New York Law School, in general, and Rick Matasar and Grace Lee, in particular. In addition, a great deal of thanks go to Larry Cunningham, Ron Sarubbi, Brent Friedman, David Dami and Steve Howard for their substantive comments and support. Lastly, I tip my hat to my "cocky and funny" research assistants, Stephen Ginsberg, Sagi Goldberg, Jon Macy, Danny Rehns, Heather Rutman, Rich Rybak, Mariam Sanni and Dimitra Tzortzatos, for their invaluable assistance and dedication.

# ABBREVIATIONS

| | |
|---|---|
| ALI–PCG | American Law Institute's Principles of Corporate Governance: Analysis and Recommendations (1994) |
| Bankruptcy Code | Bankruptcy Reform Act of 1978, as amended |
| CEA | Commodity Exchange Act of 1922, as amended |
| CERCLA | Comprehensive Environmental Response, Compensation, and Liability Act |
| CFTC | Commodity Futures Trading Commission |
| DCF | Discounted Cash Flow (Valuation) Method |
| DDM | Dividend Discount (Valuation) Method |
| DGCL | Delaware General Corporation Law |
| DIP | Debtor-in-possession under the Bankruptcy Code |
| Dodd–Frank | Dodd–Frank Wall Street Reform and Consumer Protection Act of 2010 |
| ECMH | Efficient Capital Market Hypothesis |
| ERISA | Employee Retirement Income Security Act of 1974 |
| Exchange Act | Securities Exchange Act of 1934, as amended |
| Exchange Act Rules | Rules promulgated by the SEC under the Securities Exchange Act of 1934, as amended |
| FINRA | Financial Industry Regulatory Authority |

## ABBREVIATIONS

| | |
|---|---|
| FV | Future Value |
| GAAP | U.S. generally accepted accounting principles |
| IPO | Initial public offering |
| IRC | Internal Revenue Code of 1986, as amended |
| LBO | Leveraged buy-out |
| M&A | Mergers and acquisitions |
| MBO | Management buy-out |
| MDIP | Model Debenture Indenture Provisions of the American Bar Foundation (1971) |
| MNCRD | Model Negotiated Covenants and Related Definitions (2006) |
| NYBCL | New York Business Corporation Law |
| NYSE | New York Stock Exchange |
| OTC | Over-the-counter (market) |
| P&L | Profit and loss (statement) |
| PV | Present value |
| RMBCA | Revised Model Business Corporation Act |
| RMSI | Revised Model Simplified Indenture (2000) |
| SEC | Securities and Exchange Commission |
| Securities Act | Securities Act of 1933, as amended |
| Securities Act Rules | Rules promulgated by the SEC under the Securities Act of 1933, as amended |
| SOX | Sarbanes–Oxley Act of 2002 |
| TIA | Trust Indenture Act of 1939, as amended |
| UCC | Uniform Commercial Code |

# OUTLINE

## PART III. CLAIMANTS ON THE ENTERPRISE

*OUTLINE*

## OUTLINE

# TABLE OF CASES

**References are to Pages**

---

## A

## B

# C

# D

# E

# F

# G

# M

# N

# TABLE OF CASES

# T

# U

# V

# W

# Z

# CORPORATE FINANCE

# IN A NUTSHELL

## SECOND EDITION

# PART I

# VALUING THE GOING–CONCERN

## CHAPTER 1

## DISTINCTIONS BETWEEN PUBLICLY–TRADED AND PRIVATELY–HELD COMPANIES

### § 1. PUBLICLY–TRADED COMPANIES

#### A. Overview

Publicly-traded companies have their securities–most typically shares of common stock–listed and traded on an organized stock exchange. Technically speaking, these companies are required to file periodic reports under the Exchange Act. Thus, they are also referred to as *reporting companies*. See Nutshell Section 1B. Because the reports they file are available to the public, publicly-traded companies are "public" from a disclosure standpoint as well as a trading standpoint.

The first time a company offers and sells common stock to the public is called an *initial public offering* or *IPO*. A company's sales of common stock to the public effected after its IPO are referred to as *secondary* or *follow-on offerings.* Although a company could "go public" through a sale of debt securities or preferred stock, this is rarely done. Doing so would cause the company to become a reporting company under the Exchange Act while not affording the company's founding shareholders the ability to become instantly wealthy (as is often the case with a common stock IPO). Indeed, shares in a common stock IPO are frequently underpriced when offered to the public, and thus when the shares begin to trade they "pop up" in price.

Public offerings of securities are heavily regulated in order to protect investors. The Securities Act requires each prospective issuer to register its offering on a prescribed *registration statement* filed with the Securities and Exchange Commission (SEC). The registration statement consists of two parts. The first part, called the *prospectus,* is the disclosure document that the issuer and those underwriting the offering use as a selling brochure. The second part, referred to as *information not required in the prospectus,* sets forth additional information that an issuer must file with the SEC but need not send to prospective investors. Those investors, however, may still access this information. Complete registration statements are available at the Electronic Data Gathering and Retrieval (EDGAR) section of the SEC's website located at www.sec.gov.

SEC scrutiny of a given registration statement depends on the type of offering involved as well as the issuer. For example, the SEC will review very carefully the registration statement of a company conducting a common stock IPO, while it generally will not review a follow-on offering by a Fortune 500 company. During the IPO registration process, which can take several months to complete, the SEC will provide detailed written comments on the issuer's registration statement. The issuer must address these comments to the SEC's satisfaction before the SEC will declare that issuer's registration statement *effective*. Upon receiving an order of effectiveness, that issuer may consummate sales of its securities to the public.

In order to help place its stock with investors, an issuer typically hires one or more *underwriters*. Underwriters are normally investment banks with the expertise necessary to place the issuer's stock into the hands of public investors. In other words, underwriters are an outsourced sales force that the issuer hires to get the offering sold. In return for their services, underwriters receive a commission, typically seven percent of the per share public offering price for IPOs of common stock.

Not only must a company register its securities under the Securities Act prior to sale, it also must register the *class of security* being offered under the Exchange Act (on either Form 10 or 8–A) and secure listing privileges with an organized stock exchange. A company will register under the Exchange Act and secure listing privileges while the SEC is reviewing the company's Securities Act registration statement. After the company "goes public" through the sale of shares of its stock to initial investors, those shares may be bought and sold by other investors over the organized stock exchange on which those shares are listed in the *secondary market*.

Upon registering its securities under the Exchange Act, a company must make and keep books and records which, in reasonable detail, accurately and fairly reflect the transactions and dispositions of the assets of that company. See Exchange Act § 13(b). Moreover, that company must "devise and maintain a system of internal accounting controls sufficient to provide reasonable assurances" that, among other things, its financial statements are prepared in conformity with generally accepted accounting principles (GAAP).

## B. Exchange Act Reporting Requirements

In order to level the playing field between buyers and sellers of securities in the secondary market, the Exchange Act requires each reporting company to file certain prescribed periodic reports with the SEC. Because those reports are public documents, they provide important information about the company to the marketplace.

Section 13(a) of the Exchange Act requires each reporting company to file with the SEC such information and documents as the SEC may prescribe "as necessary or appropriate for the proper protection of investors and to ensure fair dealing" in that company's securities. This includes "such annual reports, certified ... by independent public accountants, and such quarterly reports" as the SEC may prescribe. Duplicate copies of those reports must also be filed with each securities exchange on which the company's securities are listed.

Exchange Act Rule 13a–1 requires the filing of an annual report on Form 10–K. Within Form 10–K, a reporting company must, among other things:

- Discuss its business, properties, and material legal proceedings it has brought, and those brought against it;
- Set forth its financial highlights as well as its complete audited financial statements;
- Provide, from management's perspective, a thorough description of its financial condition and results of operations (referred to as *Management's Discussion & Analysis* or *MD&A*);
- Provide a report of the company's audit committee detailing information about the committee members and how they came to recommend to the company's board that the audited financial statements be included in the company's Form 10–K;
- Provide extensive information about directors, management and executive compensation if that information is not incorporated by reference from the company's definitive proxy materials;

- Provide quantitative and qualitative disclosure about its financial instruments that are sensitive to market risk (*i.e.,* derivatives);

- Disclose any disagreements with accountants and changes in accounting methods and financial disclosure;

- Disclose conclusions of the company's principal executive and principal financial officer regarding the effectiveness of the company's disclosure controls and procedures; and

- Provide a report of management on the company's internal control over financial reporting.

Exchange Act Rule 13a–13 requires a reporting company to file a quarterly report on Form 10–Q for each of the first three quarters of its fiscal year. Because the SEC allows a reporting company to include in its Form 10–K both quarterly information for its last fiscal quarter and annual information, most reporting companies do not file a separate Form 10–Q for their last fiscal quarter. Form 10–Q provides the market with a quarterly update on the financial and other affairs of a given reporting company. Within Form 10–Q, a reporting company must provide financial information for the current quarter just ended and for the same quarter for the previous fiscal year. However, that information need not be audited and rarely is due to the expense and drain on management time that an audit entails.

SOX, signed into law in 2002, requires that certifications from a company's principal executive officer and principal financial officer be included in the company's Form 10–K and 10–Q reports. Among other things, each of these executives must certify that he or she has reviewed the report in question. Then, based on his or her knowledge, each must certify that the report does not contain any untrue statement of a material fact or omit to state a material fact necessary in order to make the statements made, in light of the circumstances under which they were made, not misleading. Moreover, each of these executives must certify that, based on his or her knowledge and on the other financial information included in the report, the financial statements included in the report fairly present in all material respects the financial condition and results of operations of the company as of, and for, the time periods presented in the report. See SOX Section 302.

Exchange Act Rule 13a–11 requires reporting companies to file "current reports" on Form 8–K. That form provides the market with timely information about important events that may occur between quarterly reports; hence the name "current report." Disclosable events include, among others:

- A change in control of the company;
- The acquisition or disposition of a significant amount of assets (including financial statements for an acquired business);

- Bankruptcy or receivership;
- A change in the company's certified accountant;
- The resignation of one or more of the company's directors;
- A change in the company's fiscal year;
- Information the company elects to disclose pursuant to Regulation Fair Disclosure (Regulation FD);
- Amendments to the company's code of ethics or any waiver of a provision of that code; and
- Any other event not otherwise called for by Form 8–K but which the company at its option wishes to disclose.

Section 16(a) of the Exchange Act requires every person who is directly or indirectly the beneficial owner of more than 10% of any class of any registered equity security, or who is a director or an officer of the issuer of such security, to file with the SEC a statement of the amount of all equity securities of the issuer in question of which she is a beneficial owner. In addition, those persons must file a statement detailing a change in their ownership. Because of their reporting obligations under the Exchange Act, these individuals are referred to as *reporting persons*.

Under Section 16(a), a reporting person must file her initial statement of beneficial ownership on Form 3 within 10 days after the event that resulted in her becoming a reporting person. She must file

Form 4 to report changes in her beneficial ownership before the end of the second business day
following the day on which she executed a transaction resulting in a change in her beneficial ownership. She must file an annual statement on Form 5
on or before the 45th day after the end of the
issuer's fiscal year. Form 5 must include her total
beneficial ownership of the issuer's securities as of
the end of the issuer's fiscal year and certain transactions impacting on her beneficial ownership if not
previously reported.

## C.  Pros and Cons of "Going Public"

"Going public"—selling securities to the public
through an IPO—is not for every company. Certainly, substantial benefits result from going public.
However, serious drawbacks exist as well.

### (1) Pros

Among the benefits of "going public" are the
following:

*Lower Cost of Capital.* When equity markets are
strong, the cost of capital raised through a public
offering is typically lower—often substantially lower—than the cost of capital raised in the private
market (*e.g.,* venture capital firms, private equity
firms, etc.).

*Liquidity.* By going public and listing its securities on an organized stock exchange, a company
creates a liquid, secondary trading market for its

stock. Secondary market trading establishes a market value for the company's shares. A market-determined per share trading price is needed to set exercise prices under employee stock option or stock purchase plans, as it is an "objective" criterion with which to measure managerial performance.

*Exit Strategy.* By going public, a company gives its existing stockholders (many of whom are company founders) an avenue to "cash out," *i.e.,* turn their illiquid stock into cold hard cash. Resales of their stock, however, are subject to the holding period and other requirements of Securities Act Rule 144. Their stock also is often subject to lockup agreements with underwriters which prohibit resales typically for a six-month period following the IPO. Most investment banks underwriting an IPO insist that founding stockholders, directors and other key pre-IPO stockholders sign lockup agreements, because having these individuals selling shares shortly after an IPO is completed could undermine investor confidence in the company.

*Acquisition Currency.* By going public, a company can facilitate acquisitions of other companies by using its stock (either in a stock-for-stock deal or stock-for-assets deal). Management of a given target company feels more comfortable from a valuation perspective knowing the price at which the acquiror's stock is currently trading in the secondary market.

*Control.* The placement of shares in the hands of a large number of public stockholders, each of whom owns a relatively small number, is likely to permit current management to continue to control the company. In a private financing, by contrast, a company very often has to transfer a certain degree of control to private investors. For example, as part of a private deal, the issuer may have to yield one or more board of directors seats to the private investors or risk losing their investment.

*Prestige.* A company typically increases its exposure and prestige by going public. This may help the company in its business dealings with others. The act of going public can also serve as a marketing event for a company, thus creating additional interest in the company and its products or services.

### (2) Cons

Among the disadvantages of going public are the following:

*Commitment of Management's Time.* Preparing a Securities Act registration statement and the process of going public is terribly time consuming and absorbs significant blocks of senior management time—time it could spend running the company. It often takes anywhere from three to six months (or even longer) from the time a company first begins preparing a registration statement to the date on which the SEC declares that registration statement effective.

*Cost.* Going public is expensive. Typical costs range from $300,000 to $800,000, exclusive of underwriting commissions. These commissions, in turn, typically soak up seven percent of the gross proceeds of a common stock offering. Of course, if the public offering fails, the company never recoups the money it spent on the offering.

*Living in a "Glass House."* By going public, a company becomes a reporting company under the Exchange Act. This means the company must satisfy continuous and formal reporting requirements. Doing so is both time consuming and expensive. Moreover, the information the company discloses is open to the public, in general, and to that company's *competitors*, in particular.

*Hostile Takeovers.* Going public could open the company up to a hostile takeover attempt. If a hostile party acquires enough shares in the company through a hostile tender offer, it can oust existing senior management completely.

*Reduced Communication with Stockholders.* Once a company is public, its management cannot communicate as easily with the company's stockholders as it did when the company was privately-held. Indeed, reporting companies must adhere to the proxy rules of the Exchange Act. See Nutshell Section 56.

*Focus on Short–Term Results.* Because direct contact between management of a public company and its stockholders is limited at best, stockholder perceptions of managerial performance tend to be based on day-to-day stock price movements and published financial results, especially quarterly or annual earnings. This puts tremendous pressure on management to focus on short-term results, often to the detriment of creating long-term shareholder value. This pressure boiled over during the accounting scandals of the early 2000s, as several prominent public companies (*e.g.,* Enron, Tyco and Worldcom) were forced to restate their earnings downward before ultimately imploding due to overly aggressive accounting practices designed to show impressive earnings growth.

*SOX and the Potential for Liability.* Public companies have additional reporting and procedural obligations since the passage of SOX, many of which are costly for a company to comply with. These include, among others, requirements relating to internal control systems over financial reporting. SOX also creates some restraints on corporate governance, in that the CEO and CFO have to certify financial statements, disclose all known control deficiencies, and disclose acts of fraud. In addition, SOX requires disclosure as to whether at least one member of the company's audit committee is a "financial expert" as defined by the SEC. CEO and CFO certifications could, under certain circumstances, expose these officers to personal liability. See SOX Section 302.

*Negative Publicity.* If a public company's stock performs poorly after the company goes public, the IPO will have created negative publicity instead of positive.

## § 2.  PRIVATELY–HELD COMPANIES

### A.  Generally

All companies that are not reporting companies under the Exchange Act are, by definition, *privately-held companies*. Privately-held companies have not issued securities to the public through an IPO. Unlike publicly-traded companies, privately-held companies do not have a liquid, secondary trading market for their shares. Thus, no readily available market price exists for their shares.

Financial and other information for these companies is proprietary and cannot be viewed unless the party requesting the information has enough leverage to demand it. For example, a commercial bank contemplating loaning money to a privately-held company will insist on seeing that company's financial statements. If the company refuses, the bank simply will not make the loan.

Chart 1 below highlights some of the major differences between publicly-traded and privately-held companies.

## Chart 1
## Major Distinctions between Publicly-traded and Privately-held Companies

|  | **Public Company** | **Private Company** |
|---|---|---|
| **Capital raising** | Shares sold to public through an IPO registered with the SEC pursuant to the Securities Act | Shares sold privately through one or more exemptions to registration under the Securities Act |
| **Management & control** | Separation between ownership and control exists, as most shares are held by investors who are not directors and officers | Unity of ownership and control, as shareholders are often directors and officers as well |
| **Transferability of shares** | A liquid, secondary trading market generally exists, allowing shareholders to sell over a stock exchange through brokerage transactions | Lack of a liquid, secondary trading market; moreover, share transfers are often contractually restricted by a shareholders' agreement |
| **Transparency** | As a "reporting company" under the Exchange Act, corp must file periodic reports (*e.g.,* 10–Ks, 10–Qs, proxy statements, etc.) with the SEC which provide detailed information about the corp to the public | Corporate information is proprietary and will only be released if the corp consents |

## B.  Closely–Held Companies

### (1)  Characteristics

A very large subset of privately-held companies consists of *closely-held companies*. Closely-held companies share four key attributes. First, they have a limited number of stockholders, most of whom are individuals. Each stockholder generally had some preexisting relationship with the other stockholders prior to making her investment in the company. Indeed, stockholders may be members of the same family or close personal friends. Second, these companies are generally run by managers who are also stockholders. These stockholder-managers typically receive compensation from their companies in the form of salaries and other perquisites, rather than through the receipt of cash dividends. Third, no secondary trading market exists for shares of closely-held companies. Thus, stockholders have a difficult time cashing out of their investments. Lastly, formal (*i.e.,* contractual) restrictions typically influence their corporate governance and their stockholders' ability to transfer shares to third parties.

Because of these attributes, a closely-held company bears a striking resemblance to a partnership. In fact, these attributes, coupled with the existence in many cases of a shareholders' agreement (see Nutshell Section 2B(2)), have led commentators to refer to closely-held companies as "incorporated partnerships."

Courts and legislatures have picked up on this theme. The Massachusetts Supreme Judicial Court in *Donahue v. Rodd Electrotype Co.*, 328 N.E.2d 505 (Mass.1975), for example, stated that the relationship between stockholders in a closely-held company "must be one of trust, confidence and absolute loyalty if the enterprise is to succeed." The legal relationship between partners of a partnership is the same. See *Meinhard v. Salmon*, 164 N.E. 545 (N.Y.1928).

The legislatures of some states (*e.g.*, California and Delaware) permit a business to incorporate as a so-called "*statutory close corporation.*" A statutory close corporation is subject to special statutory governance provisions that allow it to be governed more along the lines of a partnership than a traditional corporation. See, e.g., DGCL §§ 341–356. For example, DGCL Section 351 provides that a close company's certificate of incorporation may provide that the company's business shall be managed by the stockholders rather than by a board of directors. This resembles a partnership being run by the partners.

### (2) Control and Voting

In order to address the issues peculiar to closely-held companies, it is customary for properly counseled prospective stockholders to enter into a *buy-sell* or *shareholders' agreement* at the time they make their investments. Contingencies covered by this agreement include, among others, stockholder voting and corporate governance, the alienation or transfer of stock and the valuation of stock.

A given shareholders' agreement usually contains provisions affecting the ability of stockholders to vote their shares freely. These provisions alter the traditional "majority voting" rules by requiring supermajority or even unanimous stockholder consent to certain fundamental transactions, such as a sale of all or substantially all the assets of the company or a merger. They may also provide that certain stockholders are entitled to designate one or more directors to the board. In order for this to happen, the other stockholders contractually agree to vote their shares in favor of the nominees of the stockholders with that right of designation.

Several ways exist to ensure that stockholder voting occurs according to plan. First, the shareholders' agreement can double as a *voting agreement*. Stockholders may legally enter into stockholder voting agreements. See, e.g., DGCL § 218(c) and NYBCL § 620(a). Most shareholder agreements call for a remedy of *specific performance* in the event a given stockholder does not vote in accordance with the agreement. Importantly, the voting rights of stock governed by a shareholders' agreement are not separated from the other attributes of share ownership. This is an important distinction between a shareholders' agreement and a voting trust (discussed below).

In the absence of a shareholders' agreement that covers voting, voting can be influenced through the use of irrevocable proxies and voting trusts. A stockholder who executes an *irrevocable proxy* grants the right to vote his shares to a third party for the time period stated therein or otherwise as provided by statute. See, e.g., DGCL § 212(e) and NYBCL § 609(f). The third party, rather than the stockholder, is entitled to vote the shares as she sees fit. For a proxy to be irrevocable, it must state on its face that it is irrevocable and essentially be "coupled with an interest." Typically, that "interest" is an interest in the shares themselves. Thus, a bank that receives shares as security for a loan typically receives an irrevocable proxy to vote those shares as the bank sees fit until the loan is repaid. The bank "has an interest" in the shares because it is the "pledgee" of those shares and will own them if the borrower defaults on the loan.

Under Section 212(e) of the DGCL, that "interest" could also be an interest in the corporation generally. For example, in *Haft v. Haft*, 671 A.2d 413 (Del.Ch.1995), the Delaware Chancery Court acknowledged that Herbert Haft's "senior executive officer" position with the Dart Group Corp. constituted a sufficient "interest" in the company. Thus, the irrevocable proxy that his son Ronald gave him was, indeed, "irrevocable" under Section 212(e) of the DGCL.

A final device designed to control voting actually separates voting rights from the rest of the rights of stock ownership. This device is known as a *voting trust*. Here, shares are deposited into a trust. The trust is the "record" owner of the shares and thus is entitled to vote all the shares through its trustee. The beneficiary of the trust, however, retains the right to receive dividends. Voting trusts, like shareholders' agreements, allow voting control to be allocated in a manner other than pro rata. They are also used to preserve the voting solidarity of a group of stockholders. Agreements evidencing voting trusts must be filed with the corporation. See, e.g., DGCL § 218(a) and NYBCL § 621(a).

### (3) Stock Ownership and Transfer

Because stockholders of closely-held companies desire to be in business together, shareholders' agreements often contain provisions that prevent shares from falling into the hands of strangers. These provisions include forced resale provisions and transferability restrictions.

### a. Forced Resale Provisions

A forced resale provision contained in a shareholders' agreement prevents shares from falling into the "wrong hands." Upon the occurrence of one or more specified events, the stockholder in question (or her estate) is forced to sell her shares back to the company. Thus, in the context of a forced resale, the stockholder must sell her shares back to the company even if she (or her estate) wants to continue holding them.

Typical events that trigger forced resales include:

- *Termination of employment.* The stockholder in question is allowed to retain her shares so long as she remains an employee of the company. Once she leaves (either voluntarily or involuntarily), she must sell her shares back to the company.

- *Death of a stockholder.* The estate of a deceased stockholder must sell the decedent's shares back to the company. Often, the company receives the funds necessary to repurchase the shares from the proceeds of a life insurance policy that the company took out on the decedent.

The biggest issue arising in forced resales is the price per share the company will pay. Most shareholders' agreements set forth a pricing formula to avoid disputes over price when the forced resale provision is triggered. The formula may call for a price based on the company's book value, going-concern value or appraisal value. Each of these methods has its pros and cons. Seldom are both parties pleased with the valuation derived from the application of the formula in question. However, courts are generally willing to enforce pricing provisions contained in shareholders' agreements. See Nutshell Section 24.

### b. Restrictions on Transferability

In order to control the identity of those who own shares, most shareholders' agreements severely restrict the ability of a stockholder to transfer her shares to a third party. As discussed below, these contractual restrictions are subject to certain legal exceptions. In most cases, however, courts will enforce them. A given shareholders' agreement may include one or more of the following four transfer restrictions.

The first type of restriction is a *right of first refusal*. If a stockholder receives an offer from a third party to buy her shares, she must first offer her shares for sale to the company, other existing stockholders or both on substantially the same terms (including, without limitation, the exact same price) as the third party is offering. If the offerees decline her offer, or the offer simply lapses, the stockholder can then sell her shares to the third party. The offerees may decline the offer for many reasons, including being comfortable with the third party proposing to buy the shares, or a lack of financing necessary to buy the shares. Section 202(c)(1) of the DGCL specifically authorizes the use of rights of first refusal.

The second type of restriction is a *right of first offer*. If a stockholder desires to sell her shares, she must first offer them for sale to the company, other existing stockholders or both on terms previously agreed upon and set forth in the shareholders' agreement. Only if the offerees reject that offer, or the offer simply lapses, may the stockholder thereafter offer her shares for sale to a third party. Importantly, right of first offer provisions typically contain a pricing formula for determining the price that the offerees must pay. That formula often generates a price below fair market value, much to the chagrin of the selling stockholder.

Very often a shareholders' agreement will contain both a right of first offer provision and a right of first refusal provision. Thus, a stockholder seeking to sell her shares must first offer to sell her shares to the offerees on the terms set forth in the shareholders' agreement. If the offerees decline the offer, or the offer simply lapses, the stockholder can then solicit offers for her shares from third parties. However, if a third party makes an offer, the stockholder must then *reoffer* the shares to the offerees, but this time on substantially the same terms that the third party has offered. Only if the offerees decline to buy the shares for a second time (or the offer lapses) can the stockholder actually sell her shares to the third party. Thus, in this case the offerees receive two bites of the apple.

A third type of transfer restriction is a *consent restraint*. A consent restraint prohibits a stockholder from transferring her shares unless she first obtains the permission of the company's board of directors or other existing stockholders. Section 202(c)(3) of the DGCL specifically authorizes the use of consent restraints.

As a policy matter, consent restraints could be seen as placing an unreasonable restraint on the free transferability of personal property. A court, therefore, could strike down a consent restraint if it is not carefully drafted. For example, in *Rafe v. Hindin*, 29 A.D.2d 481 (N.Y.App.Div.1968), the Appellate Division of the New York Supreme Court held that a consent restraint is valid so long as it cannot be exercised unreasonably. Thus, the language of most consent restraints reads along the following lines: "A shareholder may not transfer his shares to a third party unless the Company grants its consent to the transfer, *which consent may not be unreasonably withheld*."

By contrast, in *Quinn v. Stuart Lakes Club, Inc.*, 443 N.E.2d 945 (N.Y.1982), an incorporated club's by-laws provided that when any member ceased to be a member of the club, whether by death, resignation or otherwise, his stock would be considered void and cancelled. The New York Court of Appeals struck down this provision holding that it was void as an absolute restraint on the power of alienation violative of the public policy of New York. However, the Court indicated that while an heir of a deceased member could inherit that member's shares, the heir would be subject to all of the valid by-law provisions relating to the shares.

The final type of transfer restriction is a *group restriction*. Pursuant to it, a stockholder can freely transfer her shares, but only to designated persons or classes of persons (*e.g.,* family members). Under Section 202(c)(5) of the DGCL, group transfer restrictions are legal so long as the group designation is not "manifestly unreasonable."

In certain instances, a court will not uphold a transfer restriction. Despite a shareholders' agreement to the contrary, transfer restrictions are generally inapplicable to transfers made by operation of law. Such would be the case when shares are transferred from one former spouse to the other former spouse as part of a divorce decree.

Transfer restrictions also are ineffective against third party buyers unless the certificate representing the shares in question contains a conspicuous legend. That legend typically states that the transfer of the shares is subject to the restrictions contained in a shareholders' or other agreement. A person buying shares represented by an unlegended certificate acquires the shares free of all transferability restrictions unless the person otherwise had actual knowledge of those restrictions. See DGCL § 202(a) and UCC § 8–204.

The case of *F.B.I. Farms, Inc. v. Moore*, 798 N.E.2d 440 (Ind.2003), is illustrative of the issues implicated by transfer restrictions. Members of the Burger family had transferred their farms and related machinery to a newly-formed corporation in exchange for common stock in that corporation. At that time, Linda Burger was married to an outsider–Birchell Moore. As part of the transaction, Linda and Birchell received about 14% of the corporation's stock in exchange for their farm and equipment. When Linda's marriage to Birchell fell apart, the divorce decree awarded Linda all the shares the couple held in the corporation, while Birchell received a monetary judgment against Linda in the amount of $155,889. This judgment was secured by a lien on Linda's shares.

When Birchell's monetary award went unpaid, he sought and obtained a writ of execution of his lien. Thereafter, a sheriff's sale of Linda's shares was held, and Birchell himself purchased all the shares for $290,450. The corporation, however, refused to transfer Linda's shares to Birchell because it believed that numerous transfer restrictions relating to those shares would be violated.

The transfer restrictions in question, oddly found in the minutes of a board meeting rather than in the corporate by-laws or a shareholders' agreement, were fourfold. First, there was a *consent restraint*, whereby stock of the corporation could not be transferred "unless or until approved by the directors...." Second, there was a *right of first offer in the corporation*, whereby if any stock was to be offered for sale, assigned and/or transferred, the corporation "should have the first opportunity of purchasing the same at no more than the book value thereof." Third, there was a *right of first offer in the other stockholders*, whereby if the corporation did not exercise its rights under the right of first offer, "any stockholder of record should be given the next opportunity to purchase said stock, at a price not to exceed the book value thereof." Lastly, there was a *group transfer restriction*, whereby if the corporation or the other stockholders were not interested in buying the shares in question, "then the same could be sold to any blood member of the family ... at not more than the book value thereof."

In analyzing the case, the Indiana Supreme Court highlighted that transfer restrictions were permissible under the Indiana corporate code. Indiana's statutory provision on point recognizes the necessity of notice concerning the existence of transfer restrictions, requiring that their existence be noted conspicuously on the front or back of a stock certificate or in an information statement sent to a prospective stockholder. Otherwise, they are not en-

forceable against a person without knowledge of
them. The provision further recognizes situations
where transfer restrictions make perfect sense.
Thus, the provision allows a restriction designed
"to maintain [a] Corporation's status when [that
status] is dependent on the *number or identity* of its
shareholders." Such would be the case where a
corporation is receiving favorable "flow through tax
treatment" under Subchapter S of the IRC, a treatment contingent on a corporation having 100 or
fewer stockholders all of whom are generally U.S.
citizens or resident aliens. The provision also allows
for a transfer restriction designed "to preserve exemptions under federal or state securities law."
This is designed to ensure that a corporation can
properly take advantage of the private placement
transactional exemption to securities registration
under the Securities Act, an exemption not available if the corporation's shares are offered and sold
in a public manner. Lastly, the provision recognizes
that transfer restrictions can be imposed "for any
other reasonable purpose."

Despite the explicit statutory authority for transfer restrictions, the Court highlighted the tension
between the *desire to transfer shares* and the *need
to restrict* such transfers. Because corporate shares
are *personal property*, any restrictions on alienation
are generally disfavored. However, according to the
Court, owners of corporations have an understandable desire to control their ownership and management and prevent outsiders from infiltrating their
corporate operations. Accordingly, while transfer re-

strictions are permissible, the Court held that they are to be *narrowly construed* so as to not overly impede a person's right to alienate his or her personal property.

The Court then analyzed the four transfer restrictions contained in the minutes of the directors' meeting. In terms of the right of first offer held first by the corporation and then by the other stockholders, the corporation argued that neither Linda nor Birchell offered it or the other stockholders the opportunity to buy Linda's shares. The Court, however, disagreed, finding that the corporation and the other stockholders had effectively waived their rights in this context because they all were well aware of the sheriff's sale and did nothing to assert their right of first offer. In terms of the consent restraint, the Court disagreed with the lower court which had found the restraint unreasonable in light of the lengthy and difficult history of the parties. Instead, the Court held that under basic contract law principles, the reasonableness of a transfer restriction is measured at the time of its adoption. Clearly, all stockholders voluntarily agreed to the consent restraint at the time it was adopted as it would prevent undesirable individuals from becoming stockholders of the corporation in the future. Finally, the Court analyzed the group transfer restriction, finding that this "blood member" restriction was reasonable when adopted and thus enforceable because it protects the family's interest in maintaining ownership and operation of the corporation in the hands of only family members.

Despite upholding the validity of all four transfer restrictions as a general matter, the Court went on to analyze their applicability to involuntary transfers such as the one involved in the case. Here, the Court held that the restrictions were inapplicable. Indeed, in truly *involuntary* transfer situations, such as ones involving creditors and divorcés, transfer restrictions would lead to transferees without *any recourse whatsoever*, and thus are inapplicable. However, the Court further held that someone, such as Birchell, who acquires shares through an involuntary transfer cannot acquire greater property rights than those possessed by the transferor. Thus, the four transfer restrictions would apply to any *subsequent transfers* that Birchell attempted to make in the future.

### c. Valuation by Agreement

Please refer to Nutshell Chapter 24.

# CHAPTER 2

# WORKING WITH FINANCIAL STATEMENTS

## § 3.  INTRODUCTION

A company's financial statements consist of: (1) the balance sheet; (2) the profit and loss statement; (3) the statement of changes in shareholders' equity; and (4) the statement of cash flows. These statements quantify the company's history in monetary terms. They provide information that is useful in making investment and credit decisions and in assessing cash flow potential. Indeed, they are the primary means through which financial information is communicated to potential and current investors, creditors and regulators.

A series of footnotes are presented to help explain the items included in a company's financial statements. Among other things, these footnotes usually include: (1) a description of the company's accounting policies and the methods used in measuring the items reported in the balance sheet; (2) explanations of uncertainties and contingencies; (3) statistics that are too voluminous to include in the main body of the financial statements; and (4) disclosures regarding the substance of certain transactions (*e.g.,* related party transactions, mergers, acquisitions, and long-term contractual commitments). Because the "devil is in the details," investors should carefully review footnote disclosures before deciding to invest.

One of the most important disclosures found in the footnotes is a discussion of how a company accounts for its investments in other companies. If the investment is relatively small, the investee (*i.e.*, the company whose stock is acquired) may continue to operate as an independent entity. Thus, the investing company need only recognize the "fair value" of its investment on its balance sheet. If the investee is a public company, the investment's fair value is based on the trading price of the investee's stock in the secondary market.

Often, the investing company purchases a significant portion of the investee's outstanding shares. This allows it to exercise *significant influence* over the investee's operating and financial policies. Significant influence is exercised when a company owns 20% or more of an investee's outstanding common shares. Even when less than 20% is owned, an investing company may nevertheless be deemed to have significant influence as a result of non-quantitative factors. These include, among others, representation on the investee's board of directors, participation in the investee's policy-making process, and significant intercompany transactions.

In instances of significant influence, the investing company is required to account for its investment using the *equity method*. Thus, the amount listed on the investing company's balance sheet as the investment in the investee (the "equity method investment" line item) is adjusted as follows: (1) it is increased or decreased by the investing company's *proportionate share* of the investee's earnings (losses); and (2) it is decreased by any dividends paid out to the investing company by the investee.

When an investing company acquires a voting interest of more than 50% (a "controlling interest") in the investee, the investing company is referred to as the *parent* and the investee as the *subsidiary*. Under these circumstances, the parent usually prepares "consolidated financial statements" rather than preparing separate financial statements for the parent and the subsidiary.

Consolidated financial statements treat both the parent and the subsidiary as a single economic entity. The investment in the subsidiary is usually accounted for on the parent's books using the "equity method" discussed above. If the parent owns less than 100% of the subsidiary's outstanding stock, the parent must recognize its proportionate share of the subsidiary's revenues and expenses. Yet, when a parent consolidates a "wholly-owned" subsidiary (where the parent owns all of the subsidiary's outstanding common stock), no need exists to prorate the parent's share of the subsidiary's earnings, because the parent (as sole stockholder) is entitled to all the subsidiary's earnings. Furthermore, when consolidated financial statements are presented, a subsidiary's assets and liabilities are rolled up into the parent's balance sheet.

Transactions involving variable interest entities (VIEs) are increasingly common. VIEs generally serve only the transactions for which they were created. Special rules apply because the voting interest approach is not effective in identifying controlling financial interests in entities that are not controllable through voting interests or in which the equity investors do not bear the residual economic risks. Instead, a "risk-and-reward" model applies. An enterprise involved in a VIE needs to assess whether it is the primary beneficiary in the VIE in order to determine whether to consolidate the VIE. A primary beneficiary absorbs more than half of the VIE's expected losses or expected gains, or both, as a result of its relationship with the VIE. See Financial Accounting Standards Board (FASB) Interpretation 46(R), Variable–Interest Entities.

## § 4. ACCOUNTANTS AND THE AUDIT FUNCTION

### A. Oversight Generally

The accounting profession has adopted a common set of standards and procedures for the preparation of financial statements called *generally accepted accounting principles* (GAAP). In the United States, the Financial Accounting Standards Board (FASB) is entrusted with the primary authority to issue generally accepted accounting principles. Several other organizations are also involved in setting GAAP, including the SEC and the American Institute of Certified Public Accountants (AICPA). FASB-issued statements and interpretations along with AICPA research bulletins are considered the most authoritative guidance for what constitutes GAAP.

In light of the accounting and corporate governance scandals in the early 2000s, Congress passed the Sarbanes–Oxley Act of 2002 (SOX). SOX called for the creation of the Public Company Accounting Oversight Board (PCAOB), a private-sector, non-profit corporation that oversees the auditors of public companies in order to protect investors and the public interest by promoting informative, fair, and independent audit reports. SOX also requires accounting firms to register with the PCAOB in order to prepare, issue, or participate in audit reports of issuers. Non–U.S. accounting firms that furnish, prepare, or play a substantial role in preparing an audit report for any issuer are also subject to PCAOB rules. As of 2010, over 900 non-U.S. audit firms from more than 85 countries have registered with the PCAOB.

The five members of the PCAOB, including the Chairman, are appointed to staggered five-year terms by the SEC, after consultation with the Chairman of the Board of Governors of the Federal Reserve System and the Secretary of the Treasury. The SEC has oversight authority over the PCAOB, including the approval of the Board's rules, standards, and budget. SOX established funding for PCAOB activities, primarily through annual fees assessed on public companies in proportion to their market capitalization.

PCAOB inspects each registered public accounting firm to assess its compliance with SOX, the rules of the Board, the rules of the SEC, and professional standards, in connection with the firm's performance of audits, issuance of audit reports, and related matters involving U.S. public companies and other issuers. SOX requires the Board to conduct those inspections annually for firms that regularly provide audit reports for more than 100 issuers, and at least triennially for firms that regularly provide audit reports for 100 or fewer issuers. The PCAOB prepares a written report on each inspection and provides it to the SEC and certain state regulatory authorities. The Board also makes portions of the reports available to the public; however, certain information is restricted from public disclosure, or its disclosure is delayed, as required by SOX.

The PCAOB has the authority to investigate and discipline registered public accounting firms and persons associated with those firms for noncompliance with SOX, the rules of the PCAOB and the SEC, and other laws, rules, and professional standards governing the audits of public companies. When violations are found, the PCAOB can impose appropriate sanctions. As required by SOX, the Board's investigations are confidential and nonpublic. SOX also requires disciplinary proceedings to be confidential and nonpublic, unless and until there is a final decision imposing sanctions.

## B. Role of the Accountants

The preparation of a company's financial statements is the responsibility of company management, particularly the chief financial officer (CFO) or controller (chief accounting officer). Each piece of information in the financial statements is, therefore, a managerial "assertion" on the financial position and financial history of the company. A public accounting firm, operating as an auditor, will then objectively opine on the credibility of the statements and figures that management presents in the financial statements. Because the company selects, hires and pays for the services of the auditor, an inherent conflict of interest exists. Historically, this conflict has been kept in check by the professionalism of the accounting profession. Exceptions, however, exist. Look no further than the way in which Enron exploited its relationship with its auditing firm, the now defunct Arthur Andersen, in the late 1990s.

The financial statement audit that accountants conduct is of particular importance, because users of financial statements depend on it to lend credibility to the managerial assertions appearing in the financial statements. When conducting a financial statement audit, an auditor will gather evidence about the financial statement assertions made by management. The auditor will then compare that evidence to those assertions to determine whether the assertions adhere to GAAP. If the auditor is satisfied that the financial statements present the financial position, results of operations, and cash flows in accordance with GAAP, it will issue a clean opinion or, to use accounting terminology, an *unqualified opinion*. An unqualified opinion is the best possible opinion a company can receive.

Auditors may qualify their opinion when they encounter circumstances that prevent them from performing all necessary audit procedures or they conclude that the financial statements contain a material departure from GAAP. A *qualified opinion* is issued when, in an auditor's judgment, the subject of the qualification has a "material" effect on a given company's financial statements. Qualified opinions are uncommon, because they result from factors within the company's power to correct during the audit process. Additionally, a qualified opinion can have a negative impact on the reader's views of the accompanying financial statements.

Accountants may also perform a *compilation* for small, nonpublic companies that lack the resources to prepare financial statements on their own. The accountant essentially compiles financial information that is the representation of management and presents it in the form of financial statements. An accountant is not considered to be "independent" of the financial statements when he performs a compilation. Thus, under such circumstances, accountants may not express any opinion or other assurances on the financial statements.

The Federal securities laws require all publicly-traded companies to engage an outside auditor to perform a financial statement audit at the end of each fiscal year. Each company must receive an unqualified opinion from its auditor to stay in compliance with SEC regulations. Privately-held companies, however, are not required to have a financial statement audit performed. Nevertheless, many privately-held companies, particularly larger ones, undergo a financial statement audit because certain stakeholders, such as stockholders or creditors, demand it or because management desires it.

A financial statement audit is *not a guarantee* of the exactness or accuracy of the assertions in the financial statements. This is because most audit opinions are reached by examining only a sample of evidence supporting the dollar representations. These samples are statistically designed to provide a considerable degree of credibility and reliability. Nevertheless, conclusions drawn from examining a sample of the available evidence are subject to inherent uncertainties.

## § 5.  FUNDAMENTAL FINANCIAL STATEMENTS

### A.  Balance Sheet

#### (1) Introduction

The *balance sheet* provides a "snapshot" of a company's financial position. The term "snapshot" is used because the balance sheet provides information on a given date (*e.g.,* December 31st or March 31st) as opposed to a period of time (*e.g.,* the quarter ended September 30th). The balance sheet summarizes what a company owns (assets), what it owes (liabilities), and the difference between the two (shareholders' equity) on a given date.

#### (2) Components

The three categories of items listed on a company's balance sheet are assets, liabilities, and shareholders' equity.

##### a.  Assets

Assets are the first category of items listed on a company's balance sheet. Assets are anything that a company owns that has economic value. A company purchases assets to increase its value or benefit its operations. It may also develop other assets, such as intellectual property, internally.

Assets are listed on the balance sheet in order of decreasing liquidity, from current assets to long-lived assets. *Liquidity* refers to a company's ability to convert an asset into cash, with assets more quickly convertible into cash being viewed as more liquid than others. Thus, current assets are more liquid than long-lived assets.

A *current asset* has a useful life of less than one year. This means that the asset is fairly liquid and can be converted into cash within 12 months. Examples of current assets include accounts receivable, inventory, marketable securities, prepaid expenses and, of course, cash balances themselves.

A *long-lived asset* is one that has a relatively longer useful life and is not as easily converted into cash. These include fixed assets such as property, plant and equipment, and intangible assets such as goodwill and patents.

Under GAAP, most of the assets on the balance sheet are listed at their historical cost, or *"book value,"* unless the asset's value has been permanently impaired and is less than book value. GAAP mandates the use of historical cost because it is often more objectively measurable than market value and usually leads to more conservative figures. Limiting subjective estimates of current value ensures that the balance sheets of different companies will be similarly prepared. This allows a reader to make meaningful comparisons between different companies.

### b. Liabilities

*Liabilities* are debts that a company owes to creditors. A company's liabilities are broken down on its balance sheet in a manner similar to assets. Thus, current obligations that a company must pay in one year or less are listed first as *current liabilities*. These may include accounts payable, accrued expenses and the portion of a long-term debt due within the next 12 months. Obligations that are not due within the next 12 months are listed as *long-term liabilities*.

### c. Shareholders' Equity

*Shareholders' equity* (SE) reflects the claim of a company's owners—its stockholders—to the company's assets remaining after all the company's creditors have been paid in full. It is the difference between the total value of a company's assets and its liabilities:

$$SE = Total\ Assets - Total\ Liabilities$$

Shareholders' equity reflects the fact that if the company were to sell all its assets at the values listed on the balance sheet and use the cash to pay off its debts, the residual money that remains would belong to the stockholders.

The shareholders' equity section is generally broken down into three accounts: (1) capital stock at par value; (2) additional paid-in capital (APIC), sometimes referred to as "capital surplus"; and (3) retained earnings. The first two categories, capital stock at par value and APIC, together constitute the capital contributed by the investors who bought shares of stock *directly* from the company. Investor consideration for stock is split between the capital stock at par value account and the APIC account. Consideration equal to the par value of each share is allocated to the capital stock at par value account, while the remainder of the consideration, if any, is allocated to the APIC account.

When a company has issued more than one class of capital stock, the capital stock at par value account is often split into two or more sub-accounts. For example, if a company has both common stock and Series A preferred stock outstanding, the aggregate par value attributed to outstanding shares of common stock will be reflected in the "Common Stock" account. Similarly, the aggregate par value of the Series A preferred stock will be reflected in the "Series A Preferred Stock" account. Consideration, if any, paid for shares of both common stock and Series A preferred stock in excess of par value, however, will be aggregated into the APIC account.

For a more detailed discussion of par value and the legal capital rules applicable to corporations, see Nutshell Section 49B.

When the initial investors in a company resell their shares to other investors, either privately or over a stock exchange in the secondary market, the company's capital stock at par value account and APIC account are *not* affected. Only initial issuances of stock by the company itself (so-called *primary offerings*) affect these accounts. Moreover, if shares trade in the secondary market, changes in their market value do not affect these accounts. Therefore, the value listed in the capital stock at par value and APIC accounts (*i.e.,* the accounting value of a company's stock) and the aggregate value of the stock trading in the secondary market are usually not related. For financial analysts and corporate executives, the accounting value of the stock is not important; it is the market value that matters.

The third category of shareholders' equity is *retained earnings*. Retained earnings represent the earned capital of the company that has not been distributed to the stockholders. The main source of retained earnings is income from a company's operations. Any income not distributed to the company's stockholders in the form of a dividend may be used in the operations of the business (hence the term "retained earnings").

Pursuant to FASB Statement No. 130, *Reporting Other Comprehensive Income*, entities may also present a fourth category in the shareholders' equity section called "Accumulated Other Comprehensive Income." This section captures extraordinary and nonrecurring earned income items. These items tend to be volatile and do not relate to a company's core operations. Retained earnings and accumulated other comprehensive income should be added together in figuring out a company's total earned income.

### (3) Limitations of the Balance Sheet

The usefulness of the balance sheet is limited for four reasons. First, the historical approach to valuing assets and liabilities requires the omission of the current fair values of most assets and liabilities. Exceptions include accounts receivable and certain financial instruments with readily ascertainable market values, such as publicly-traded securities. Yet key assets, such as land held for use in the company's operations, are always valued at their historical cost. Over time, however, land generally appreciates in value, sometimes quite significantly.

Second, depreciation of tangible long-lived assets, such as plant and equipment (but not land used in a company's operations), also contributes to the understatement of asset values on the balance sheet. *Depreciation* is an accounting process that allocates the cost of long-lived assets to expense (a line item on the profit and loss statement) in a systematic manner over the time period expected to benefit from the use of those assets. As the cost is allocated to expense, the dollar amount reflected on the balance sheet decreases. Although the market value of the long-lived asset may fluctuate either up or down, the total depreciation expense for a particular asset always accumulates from one period to the next. Thus, there is no attempt to reflect the fair value of those assets accounted for according to the depreciation method.

Depreciation only applies to tangible long-lived assets. The cost of intangible assets with a *finite useful life* (*e.g.,* copyrights and patents) is allocated in a similar manner but is known as *amortization*. An intangible asset's useful life is the period over which the asset is expected to contribute directly or indirectly to the future cash flows of the entity which owns it. Intangible assets with *finite useful lives* are amortized systematically. For example, the price paid to obtain a patent can only benefit a company for a maximum of 20 years. Therefore, the price of obtaining the patent is allocated to expense systematically over a period of no more than 20 years. Intangible assets with an *indefinite life* (*e.g.,* trademarks) are not amortized, although their value is allocated to expense once their value becomes impaired.

Third, management's subjective estimates of, and assumptions about, the current value of certain items further erodes the usefulness of the balance sheet. For example, a company's accounts receivable balance will be offset by an amount representing management's estimate of receivables that will not be paid and, therefore, are not collectible. Management may have arrived at this offset by using facts available to it, or using past performance to predict future results.

Finally, the balance sheet also omits many items that are of tremendous financial value to the business but cannot be objectively quantified. Items of value that may not be reported include a company's workforce, managerial skills, research superiority and reputation with consumers.

### (4) Working with the Balance Sheet

A company's balance sheet provides a basis for computing its rates of return, measuring its exposure to debt, evaluating its capital structure, and assessing its liquidity and financial flexibility. Investors, creditors and others can also use balance sheet information for comparing financial features of one company to another, as each company's balance sheet will have been prepared in accordance with GAAP. This remains true even if the companies are different in size or operate in different industries.

### a.   Rates of Return

The two primary rates of return are *return on assets* (ROA) and *return on equity* (ROE). ROA indicates how much income was generated from each dollar of assets. Similarly, ROE indicates how much income was generated from each dollar of shareholders' equity. Because net income, a profit and loss statement item, is an essential component in these rates of return, see Nutshell Section 5B(4) for a complete discussion on how to calculate them.

### b.  Exposure to Debt

Long-term solvency ratios measure a company's *leverage,* and thus help predict a company's long-run ability to service its debt obligations. Leverage represents the portion of a company's assets financed with debt (*e.g.,* a bank loan, bonds or debentures) and therefore involves contractual obligations to pay interest and principal. See Nutshell Section 33. While long-term solvency ratios are important to potential creditors, they also indicate part of the risk involved in investing in the common stock of a given company. The more debt that is added to the company's capital structure, the more uncertain the return on common stock.

The *total debt ratio* provides creditors with some idea of a company's ability to withstand losses without impairing the interests of creditors, primarily the timely payment of interest and principal on loans. The lower the ratio, the better for creditors as there are fewer contractual claims on the assets of the company. A high ratio indicates that the company is highly-leveraged and further growth financed with additional debt may not be possible. The ratio is computed as follows:

$$\text{Total Debt Ratio} = \frac{\text{Total Liabilities}}{\text{Total Assets}}$$

The *debt-to-equity ratio* helps stockholders determine the risk of their investment in the company becoming impaired. This ratio is calculated by dividing a company's total debt by shareholders' equity.

The higher the ratio, the more risky the equity investment:

Debt-to-Equity Ratio   =   $\dfrac{\text{Total Debt}}{\text{Shareholders' Equity}}$

Another common measure of long-term solvency is the *times interest earned ratio* (TIER). This ratio measures a company's ability to cover all interest payments. The higher the ratio, the more protection creditors have. The ratio is computed as follows:

TIER   =   $\dfrac{\text{Income Before Taxes and Interest Charges}}{\text{Interest Charges}}$

### c.   Measures of Liquidity

#### i.   *Working Capital*

An excellent measure of a company's liquidity, *working capital* (WC) equals the excess of current assets (CA) over current liabilities (CL):

$$WC = CA - CL$$

Based on the definitions of current assets and current liabilities, a positive working capital amount means that a company should have enough cash over the next 12 months to cover its maturing obligations (assuming business conditions do not change significantly for the worse). Working capital, however, is seldom disclosed on the face of the balance sheet. In order to determine the actual liquidity and availability of working capital to meet current obligations, therefore, one must analyze the composition of the current assets and their nearness to cash.

## ii.   Liquidity Ratios

Liquidity ratios also provide meaningful comparative information about a company's ability to pay its bills over the short run without having to rely on cash infusions from outside investors or creditors. One of the best known and most widely used ratios is the *current ratio*. The current ratio is the ratio of current assets to current liabilities, expressed as:

$$\text{Current Ratio} \quad = \quad \frac{\text{Current Assets}}{\text{Current Liabilities}}$$

The current ratio is sometimes called the *working capital ratio,* because the definition of working capital incorporates both current assets and current liabilities. The higher the current ratio, the better the financial condition of the company. A high ratio may also indicate an efficient use of cash and other short-term assets.

It is important to realize that, like all other ratios, the current ratio can be easily manipulated by certain transactions. For example, a company may obtain a long-term loan that increases its cash reserves and long-term debt. Because current liabilities would only be marginally affected (*i.e.,* increased only by the amount of the additional long-term debt payable within the next 12 months), the current ratio would rise.

While useful, the current ratio does not answer how liquid a company's receivables and inventory are, or what effect the omission of inventory may have on the liquidity analysis. The liquidity of inventory is a primary concern because there is always a question of how long it will take to transform the inventory into cash through sales. For this reason, inventory's book value, or historical cost, is an unreliable measure of its value. In addition, relatively large inventories may be a sign of short-term trouble. A company may have overestimated demand and, as a result, produced too many goods. In this event, the company may have a substantial portion of its liquidity tied up in slow moving inventory that may become damaged or obsolete. The *quick ratio* or *acid test* is used to recognize this problem. This ratio is computed like the current ratio, except inventory is omitted:

$$\text{Quick Ratio} = \frac{\text{Current Assets} - \text{Inventory}}{\text{Current Liabilities}}$$

Neither the current ratio nor the quick ratio gives a complete explanation of the current debt-paying ability of a company. The *defensive-interval ratio* supplements the other liquidity ratios because it measures the time-span during which a company can operate using present liquid assets without resorting to revenues from future periods. This ratio is computed by dividing defensive assets (cash, marketable securities, and net receivables) by projected daily expenditures from operations. Projected daily expenditures are computed by dividing the cost of goods sold and all ordinary cash expenses (both based on past expenditures) by 365 days. Non-cash charges such as depreciation and amortization are excluded from this computation:

$$\text{Defensive–Interval Ratio} \; = \; \frac{\text{Defensive Assets}}{\text{Projected Daily Operational Expenditures} - \text{Non–Cash Charges}}$$

Another way of evaluating liquidity is by examining how efficiently a company uses its assets. An efficient company is able to quickly convert assets into cash. The *total asset turnover ratio* determines the amount of net sales (total sales less returns) that is generated from each dollar of assets. A high asset turnover ratio means a company is receiving a higher return on its assets. The ratio is calculated as follows:

$$\text{Total Asset Turnover Ratio} \; = \; \frac{\text{Net Sales}}{\text{Total Assets}}$$

Sometimes it is helpful to break down the total asset turnover ratio into several components to better compare financial statements of different companies. The *fixed asset turnover ratio,* a component of the total asset turnover ratio, measures the amount of sales that are generated from every dollar of fixed assets. Sometimes companies may have similar total asset turnover ratios but very different fixed asset turnover ratios. For example, the airline industry invests heavily in fixed assets, while most Internet businesses do not. Thus, an airline company with the same amount of net sales as an Internet company will probably have a substantially lower fixed asset turnover ratio. Similar ratios may also be calculated for other asset line items on the balance sheet, including accounts receivable and inventory.

## B.  Profit and Loss Statement

### (1) Introduction

The *profit and loss statement* (or *P&L* for short) measures the financial performance of a company over a given period of time. It includes a company's total revenue and expenses and then presents the difference as net income or loss. To further their basic principle of conservatism, accountants limit the components of income to amounts that are objectively measurable and restrict the use of subjective assumptions. Therefore, qualitative items that contribute to the general growth of a company but cannot be quantified with any degree of reliability are not included in a P&L statement.

A P&L statement lists revenue and expenses from operations first. This is followed by a listing of nonoperating revenue and expenses, such as interest generated through investments and taxes. The difference between all the revenues and expenses is presented as net income or loss (the *bottom line*).

A P&L statement prepared using GAAP must follow fundamental realization and matching principles. Under the *realization principle,* a company recognizes revenue when it is *earned*. Thus, a company records revenue at the time a sale or service is completed, which may or may not be (and very often is not) the time the company receives actual payment from a customer.

Expenses shown on the P&L statement are based on the *matching principle*. Once revenues are earned, they are matched with the costs associated with producing them. For example, if a company manufactures a product and sells it on credit, the revenue is recognized at the time of sale. The production and other costs associated with the sale of the product are also recognized at the time of sale even though the associated cash outflows occurred at some other time. As a result of the way revenues and expenses are recorded, the figures shown on the P&L statement may not be representative of the actual cash inflows and outflows that occurred during a particular period. The statement of cash flows covers this. See Nutshell Section 5D.

A primary reason that accounting for income differs from cash flows is that a P&L statement contains non-cash items, while a statement of cash flows obviously does not. The most common non-cash item reflected on the P&L statement is depreciation. In accordance with the matching principle, a company may not recognize an expense when it purchases fixed assets such as plant and equipment. Rather, the expense is periodically recognized over the useful life of the asset. See Nutshell Section 5A(3).

The "quality" of earnings reported on a P&L statement is extremely important. This was clearly underscored by the debacles involving Enron, Tyco, Worldcom and Adelphia Communications during the early 2000s. Companies can affect reported income by employing different accounting methods. For example, one company may choose to depreciate its plant assets on a straight line basis while its competitor may depreciate plant assets on an accelerated basis. Assuming all other factors are equal, the income of the latter company in earlier periods will be less than the former company, because the latter's expenses are higher in those periods. Companies that use aggressive accounting policies report higher net income numbers in the short run, but the quality of the earnings suffers as a result.

(2) Earnings Per Share (EPS)

Pursuant to FASB Statement No. 128, *Earnings per Share*, all public companies are required to present net income/loss on a per share basis as well as on an aggregate basis. A per share presentation of net income/loss is known as *earnings per share* (EPS).

A company's capital structure determines the manner in which earnings per share is disclosed. For example, a company with a simple capital structure (*i.e.*, one with only common stock and preferred stock outstanding) is required to disclose "basic" EPS. *Basic EPS* is computed by dividing income available to common stockholders by the weighted-average number of shares of common stock outstanding. (A weighted-average number of shares is used because the company may have issued, or retired, shares of common stock during the period of time in question). Thus:

$$\text{EPS} = \frac{\text{Net Income} - \text{Declared Preferred Dividends}}{\text{Weighted Avg. No. of Common Shares Outstanding}}$$

As seen in the formula above, income available to common stockholders is computed by deducting dividends declared in the period on any preferred stock (whether or not paid) from net income. For example, assume Company A reports net income of $4.5 million during the past fiscal year. Company A also has 6 million shares of preferred stock outstanding, and the annual dividend on the preferred stock is $0.20 per share. The calculation of net income available to common stockholders for Company A would be:

| | |
|---|---:|
| Net Income | $ 4,500,000 |
| *Less:* | |
| Preferred stock dividends | |
| $(6,000,000 \times \$0.20)$ | (1,200,000) |
| Income available to common stockholders | $ 3,300,000 |

As discussed in greater detail in Nutshell Section 43B, companies may issue cumulative or noncumulative preferred stock. The dividend rate listed on cumulative preferred stock must be factored into the above equation, regardless of whether the board of directors has actually declared a dividend. Therefore, in the above example, if Company A's preferred stock were cumulative, the $1.2 million in preferred dividends would always be deducted from net income, even if the board never declared a dividend. This is because skipped cumulative preferred stock dividends are not eliminated but rather accrue into a dividend arrearage.

By contrast, if a company's preferred stock is noncumulative, then the dividend rate is only factored into the equation if the board of directors actually declared a dividend. In that event, net income should be decreased by the actual dividend declared.

Companies with more complex capital structures must report both "basic" and "fully diluted" EPS on the face of the P&L statement. *Fully diluted EPS* is based on outstanding common shares and *common stock equivalents*. Common stock equivalents are securities (such as options, warrants, convertible debt and convertible preferred stock) that allow their holders to exercise or convert them into shares of common stock. Until those holders do so, however, they cannot participate fully in the earnings of the company available to common stockholders. Because these securities will dilute (*i.e.,* reduce) earnings on a per share basis when exercised or converted, accounting rules require companies to recognize this fact by stating earnings per share on a "fully diluted" basis. These securities dilute EPS because the additional shares of common stock into which they can be converted are added to the denominator in the EPS calculation.

## (3) EBITDA

Users of financial statements can ameliorate the arbitrary results that may arise when comparing P&L statements prepared using different accounting methods. They can do so by determining a company's *"earnings before interest, taxes, depreciation and amortization"* are deducted. This amount is called *EBITDA*. (Many pronounce EBITDA as one word (ebitda); others pronounce it as three words (ebit-D–A)).

No matter how you pronounce it, EBITDA is important because it evidences a company's positive cash flow from its core operations. Excluded, therefore, are cash flows from non-core or non-recurring operations. Also excluded are certain financial items, such as taxes, which are variable and usually based on political rather than economic factors. Because depreciation methods may vary between companies, EBITDA also removes distortions that prevent accurate comparisons of different companies. Furthermore, because depreciation and amortization are non-cash charges, EBITDA provides a better picture of the cash generated by a company's core operating activities.

EBITDA is often used by investment bankers to analyze profitability between companies and industries. Because it eliminates the effects of financing and accounting decisions, EBITDA can provide a good "apples-to-apples" comparison. For example, EBITDA as a percentage of sales (the higher the ratio, the higher the profitability) can be used to find companies that are the most efficient operators in an industry.

Moreover, commercial bankers often use EBITDA to determine whether to extend new loans to a company, while investment bankers may use it in deciding whether or not to underwrite a new debt offering by a company. Because EBITDA disregards the effects of accounting decisions (*i.e.,* depreciation and amortization), EBITDA often provides a clearer picture of how much earnings or cash flow a company has that can be used to service a contemplated debt offering or loan.

### (4)  Measures of Profitability

The P&L statement is also used to calculate a company's profitability ratios. Common profitability ratios include earnings per share (see Nutshell Section 5B(2)), profit margin on sales, return on assets, and return on equity. These ratios measure how well a company has performed during the past period. They are widely used because profitability is the ultimate measure of how well a company is managing its operations.

*Profit margin on sales* is computed by dividing net income by net sales (both from the P&L statement) for the period:

$$\text{Profit Margin on Sales} \quad = \quad \frac{\text{Net Income}}{\text{Net Sales}}$$

A high profit margin indicates that a company is incurring minimal expense to achieve each dollar of sales and has flexibility to either lower its sales prices and/or absorb additional expenses while still remaining profitable. Conversely, a low profit margin indicates that a company is incurring substantial expense to achieve each dollar of sales. Thus, it may not be able to weather economic developments that lead to lower sales prices and/or higher expenses.

*Return on assets* (ROA) is useful because it indicates how profitable a company is relative to its total assets. It is calculated as follows:

$$\text{Return on Assets} = \frac{\text{Net Income}}{\text{Total Assets}}$$

This ratio measures how much profit is generated from each dollar of assets. Thus, higher profit margins, which increase net income, may result in a relatively higher return on assets. Remember, however, that GAAP requires companies to list most balance sheet items at their historical cost. Therefore, the figure for total assets in the ROA equation is generally conservative, thus leading to an artificially inflated ROA. For this reason, ROA is considered an accounting rate of return as opposed to a true financial rate of return.

*Return on equity* (ROE) measures how well the stockholders fared during the previous fiscal year. As equity equals the difference between a company's total assets and total liabilities, ROE measures how effectively management is using the investment of the stockholders to generate income. It is computed as follows:

Return on Equity $=$ $\dfrac{\text{Net Income}}{\text{Average Shareholders' Equity}}$

A ROA lower than ROE is an indication that the company is financing its operations partially through the use of debt (*i.e.,* leverage). Because debt is a liability, and liabilities are subtracted from a company's assets to determine equity, ROE will be higher as more leverage is used. Of course, leverage also increases a company's financial risk. During an economic downturn, a company may find it more difficult to make its interest and principal payments. Nevertheless, leverage will increase earnings as long as a company's ROA is greater than the cost of borrowing. See Nutshell Section 33.

## C. Statement of Changes in Shareholders' Equity

As its name indicates, a *statement of changes in shareholders' equity* reveals changes in the categories listed in the shareholders' equity section of the balance sheet. Those categories are the capital stock at par value account, the additional paid-in-capital (APIC) account, and retained earnings.

This particular financial statement is a reconciliation (technically a "roll forward") of the balance of each of these categories at the beginning and end of the year. The statement assists in the assessment of overall performance by providing additional information on why net assets increased or decreased during the year. For example, the statement lists each issuance of stock and the distribution of dividends. In addition, each component that resulted in a change to retained earnings is itemized within the statement.

Capital stock may be (1) authorized, (2) authorized and issued, or (3) authorized, issued, and outstanding. A corporation's certificate of incorporation or "charter" contains the types and number of shares of stock that the corporation can issue. These shares constitute the *authorized* capital stock of the corporation. Shares of authorized capital stock that a corporation distributes are classified as *issued*. Because a corporation may own shares of its issued capital stock in the form of *treasury stock*, shares of issued capital stock in the hands of stockholders (*i.e.*, those other than the corporation) are called *outstanding*.

A corporation's earned capital is reflected in the retained earnings account. A corporation generally uses its retained earnings to finance its operations, invest in new projects or pay dividends to its stockholders. Because the corporation's net profits are reflected in the retained earnings account, that account grows over time if the corporation is profitable. However, the corporation's net losses are also reflected in that account, and thus the account shrinks, disappears altogether or reflects an accumulated deficit if the corporation is unprofitable over time. The account also shrinks by the amount of any dividend a corporation pays out to its stockholders.

A corporation may pay dividends out of retained earnings in the form of cash, promissory notes (scrip), property or stock. If a corporation does not have any retained earnings and chooses to pay a dividend, it must reduce APIC. Such distributions are known as liquidating dividends. Sometimes, restrictions may be placed on a corporation's use of retained earnings by loan agreements, bond indentures or regulatory requirements. These restrictions are intended to offer additional protection to creditors by reducing amounts available for dividend distributions or reinvestment in operations.

Pursuant to FASB Statement No. 130, *Reporting Comprehensive Income*, certain income items that were previously recorded in the P&L statement are now recognized in the shareholders' equity section. These items are extraordinary and nonrecurring gains and losses that tend to be inherently volatile and unrelated to a corporation's core operations. These items, therefore, are "accumulated" from one time period to the next as a direct adjustment to capital. Together with retained earnings, *accumulated other comprehensive income* comprises an entity's total earned income. Other comprehensive income includes foreign currency translation adjustments, minimum pension liability adjustments, and unrealized gains and losses on certain investments in debt and equity securities. The effects on earned income are still appropriately captured, but the volatility that is associated with these items is removed from the P&L statement. This stabilizes a corporation's reported earnings, and thus better reflects its true performance.

## D. Statement of Cash Flows

### (1) Introduction

The balance sheet and P&L statement are prepared using the *accrual basis* of accounting. Under this method, revenues are recognized when earned and are matched up with the expenses associated with them. Matching is done without regard to the actual timing of cash receipts or payments.

The *statement of cash flows* presents a company's financial information under the *cash basis* of accounting. This statement is useful because it provides answers that the other accrual-based financial statements cannot. These include: (1) From what sources did the company generate cash during the period? (2) How did the company use cash during the period? (3) What was the change in the company's cash balance during the period?

The primary purpose of a statement of cash flows is to provide information about a company's cash receipts and cash payments during a period. A secondary objective is to provide information on a cash basis about a company's operating, investing and financing activities. The information that the statement provides should help a reader of the financial statements assess: (1) a company's ability to generate positive future net cash flows; (2) a company's ability to meet its obligations and pay dividends; (3) a company's need for external financing; (4) the reasons for differences between a company's net income and associated cash receipts and payments; and (5) the effects on a company's financial health stemming from both its cash and non-cash investing and financing transactions during a period.

### (2) Composition

In order to grasp fully how the statement of cash flows is useful to a reader, one must understand its composition. The statement of cash flows classifies cash receipts and cash payments as operating, investing and financing activities based on the following:

*Operating activities* include the cash effect of transactions that enter into the determination of net income, such as cash receipts from operating revenues (*e.g.,* sales of inventory) and cash payments for operating expenditures (*e.g.,* payments to vendors and employees). Operating cash flow is probably the most important number because it tells a reader whether a company's cash inflows from its core operations are sufficient to cover its everyday cash outflows. A positive operating cash flow figure means that the company's core operations contributed to the company's liquidity. A negative operating cash flow figure means that a company used more cash than it earned in order to produce the net income (or loss) reported in its P&L statement. For this reason, a negative operating cash outflow is troubling.

*Investing activities* involve long-lived assets. These activities include the purchase and sale of property, plant and equipment, investment securities, and other long-lived assets. For example, the purchase of a piece of machinery would result in a cash outflow, while the sale of an investment security would generate cash inflow.

*Financing activities* involve long-term liability and shareholders' equity items. Typical sources of cash include cash raised by selling stocks and bonds or borrowing from banks. Likewise, paying back a bank loan would show up as a use of cash.

### (3) Measures of Liquidity

Like the balance sheet, the statement of cash flows is also used to measure a company's liquidity. While balance sheet-based ratios only measure how liquid a company was on a given day in the past, cash flow ratios can be used to evaluate how much cash a company generated over a period of time and compare that figure to its current obligations. For this reason, many financial analysts place more reliance on cash flow-based liquidity ratios.

The *operating cash flow ratio* (OCF) measures a company's ability to generate the resources required to meet its current liabilities. The equation is:

$$\text{OCF Ratio} \quad = \quad \frac{\text{Cash Flow from Operations}}{\text{Current Liabilities}}$$

The purpose of this ratio is to assess whether a company's operations are generating enough cash to cover its current liabilities. If the ratio falls below 1.00, then the company is not meeting this goal. In order to do so, the company will have to find other sources of cash to finance its operations or slow the rate at which it is spending its cash.

The *current cash debt coverage ratio* (CCD) is another cash flow-based ratio used to measure a company's ability to repay its current debt. CCD is calculated as follows:

$$\text{CCD Ratio} \quad = \quad \frac{\text{Cash Flow from Operations} - \text{Cash Divs.}}{\substack{\text{Current Interest Bearing Debt} \\ \text{(including current interest)}}}$$

The numerator of this equation represents a company's retained operating cash flows (*i.e.,* the portion that will not be distributed to its stockholders). Like the OCF ratio, a CCD ratio of less than 1.00 indicates that a company is not generating enough cash to repay its current debt obligations.

# CHAPTER 3

# TIME VALUE OF MONEY

## § 6. OVERVIEW

No doubt your parents have complained that a "dollar just doesn't go as far as it used to." Whether they knew it or not, their lamentations were really about the *time value of money*. This concept is arguably the most fundamental in the world of finance and investing.

The time value of money rests on the fact that a dollar generally will be less valuable a year from now than it is today. The reason for the declining value of a dollar is inflation. *Inflation* is the erosion of a dollar's purchasing power that naturally occurs over time as prices for consumer goods and services rise. As these prices increase, the purchasing power of a single dollar declines. Thus, your parents were right. A dollar did, indeed, have greater purchasing power when they were younger than it does today.

Inflation is caused by too many dollars chasing too few goods and services. This occurs during periods of economic expansion when the economy is flush with cash and consumer spending is in full swing. In order to balance the supply and demand for goods and services, merchants and service providers raise their prices until demand levels off to match supply. The U.S. Federal Reserve, discussed below in Nutshell Section 8, is responsible for maintaining price stability (*i.e.,* low inflation).

The U.S. economy has generally suffered from mild to more severe bouts of inflation throughout the 20th Century up until today. During the 1970s and early 1980s, the U.S. suffered from double-digit inflation primarily due to an artificial stimulus. That stimulus was the oil embargo that the oil cartel known as OPEC (Organization of the Petroleum Exporting Countries) unleashed on developed nations in 1973. In what turned out to be a wildly successful bid to enhance its members' profits, OPEC limited the supply of oil through the embargo while quadrupling the price on the barrels it did sell. Because the number of petroleum dependent products and services are vast, overall prices on goods and services ballooned as well.

Inflation in the 1970s was often a self-fulfilling prophesy. Sellers of goods and services, anticipating that their suppliers and vendors would be raising prices, increased their prices preemptively. Thus, rising prices became a vicious cycle. To combat the "psychological" nature of inflation, President Gerald Ford in 1974 encouraged citizens on a grassroots-basis to engage in disciplined spending habits and to increase personal savings. To promote solidarity, Ford urged citizens to wear "WIN" buttons, which stood for "Whip Inflation Now." Former Fed Chairman Alan Greenspan referred to the program as "unbelievably stupid," and not surprisingly inflation remained a threat to the economy well into the 1980s during the presidency of Ronald Reagan.

Although its occurrence is rare, *deflation* can occur when too few dollars are chasing available goods and services. This can happen when the economy is in a severe recession or depression and consumer spending dries up. A *recession* occurs when there is negative growth in gross domestic product (GDP) for at least two consecutive quarterly periods. A *depression* occurs when GDP declines in excess of 10% or a recession lasts for two or more years. When spending dries up, merchants and service providers are forced to lower their prices to the point where demand matches supply. In a deflationary environment, the purchasing power of a dollar actually rises. Cruelly, deflation can exacerbate or prolong a recession or depression, as consumers—believing prices will drop further in the near future—delay major purchases (homes, refrigerators, cars, etc.) thus further dampening economic activity.

The U.S. economy has experienced periods of deflation only occasionally. The last significant period occurred during the Great Depression of the 1930s. During that time, few people had discretionary funds to spend on nonessential goods and services. Prices of goods and services declined—sometimes gradually, sometimes precipitously—as a result. The U.S. also experienced deflation in the early and late 1920s, 1949 and in the mid–1950s.

## § 7.  INTEREST RATE COMPONENTS

Suppose you are thinking about loaning $20,000 to a colleague for a year. What are the factors that go into determining the rate of interest you should charge? As described below, the rate of interest that a lender charges typically reflects three variables: (1) the anticipated average rate of inflation during the duration of the loan; (2) the opportunity cost of the loaned money; and (3) the credit or default risk of the borrower.

Because of inflation, lenders must charge a rate of interest at least equal to the anticipated average rate of inflation during the loan. This way the money they receive back in the future from their borrowers will have the same purchasing power it has today. A failure to do so would mean they receive back less purchasing power than they lent, certainly an unacceptable result.

But simply charging a rate of interest designed to cover the erosive effects of inflation is insufficient to most lenders. Indeed, when they lend money they forgo the opportunity to use that money for other purposes. In the case of your loan to your colleague, you could do many things with that money rather than lend it. You could purchase a new car, take a vacation, or pay for a child's education, among other things. What you forgo when you lend money to your colleague—your delayed gratification—is the *opportunity cost* associated with that loan. To compensate themselves for opportunity costs, lenders charge a rate of interest above and beyond the anticipated average rate of inflation.

Lenders, however, must also factor in the possibility that the borrower will be unable to repay the loan when it comes due. In the case of your colleague, what is the likelihood that she will have the money needed to pay interest and principal on the loan? The risk of nonpayment of principal and/or interest is called *credit* or *default risk*.

Credit risk varies from borrower to borrower. Lenders typically charge riskier borrowers a higher rate of interest than they charge more creditworthy borrowers. A higher rate compensates lenders for accepting the additional risk associated with less creditworthy borrowers. However, raising rates to reflect default risk creates a Catch–22. The higher the rate of interest charged on a loan to a less creditworthy borrower, the more likely she will actually default on that loan.

## § 8.  THE IMPORTANCE OF THE FEDERAL RESERVE

### A.  Background

The *U.S. Federal Reserve System,* better known as the *"Fed,"* is the central bank of the United States. Created by Congress back in 1913 with the passage of the Federal Reserve Act, the Fed is comprised of a central, governmental agency—the *Federal Reserve Board* or *"Board of Governors"*—

and 12 regional Federal Reserve Banks located in major U.S. cities. The Fed has counterparts around the globe, such as the European Central Bank.

The Fed is considered an "independent" central bank. The reasons for this are threefold. First, its decisions do not have to be ratified by the executive or legislative branches of the U.S. government. Second, it does not receive funding from Congress. The Fed is self-funding through, among other sources, the receipt of interest income on U.S. government securities it has acquired through open market purchases. Third, the terms of its members on the Board of Governors span multiple presidential and congressional terms. Nevertheless, the Fed remains subject to congressional oversight and, if Congress so desired, it could alter the Fed's statutory authority. For example, pursuant to the Dodd–Frank Wall Street Reform and Consumer Protection Act of 2010, Congress appointed the Fed as the lead regulator for the biggest, most interconnected financial companies–those whose failures could threaten the entire financial system. However, the Act required greater transparency from the Fed with respect to its emergency lending powers and required the Government Accountability Office (GAO) to audit the Fed's emergency lending programs that were used to stabilize the markets during the financial crisis of 2008. That audit included the Fed's discount lending to banks.

There are seven members of the Board of Governors. They are nominated by the President and must be confirmed by the Senate. From among the sitting members, the President chooses a Chairman and a Vice Chairman. The current Chairman is Ben Bernake. Given the importance of the Fed in the national and world economies, many view the Fed's Chairman as the most powerful person on the planet, economically speaking.

In addition to the 12 regional Federal Reserve Banks, thousands of other financial institutions are "members" of the Federal Reserve System. Banks chartered by the Office of the Comptroller of the Currency in the U.S. Department of the Treasury are, by law, automatically members of the system. Assuming they meet the membership requirements set by the Board of Governors, state-chartered banks and trust companies also may become members through an application process. Financial institutions that are members of the Federal Reserve System are referred to as *member banks*.

Member banks must subscribe for stock in their regional Federal Reserve Bank. The subscription is for an amount equal to six percent of each member bank's capital and surplus, of which three percent must be paid into the Fed. The remaining amount is subject to call by the Board of Governors. This "stock," however, does not convey ownership like stock in a for-profit corporation. Rather, it is simply a legal obligation that membership imposes. Nevertheless, member banks do receive a legally-mandated six percent annual dividend and do vote for some of the directors of their regional Federal Reserve Bank.

## B.  The Fed's Role in the Economy

According to the Federal Reserve Act, the Fed should seek "to promote effectively the goals of maximum employment, stable prices, and moderate long-term interest rates." To accomplish this, the Fed conducts this nation's monetary policy. By influencing the availability and cost of money and credit through monetary policy, the Fed pursues the twin long-term goals of sustainable economic growth and low inflation.

The Fed has three primary tools of monetary policy at its disposal: open market operations, reserve requirements and the discount rate. It wields these tools in an attempt to influence the demand for, and the supply of, balances that depository institutions hold on deposit at Federal Reserve Banks. By doing so, the Fed influences the "federal funds rate" of interest.

### (1)  The Federal Funds Rate of Interest

The *federal funds rate* is the interest rate at which depository institutions lend immediately available funds (balances they hold at the Federal Reserve) to other depository institutions on an overnight basis. Because federal funds lending is not collateralized, different depository institutions pay different rates for loans depending on their creditworthiness. Institutions can arrange loans directly between themselves or, in the case of large loans, through a federal funds broker. As reported in the press, the "federal funds rate" typically is the rate at which the most creditworthy institutions borrow and lend balances in the brokered market for fed funds.

Changes in the federal funds rate trigger a chain of events that affect other short-term interest rates, foreign exchange rates, long-term interest rates, and the available amount of money and credit. These variables, in turn, impact upon other economic variables, such as employment, the production of goods, and the prices of services and goods.

By altering the federal funds rate, the Fed influences economic growth and price stability. A decrease in the federal funds rate stimulates economic growth essentially by easing credit conditions and making more money available on a less costly basis. An easing in that rate, however, could cause the economy to overheat, thus leading to higher inflation.

By contrast, an increase in the federal funds rate will dampen economic growth essentially by making borrowing more costly and thus decreasing the supply of available money. An increase, therefore, tends to ease inflationary pressures.

### (2) Open Market Operations

*Open market operations* are the Fed's principal tool in influencing the federal funds rate. These operations consist of the buying and selling of U.S. government securities and Federal agency securities. Nearly all of the securities held by the Fed are U.S. Treasury securities, roughly split equally between Treasury Bills, on the one hand, and Treasury Notes and Bonds, on the other. See Nutshell Section 9A.

The *Federal Open Market Committee* (FOMC) oversees open market operations. Because of this, the FOMC is the Fed's primary monetary policy-making body. FOMC consists of 12 voting members. These members include the seven members of the Board of Governors and five of the 12 presidents of the regional Federal Reserve Banks. Nevertheless, the other seven non-member presidents typically attend FOMC meetings, participate in discussions and contribute to the FOMC's economic analysis.

At the instructions of the FOMC, the *Open Market Trading Desk* (Desk) at the Federal Reserve Bank of New York will purchase or sell securities. When the Desk purchases securities, the Fed credits the account of the seller's depository institution at its Federal Reserve Bank. This increases the quantity of Federal Reserve balances which can then be lent to other depository institutions in the federal funds market. Because an increase in balances puts downward pressure on the federal funds rate, the Desk's purchases of securities tend to have a stimulating effect on economic development.

When the Desk sells securities, by contrast, the Fed debits the account of the purchaser's depository institution at its Federal Reserve Bank. This decreases the quantity of Federal Reserve balances which can be lent to other depository institutions in the federal funds market. Because a decrease in balances leads to an increase in the federal funds rate, the Desk's sales of securities tend to have a dampening effect on economic development.

### (3) Reserve Requirements

While the FOMC is responsible for open market operations, the Board of Governors is responsible for establishing *reserve requirements*. *Reserves* are the funds depository institutions must legally retain against specified deposits made by their customers (*i.e.,* depositors). The Board of Governors has sole authority over increases and decreases in reserve requirements, but can only make changes within limits established by law. The key component of reserves consists of balances that depository institutions hold at Federal Reserve Banks.

An increase in the reserve requirements decreases the supply of funds available for lending. This has a dampening effect on economic growth, but helps ease inflationary pressures. A decrease in the reserve requirements, by contrast, increases the supply of funds available for lending. This helps stimulate economic growth, but leads to increased inflationary pressures.

A given depository institution's reserve requirement, in dollar terms, is calculated by applying the reserve ratios specified in the Federal Reserve

Board's Regulation D to that institution's *reservable liabilities*. In the world of banking, it is important to remember that deposits you make in your bank represent "liabilities" of that bank because the bank owes you that money. Not all liabilities, however, are subject to reserve requirements; hence, the term "reservable" liabilities is used.

### (4) Discount Rate

The Board of Governors also sets the *discount rate*. This is the rate of interest a Federal Reserve Bank's lending facility (referred to as its *"discount window"*) charges eligible depository institutions which borrow directly from the Fed. These institutions borrow extremely short-term funds (typically overnight) on a fully secured basis in order to meet their short-term liquidity needs. The Board of Governors can influence the money supply by increasing or decreasing the discount rate.

While each Federal Reserve Bank offers three discount window programs—primary credit, secondary credit and seasonal credit—the Fed typically is referring to the primary credit rate when it uses the term "discount rate." Depository institutions in generally sound financial condition qualify for primary credit. Those not eligible for primary credit may apply for secondary credit. Small depository institutions operating in agricultural or seasonal resort communities may apply for seasonal credit. Not surprisingly, primary credit is less expensive than secondary credit. Seasonal credit, by contrast, is usually set at an average of selected market rates.

Generally, the Fed sets the discount rate for primary credit slightly below the federal funds rate. While ordinarily this would create an incentive for depository institutions to borrow at the discount window at the discount rate rather than from other institutions at the federal funds rate, the Fed restricts access to discount window credit. Indeed, a depository institution is required to pursue all other reasonably available sources of funds, including those in the federal funds market, before the Fed will grant it credit through the discount window.

### (5) The Financial Crisis of 2008 and Expanded Fed Powers

Beginning in 2008 through 2010, the United States experienced an unprecedented credit crisis that quickly spread globally. The main genesis behind the crisis was an overvaluation of assets, particularly homes. Prior to 2008, lending institutions became more lax in their credit standards with respect to home mortgages. Many borrowers who under normal circumstances would not be given a mortgage qualified for so-called "subprime" mortgages where the creditworthiness of a borrower was highly suspect. As more and more individuals purchased homes (some purchased multiple homes with the intent to "flip" them for a quick profit), home prices were bid up to the highest levels in history. Significant price increases in homes were ultimately unsustainable. Eventually, many homeowners found themselves "underwater," *i.e.*, the value of their homes was less (sometimes significantly less) than the outstanding balances on their mortgages. This rendered many mortgages, and the mortgage-backed securities secured by them, substantially less valuable and, in many cases, worthless.

Those holding these mortgages and securities suffered tremendously as a result of the declining value of homes. Lehman Brothers, one of the leaders in the mortgage-backed securities industry, collapsed completely and was liquidated. Bear Stearns and Merrill Lynch were sold at bargain-basement prices, while Goldman Sachs and Morgan Stanley converted into commercial banks in order to access credit through the Fed. All these financial firms—save Lehman Brothers—received government bailouts in order to stay afloat. American International Group, Inc. (AIG), one of the largest public companies in the world, suffered a liquidity crisis after its credit rating was downgraded substantially. AIG, which had issued substantial amounts of credit default swaps (essentially insurance that debt securities would be repaid), was required to pay over $100 billion to major global financial institutions as a result.

Due to the financial crisis, the Fed took on a new role and used its independent authority to purchase various distressed financial assets and implement emergency loan programs. As part of a $700 billion bailout plan approved by Congress and signed into law by then President George W. Bush in 2008, the Fed was given the power for the first time to pay interest on the reserves of commercial banks in order to encourage banks to continue lending money to businesses and consumers. The Fed also created a Term Asset–Backed Securities Loan Facility (TALF). The facility was created to help market participants meet the credit needs of households and small businesses by supporting the issuance of asset-backed securities (ABSs) collateralized by student loans, auto loans, credit card loans, and loans guaranteed by the Small Business Administration.

The Fed also purchased $600 billion in mortgage-related debt guaranteed by Fannie Mae, Freddie Mac, and Ginnie Mae, in an attempt to boost the housing market. This was the first time the Fed tried to influence interest rates by injecting large amounts of money into the mortgage markets. Because the fed funds rate was already at one percent, buying up mortgage-related debt was one of the few options left for the Fed in this regard. As 2008 came to a close, the federal funds rate was at 0.25% and the Fed had increased its lending and purchases of debt to $2.2 trillion.

## § 9. KEY INTEREST RATES

In addition to the fed funds rate and discount rate discussed in Nutshell Sections 8B(1) and (4), respectively, the other key interest rates in corporate finance are the rates paid on U.S. Treasury instruments, the prime rate and the London Interbank Offered Rate (LIBOR). In order to find out what current rates are, one need only look in *The Wall Street Journal* or in another daily financial publication, such as *Investor's Business Daily*. On-line sources, such as Google Finance and Yahoo Finance, also provide this information.

In the world of finance, interest rates are measured in *basis points*. Each basis point is 1/100th of one percent. Thus, an interest rate of 5% is 500 basis points. An interest rate of 9.24% is 924 basis points.

## A.   Rates Paid on U.S. Treasury Instruments

The U.S. government borrows money in order to pay off maturing government debt securities and raise cash needed to run the Federal government. It does so by selling three types of debt instruments which are primarily distinguished from one another by their term.

*Treasury Bills* (T–Bills) mature in a short period of time. Terms generally run from as little as three months up to a maximum term of one year. T–Bills trade on a discount basis. This means that investors purchase T–Bills at a price below their face value. The yield (or profit) the investor receives is the difference between the purchase price she paid and the face value of the T–Bill she receives at maturity. (As seen in Nutshell Section 16, this is similar to zero-coupon bonds.) The government sells T–Bills in minimum units of $10,000. A very active secondary market exists for T–Bills.

Other government securities have longer terms. *Treasury Notes* (T–Notes) have intermediate terms, maturing from one to 10 years. *Treasury Bonds* (T–Bonds) are long-term obligations issued with a term of more than 10 years. Unlike T–Bills, T–Notes and T–Bonds provide fixed interest, paid semi-annually, and trade in units of $1,000 or higher. The yield on 10–year Treasury Notes is particularly influential, as it directly influences home mortgage interest rates.

The U.S. Treasury also offers 10–year notes that protect purchasers from the effects of inflation by indexing the interest rate to inflation. These notes are called *Treasury Inflation Protection Securities* (TIPS). TIPS provide two forms of return. The first is interest that is paid out semi-annually. The second is an automatic increase in the principal, or maturity value, to account for inflation.

## B. Prime Rate

The *prime rate* is the rate of interest banks charge their largest and most stable (and therefore most creditworthy) borrowers (typically large companies). The prime rate major banks publicize is usually always the same. In reality, however, banks charge some borrowers slightly higher or lower rates of interest.

Banks make changes to the prime rate infrequently. When changes to the prime rate are made, the change is typically initiated by a large regional bank. Major money center banks then quickly follow suit.

The financial community closely watches the prime rate, as it is a useful indicator of the direction of interest rates generally. Moreover, many other rates charged to borrowers are based on the prime rate. For example, a given credit card company may charge borrowers a rate of interest equal to the prime rate plus a set number of basis points, such as 550 (or 5.5%). Thus, holders of that credit card pay a rate of interest that fluctuates with the prime rate.

## C.  LIBOR

*LIBOR* is the acronym for the *London Interbank Offered Rate.* It is the rate of interest that London banks charge each other for short-term loans. Each business day, rates are provided for 10 different currencies, and 15 maturities are quoted for each currency (ranging from overnight to 12 months). Thus, 150 rates are quoted each business day.

LIBOR essentially is the United Kingdom equivalent to the U.S. federal funds rate. London banks with surplus reserves lend those surpluses to other London banks in need of liquidity. The rate they charge is LIBOR. This enables banks to avoid holding excessively large amounts of their asset base as liquid assets. LIBOR is compiled by the British Bankers' Association and released publicly once each business day.

In the world of commercial lending, LIBOR is very important. Many loan or credit agreements utilize LIBOR as the base interest rate in a loan with a floating or fluctuating rate of interest. The specific rate of interest on a given loan will be LIBOR plus a specified number of basis points negotiated between the lender and the borrower. For example, the rate could be set at LIBOR plus an additional 350 basis points (or 3.5%).

## § 10.   SIMPLE INTEREST VERSUS COMPOUND INTEREST

### A.   Generally

There are two ways to calculate interest earned on an invested sum of money. The first is called *simple interest* and the second *compound interest*. When simple interest is earned on an investment, it means that interest will only be earned on the invested sum itself over the course of the investment. In other words, the interest earned on the invested sum during one period does not itself earn interest in subsequent periods.

For example, suppose you invest $5,000 in a savings account that pays four percent *simple interest* annually over a three-year period. As detailed below, at the end of the period you will have earned $600 in interest:

| Year | Amount Invested | Interest Earned |
|:----:|:---------------:|:---------------:|
| 1 | $5,000.00 | $200.00 |
| 2 | $5,000.00 | $200.00 |
| 3 | $5,000.00 | $200.00 |
| | Total Interest | $600.00 |

This example shows that the $200 of interest earned during Year 1 is *not* added to the amount invested, and thus does *not* itself earn interest during Years 2 and 3. Likewise, the $200 of interest earned during Year 2 *does not* itself earn interest during Year 3.

When an investment earns *compound interest*, interest earned on the invested sum during one period will itself earn interest in subsequent periods. This is called *compounding*. Interest earned during one period is reinvested and earns interest on itself in subsequent periods. Interest can be compounded annually (once a year), semi-annually (every six months, or twice a year), quarterly (every three months, or four times a year), monthly (every month, or 12 times a year) or even daily (every day, or 365 times a year).

For example, suppose you invest $5,000 in a savings account that pays four percent interest *compounded annually* over a three-year period. As detailed below, at the end of the period you will have earned $624.32 in interest:

| Year | Amount Invested | Interest Earned |
|------|-----------------|-----------------|
| 1 | $5,000.00 | $200.00 |
| 2 | $5,200.00 | $208.00 |
| 3 | $5,408.00 | $216.32 |
| | Total Interest | $624.32 |

The compound interest example yielded an extra $24.32 in interest over the example using simple interest. That $24.32 represents interest earned on previously earned interest. As seen above, the $200.00 in interest earned in Year 1 was added to the amount invested in Years 2 and 3, and thus itself earned interest during Years 2 and 3. Likewise, the $208.00 in interest earned during Year 2 was added to the amount invested in Year 3, and thus itself earned interest during Year 3.

## B.   Rule of 72s

The *Rule of 72s* is a useful tool for determining how long it would take a given sum of money to double in value assuming various rates of interest *compounded annually*. The result of dividing the number 72 by the rate of compound interest to be earned *approximates* the number of years it would take for a given sum of money to double. (Actually, the number 69.315, which is based on the natural log of 2, would be more precise, but 72 is simply easier to use in the calculations).

Using the Rule of 72s, it would take an investment earning compound interest at an annual rate of 10 percent a little over 7 years to double [72 ÷ 10]. An investment earning compound interest at an annual rate of six percent would double in about 12 years [72 ÷ 6]. And an investment earning compound interest at an annual rate of only three percent would double in around 24 years [72 ÷ 3].

## C.  Rule of 110

Similarly, the *Rule of 110* is used to determine how long it would take a given sum of money to triple in value based on various rates of interest *compounded annually*. (110 is based on the rough estimate of the log of 3). Thus, it would take an investment earning compound interest at an annual rate of 15 percent about 7 years, 3 months to triple [110 ÷ 15]. An investment earning compound interest at an annual rate of eight percent would triple in just under 14 years [110 ÷ 8]. And an investment earning compound interest at an annual rate of only five percent would triple in around 22 years [110 ÷ 5].

# CHAPTER 4

# FUTURE VALUE AND PRESENT VALUE

The "time value of money" is directly related to two concepts in corporate finance known as "present value" and "future value." As you will see, these concepts are basically *two sides of the same valuation coin*.

## § 11. FUTURE VALUE

*Future value* (FV) is simply the value of a current sum of money on some *future date*, assuming it was invested and earns a specified rate of interest between now and that future date. To determine FV, one must know four pieces of information: (1) the current sum of money to be invested; (2) the future point in time; (3) the rate of interest to be earned on the current sum of money between today and that future date; and (4) the frequency at which interest will be compounded. An example provides the best way to understand FV.

Suppose you place $1,000 for one full year in a savings account that pays interest at the rate of five percent per annum. At the end of the year, how much money will be in the savings account? The answer is $1,050. $1,000 was your original investment and $50 [$1,000 × .05] was the interest you earned during the one-year period. Thus, the "future value" of the current sum of $1,000 one year into the future, assuming a rate of interest of five percent per annum, is $1,050.

Calculating FV is relatively easy because there is a formula to follow:

$$FV_n = x(1 + k)^n$$

where:    $FV_n$ is what is being determined. It represents the future value of the current sum at the end of "n" periods of time. The subscript "n" does not affect the calculation. It is simply a mathematical designation indicating that "FV" is a future rather than present sum.

$n$ following the term $(1 + k)$ is the period of time into the future that FV will be determined. Because FV can be calculated based on years, months or other time periods, "n" is used instead of "years." "n" appears as an *exponent* when it follows the term $(1 + k)$, and thus $(1 + k)^n$ reads $(1 + k)$ to the "n$^{th}$" power. Accordingly, it is *incorrect* to simply multiply $(1 + k)$ by "n." For example, $(1 + .05)^3$ is not simply $1.05 × 3$ (which equals 3.15); rather, it is $1.05 × 1.05 × 1.05$ (which equals 1.1576).

$x$ is the current sum of money to be invested.

> $k$ is the rate of interest *compounded an-nually* to be earned on the current sum of money. It is expressed as a decimal, and thus 14 percent would appear as .14 in the formula.

Virtually all financial calculators calculate FV in a few simple key strokes. For your convenience and for those without a financial calculator, the term $(1 + k)^n$, which is referred to as the *future value factor* when used in the future value formula, has been calculated based on many different time periods and many different interest rates. The results are set forth in the "Future Value of $1 at the End of 'n' Periods" table that appears in *Exhibit I*.

Looking at that table, notice that the future value factor when "n" equals 20 years and the interest rate is seven percent is 3.8697. Accordingly, the future value of $10,000 placed into a savings account earning interest of seven percent per annum compounded annually for 20 years would be calculated as follows:

$$FV_{20} = \$10,000 \ (1 + .07)^{20}$$
$$= \$10,000 \ (3.8697)$$
$$= \underline{\$38,697.00}$$

The FV formula presented above assumes that interest will be compounded *annually*. To determine FV based on compounding more frequent than annual, the FV formula must be modified. (For an explanation of "compounding," see Nutshell Section 10.) To do so, first divide the interest rate (k) by the frequency of compounding (m), and then multiply the number of time periods (n) by the same. Thus:

$$FV_n = x(1 + k/m)^{n \cdot m}$$

Once again, interest can be compounded semi-annually, quarterly, monthly or even daily. Thus, if interest was compounded semi-annually, quarterly, monthly or daily, "m" would equal 2, 4, 12 and 365, respectively.

Suppose you invest $2,000 in a certificate of deposit (CD) for five years. That CD pays 16 percent annual interest *compounded quarterly*. How much money would you receive at the end of the five-year period?

$$
\begin{aligned}
FV_5 \quad &= \quad \$2{,}000\,(1 + .16/4)^{5 \cdot 4} \\
&= \quad \$2{,}000\,(1 + .04)^{20} \\
&= \quad \$2{,}000\,(2.1911) \\
&= \quad \underline{\$4{,}382.20}
\end{aligned}
$$

Thus, the future value of $2,000 invested for five years in a CD paying 16 percent interest compounded quarterly is $4,382.20. Picking up on the use of "n" rather than years, one could also say that the future value of $2,000 invested for *20 quarterly periods* [5 × 4] paying four percent interest per quarter [.16 ÷ 4] is $4,382.20.

If that same $2,000 were invested in a similar five-year CD that only paid 16 percent interest compounded *annually*, it would yield only $4,200.60 [$2,000 × 2.1003 = $4,200.60]. This is $181.60 *less* than the $4,382.20 earned using quarterly compounding.

Accordingly, savvy investors seek to have interest on their invested money compounded more frequently than annually. In the context of FV, *the more frequent the compounding, the greater the resulting future value.*

## § 12. PRESENT VALUE

If future value lies on one side of the valuation coin, then *present value* (PV) lies on the other. PV is simply a lump sum of money to be received or paid in the future *valued in today's dollars*. As seen below, PV can be calculated for a single future sum of money or for a stream of future payments, known as an *annuity*. In determining PV, we move backward in time—from a future date back to today—through the process of *discounting*.

### A. PV of a Lump Sum

How much is a lump sum of money to be paid or received on a future date worth in today's dollars? Suppose, for example, you estimate that one year of college tuition 20 years from today will cost $65,000. How much money must you invest today to have $65,000 at that future date? Alternatively, suppose a trust your parents set up is to pay you $100,000 when you turn 40 years old, which is 15 years from now. How much is that $100,000 worth in today's dollars?

Present value answers both of these questions. In order to determine PV, we need to know four pieces of information: (1) the future sum of money to be received or paid; (2) the future point in time that sum is to be received or paid; (3) the rate of interest that will be earned on investments between today and that future date; and (4) the frequency at which interest will be compounded.

To calculate PV, use the following formula:

$$PV = \frac{x_n}{(1 + k)^n}$$

where:    *PV* is what is being determined. It represents the present value (the value measured in today's dollars) of the future sum to be received or paid at a future date.

*n* following the term $(1 + k)$ is the period of time into the future that the future sum is to be paid or received. Because the period of time between now and the future date can be measured in years, quarters, months or other time periods, "n" is used instead of "years." "n" appears as an *exponent* when it follows the term $(1 + k)$, and thus $(1 + k)^n$ reads $(1 + k)$ to the "$n^{th}$" power. Accordingly, it is *incorrect* to simply multiply $(1 + k)$ by "n." For example, $(1 + .05)^3$ is not simply $1.05 \times 3$ (which equals 3.15); rather, it is $1.05 \times 1.05 \times 1.05$ (which equals 1.1576).

$x_n$ is the future sum of money. The subscript "n" does not affect the calculation. It is simply a mathematical designation indicating that "x" is a future rather than present sum.

$k$ is the rate of interest *compounded annually* to be earned on investments between the present and future date. It is expressed as a decimal, and thus 14 percent would appear as .14 in the formula. When used in the present value formula, "k" is referred to as the "*discount rate.*"

Virtually all financial calculators calculate PV in a few simple key strokes. For your convenience and for those without a financial calculator, the term $(1 + k)^n$, which is referred to as the *present value factor* when used in the present value formula, has been calculated based on many different time periods and many different interest rates. The *reciprocals* of these factors are set forth in the "Present Value of a \$1 at the End of 'n' Periods" table that appears in *Exhibit I*. Thus, a given reciprocal must be *multiplied against,* rather than divided into, the future sum. For example, the number the table provides when "n" equals 14 years and the discount rate is nine percent is 0.2992. This number is the *reciprocal* of the present value factor:

$$\frac{1}{(1 + .09)^{14}} = .2992$$

Suppose your five-year old daughter will be starting college in 13 years. You estimate that her first year at Syracuse University at that point in time will cost $65,000. Between then and now, you expect to earn 11 percent per annum on your money. How much do you have to invest *today* to have the $65,000 you will need 13 years from now? In other words, what is the present value of that $65,000 based on a discount rate of 11 percent?

$$PV = \frac{\$65,000}{(1 + .11)^{13}}$$

$$= \$65,000 \times .2575$$

$$= \underline{\$16,737.50}$$

The PV formula presented above assumes that interest will be compounded *annually*. To determine PV based on compounding more frequent than annual, the PV formula must be modified to reflect the frequency of compounding. (For an explanation of "compounding," see Nutshell Section 10.) To do so, first divide the interest rate (k) by the frequency of compounding (m) and then multiply the number of time periods (n) by the same:

$$PV = \frac{x_n}{(1 + k/m)^{n \cdot m}}$$

Once again, interest can be compounded semi-annually, quarterly, monthly or even daily. Thus, if interest was compounded semi-annually, quarterly, monthly or daily, "m" would equal 2, 4, 12 and 365, respectively.

Suppose a trust your parents set up is to pay you $100,000 when you turn 40 years old, which is 15 years from now. Between then and now, you expect to earn eight percent per annum compounded semi-annually on your investments. How much is that $100,000 worth to you in *today's* dollars? In other words, what is the present value of that $100,000 based on a discount rate of eight percent compounded semi-annually?

$$\begin{aligned} PV &= \frac{\$100,000}{(1 + .08/2)^{15 \cdot 2}} \\[2mm] &= \frac{\$100,000}{(1 + .04)^{30}} \\[2mm] &= \$100,000 \times 0.3083 \\[2mm] &= \underline{\underline{\$30,830.00}} \end{aligned}$$

If that same $100,000 were discounted at eight percent compounded *annually*, instead of semi-annually, the present value would be $31,520.00 [$100,000 × .3152 = $31,520.00]. Of course, this is $690.00 *more* than the $30,830.00 resulting from semi-annual compounding.

In the context of PV, *the more frequent the compounding, the lower the resulting present value will be.*

## B. PV of an Annuity

Present value can also be calculated for an *annuity*. An annuity is the payment of a constant sum of money at fixed intervals over a period of years. Thus, an annuity requires the periodic cash flows to be equal, the intervals between cash flows to be the same, and interest to be computed once each period. The cash flows in an *ordinary annuity* occur at the end of each period (in *"arrears"*). Thus, an ordinary annuity is also called a "deferred" annuity. The cash flows of an *annuity due,* by contrast, occur at the beginning of each period.

## (1) Ordinary ("Deferred") Annuity

Winners of some lotteries can choose to receive a lump sum payment of $1 million this year or payments of $150,000 per year over the next ten years. The receipt of $150,000 a year for the next ten years is an annuity. Should you choose the $1 million lump sum or the $150,000 yearly payments made over the next ten years? (For purposes of the example, taxes are ignored). The answer to this depends on the rate of interest that will be earned on investments during that 10–year period. Suppose you think interest rates will average around eight percent per year. What is the present value of that $150,000 per year income stream if payments are made at the end of each year (an ordinary annuity)?

One way to figure this out is to use the present value formula to determine the present value of each $150,000 payment over the 10-year period:

$$PV = \frac{x_1}{(1 + k)^1} + \frac{x_2}{(1 + k)^2} + \ldots \frac{x_{10}}{(1 + k)^{10}}$$

Fortunately, the following formula has been developed to simplify this calculation:

$$PV_a = \sum \frac{x_n}{(1 + k)^n}$$

where:    $PV_a$ is what is being determined. It represents the present value (the value measured in today's dollars) of a constant sum of money ("$x_n$") received at the end of fixed intervals over a period of time ("$n$"). The subscript "a" does not affect the calculation. It is simply a mathematical designation indicating that "PV" is the present value of an annuity rather than a sum certain.

$\sum$ (the Greek letter "sigma") means the *summation* of present values for "$n$" periods of time.

$n$ following the term $(1 + k)$ is the period of time into the future that the annuity will be paid. Because the period of time between now and the future date can be measured in years, quarters, months or other time periods, "$n$" is used instead of "years."

$x_n$ is the constant sum of money paid at the end of fixed intervals into the future. The subscript "$n$" does not affect the calculation. It is simply a mathematical designation indicating that "x" is a future rather than present sum.

> *k* is the rate of interest *compounded annually* to be earned on investments between the present and future date. Once again, it is referred to as the "*discount rate.*"

Virtually all financial calculators calculate PV for an ordinary annuity in a few simple key strokes. For those without a financial calculator, the term $(1 + k)^n$, which is referred to as the *present value factor of an ordinary annuity* when used in the present value of an annuity formula, has been calculated based on many different time periods and many different interest rates. The *reciprocals* of these factors are set forth in the "Present Value of an Ordinary Annuity of $1 per Period for 'n' Periods" table that appears in Exhibit I. For example, the number the table provides when "n" equals 10 years and the discount rate is eight percent is 6.7101. This number must be *multiplied against,* rather than divided into, the constant sum when determining the present value of an annuity.

Taking our example of a 10–year annuity paying $150,000 a year and a discount rate of eight percent, the calculation is as follows:

$$PV_a = \sum \frac{\$150,000}{(1 + .08)^{10}}$$

$$= \$150,000 \times 6.7101$$

$$= \underline{\$1,006,515}$$

Thus, an annual payment of $150,000 for the next 10 years when interest rates are averaging eight percent is worth $1,006,515 to you today. This is more (but barely more) than your other option of the $1 million lump sum. Therefore, the lottery winner should select the annuity over the lump sum payment, unless tax consequences or other considerations (your health, for example) dictate otherwise.

What if, in that same example, you assumed more frequent compounding than annual? Suppose interest was compounded semi-annually? Would the same result follow? Based on what we know about discounting, the answer is no. More frequent compounding would result in a lower present value than that calculated using less frequent compounding.

Calculating the PV of an ordinary annuity based on compounding more frequent than annual is a two-step process. First, you must determine what the effective annual interest rate (EAIR) is, because a portion of the annual interest is being compounded. EAIR is calculated as follows:

$$\text{EAIR} = (1 + i/m)^m - 1$$

where:    "$i$" is the annual interest rate.
          "$m$" is the frequency of compounding.

Thus, when the annual interest rate is eight percent and compounding is semi-annual, EAIR is calculated as follows:

$$\begin{aligned}
\text{EAIR} &= (1 + .08/2)^2 - 1 \\
&= (1 + .04)^2 - 1 \\
&= 1.0816 - 1 \\
&= \underline{.0816} \text{ or } \underline{8.16\%}
\end{aligned}$$

Second, perform the regular calculation for an ordinary annuity, replacing "k" with "EAIR." However, because EAIR is unlikely to be a whole number, you must use a *financial calculator* rather than the table to perform the calculation:

$$PV_a = \sum \frac{\$150,000}{(1 + .0816)^{10}}$$

$$= \$150,000 \times 6.6619$$

$$= \underline{\$999,285}$$

As seen above, the present value of an annuity paying $150,000 a year for ten years when the rate of interest is eight percent compounded semi-annually is $7,230 less than if interest was compounded annually. This result is expected, as more frequent compounding yields lower present values.

### (2) Annuity Due

The cash flows in an ordinary annuity occur at the end of each period (in *"arrears"*). Annuities where the cash flows occur at the *beginning* of each period are called *annuities due*. Thus, while the same number of payments are received in an ordinary annuity and an annuity due, the first payment in the annuity due is received *one time period earlier*. Because of this, the present value of the cash flow of an annuity due is exactly one interest payment *greater* than the present value of an ordinary annuity. Therefore, an annuity due is more valuable than an ordinary annuity.

In an annuity due, each payment is discounted for one less period. Therefore, to calculate the present value of an annuity due, simply multiply the present value of an *ordinary* annuity by 1 plus the interest rate:

$$PV_{ad} = \sum \frac{x_n}{(1+k)^n} \bullet (1+k)$$

Notice the difference in present values below when the facts of the previous example (assuming annual compounding) are applied to a series of cash flows that occur at the beginning of the period rather than at the end:

| | | | Factor | | Amount * | |
|---|---|---|---|---|---|---|
| | Cash | | Ordinary | Annuity | Ordinary | Annuity |
| Period | Flow | Rate | Annuity | Due | Annuity | Due |
| 1 | $150,000 | 8% | 0.92593 | 1.00000 | $ 138,890 | $ 150,000 |
| 2 | $150,000 | 8% | 0.85734 | 0.92593 | 128,601 | 138,890 |
| 3 | $150,000 | 8% | 0.79383 | 0.85734 | 119,075 | 128,601 |
| 4 | $150,000 | 8% | 0.73503 | 0.79383 | 110,255 | 119,075 |
| 5 | $150,000 | 8% | 0.68058 | 0.73503 | 102,088 | 110,255 |
| 6 | $150,000 | 8% | 0.63017 | 0.68058 | 94,525 | 102,088 |
| 7 | $150,000 | 8% | 0.58349 | 0.63017 | 87,525 | 94,525 |
| 8 | $150,000 | 8% | 0.54027 | 0.58349 | 81,040 | 87,525 |
| 9 | $150,000 | 8% | 0.50025 | 0.54027 | 75,037 | 81,040 |
| 10 | $150,000 | 8% | 0.46319 | 0.50025 | 69,479 | 75,037 |
| | | | | | $1,006,515 | $1,087,036 |

* Amounts may be off by $1 due to rounding errors

## C.  Using PV to Determine Rate of Return

The discount rate used in the basic PV formula is also called the *rate of return* of an investment. Thus, the formula can also be used to determine the rate of return of an investment when certain variables are known or assumed.

For example, assume an investor contributes $1,000 and wants to double the value of her investment in four years. What rate of return must she earn to achieve this result? By using the basic PV formula, "k" (the discount rate or "rate of return" in this example) can be determined based on what we know:

$$PV = \frac{X_n}{(1 + k)^n}$$

$$\$1,000 = \frac{\$2,000}{(1 + k)^4}$$

$$\$1,000 (1 + k)^4 = \$2,000$$

$$(1 + k)^4 = \frac{\$2,000}{\$1,000}$$

$$\sqrt[4]{(1 + k)^4} = \sqrt[4]{2}$$

$$k = \underline{0.1892} \text{ or } \underline{18.92\%}$$

Obviously, a financial calculator can calculate "k" in a few easy key strokes, and thus it is essential to use one.

# CHAPTER 5

# BOND VALUATION

## § 13. INTRODUCTION TO BOND VALUATION

A corporate bond normally has a face or "par" value of $1,000 and pays interest semi-annually at its stated rate of interest (its *coupon rate*). During its life, it is an *interest-only* bond. This means that its corporate issuer pays interest over the bond's life. When the issuer makes the final interest payment upon the bond's maturity, it also repays the principal (the bond's $1,000 face value) in one lump-sum.

If the bond's original purchaser holds the bond until its maturity, she will receive the full $1,000 face value plus, of course, interest along the way. However, that purchaser need not hold onto the bond until its maturity. Instead, if the bond is listed on a stock exchange for trading purposes, she can resell it in the secondary market to another investor. The important question is, "at what price?"

Although the corporate issuer is obligated to pay interest at the bond's coupon rate to any secondary market purchaser of the bond, investors seeking to buy bonds in the secondary market demand an interest rate (a *yield to maturity* or *YTM*) competitive with the current market rate on similar, newly-issued bonds. That rate, however, may be higher or lower than the existing bond's coupon rate. Because the existing bond's coupon rate cannot be changed, the only way to raise or lower its YTM in response to current market conditions is for the bond to sell above (*i.e.*, at a *premium*) or below (*i.e.*, at a *discount*) its $1,000 face value.

In order to calculate the value of a particular bond in the secondary market, *three steps* must be completed. First, calculate the present value of the one-time principal payment at the end of the bond's life. To do so, simply calculate the present value of a future lump sum. (See Nutshell Section 12A). Second, calculate the present value of the remaining interest payments due on the bond. To do so, simply calculate the present value of an ordinary annuity. (See Nutshell Section 12B(1)). Third, add the two present values together. Examples follow below in Nutshell Sections 14A and B.

## § 14. INVERSE RELATIONSHIP BETWEEN INTEREST RATES AND BOND VALUES

Bond values in the secondary market fluctuate *inversely* with changes in interest rates. When interest rates increase beyond the coupon rate of an existing bond ("Bond A"), Bond A's value in the secondary market declines. Those selling Bond A at that time must do so at a discount to its face value. This occurs because investors will discount Bond A's value at the current (and higher) coupon rate on a similar, newly-issued bond, thus leading to a market value for Bond A below its face value. When considered together with Bond A's below-market coupon rate, the discounted price an investor pays will cause Bond A's YTM to match the higher coupon rate of a similar, newly-issued bond.

When interest rates decrease below the coupon rate of Bond A, Bond A's value increases. Those selling Bond A at that time charge a price greater than Bond A's face value, because investors will pay a premium for a bond with an above-market coupon rate. When considered together with Bond A's above-market coupon rate, the premium price an investor pays will cause Bond A's YTM to match the lower coupon rate of a similar, newly-issued bond.

The examples below illustrate the inverse relationship between bond valuations and market interest rates. Note that rounding is to the fourth decimal, except with respect to the final dollar amount, which is rounded to the penny.

## A. Lower Valuation When Interest Rates Increase

Assume that three years after SJG Corp. issued a 20–year bond with a seven percent coupon, similar, newly-issued bonds have a coupon of 10 percent. In other words, interest rates have risen during the last three years. What will the SJG bond be worth at that time in the secondary market given its now below-market coupon rate? To calculate this, simply follow the three steps mentioned above in Nutshell Section 13.

First, calculate the present value of the bond's face value of $1,000 (present value of a future lump sum, see Nutshell Section 12A) discounted at the *current market rate* of 10 percent for the remaining 17–year life of the bond:

$$
\begin{aligned}
PV &= \frac{x_n}{(1 + k)^n} \\[2ex]
&= \frac{\$1,000}{(1.10)^{17}} \\[2ex]
&= \$1,000 \times 0.1978 \text{ [from Exhibit I]} \\[2ex]
&= \$197.80
\end{aligned}
$$

Next, calculate the present value of the remaining interest payments (present value of an annuity, see Nutshell Section 12B(1)) discounted at the *current market rate* of 10 percent. Recall that the bond will pay $70 [.07 x $1,000] annually for the next 17 years:

$$PV_a = \sum \frac{x_n}{(1 + k)^n}$$

$$= \sum \frac{\$70}{(1.10)^{17}}$$

$$= \$70 \times 8.0216 \text{ [from Exhibit I]}$$

$$= \$561.51$$

Finally, add the two present values together:

$$PV_{bond} = \$197.80 + \$561.51$$
$$= \underline{\$759.31}$$

This demonstrates that as interest rates rise, the value of an existing bond declines in the secondary market. By purchasing the SJG bond for $759.31 rather than $1,000 from its seller, a new purchaser receives a YTM of 10 percent.

## B.  Higher Valuation When Interest Rates Decrease

What would the SJG bond be valued at if the interest rate for similar, newly-issued bonds decreased to four percent over the three-year period? (Assume that all other variables remain the same as in the prior example). Follow the three steps mentioned in Nutshell Section 13.

First, calculate the present value of the bond's face value of $1,000 discounted at the *current market rate* of four percent for the remaining 17–year life of the bond:

$$PV = \frac{x_n}{(1 + k)^n}$$

$$= \frac{\$1,000}{(1.04)^{17}}$$

$$= \$1,000 \times 0.5134 \text{ [from Exhibit I]}$$

$$= \underline{\$513.40}$$

Next, calculate the present value of the remaining interest payments discounted at the *current market rate* of four percent. Recall that the bond will pay $70 [.07 $\times$ $1,000] annually for the next 17 years:

$$PV_a = \sum \frac{x_n}{(1 + k)^n}$$

$$= \sum \frac{\$70}{(1.04)^{17}}$$

$$= \$70 \times 12.1657 \text{ [from Exhibit I]}$$

$$= \$851.60$$

Finally, add the two present values together:

$$PV_{bond} = \$513.40 + \$851.60$$
$$= \underline{\$1,365.00}$$

As you can see, the SJG bond's valuation is higher than its face value when the current interest rate on similar, newly-issued bonds decreases to 4 percent. By paying a "premium" of $365 over the $1,000 face value of the SJG bond, the purchaser obtains a bond with a seven percent stated interest rate, but a YTM of only four percent. While the YTM on the bond is substantially below its coupon rate, the purchaser is no worse off than if he had purchased a similar, newly-issued bond with a four percent coupon at its $1,000 face value.

## C.  Predicting Sensitivity

### (1) Sensitivity to Changing Interest Rates

The sensitivity of a bond's value to changing interest rates is referred to as a bond's *duration*. The greater a bond's duration, the more sensitive the bond is to interest rate changes. Duration is the weighted average of the times when a bond's cash payments are to be received. A bond with a duration of 3.0 will be less sensitive to interest rate changes than will a bond with a duration of 7.0. Duration is a useful concept to know, because a bond's maturity only indicates when its final payment is to be made, not the average time to each payment.

A bond with a longer maturity will be more sensitive to interest rate changes than a bond with a shorter maturity. This stems from the fact that more of the value of the longer term bond is derived from discounting the face value of that bond. The longer the time to maturity, the more time periods the face value is discounted back. Thus, the denominator in the PV formula is greater for a bond with a longer term than it is for a bond with a shorter term.

A bond's sensitivity to interest rate changes is also a function of its coupon rate. If two bonds have the same characteristics except that one bond has a lower coupon rate than the other (because, for example, its issuer is a better credit risk), the value of the bond with the lower coupon rate will be more sensitive to fluctuations in interest rates. This is because the lower coupon rate bond derives a greater proportion of its value from its face value to be received at maturity than does the higher coupon rate bond. The higher coupon rate bond, by contrast, derives a greater proportion of its value from its interest payments than does the lower coupon rate bond. The result is that the value of the lower coupon rate bond is more sensitive to changes in interest rates.

### (2) Sensitivity to Changes in an Issuer's Creditworthiness

A bond's value may also fluctuate due to a change in the creditworthiness of its issuer. If the issuer's creditworthiness diminishes (the issuer is seen as less likely to service the interest and principal payments on its bonds), then investors will discount the bond's face value and interest payments at a higher discount rate that reflects the increase in risk. A higher discount rate, in turn, results in a lower bond valuation. This is what happened in *Metropolitan Life Ins. Co. v. RJR Nabisco, Inc.*, 716 F.Supp. 1504 (S.D.N.Y.1989), where bondholders sued over the decline in their bonds' value that resulted from an increase in the issuer's default risk.

Conversely, if the bond issuer's creditworthiness increases, then investors will discount the bond's face value and interest payments at a lower discount rate that reflects the decrease in risk. A lower discount rate, in turn, results in a higher bond valuation. For example, in 2005 investors in MCI debt were delighted when Verizon Communications, a company with an A2 credit rating from Moody's and an A+ rating from Standard and Poor's, decided to purchase MCI. With Verizon's support, MCI's creditworthiness would increase and its bonds would become less risky, causing the value of the MCI bonds to increase as they rose from junk to investment grade status.

## § 15. CALCULATING YIELD TO MATURITY

Existing bonds are always priced in the secondary market to reflect current market interest rates. Therefore, if you know the current price of an outstanding bond, you can work backwards to determine its yield to maturity. For example, suppose SJG Corp. issued 20–year bonds, each with a seven percent coupon rate and a $1,000 face value. Five

years later, each SJG bond is valued at $838.79 in
the secondary market. What is the YTM on the SJG
bonds?

Because each bond is trading at a discount to its
$1,000 face value, its yield to maturity has to be
greater than seven percent, the bond's coupon rate.
The inverse relationship between outstanding bond
values and interest rates tells us that. (See Nutshell
Section 14). One could attempt to solve this problem algebraically by plugging in various numbers
for the interest rate on a trial and error basis.
However, most financial calculators have the capacity to calculate a bond's yield to maturity easily.
Usually, the financial calculator requires the following method of calculation: enter $70 as the coupon
payment (PMT); 15 as the number of periods (n);
$838.79 as the present value (PV); and $1,000 as
the future value (FV). The final step is to solve for
the interest rate (i). The answer is 8.98 percent.

## § 16.  ZERO COUPON BONDS

A *zero coupon bond* (referred to as a *"zero"*) is a
bond that pays no annual interest (hence the phrase
"zero coupon" in its name). The bond, however, is
sold at a significant discount to its face value. Upon
maturity, its issuer must pay back the full face
value, and thus its holder's compensation is the
difference between the zero's face value and the
discounted price at which it was originally issued.

Zeros have an implicit rate of interest associated
with them. For example, suppose SMH Corp. issues

five-year zeros with a $1,000 face value for $747.26 each. Using the present value of a lump sum formula, plug in $1,000 for the future sum, $747.26 for the present value, five years for the time period, and then calculate the discount rate. Using a financial calculator, the implicit rate of interest in this example is six percent assuming annual compounding. Another way of looking at this is to say that $747.26 compounded annually at six percent interest will grow to $1,000 five years from now.

Although an investor receives no interest payments during the life of a zero, she must recognize the *imputed income* from the zero on her tax return. This means she pays tax on that income even though she receives no cash interest payment from the issuer. Because of this, most investors in zeros are pension funds, other tax-exempt entities, and individuals buying zeros for their individual retirement accounts.

A company which prefers not to pay interest during the term of its outstanding debt securities is a prime candidate for issuing zeros. While zeros allow the company to avoid cash outlays in the form of interest payments, the Internal Revenue Code nevertheless permits it to deduct interest expense each year as if it had. For example, suppose SMH Corp. needed $80 million to purchase a large tract of land. It plans on improving that land over a five-year period and then reselling it at a sizeable profit. Because SMH will not receive any return from its investment in the land until it resells it, issuing zeros makes sense for SMH. Indeed, SMH pays no interest over the five-year period yet deducts interest expense as if it had. When the aggregate face value of the zeros matures, SMH will have the funds necessary to pay investors after it sells the improved land.

## § 17. BOND MARKET PRICING TERMINOLOGY

When buying and selling bonds in the secondary market, one must understand the terms "bid price," "asked price," "bid-ask spread" and "tick." The *bid price* represents what a purchaser is willing to pay for a given bond. The *asked price* represents the price at which the seller is willing to sell the bond. The difference between the two prices is referred to as the *bid-ask spread*. Bond dealers receive the spread rather than charge commissions.

Generally, bond prices are listed as a percentage of par value to allow bonds with different face values to be compared directly. Under this pricing convention, a bond with a face value of $1,000 that is selling for par and a bond with a face value of $10,000 that is also selling for par will each have its price listed as 100. This simply means that their prices are equal to 100% of par value. For example, if a $1,000 corporate bond was listed at 90 and a $5,000 municipal bond was listed at 95, it can be easily seen that the $1,000 bond is selling at a bigger discount. To calculate the bond's actual price, turn the list price into a percentage and then multiply by the face value of the bond. Thus, the price of the $1,000 corporate bond is 90% times $1,000, or $900.00, while the price for the $5,000 municipal bond is 95% times $5,000, or $4,750.00.

Bond prices in the secondary market are rounded to the 32nd rather than the penny. The smallest price change is 1/32 and is referred to as a *tick*. A bond quoted at a price of 100:10 is, in actuality, 100–10/32 or 100.3125. This, however, is not the price of the bond; rather, this means the price of the bond is 100.3125% of its face value. Therefore, if the bond has a $1,000 face value, multiply 100.3125 by $10 to determine that the price of the bond is $1,003.13 (rounded to the penny). Thus, the price of a $1,000 face value bond quoted at 97:12 is, in actuality, 97–12/32 or 97.375% of its face value. Its price is thus $973.75 [97.375 x $10].

Because trading volume in U.S. Treasuries is much greater than for other bonds, they sometimes trade in 1/64 increments. An increment of 1/64 is denoted by a plus sign next to the listed price. Thus, a U.S. Treasury bond with a $1,000 face value that is listed at "100:1 + " is equal to 100 + 1/32 + 1/64, or 100 + 3/64. This equals 100.04875 thus making the bond worth 100.04875% of its $1,000 face value, or $1,000.49 (rounded) [100.04875 x $10].

The prices of listed bonds are set forth at their *flat (or clean) prices*. That is, the prices do not reflect any accrued interest. Bonds generally pay interest on a semi-annual basis, and therefore interest accrues between interest payment dates. Bonds purchased on interest payment dates are priced at their flat prices. However, prices of bonds purchased between interest payment dates are equal to their flat prices *plus* accrued interest, a collective amount referred to as the *full* or *dirty price*. When a bond is purchased in the secondary market between interest payment dates, the buyer must pay the seller the full or dirty price.

Accrued interest is calculated as follows:

$$\text{accrued interest} = \text{interest payment} \times \frac{\text{number of days since last payment}}{\text{number of days between payments}}$$

# CHAPTER 6

## VALUING COMPANIES

When it comes to valuing a business, valuation methods abound. On one end of the continuum are those methods that are highly-developed and utilize complex computer models. In fact, those in the business of valuing companies, most notably investment banking firms, consider their approaches to valuation highly-proprietary. On the other end of the valuation continuum are methods that are extremely easy to apply. Those involved with smaller businesses most frequently employ these methods, as their usefulness resides primarily in their simplicity.

The valuation methods described below attempt to identify what the *intrinsic* or *true value* of a business is. However, *valuing a company is an art, not a science*. Be wary of those who insist that the value of a business is "$X" rather than "$Y." There is really no right answer. In fact, the best test of "value" is whether someone is actually willing to buy a company at a price established by a given valuation method. If not, is the intrinsic value provided by that method truly reflective of that company's worth?

Having said that, certain valuations are, depending on the surrounding circumstances, more compelling or persuasive than others. Proponents for one valuation will get their chance, either at the negotiating table or in court, to advocate why their valuation is more appropriate than another's for the business under consideration.

The valuation methods described below are broken down into: (a) balance sheet-based valuation methods; (b) profit and loss (P&L) statement-based valuation methods; and (c) cash flow-based valuation methods. It is usual for someone in the business of valuing a company, such as an appraiser or an investment bank, to employ several valuation methods in order to determine a range of possible values for that company. Once that range is developed, the appraiser or investment bank will assign weights to those values based on variables both internal and external to that company. The appraiser or investment bank will then present the weighted average valuation as the appropriate valuation for that company.

The valuation methods described below can be used to value either privately-held or publicly-traded businesses. As mentioned above, these methods attempt to identify what the "intrinsic" or "true" value of the business is. Unlike in the case of a privately-held business, public companies enjoy a market-generated share price for their stock. Accordingly, this market price can be used to help refine the valuation of a publicly-traded company. Market price, however, should not be the only valuation factor looked at when valuing an entire company, because it only reflects the value of one share of that company's stock. A controlling stake, by definition, allows its owner to exercise control. Because control is valuable, an acquiror typically pays a price well above the market price per share for that stake.

## § 18.  BALANCE SHEET–BASED VALUATION METHODS

Balance sheet-based valuation methods utilize the numbers contained in a company's balance sheet to determine a company's value. The balance sheet is a financial statement that lists a corporation's assets, liabilities and shareholders' equity. Importantly, it lists the value of the company's assets at their historical cost (or lower current market value if their value has been permanently impaired). The balance sheet provides values as of a specific date in time, such as December 31st. Thus, the balance sheet gives a "snapshot" of a company's assets, liabilities and shareholders' equity on a given day (*i.e.,* the last day of a fiscal quarter or year). See Nutshell Section 5A.

Because virtually all businesses, including small businesses, create a balance sheet at least once a year, balance sheet-based valuation methods are popular valuation methods. For example, it is usual to see a balance sheet-based valuation method appear within a "shareholders' agreement" or "buy-sell agreement" entered into by the stockholders of a closely-held company. Such an agreement often requires a stockholder to sell her shares back to the company upon the occurrence of certain events; therefore, having a pricing formula or method specified in the agreement is imperative. See Nutshell Section 2B(3)a.

## A. Book Value

*Book value* (BV) is the simplest valuation method because it is derived from the "books" of the company (*i.e.,* the company's balance sheet). The book value of a company on any given date is simply the value of its total assets (TA) *less* the value of its total liabilities (TL) on that date. In other words, book value is the amount of the company's assets that would be left after the company's creditors are paid off in full (an amount also know as "shareholders' equity"):

$$BV = TA - TL$$

To determine book value on a per share basis, simply take a company's book value on a given date and divide it by the number of outstanding shares of common stock on that date:

$$BV \text{ per share } = \frac{BV}{\# \text{ of outstanding shares}}$$

In the case of a business whose assets consist of a large amount of intangible assets, one normally values the business based on its *net tangible book value*. This is because intangible assets cannot easily be converted into cash. Thus, if the business were to be split up and its assets sold off piecemeal, the intangible assets may not generate much cash. To determine the net tangible book value for a given company, simply deduct the value of the company's intangible assets (IA) from the company's total assets, and then proceed to subtract the value of the company's total liabilities:

Net Tangible Book Value = (TA − IA) − TL

The book value approach suffers from two big flaws. First, because it utilizes numbers from the balance sheet, it falls prey to the accounting convention that requires assets to be listed on the balance sheet at their historical costs (subject to a reduction if an asset's value has been permanently impaired). The problem with this is highlighted by the asset category of "plant (or buildings) and equipment." Because a building may appreciate in value over time, the gap between the building's fair market value and its value as listed on the balance sheet can become quite substantial. If this were not problematic enough, accounting rules also require a company to *depreciate* its buildings and equipment over a two– to 30–year period, depending on the asset in question. Thus, over time, the accounting value of a company's plant and equipment as listed on the balance sheet slowly dwindles in value due to depreciation. Accordingly, the balance sheet typically understates—often quite substantially—the true value of a company's plant and equipment, as well as other assets.

Second, book value does not recognize that the company is a "going-concern." Book value assumes that a company's assets will be sold off at the values reflected on the balance sheet, the proceeds will then be used to pay off the company's creditors in full, and any remaining proceeds will be distributed to the company's stockholders. In other words, book value is synonymous with *liquidation value*. A company, however, utilizes its assets to generate income over time. Book value's failure to recognize this fact—*i.e.,* that the company is a "going-concern"— undermines the utility of this valuation method. As the Pennsylvania Supreme Court has noted, normally a company's "total assets are worth more than the sum of their parts, because they include qualities useful in the context of a particular business that they would lose if put to different uses." *O'Connor Appeal*, 304 A.2d 694 (Pa.1973).

Because of these flaws, book value tends to provide a *minimum value* for a company. Thus, those seeking to purchase shares at book value favor this valuation method because it minimizes the cost of the shares. Those receiving payment for their shares, however, tend to disfavor this method because they do not believe they are receiving full value for their shares.

## B. Adjusted Book Value

The adjusted book value approach attempts to keep the simplicity of the book value method while eliminating that method's emphasis on conservative asset valuation. Under the adjusted book value approach, asset values listed on the balance sheet are restated to reflect their current market value (CMV). Once this is done, the adjusted asset values are plugged into the basic book value formula:

$$\text{Adjusted BV} = (\text{CMV of TA}) - \text{TL}$$

While the adjusted book value approach solves the conservative asset valuation problem of the book value method, it still suffers from the "going-concern" problem. That is, adjusted book value measures the value of a business as if the assets were to be *individually sold*, rather than valuing the business as a *"going-concern"* that generates income.

## C.  Net Asset Value

The net asset value method seeks to improve upon the book value and adjusted book value methods by valuing the business as a going-concern. It does so by determining what it would cost to *duplicate* the company in question. Thus, it considers more than simply what it would cost to purchase the same group of assets. It also considers the costs associated with establishing name recognition, hiring and training the company's employees, developing its products, creating brand awareness, and attracting and retaining its customer base, among other things. All of these reflect the "going-concern" concept.

Another way to consider "going-concern" value is to consider the accounting concept of *goodwill*. Goodwill reflects the value of a business as a going-concern, and it typically arises in the context of a corporate acquisition. Whenever an acquiror pays more to purchase a target company than the target company's book value, the *overage* is called goodwill.

Goodwill thus represents the "going-concern" value of the target company, because presumably an acquiror would only pay book value or adjusted book value for a target company that had no future as a viable, earnings-generating enterprise. Once the acquisition is completed, accounting rules mandate that the acquiror reflect the amount of overage on its balance sheet as an intangible asset called "goodwill."

When goodwill is accurately valued it is considered to be an asset that has an indefinite useful life to the acquiror. Occasionally, a company will miscalculate the projected benefit an acquisition will produce and overpay to acquire another company. When this occurs, the expected synergies from the acquisition do not materialize and the value of the goodwill is said to be *impaired*. FASB Statement No. 142, *Goodwill and Other Intangible Assets*, requires a company to determine if the goodwill that appears on its balance sheet is impaired at least annually. Impairment occurs when the expected "discounted cash flows" (see Nutshell Section 20B) of an acquired company or business unit fall below the purchase price.

The portion of goodwill that is impaired must be *amortized* (*i.e.*, expensed) and reflected on a separate line item of the acquiror's P&L statement. The amortized amount is a *non-cash* expense, in that there is no associated cash outflow. Because of the potential of amortizing goodwill, an acquiror has a built-in incentive not to overpay for a target company. Indeed, due to amortization, any overpayment will have a negative impact on the acquiror's earnings going forward.

Perhaps the easiest way to determine the net asset value of a privately-held company is to take a *benchmark* from a similar, yet *publicly-traded* company, and then apply it to financial variables of the *privately-held* company. In other words, deliberately mix apples and oranges to determine a more accurate value for the privately-held company.

One useful benchmark is the *market-to-book ratio* (the *M/B Ratio*). This ratio is calculated as follows:

$$M/B \text{ Ratio} = \frac{\text{market price per share}}{\text{book value per share}}$$

The variable "market price per share" in the above formula is a *going-concern* concept, because it reflects what the market thinks a single share of a given publicly-traded company's stock is worth. The variable "book value per share," by contrast, is an accounting-based concept that one can determine by referencing the company's balance sheet.

Of course, in the context of a privately-held company, a problem quickly arises with respect to the M/B Ratio. That company has no "market price per share" because it is privately-held and thus its shares do not trade in the secondary market. Nevertheless, one can take the M/B Ratio of a *comparable, publicly-traded company* and use it to determine the per share price of the privately-held company. This is the mixing of "apples and oranges" referred to earlier. By rearranging the M/B Ratio formula, one gets:

| market price per share (for private co.) | = | M/B Ratio (for public co.) | x | book value per share (for private co.) |
|---|---|---|---|---|

Because a publicly-traded company has, by definition, a readily available stock price and publicly-available financial statements, its M/B Ratio is relatively easy to calculate. By multiplying the book value per share of a privately-held company by that M/B Ratio, one can determine a market price for a share of stock of that privately-held company. Armed with this knowledge, one can at least approximate the value of the entire privately-held company by multiplying that price by the number of outstanding shares of stock of that company. It often is appropriate to reduce that value by 10 to 20 percent because of the illiquidity associated with an investment in a privately-held company.

Difficulty lies in determining which publicly-traded company's M/B Ratio to use. One must select a publicly-traded company that is *comparable* to the privately-held company. Choosing a comparable company is an art, not a science. Several publicly-traded companies may be candidates in this regard, and one has to use her gut feeling to settle on a choice.

When picking a comparable company, start first with publicly-traded companies operating within the same industry as the privately-held company. In other words, look at publicly-traded *competitors*. Next, examine the competitors' financial statements. Which one is most similar to the privately-held company in terms of revenue per share? Earnings per share? Asset size? Which one seems to have the same history? Trajectory? Because no one competitor will mirror the privately-held company exactly, individuals may very well disagree over the appropriate comparable.

## § 19.   PROFIT AND LOSS STATEMENT–BASED VALUATION METHODS

P&L statement-based valuation methods utilize information from a company's P&L statement in order to generate a value for the company. The main method is the *capitalization of earnings method*. This method utilizes representative earnings of a company, as reflected on that company's P&L statement, to generate a valuation. Typically, *normalized earnings per share* are used. These earnings are simply the average of the earnings per share of that company generated over a period of time, such as the previous five years.

The formula used in the capitalization of earnings method is as follows:

$$V_e = \frac{E}{R}$$

The formula tells us that the value of the company $(V_e)$ based on earnings is simply the company's earnings per share (E) divided by the company's capitalization rate (R).

Picking representative earnings per share involves a measure of subjectivity. Earnings per share are typically averaged or "normalized" over a period of years. Thus, the time period chosen has a significant impact on the calculation of the company's value. For example, if the period chosen includes early years of a company's existence, when earnings were modest or nonexistent, the company's normalized earnings will be lower than they would be if those early years were excluded from the calculation. Hence, picking the time period adds a subjective element to the valuation of the company.

A company's *capitalization rate* (R) is a rate of return that is representative of the risks inherent in that company. The capitalization or "cap" rate is expressed as a decimal in the formula above. Choosing a representative cap rate adds an additional layer of subjectivity to the valuation of that company.

One way to help ensure that the chosen cap rate is more objective is to deliberately mix apples and oranges. That is, take a market-driven variable of a *comparable, publicly-traded* company and apply it when determining the value of a privately-held company. The variable to use is the *price-to-earnings* or *P/E ratio* of the publicly-traded company. This is because the P/E ratio of that company is the *reciprocal* of that company's cap rate.

Like the cap rate, the P/E ratio reflects risk based upon the relationship between a stock's market price and its historical earnings. Thus:

$$\text{P/E ratio} = \frac{\text{Price per share}}{\text{Earnings per share}}$$

The P/E ratios for publicly-traded companies are easily determined, as they are published daily by leading financial publications such as *The Wall Street Journal* and *Investor's Business Daily*.

Because the P/E ratio of a given company's stock is the reciprocal of that company's cap rate, the cap rate for that company can easily be determined by dividing its P/E ratio into the number 1:

$$R = \frac{1}{\text{P/E ratio}}$$

Once the cap rate for the comparable, publicly-traded company is calculated, it can be plugged into the capitalization of earnings formula to determine the per share value of the privately-held company. In true "apples and oranges" fashion, however, the earnings plugged into that formula are the normalized earnings per share for the privately-held company. Once again, the value calculated could be reduced by 10 to 20 percent to reflect the illiquidity of the privately-held company's shares.

While useful, the capitalization of earnings method suffers from a number of problems. First, this method does not consider whether earnings will be paid out to stockholders in the form of dividends or plowed back (*i.e.,* reinvested) into the company to fund future expansion. Second, it is heavily dependent on past earnings, and thus the quality of those earnings is crucial. The quality of the earnings suffer from the fact they are "accounting" earnings, which factor in non-cash expenses. For example, depreciation expense is subtracted from revenues when determining earnings, yet that expense does not represent a cash outflow of the company.

Perhaps a bigger potential problem relating to the quality of past earnings is a concern about the manipulation of those earnings. In the context of publicly-traded companies, the late 1990s and early 2000s were filled with prominent public companies that were forced to restate their earnings from prior years. Some became demonized, like Enron, Tyco and Adelphi, and rightly so. Others, like Cisco, IBM and Lucent, highlighted that the problem was more extensive than originally thought.

Earnings manipulation can also be acute in the context of closely-held companies, where stockholders are often managers as well. As managers, these stockholders draw salaries and receive other perquisites, and typically control the timing of both. They also seek reimbursement for many daily and seemingly ordinary expenses ("goodies") like dinners that are often of dubious value to the business. Non-manager stockholders are not afforded equal treatment in this regard. Costs associated with salaries, perquisites and other goodies are subtracted from company revenues in determining company earnings. To the extent one is using a valuation method dependent on past earnings, excessive salaries, perquisites and other goodies will reduce earnings and thus result in a lower valuation of the company as a whole.

Such was the case in *Donahue v. Draper*, 491 N.E.2d 260 (Mass.App.Ct.1986). A disgruntled stockholder, Donahue, sought to cash out of the company. Donahue's valuation expert added the amount of salaries he considered excessive back into earnings before valuing the company. This resulted in a higher valuation of the company in question, and thus benefitted his client, Donahue. See Nutshell Section 25 for more on *Donahue*.

A *sweetheart deal* can also affect earnings negatively. A sweetheart deal is a transaction between a company (Company A) and one of its significant stockholders (or another company, Company B, controlled by that stockholder). The transaction calls for Company A to pay that stockholder (or Company B) an overly-generous amount for services or goods. While the transaction's lopsidedness favors the one stockholder (or Company B) with whom the transaction is made, its harm is spread out over all stockholders of Company A. The excessive expense negatively impacts Company A's earnings, and thus results in a lower valuation of Company A if the valuation method employed is based on past earnings.

## § 20.  CASH FLOW–BASED VALUATION METHODS

Cash flow-based valuation methods were designed to solve many of the problems associated with balance sheet-based and P&L statement-based valuation methods. Cash flow-based methods basically require one to determine the *present value,* or *discounted value,* of a company's future cash flows. The two traditional cash flow-based valuation methods are (1) the Dividend Discount Method (DDM) and (2) the Discounted Cash Flow Method (DCF). Each is explored below.

### A.  Dividend Discount Method (DDM)

According to the *Dividend Discount Method* (DDM), the value of a share of common stock resides solely in its expected stream of cash dividends. Accordingly, this method calculates share value by determining the present value of a company's stream of future dividend payments.

Three steps are required to calculate a company's value based on DDM. First, you must forecast expected dividends to be received by stockholders in the future. This, of course, is very difficult, because dividend payments are not only based in large part on earnings (which are tough enough to estimate), but also are payable at the discretion of a company's board of directors. Nevertheless, forecasting dividends is not impossible, especially for a mature company that has paid dividends consistently over a number of years.

The second step is to choose an appropriate discount rate for use in discounting the forecasted dividend stream back to today's dollars. The chosen discount rate must reflect the risk inherent in the company. The relationship of the discount rate to company risk was underscored in a Delaware appraisal proceeding. In determining the value of the company in question, the Delaware Chancery Court used the "build-up" method to determine the discount rate. This method begins with a risk-free rate of return as a base. Then, additional rates that represent the company's security's unique risks are added to that risk-free rate to determine a discount rate. See *Henke v. Trilithic, Inc.*, 2005 WL 2899677 (Del.Ch.).

The final step is to make a determination about the company's growth prospects. Is it a "zero growth" company (where earnings are flat), a "constant growth" company (where earnings are growing at a steady increment), or a "nonconstant (variable) growth" company (where the company has earnings in some years and losses in others)? This is important because the growth prospects of the company in question impact the ability of a company to pay dividends in the future.

One way to determine the growth rate of a company is to calculate the pattern of growth in its sales over a historical period of time. For example, one could use the geometric average of sales for the previous five years and then compare it to the geometric average of sales over the previous ten years. To illustrate, assume that a company's sales for the previous 10 years (year 1 being the most recent year) are as follows:

| Year 1 | $2,000,000 |
| Year 2 | $2,100,000 |
| Year 3 | $2,100,000 |
| Year 4 | $1,800,000 |
| Year 5 | $1,600,000 |
| Year 6 | $1,500,000 |
| Year 7 | $1,400,000 |
| Year 8 | $1,280,000 |
| Year 9 | $1,180,000 |
| Year 10 | $1,000,000 |

The geometric average for the most recent *five-year* period is:

$$(1 + g)^4 = \text{Year 1 Sales} \div \text{Year 5 Sales}$$
$$(1 + g)^4 = \$2,000,000 \div \$1,600,000$$
$$(1 + g)^4 = 1.25$$
$$1 + g = 1.057$$
$$g = 5.7\%$$

The geometric average for the previous *ten-year* period is:

$$(1 + g)^9 = \text{Year 1 Sales} \div \text{Year 10 Sales}$$
$$(1 + g)^9 = \$2,000,000 \div \$1,000,000$$
$$(1 + g)^9 = 2.00$$
$$1 + g = 1.08$$
$$g = 8.0\%$$

Subjective judgment is necessary to estimate what the future growth rate will be. One could emphasize the current five-year trend in sales to project approximately a 5.7% growth rate. However, one could also attempt to take into consideration the apparent effects of business cycles and random factors. The resulting long-term growth rate would be approximately 8%. A rate somewhere in between 5.7% and 8% will most likely represent the company's growth rate in the future.

The basic DDM formula is as follows:

$$P_o = \frac{D_1}{(1 + K_e)^1} + \frac{D_2}{(1 + K_e)^2} + \frac{D_3}{(1 + K_e)^3} + \dots \frac{D_\infty}{(1 + K_e)^\infty}$$

where:  $P_o$ is the price of the stock, which is being calculated.

D is the dividend for each year.

$K_e$ is the required rate of return for the stock (discount rate).

This formula is basically the formula for an annuity, which was discussed previously in Nutshell Section 12B. The formula, however, has been adjusted to play out to infinity. That is, the formula assumes that the company will pay out dividends forever. An annuity that goes on forever is called a *perpetuity*.

This formula, with modification, is generally applied to the three different growth scenarios described above: (1) zero growth, (2) constant growth, and (3) nonconstant (or variable) growth.

Under the "no-growth" scenario, a company pays a constant dividend on its stock each year. This is shown as:

$$P_o = \frac{D}{K_e}$$

Suppose the market value of Company A's common stock is $20 per share. Company A's current annual dividend is $1.80 per share and your required rate of return is 12 percent. Should you purchase Company A's common stock? Based on the above formula, the price ($P_o$) you would be willing to purchase a share of Company A's common stock is:

$$P_o = \frac{\$1.80}{0.12}$$

$$P_o = \$15.00$$

Thus, you would not want to purchase the stock at the current price of $20 per share.

In a "constant growth" scenario, Company A may decide to increase its dividend by seven percent per year. The valuation approach would be shown as:

$$P_0 = \frac{D_1}{K_e - g}$$

where: $D_1$ is the dividend at the end of the first year.

$K_e$ is the required rate of return for the stock (discount rate).

$g$ is the constant growth rate of dividends.

If the current dividend was $1.80, then a seven percent increase would result in a dividend at the end of the year of $1.93. Therefore, the price per share you would be willing to pay is:

$$P_0 = \frac{\$1.93}{0.12 - 0.07}$$

$$P_0 = \$38.60$$

Thus, you would clearly accept the opportunity to purchase Company A's stock at the current market price of $20 per share.

DDM suffers from several problems. First, it is useless in valuing a company, such as Warren Buffet's Berkshire Hathaway, that does not currently pay dividends and does not expect to do so in the foreseeable future. Indeed, based on DDM, the value of Berkshire Hathaway would be zero because that company has no future dividend stream that can be discounted. Yet, no one would rationally suggest that Berkshire Hathaway has no value.

A second problem is with the forecasting of future dividends. As no one has a crystal ball, the forecasting process is inherently subjective. For a company with nonconstant or variable growth, predicting dividends is often an exercise in futility.

A final problem is in choosing an appropriate discount rate. One can use a given company's capitalization rate, however, in discounting forecasted dividends. To the extent the company is privately-held, one can use the reciprocal of a comparable, publicly-traded company's P/E ratio for discounting purposes. See Nutshell Section 19.

## B.  Discounted Cash Flow Method (DCF)

The *Discounted Cash Flow* (DCF) method, or a variant thereof, is the most common valuation method employed by the financial community today. Similar to DDM, DCF is based on discounting. DCF, however, determines the present value of a company's future net cash flows as opposed to its future dividend stream. Thus, DCF is particularly helpful in valuing companies that do not currently pay cash dividends and do not plan to do so in the foreseeable future.

Calculating value based on DCF involves four steps:

- *First*, forecast the company's annual net cash flows (*i.e.,* annual inflows less outflows) for the time period you expect to own shares of its common stock.

- *Second*, estimate a terminal or residual value of the company at the end of your holding period.
- *Third*, discount at an appropriate discount rate the present value of each of (a) the projected net cash flows determined in step one and (b) the terminal value determined in step two.
- *Fourth*, add the discounted net cash flows to the discounted terminal value to arrive at the present value of the company.

The first step in DCF is to forecast the company's annual net cash flows for the time period you expect to own shares of its common stock. A cash flow is a change in a company's cash position over a specified period of time. There are two primary forms of cash flow: operating cash flow and financial cash flow. Operating cash flows are derived from a company's operations, and thus stem from the sale of products or services. Financial cash flows are derived from raising capital funds, such as through the issuance of bonds. Typically, cash flows are forecasted annually based on a projected growth rate for the period you intend to hold the stock.

Several formulae may be utilized to project a company's future net cash flows. They range from simple to complex, and all tend to be much more accurate in projecting short-term rather than long-term cash flows. Cash budget analysis is a simple method often employed by startup companies to project liquidity and assess value. Cash budget anal-

ysis is based on direct estimates for every receipt
and expenditure of cash a company expects to occur
in the near future.

Another model is the free cash flow method. This
method requires you to calculate net cash flows
after taking into account tax consequences and accounting expenses that do not affect a company's
cash flow. Thus, free cash flow is determined by
adding depreciation and amortization expense back
to a company's net income, subtracting capital expenditures and then factoring in changes in working capital.

The second step in DCF requires you to estimate
a terminal or residual value of the company. The
terminal value is the price you expect to receive for
your shares when you sell them at the end of your
anticipated holding period. This number is typically
determined by applying a multiple to the company's
projected net cash flow during the final year of the
holding period. A multiple is usually based on a
company's earnings, growth and business risks. On
the one hand, stocks of high-tech companies usually
sell at higher multiples to reflect higher growth
rates. On the other hand, stocks of brick and mor-
tar companies in more mature industries typically
sell at lower multiples to reflect lower growth rates.
Most importantly, a multiplier for a specific company must be based on a key revenue driver and be
comparable to those of other companies within its
industry. One multiple that the financial communi-

ty frequently uses is based on a company's price-to-earnings (P/E) ratio.

The third step of DCF is to discount at an appropriate discount rate the present value of each of (a) the projected net cash flows determined in step one and (b) the terminal value determined in step two. The discount rate employed in this analysis is typically the rate of return for a company with a similar level of risk as the company being valued.

The last step of DCF is to add the discounted net cash flows to the discounted terminal value to arrive at the present value of the company being valued. An example will illustrate the process involved in calculating a valuation based on the DCF method.

Suppose that Peter acquired all the outstanding shares of PNH Corp. on December 31, 2010. Peter plans to hold his shares for five years and then sell them all. Peter projects that PNH will provide $100 million in net cash flow during 2011, and that PNH's net cash flow will increase at an annual rate of 10% thereafter. PNH's projected terminal value in 2015 is expected to be $1.46 billion based on a cash flow multiple of 10 in its fifth year of the forecast. Assume further that the rate of return for companies with a risk profile similar to PNH's is five percent. What is the value of PNH today applying DCF?

First, calculate the present value of the projected net cash flows discounted at the discount rate for companies with a similar risk profile as PNH's (dollar amounts below are in millions):

$$PV_{cash\ flow} = \frac{\$100}{1.05} + \frac{\$110}{1.05^2} + \frac{\$121}{1.05^3} + \frac{\$133}{1.05^4} + \frac{\$146}{1.05^5}$$

$$= \$95.24 + \$99.77 + \$104.52 + \$109.42 + \$114.39$$

$$= \$523.34$$

Next, calculate the present value of the terminal value discounted at the discount rate for companies with a similar risk profile as PNH's (dollar amounts below are in millions):

$$PV_5 = \frac{\$1,460}{1.05^5}$$

$$= \$1,143.91$$

Finally, add the two present values together:

$$\$523.34 + \$1,143.91 = \underline{\$1,667.25}$$
$$(or\ \underline{\$1,667,250,000})$$

Like DDM, DCF suffers from several flaws. First, you must forecast future net cash flows, a process that is inherently subjective and rarely accurate. Second, you must subjectively choose an appropriate discount rate. Once again, you can use a discount rate that reflects a rate of return for a company with a comparable level of risk as the company you are valuing. If the company is privately-held, you can use the capitalization rate of a *comparable, publicly-traded* company. This rate simply the reciprocal of that public company's P/E ratio. (See Nutshell Section 19). Lastly, estimating a terminal value for a company in the future is very difficult because of the myriad of uncertainties in the business, financial and economic environment.

*In re Zenith Electronics Corp.*, 241 B.R. 92 (Bankr.D.Del.1999), provides an interesting discussion on choosing an appropriate discount rate. The Bankruptcy Court needed to determine the going-concern value of Zenith (in bankruptcy at the time) before it could resolve the issue of whether Zenith's proposed plan of reorganization was fair and equitable under Section 1129 of the Bankruptcy Code. All interested parties conceded that Zenith's future depended on a new technology Zenith had developed ("VSB technology"). Zenith's expert used DCF to value that technology at $155 million after using a discount rate of 25%. The expert for Zenith's equity committee used DCF as well in calculating a $833 million value for that technology after using a discount rate of only 17%. The higher the value, the more likely Zenith's existing equity holders would receive something in the plan of reorganization.

As the Court commented:

[Zenith's expert's] valuation uses a discount rate ... of 25%, which was selected from the middle range of rates for venture funds and hedge funds. Further, [the expert] compared risk inherent in VSB technology to start-up biotech firms, which have a new product near regulatory approval but without any established sales....

In contrast, the Equity Committee's valuation expert ... used a discount rate of 17%.... [It] also used the capital asset pricing model to determine that discount rate, but selected different companies for comparison.... [I]ts discount rate is the same as Microsoft's.

We agree with the conclusion of [Zenith's expert] that the discount rate for Zenith is more appropriately 25% than 17%. Zenith, although an established company in the consumer electronics industry, has clearly not been a leader in recent years. It is no Microsoft and no source of capital would view it as such. In fact, its inability to raise capital, at any rate, is one of the reasons it is in chapter 11 today. Further, the [VSB technology] is new and untried in the market. There are significant risks inherent in its future.... We conclude that [Zenith's expert] properly assessed risk inherent in this technology by comparing it to hedge funds and biotech firms.

# CHAPTER 7

# EFFICIENT CAPITAL MARKET HYPOTHESIS (ECMH)

## § 21. OVERVIEW

The *Efficient Capital Market Hypothesis* (ECMH) is an information-based economic model. It posits that a price of a share of stock trading in the secondary market accurately reflects information relating to that stock. Thus, changes in a stock's price result from changes in information concerning that stock.

Under ECMH, past price movements constitute information already embedded in current stock prices. Therefore, ECMH comports with Burton Malkiel's "random walk" model of stock price movements. Malkiel demonstrated that securities prices follow a "random walk" from day-to-day. This means that future price changes in a security cannot be predicted merely by looking at past price changes. In other words, a future price change with respect to a given security is statistically independent from past price changes. Thus, just because the trading price of a given stock has risen in each of the last 20 trading days, this does not mean that its price will rise on the 21st trading day.

*Chartists* or *technical analysts* disagree with the random walk model and piece together elaborate charts detailing past price movements in an attempt to discern future price movements. They note that stock prices over time undulate between high points and low points, which they refer to as *resistance points*. Whenever a given stock's price trends downward towards the lower resistance point, technical analysts predict an upturn. Whenever the price approaches the higher resistance point, they predict a downturn. Not until a given stock's price has "broken through a resistance point" do they predict a new trading range with new resistance points.

While some may call chartists "witchdoctors," it is important to recognize that chartists have many adherents. Therefore, when the price of a given stock trends downward towards its lower resistance point, many investors will begin purchasing the stock thus creating upward pressure on its price. When the price of that stock trends upward towards its higher resistance point, many investors will begin selling the stock thus creating downward pressure on its price. In other words, at times there are enough "believers" to make a chartist-predicted upturn or downturn in a given stock's price a self-fulfilling prophecy.

Turning back to ECMH, economists have broken down this hypothesis into three distinct forms:

    (1) *Weak Form.* The "weak" form of ECMH posits that current security prices fully reflect all information concerning past securi-

ty prices. This, of course, is entirely consistent with the basic premise of the "random walk" model.

(2) *Semi–Strong Form.* The "semi-strong" form of ECMH posits that current security prices fully reflect all information that is currently publicly available. This information not only includes past security prices, but all publicly-available information distributed by public companies in their periodic reports filed with the SEC under the Exchange Act.

(3) *Strong Form.* The "strong" form of ECMH posits that current security prices reflect all currently existing information, including both public and non-public information. Non-public information is called *inside information* in securities jargon. Thus, the "strong form" encompasses not only all the information that the other two forms cover, but also all information that public companies have not yet made public.

Empirical testing of the three forms of ECMH has revealed the following:

(1) *Weak Form.* Evidence demonstrates that the "weak" form of ECMH is valid. It generally is not possible to achieve superior returns by investing based solely on price histories of securities.

(2) *Semi–Strong Form.* Evidence demonstrates that the "semi-strong" form of ECMH is

valid in most cases. As a general matter, most studies have shown that investors cannot consistently outperform the market based solely on their analyses of publicly-available information. Some anomalies exist, however, as certain investors are able to interpret publicly-available information in a way that allows them to achieve above market returns.

(3) *Strong Form.* Evidence demonstrates that the "strong" form of ECMH is not valid. Corporate insiders and market specialists continue to trade on "non-public" information despite legal prohibitions against insider trading. If not caught, they are rewarded with above market returns.

Strict adherence to ECMH creates a conundrum known as the *efficiency paradox*. If, under ECMH, information concerning a stock is quickly analyzed and then incorporated into its price, then why would anyone spend time and money analyzing information? And if no one is willing to spend resources to uncover information, how will information come to be reflected in a given stock's price? The fact that investors do expend resources to analyze information is perhaps the best clear evidence that the market is not purely efficient. How investors view a particular piece of information (such as a public company's annual report on Form 10–K) may differ. Some investors may see opportunities embedded in that information while others may not.

More evidence of an inefficient market is found in James Tobin's *noise theory.* Tobin asserts that the public capital markets will not reflect fundamental asset values (*i.e.,* the intrinsic values of public companies) because those markets are infected by substantial trading based on information unrelated to fundamental asset values. Tobin calls this trading *noise trading,* which is trading conducted by ill-informed investors who do so based on rumor, innuendo or misinformation.

Tobin noted that the public capital markets are not truly efficient because they often reflect information in stock prices without regard to the *quality* of that information. While information relating to the fundamental value of a stock is reflected in its price, so too is information wholly-unrelated to that fundamental value. Because of this, the price of a given stock will never reflect its true intrinsic value.

## § 22.　ECMH IN THE COURTROOM

The U.S. Supreme Court tipped its hat to ECMH in the seminal case of *Basic, Inc. v. Levinson,* 485 U.S. 224 (1988). The case involved a publicly-traded company (Basic, Inc.) that made three public announcements over a period of two years denying that it was engaged in merger negotiations when in fact it was. Several former Basic common stockholders sued Basic after they sold their shares after Basic's first denial of a pending merger, but before Basic finally admitted to it. They alleged that the three press releases issued by the defendants were false and misleading and thus violated the antifraud provisions of the Exchange Act. They allegedly suffered injury because those releases artificially depressed the prices at which they sold their Basic shares. (The plaintiffs actually made a small profit when they sold their shares but apparently not enough in their view).

Normally, a plaintiff must show that she relied on the false and misleading statements in order to prove an allegation of fraud. Reliance is important because it provides the requisite causal connection between a defendant's misrepresentations and a plaintiff's injury. In this case, however, the plaintiffs did not need to show reliance, because the Court embraced the *fraud on the market theory*.

The fraud on the market theory creates a rebuttable presumption that the plaintiffs had relied on Basic's press releases. The theory is based on the hypothesis that, in an open and developed securities market, the price of a company's stock is determined by the available material information regarding the company and its business. Thus, the theory embraces the semi-strong form of ECMH, as the Court implied that stock prices reflect all available (*i.e.,* public) material information.

According to the Court, the market is interposed between a buyer and seller of securities and, ideally, transmits information to the buyer "in the processed form of a market price." Misleading statements from issuers, therefore, indirectly defraud purchasers. While purchasers may not have relied directly on issuer misstatements, they did rely on a stock price that incorporated those misstatements.

The fraud on the market theory only creates a presumption of reliance which can be rebutted by the defendants. Rebutting the presumption, however, is difficult. However, the defendants can attempt to show four things. First, the defendants could attempt to show that the market for the common stock of Basic was "inefficient." Second, they could attempt to show that their misrepresentations did not lead to a material change in the trading price of Basic common stock. Third, they could attempt to show that securities traders already knew that Basic was in merger talks (*i.e.*, that this "private" information was already reflected in Basic's stock price). Finally, they could attempt to prove that the plaintiffs would have sold their shares even without relying on the integrity of the market.

*In re PolyMedica Corp. Securities Litigation*, 432 F.3d 1 (1st Cir.2005), involved a suit by a plaintiff shareholder of PolyMedica Corp. The plaintiff alleged that PolyMedica artificially inflated the market price of its stock by misrepresenting sales, revenues and accounts receivable and by issuing false press releases. This caused the plaintiff and other shareholders to purchase PolyMedica stock at artificially inflated prices. When the "truth came out," the plaintiff alleged that PolyMedica's stock lost more than 80% of its value. On the issue of "reliance," the plaintiff relied on *Basic's* fraud on the market theory. The District Court had disregarded the defendants' expert's opinion that the market for PolyMedica stock was "inefficient" and thus the fraud on the market theory was inapplicable.

In reversing the District Court, the First Circuit made clear that, in the context of *Basic*, "efficiency refers to the flow of information in the relevant market and the effect of that information on the price of the stock." It added that "when a market lacks efficiency, there is no assurance that the market price was affected by the defendant's alleged misstatement at all. Instead, the price may reflect information wholly unrelated to the misstatement."

The First Circuit then rejected the plaintiff's definition of an "efficient market," a definition taken directly from language found in *Basic* and which had been accepted by the District Court. According to the plaintiff, an "efficient market" is simply one in which "market professionals generally consider *most* publicly announced material statements about companies, thereby affecting stock market prices." (Emphasis added.) Instead, the First Circuit accepted the definition proffered by the defendants: an "efficient market" is "one in which the market price of the stock *fully reflects all* publicly available information." (Emphasis added.)

Commentators and state courts have not been kind to the fraud on the market theory. For example, in *Kaufman v. i-Stat Corp.*, 754 A.2d 1188 (N.J.2000), the New Jersey Supreme Court addressed the theory in a case alleging fraud under New Jersey's state securities laws. New Jersey requires a showing of direct or indirect reliance on a fraudulent misstatement. The plaintiff attempted to eliminate the need for reliance altogether based on the fraud on the market theory. Alternatively, he tried to demonstrate that reliance on a publicly available stock price that incorporated material corporate misstatements was equivalent to "indirect reliance" under New Jersey law. The Court, however, was not persuaded. It explained:

> Indirect reliance occurs when a single communication, an inducement to engage in a fraudulent transaction, is clearly communicated to the defrauded party. The price of a publicly traded stock, however, synthesizes a great variety of information and conveys as much of that information as possible. But the information is jumbled. No one piece of information survives clearly enough that the share price can be said to have passed it on clearly. Until study or experience can prove that an impersonal mechanism can communicate a single idea clearly, indirect reliance should not be expanded to include this theoretical model of market performance....

New Jersey keeps good company. The courts in California, Colorado, Delaware, Florida, Georgia, Pennsylvania, and Tennessee have all rejected the fraud on the market theory. To date, no state court has accepted it.

# CHAPTER 8

# VALUATION IN THE COURTROOM

Valuation is important inside as well as outside the courtroom. Judges are called upon to determine the value of shares in the hands of a given stockholder in several situations. First, a judge must value shares in an appraisal proceeding commenced by a stockholder who dissented to a merger involving her company. Second, a judge must interpret a valuation formula set forth in a shareholders' agreement when a stockholder challenges its applicability. Third, a judge must value the shares in the hands of a disgruntled stockholder who is alleging that she has been unfairly "oppressed" by one or more other stockholders. Lastly, valuation issues arise in other situations, including divorce, probate and taxation cases. This chapter addresses these situations.

## § 23.  APPRAISAL OR "DISSENTERS'" RIGHTS

### A.  Background

Sometimes referred to as *dissenters' rights* or *buy-out rights, appraisal rights* entitle stockholders who disfavor certain mergers to seek a judicial determination of the *fair value* of their shares. Once that determination is made, the surviving entity must then pay that amount to these stockholders in *cash*.

The origin of the appraisal remedy is tied to a shift in stockholder voting rights. Historically, corporate law required unanimous stockholder approval of all fundamental corporate transactions. Over time, the law moved away from unanimity to mere majority approval. The law embraced appraisal rights as a quid pro quo for taking away a stockholder's veto power over such transactions. Any stockholder who did not want to go along with the majority of stockholders who approved the transaction could cash out at fair value and move on.

## B. Availability of the Appraisal Remedy

One of the most common mistakes involving the appraisal remedy relates to the remedy's availability. While many believe it is always available to stockholders whose companies are involved in a merger, this simply is not the case. Therefore, once a given transaction structure is agreed upon, the lawyers involved must then answer the question as to whether stockholders of the constituent companies receive appraisal rights.

Section 262 of the DGCL is the appraisal rights provision applicable to Delaware corporations. One glance reveals it is highly, and perhaps unnecessarily, complex. The general rule gleaned from Section

262(b) is that, except in limited instances, dissenting stockholders in statutory mergers do receive appraisal rights. This includes stockholders being "squeezed out" through short-form mergers conducted under Section 253 of the DGCL, even though those stockholders are not entitled to vote on the merger and thus, as a technical matter, cannot "dissent." See DGCL §§ 253(d) & 262(b)(3).

Unlike stockholders of corporations formed in certain other states, dissenting stockholders of a Delaware corporation do not receive appraisal rights when their corporation sells assets. This is true even if the sale is of "all or substantially all" of the corporation's assets—a transaction requiring stockholder approval under Section 271 of the DGCL. Nor do stockholders of a Delaware corporation receive appraisal rights when the corporation's charter is amended, although they do receive voting rights under Section 242(b) of the DGCL. However, any Delaware corporation can provide its stockholders, through a charter provision, with additional appraisal rights that cover these actions. See DGCL § 262(c).

Despite the general rule, mergers involving Delaware corporations do not give rise to the appraisal remedy in three notable instances. The first involves the *market-out exception* under Sections 262(b)(1) and (2) of the DGCL. Pursuant to this exception, stockholders whose shares are currently listed on a national securities exchange or, if not listed, are held of record by more than 2,000 stockholders *do not* receive appraisal rights if they are to receive as merger consideration: (a) shares of stock in the surviving corporation; (b) shares of stock of another corporation (*e.g.,* a parent company) so long as those shares are listed on a national securities exchange or, if not listed, are held of record by more than 2,000 stockholders; (c) cash in lieu of fractional shares; or (d) any combination of the foregoing.

Importantly, the market-out exception does not apply to stockholders of a public company who receive cash (other than for fractional shares) and/or debt securities as merger consideration. Those public stockholders have their appraisal rights restored under Section 262(b)(2) of the DGCL. This, therefore, is an "exception to the exception."

The market-out exception recognizes that the market is superior to a judge when it comes to fairly valuing the shares of dissenting public stockholders. If those stockholders are to receive stock as merger consideration, the market-out exception encourages them to simply cash out before the merger is consummated by selling their shares in the open market. When dissenting public stockholders are forced to receive cash as merger consideration, by contrast, the market may not provide a fair valuation. Indeed, the trading price of a target company's stock typically trades within a narrow band of the per share cash price being offered by the prospective acquiror. Dissenting public stockholders in that situation should (and do) receive appraisal rights because the market price at which they otherwise could cash out is overly influenced by the cash merger consideration being offered by that acquiror. That consideration may not be fair to the target's stockholders.

The second exception is the *no vote exception* under Section 262(b)(1) of the DGCL. It states that stockholders of the surviving corporation in the merger do not receive appraisal rights if they *were not* entitled to vote on the merger under Section 251(f) of the DGCL. Section 251(f) states that stockholders of the surviving corporation are not entitled to vote if (a) the merger agreement does not amend the charter of the surviving corporation, (b) each share of stock after the merger is identical in terms of rights, preferences, privileges, etc. as each share was prior to the merger, and (c) either (1) no shares of the surviving corporation are to be issued in the transaction or (2) the additional shares of the surviving corporation to be issued do not exceed 20% of the outstanding shares of the surviving corporation prior to the merger.

The third exception is the *holding company exception* under Section 262(b) of the DGCL. Pursuant to it, stockholders of companies engaged in a merger effected solely to create a holding company structure in accordance with Section 251(g) of the DGCL do not receive appraisal rights.

# C. Perfection and Forfeiture of Appraisal Rights

Stockholders entitled to appraisal rights forfeit those rights under Delaware law in three situations. First, under Section 262(a) of the DGCL, any stockholder who either votes in favor of the merger in question or consents to the merger through a written consent can no longer seek the appraisal remedy. However, voting against the merger, abstaining or not voting at all does not cause a forfeiture of appraisal rights. See *Lewis v. Corroon & Reynolds Corp.*, 57 A.2d 632 (Del.Ch.1948). This makes perfect sense in that a truly disgruntled stockholder would not cast a vote in favor of the merger which caused her disgruntlement in the first place.

Second, under Section 262(a), a stockholder entitled to appraisal rights forfeits those rights if she fails to continue to own her shares from the time she demands her appraisal rights (which occurs prior to the merger) until the effective date of the merger.

The third way for a stockholder to forfeit her appraisal rights is for her to fail to *perfect* those rights in accordance with the strict procedures set forth in Section 262(d) of the DGCL. To the extent a stockholder forfeits her rights, more likely than not it is because she failed to properly perfect those rights.

The perfection process involves actions by both the corporation in question and dissenting stockholders. First, if a particular merger gives rise to appraisal rights, the corporation must notify all its record stockholders that they are entitled to those rights at least 20 days before the corporation submits the transaction to stockholders for their approval. Second, each dissenting stockholder must make a written demand for appraisal of that stockholder's shares on the corporation before the vote on the merger occurs. Simply voting against the merger *does not* constitute a sufficient demand in this regard. Third, if the merger is approved by a stockholder vote, then, within 10 days after the effective date of the merger, the surviving corporation must notify only those stockholders who properly demanded appraisal rights and who did not vote in favor of the merger that the merger has been consummated. See DGCL § 262(d)(1).

Thereafter, either the surviving corporation or a dissenting stockholder may file a petition in the Delaware Chancery Court demanding a judicial determination of the value of the stock held by all dissenting stockholders. The petition must be filed within 120 days of the merger's effective date. Needless to say, the surviving corporation has zero incentive to file such a petition, so it is incumbent upon a dissenting stockholder to do so. Any dissenting stockholder who has second thoughts has 60 days from the effective date of the merger to withdraw her demand for the appraisal remedy and receive the merger consideration instead. See DGCL § 262(e).

Pursuant to Section 262(k) of the DGCL, from and after the effective date of the merger a dissenting stockholder is not entitled to vote her shares during the pendency of an appraisal proceeding. Nor is that stockholder entitled to receive any dividends or other distributions payable on those shares. For all intents and purposes, shares in the hands of a dissenting stockholder represent the right to receive either fair value in an appraisal proceeding before the Delaware Chancery Court or the merger consideration from the surviving corporation, but nothing more.

A dissenting stockholder must wait until the bitter end of a Delaware appraisal proceeding for payment for her shares. The wait is often as long as several years. This fact alone deters many stockholders from seeking the appraisal remedy. However, once the case is decided, the court will award the dissenting stockholder interest on the value of her shares measured from the effective date of the merger. See Nutshell Section 23D(7). Surprisingly, the Delaware Chancery Court generally awards simple interest rather than compound interest. See Nutshell Section 10 for the distinction between the two. Compound interest may be awarded at the discretion of the court only upon a finding of *exceptional circumstances*, and for the court's determination to withstand challenge it must explain its choice. See *M.G. Bancorporation, Inc. v. Le Beau*, 737 A.2d 513 (Del.1999).

The court will not shift the dissenting stockholder's expenses—mainly attorney's fees and expert witness fees—to the surviving corporation; however, under Section 262(j) of the DGCL, the court may spread those expenses pro rata over all the shares for which appraisal is sought.

By contrast, Section 13.24 of the RMBCA requires the surviving corporation to pay the corporation's estimated value of the shares in the hands of dissenting stockholders within 30 days of the effective date of the merger. If a dissenting stockholder is dissatisfied with the amount he receives, he can then convey his estimate of the value of those shares back to the corporation. If the corporation and the dissenting stockholder fail to settle their disagreement over value, the corporation (not the stockholder) must commence a proceeding in court. Section 13.31(a) of the RMBCA also requires a court to assign the plaintiff stockholder's attorney's and expert witness fees to the surviving corporation, unless the court finds that the plaintiff stockholder has acted arbitrarily, vexatiously or in bad faith.

## D.  Valuation in an Appraisal Proceeding

### (1) Introduction

The DGCL and Delaware case law provide the valuation guidelines followed by most courts around the country. From a statutory perspective, Section 262(a) of the DGCL requires the Delaware Chancery Court to decide the "fair value" of the dissenting stockholder's shares. But what is "fair value" in this context? The dissenting stockholder, on the one hand, would like the court to determine that her shares are worth the highest possible per share price within the realm of reason, and thus she parades in expert witnesses supporting her position. The surviving corporation, on the other hand, would like the court to determine that the dissenting stockholder's shares are worth exactly the per share price paid in the merger, and thus it parades in expert witnesses supporting its position.

The surviving corporation has the most at risk during the proceeding as it attempts to avoid the "egg on the face" problem. This problem arises if the judge determines a value per share that is too different than the per share price offered in the merger. Indeed, if the judge's valuation is significantly higher than the merger consideration, this could give rise to lawsuits against the seller's board for breach of fiduciary duty under the mantra of "you sold too low!" If the valuation is significantly lower than the merger consideration, then it looks like the surviving corporation overpaid for the target company.

### (2) Burden of Proof on Issue of Valuation

In a statutory appraisal proceeding, both sides have the burden of proving their respective valuation positions by a preponderance of the evidence. The court may exercise independent judgment to assess the fair value of the dissenting stockholder's shares if neither party meets its burden. See *M.G. Bancorporation, Inc. v. Le Beau*, 737 A.2d 513 (Del.

1999); *Cooper v. Pabst Brewing Co.*, 1993 WL 208763 (Del.Ch.).

### (3) Valuation Methodology

The key statutory language on valuation appears in Section 262(h) of the DGCL:

> [T]he Court shall appraise the shares, determining their fair value exclusive of any element of value arising from the accomplishment or expectation of the merger or consolidation, together with a fair rate of interest, if any, to be paid upon the amount determined to be fair value. In determining ... fair value, the Court shall take into account all relevant factors....

Prior to the seminal case of *Weinberger v. UOP, Inc.*, 457 A.2d 701 (Del.1983), the Delaware courts used the *Delaware Block Method* of valuation as the exclusive method to determine fair value in an appraisal proceeding. This method was a weighted average method of valuation.

When employing the Delaware Block Method, the court would value the company by examining: (1) market value, which was based on the trading price of the stock of the company in question; (2) earnings value, which was based on an estimate of what the company would earn in the future; and (3) net asset or "book" value (equal to the company's total assets less its total liabilities taken from its balance sheet). The court would then accord each of these three values a weight. Each weight would equal a percentage out of 100% based on the perceived accuracy of that particular value in light of the circumstances surrounding the company in question. The higher the weight, the more impact a given value would have in the ultimate valuation of that company. The three weights collectively would equal 100%. Once the three values had been weighted (*i.e.,* multiplied by their respective percentages), they would be added together to arrive at a final valuation. For an elaborate explanation of the Delaware Block Method, see *Piemonte v. New Boston Garden Corp.,* 387 N.E.2d 1145 (Mass.1979).

*Weinberger* changed the valuation landscape. The Delaware Supreme Court held that the "inflexible" Delaware Block Method of valuation would be abandoned as the exclusive method of determining value in appraisal proceedings. Instead, the Court held that the Delaware Chancery Court must use a "more liberal approach [that] must include proof of value by any techniques or methods which are generally considered acceptable in the financial community and otherwise admissible in court."

Thus, in *M.G. Bancorporation, Inc. v. Le Beau,* 737 A.2d 513 (Del.1999), the Delaware Supreme Court reviewed a number of different valuation methods proffered by the financial experts of the respective parties. The case itself revolved around a "short-form" merger conducted pursuant to Section 253 of the DGCL. Southwest Bancorp owned over 91% of the stock of M.G. Bancorporation (MGB). MGB itself was a holding company. Its primary assets were stock in two subsidiaries, both of which were banks.

In order to rid itself of the minority stockholders of MGB, Southwest merged MGB with and into itself pursuant to Section 253 of the DGCL. Southwest paid the minority stockholders $41 per share as merger consideration. Pursuant to Section 262(b) of the DGCL, the minority stockholders were entitled to appraisal rights, and some of them perfected them. At issue, therefore, was the "fair value" of the shares held by the dissenting stockholders. After a trial featuring extensive testimony from the experts for both sides, the Delaware Chancery Court determined that the shares were worth $85 per share, a dramatically different number from the $41 per share that MGB offered in the merger.

The valuation methods proffered by the experts fell into four main categories. The first category included comparable valuations. This involved determining MGB's value based on the values of other comparable companies. The second category included valuations based on book value. Book value is a balance sheet-based valuation method that is calculated by subtracting a company's total liabilities from its total assets. The third category included valuations based on earnings. This involved looking at earnings multiples and price-to-earnings (P/E) ratios to determine value. The final category included valuations based on discounted cash flow (DCF).

In *LeBeau,* the Delaware Supreme Court made it clear that the lower court is not bound to accept a particular expert's valuation or methodology *in toto*. Rather, the court can make its own independent calculation by either adapting or blending the factual assumptions of the parties' experts. The ultimate selection of a valuation framework is within the court's discretion. Indeed, definitively adopting the valuation of one expert as part of an "either/or" approach is at variance with the court's statutory obligation to engage in an independent valuation exercise. See *Gonsalves v. Straight Arrow Publishers, Inc.*, 701 A.2d 357 (Del.1997).

Furthermore, the Delaware Supreme Court underscored that the lower court's valuation will be accorded a high level of deference. In the absence of legal error, the standard of review is "abuse of discretion." The lower court will be found to have abused its discretion when either its factual findings do not have support in the record or its valuation is not the result of an orderly and logical deductive process. See also *Rapid–American Corp. v. Harris*, 603 A.2d 796 (Del.1992).

### (4) Minority Discount and Control Premium

Surviving companies have argued that courts should only value the specific shares held by a dissenting stockholder during an appraisal proceeding. See, e.g., *Pueblo Bancorporation v. Lindoe, Inc.*, 63 P.3d 353 (Colo.2003). Those shares, of course, typically represent only a small stake or "minority position" in the company. The holders of small blocks of stock have little influence over the company because the voting power their shares carry is insignificant. By contrast, a large block of stock—especially a majority stake—carries with it a large element of control. Because "control" is valuable, surviving companies have argued that courts should assign a lower per share valuation to a small block of stock. In other words, these companies want the courts to apply a *minority discount* when they value small blocks of stock.

Courts, however, have rejected this argument in the majority of jurisdictions. Most refuse to equate "fair value," as such appears in their appraisal statutes, with "fair market value." According to the *Pueblo Bancorporation* court:

> Under a fair market value standard ... [,] the court is, by definition, determining the price at which a specific allotment of shares would change hands between a willing buyer and a willing seller. However, in a dissenter's rights action, the dissenting shareholder is not in the same position as a willing seller on the open market—he is an unwilling seller with little or no bargaining power. We are convinced that "fair value" does not mean "fair market value."

. . .

The clear majority trend is to interpret fair value as the shareholder's proportionate ownership of a going concern and not to apply discounts at the shareholder level. . . .

Thus, when valuing the shares held by a dissenting stockholder, most courts start first by valuing the *entire corporation* itself. By valuing the entire corporation prior to valuing the shares in the hands of a dissenting stockholder, the court ensures that the dissenting stockholder will receive a *control premium* for her shares. As articulated in *Cavalier Oil Corp v. Harnett*, 564 A.2d 1137 (Del.1989), the objective of an appraisal under Section 262 of the DGCL is to value the corporation itself as distinguished from a specific fraction of its shares as they may exist in the hands of a dissenting stockholder. That stockholder is entitled to her proportionate interest in the overall fair value of the entire corporation appraised as a going-concern. Indeed, the valuation must be based on the assumption that a dissenting stockholder would be willing to continue with her investment position, however slight, had the merger never occurred.

Once a court has valued the entire corporation, it then must determine the value of the dissenting stockholder's stake. This is done by simply dividing the value of the entire corporation by the number of outstanding shares to arrive at a per share valuation. Next, simply multiply that per share valuation by the number of shares held by the dissenting stockholder:

$$\text{Value of dissenter's shares} = \frac{\text{Value of Corp}}{\text{\# of o/s shs.}} \times \text{\# of shares held by dissenter}$$

Courts also discount the usefulness of the per share trading price of a publicly-traded company in determining the value of a dissenting stockholder's shares. This stems from the fact that the quoted stock price of a publicly-traded company represents a market valuation of only a single share of stock. Thus, that price has a minority discount built into it. Because of this, it is not appropriate to simply multiply the number of outstanding shares of stock held by a dissenting stockholder by that price to determine the value of her shares.

Nor is it appropriate to multiply the total number of outstanding shares of a given company by its per share trading price to arrive at a valuation for the entire company. That calculation yields a publicly-traded company's *market capitalization*. Market capitalization, however, does not reflect what a third party would have to pay to acquire control of that company. Control is valuable, and acquirors seeking it must pay for it in the form of a control premium. That is why a bidder conducting a tender offer always offers more (sometimes substantially more) per share than the target company's per share trading price.

Control premiums also come into play when the company being valued is a holding company, as was the case in *M.G. Bancorporation, Inc. v. Le Beau*, 737 A.2d 513 (Del.1999). One of the issues addressed by the Delaware Supreme Court was whether a control premium should be applied when valuing the *subsidiaries* owned by a holding company.

The Court held that it is appropriate to include a control premium when the holding company owns a majority stake in the subsidiary. According to the Court, the value of the holding company must reflect a control premium attributable to the control of a subsidiary if the Court is valuing the holding company from the bottom up (*i.e.,* valuing each subsidiary and then adding those values to determine the value of the holding company itself). Indeed, it makes intuitive sense that if a holding company owns a majority stake in a subsidiary, this fact alone makes the holding company more valuable.

### (5) Synergies and Other Benefits of the Merger

When two companies combine, management of both often point to *synergies* as the reason for the merger. A *synergy* is a benefit that arises when complimentary operations are combined. For example, assume that Company A is going to merge with and into Company B. Company A sells computer equipment only through retail outlets but would like to begin selling through mail order as well. Company B owns as an asset the largest data base of mail order customers in the world. Needless to say, the combination of Company A and Company B makes sense because their businesses are complimentary. Together, they will create more value than they would operating independently.

Should a court in an appraisal proceeding consider potential synergies and other benefits of a merger when valuing the shares of a dissenting stock-holder? What is to say that the premium price paid by the surviving company did not already reflect the synergistic effect of the merger? Section 262(h) of the DGCL requires the Delaware Chancery Court to "appraise the shares, determining their fair value exclusive of any element of value arising from the accomplishment or expectation of the merger or consolidation...." But it also adds, "In determining ... fair value, the Court shall take into account all relevant factors...." Are these two statutory statements in conflict?

In *Weinberger v. UOP, Inc.*, 457 A.2d 701 (Del. 1983), the Delaware Supreme Court stated that since fair value was to be based on all relevant factors, "[o]nly the speculative elements of value that may arise from the 'accomplishment or expectation' of the merger are excluded." This narrow exception to the appraisal process is, according to the Court:

> designed to eliminate use of *pro forma* data and projections of a speculative variety relating to the completion of the merger. But elements of future value, including the nature of the enterprise, which are known or susceptible of proof as of the date of the merger and not the product of speculation, may be considered.

In *M.G. Bancorporation, Inc. v. Le Beau*, 737 A.2d 513 (Del.1999), the Delaware Supreme Court clarified its holding in *Weinberger*. It first stated that the underlying assumption in an appraisal valuation is that the dissenting stockholders would be willing to maintain their investment position had the merger not occurred. It then added, "the corporation must be valued as a going concern based upon the 'operative reality' of the company as of the time of the merger." See also *Delaware Open MRI Radiology Assocs., P.A. v. Kessler*, 898 A.2d 290 (Del.Ch.2006).

This notion of "operative reality" had appeared earlier in *Cede & Co. v. Technicolor, Inc.*, 684 A.2d 289 (Del.1996). This case involved a two-step acquisition of Technicolor by Ronald Perelman's McAndrews & Forbes (MAF). Step one consisted of a friendly tender offer in which MAF purchased 82.19% of Technicolor's stock for $23 per share in cash. Step two consisted of Macanfor Corp., a newly-formed, wholly-owned subsidiary of MAF, merging with and into Technicolor (a reverse triangular merger). Technicolor's remaining stockholders were squeezed out through the merger and received $23 in cash as merger consideration.

Prior to its involvement with MAF and Perelman, Technicolor's business strategy was driven by a plan championed by its Chairman, Morton Kamerman. This strategy—the Kamerman Plan—remained in effect until step one of MAF's takeover was completed. Ronald Perelman had developed a strategy for Technicolor (the Perelman Plan) that called for Technicolor to sell off many of its businesses while focusing on only two. After step one of MAF's takeover was completed, but *before* the second step merger was effected, Perelman had Technicolor begin implementing his strategic plan.

Cinerama, a beneficial owner of Technicolor stock, sought appraisal rights in the Delaware Chancery Court. It argued that Technicolor should be valued as it existed on the date of the merger. This would mean that Technicolor would be valued based on the implementation of the Perelman Plan rather than the Kamerman Plan. Technicolor, in turn, argued that it should be valued as if the strategies of the Kamerman Plan remained in place.

The Delaware Chancery Court agreed with Technicolor. It reasoned that, as a matter of policy, the valuation process in an appraisal proceeding should be the same irrespective of whether a merger is accomplished in one step or two steps. Therefore, the Perelman Plan should not be taken into consideration because it encompasses value resulting from the accomplishment of the merger.

The Delaware Supreme Court, however, disagreed. It highlighted that in a two-step acquisition, the buyer typically controls the target after the first step tender offer. Accordingly, the buyer is in a position to implement its plans for the target immediately—even before the second step merger. To the extent value has been added to the target following a change in majority control, that value accrues to the benefit of all stockholders of the target—majority as well as minority—and must be included in the appraisal process on the date of the merger. According to the Court, the narrow exclusion in Section

262(h) of the DGCL does not encompass known elements of value, including those which exist on the date of the merger because of a majority acquiror's interim action in a two-step cash-out transaction.

### (6) Subsequent Events

Dissenting stockholders who cashed out in an appraisal proceeding have sometimes asked the court to reconsider its valuation decision after subsequent events indicated that the court's valuation was too low. For example, assume that Company A is sold to Company B for $100 million. One year later, Company A is resold by Company B to Company C for $300 million. Should dissenting stockholders from the original deal between Company A and Company B be allowed to petition the court to receive more money based on the subsequent deal between Company B and Company C? What if the subsequent deal was for far less money? Should dissenting stockholders from the original deal be required to give back money?

Not surprisingly, the courts have declined to reopen valuation cases in the absence of fraud. Such was the case in *Metlyn Realty Corp. v. Esmark, Inc.*, 763 F.2d 826 (7th Cir.1985). According to the Seventh Circuit, only facts discernible when the appraisal occurs can and should be considered. Subsequent facts should not be considered. The Court, however, noted that the existence of fraud would lead to a different conclusion. Indeed, a court must ensure that an acquiror did not withhold facts that would help establish value at the time of the acquisition.

### (7) The Issue of Interest

Should a dissenting stockholder receive interest along with the fair value of her shares once the appraisal proceeding concludes? If so, at what rate? And should it be simple or compound interest? Section 262 of the DGCL addresses the issue of interest twice. Section 262(i) states that the Delaware Chancery Court "shall direct payment of the fair value of the shares, *together with interest, if any,* by the surviving or resulting corporation to the stockholders entitled thereto. *Interest may be simple or compound, as the Court may direct.*" (Emphasis added.) As seen in Nutshell Section 10, simple interest entails the payment of interest only on the amount of money actually owed. Compound interest, by contrast, entails the payment of interest not only on the amount owed, but on interest itself as it accrues. Section 262(h) states that "[u]nless the Court in its discretion determines otherwise for good cause, interest from the effective date of the merger through the date of payment of the judgment shall be compounded quarterly and shall accrue at 5% over the Federal Reserve discount rate (including any surcharge) as established from time to time during the period between the effective date of the merger and the date of payment of the judgment." This rate is referred to as the "legal" rate of interest in Delaware.

Despite this statutory guidance, the Delaware Supreme Court has indicated that the Delaware Chancery Court has broad discretion in awarding interest in the first place, as well as in picking the actual rate of interest and the frequency of compounding. For example, in *Gonsalves v. Straight Arrow Publishers, Inc.*, 701 A.2d 357 (Del.1997), the Delaware Supreme Court indicated that the Delaware Chancery Court has broad discretion under Section 262(i) to award either simple or compound interest. The Chancery Court, however, must explain its selection of one type of interest over another and cannot choose one type of interest over another as a matter of course.

In the subsequent case of *M.G. Bancorporation, Inc. v. Le Beau*, 737 A.2d 513 (Del.1999), the Delaware Supreme Court seemingly made it more difficult for dissenting stockholders to receive compound interest. It held that an award of compound interest must be based on the Chancery Court's finding of "exceptional circumstances." For the Chancery Court's determination to withstand challenge, the Chancery Court must explain its choice.

In making its case that compound interest should always be awarded, the Delaware Chancery Court in *Taylor v. American Specialty Retailing Group, Inc.*, 2003 WL 21753752 (Del.Ch.) (citations omitted) said the following:

An award of compound interest is generally the form of interest most likely to fulfill the purposes of Delaware's appraisal statute. This is so because the award of interest pursuant to [Section 262(h)] supports two goals: first, the award compensates the petitioner for the loss of the use of the fair value of his or her shares during the pendency of the proceeding; and second, the award forces the corporation to disgorge any benefits it obtained from the use of the fair value of the petitioner's shares during the pendency of the proceeding.

An award of simple interest does not satisfy the first goal of Section 262(h) because "it is simply not credible in today's financial markets that a person sophisticated enough to perfect his or her appraisal rights would be unsophisticated enough to make an investment at simple interest." Moreover, an award of simple interest does not satisfy the second goal of Section 262(h) because "as for the defendant company in an appraisal action, it is even harder to imagine a corporation today that would seek simple interest on the funds it holds.... Nor is it conceivable that [the defendant company's] lenders were providing ... capital at simple rates of interest." Thus, awarding simple interest "would not force the defendant company to disgorge the full benefit it received from having use of the plaintiff's funds." (Citations omitted.)

*APPRAISAL RIGHTS*

## E. Exclusivity of Appraisal Rights

An important issue relating to appraisal rights is the exclusivity of that remedy. It seems clear that a dissenting stockholder, whose complaint is with the magnitude of the merger consideration she is to receive, should be limited to the appraisal remedy. However, should that same stockholder be precluded from bringing another cause of action against her corporation and its board of directors if one exists? For example, should the availability of appraisal rights cut off a stockholder's ability to claim that directors of her company approved a merger in violation of their fiduciary duties?

According to *Weinberger v. UOP, Inc.*, 457 A.2d 701 (Del.1983), the answer is yes so long as the appraisal remedy is "adequate" under the circumstances. In so holding, however, the Delaware Supreme Court stated, "we do not intend any limitation on the historic powers of the [Delaware Chancery Court] to grant such other relief as the facts of a particular case may dictate. The appraisal remedy we approve may not be adequate in certain cases, particularly where fraud, misrepresentation, self-dealing, deliberate waste of corporate assets, or gross and palpable overreaching are involved." See also Comment 5 to RMBCA § 13.02(d).

Plaintiff security lawyers have fought against the general supremacy of the appraisal remedy. Instead, they want it to be but one weapon in an arsenal of weapons with which to attack a merger. Included in that arsenal are challenges based on breach of fiduciary duties, securities law violations, and fraud. Since *Weinberger,* the Delaware courts have allowed additional causes of action only when plaintiffs uncover evidence of such a course of action during the discovery phase of a pending appraisal proceeding. That evidence, however, must support claims that transcend those of ordinary breaches of fiduciary duty. The remedy in non-appraisal proceedings attacking a merger is limited to injunctive relief and rescissory damages.

## § 24.  VALUATION BY AGREEMENT

Valuation issues arise frequently in the context of a closely-held corporation. In order to control the identity of those who own shares of a closely-held corporation, founding stockholders often enter into a shareholders' agreement at the time they make their investments. Among other things, this agreement may require a stockholder (or her estate) to sell her shares back to the corporation (a so-called *forced resale*) upon the occurrence of certain events. See Nutshell Section 2B(3)a. The shareholders' agreement typically specifies a formula or method for determining the price that the corporation will pay for that stockholder's shares.

A stockholder forced to resell her shares is generally in no position to complain about the price determined by the valuation formula contained in a shareholders' agreement. Indeed, she is a signatory to that agreement. Moreover, the agreement applies equally to all other stockholders.

In *Allen v. Biltmore Tissue Corp.*, 141 N.E.2d 812 (N.Y.1957), the company's by-laws contained a provision granting the company, upon the death of any stockholder, a 90–day option to repurchase the deceased stockholder's shares at the price at which that stockholder had originally purchased them. This provision was clearly reflected in a legend set forth on the stock certificates held by the stockholders.

The son of a deceased stockholder sent a letter seeking to find out if the company was interested in purchasing his deceased father's 20 shares and at "what price." The board decided to exercise the company's option pursuant to the by-laws, and even offered $20 per share, which was more than the company was required to pay under the by-laws. The decedent's executors, however, declined to sell the shares to the company. Instead, they brought suit arguing that the by-law was void as an "unreasonable restraint" on the transfer of personal property. The company counterclaimed for specific performance.

While noting that outright prohibitions on share transfers are illegal, the New York Court of Appeals disagreed with the executors' position. The Court noted that the restriction was not a prohibition on resale. Under the by-law, if the company did not exercise its option within 90 days, then the executors could resell to whomever they saw fit. Moreover, the Court noted that the executors had to prove more than a mere disparity between the option price and the current market value of the shares. This is especially true when the parties agree on a pricing formula which suits their needs in advance.

*Evangelista v. Holland*, 537 N.E.2d 589 (Mass. App.Ct.1989), also involved a forced resale provision in a shareholders' agreement. After a stockholder died, the company brought suit to force the decedent's estate to sell the decedent's stock back to the company at the price determined by a formula set forth in the agreement. Even though a large disparity existed between the price for the decedent's shares determined by the formula and their fair market value, the Massachusetts Appeals Court found for the company. It stated, "Questions of good faith and loyalty do not arise when all the stockholders in advance enter into an agreement for the purchase of stock of a withdrawing or deceased stockholder." It added, "That the price [of shares] established in the stockholders' agreement may be less than the appraised or market value is unremarkable.... When the agreement was entered into in 1984, the order and time of death of stockholders was an unknown. There was mutuality of risk." (Internal citations omitted.)

A court is even less likely to step in when a stockholder has the choice on whether to sell his shares back to the company at the price specified in an agreement. In *Nichols Construction Corp. v. St.*

*Clair*, 708 F.Supp. 768 (M.D. La.1989), for example, the defendants had redeemed the shares of a closely-held corporation from the plaintiff at their book value in accordance with multiple stock redemption agreements between the parties. Later, the plaintiff claimed that the defendants should have paid fair market value for his shares. He argued that as a minority stockholder the defendants owed him a fiduciary obligation to pay a higher price for his stock.

The District Court, however, disagreed, claiming that no fiduciary duties were owed in this regard. Because the plaintiff entered into the agreements in an atmosphere free of fraud, mistake or error, the agreements themselves were fully enforceable. Pursuant to the agreements, the defendants could only offer to purchase the plaintiff's shares at book value; they could not force the plaintiff to sell. Once the plaintiff accepted the defendants' offer, the plaintiff was in no position to complain about the price.

By contrast, *Helms v. Duckworth*, 249 F.2d 482 (D.C. Cir.1957), indicates that the courts may police the pricing provisions of a shareholders' agreement when inequitable conduct occurs. Here, Easterday, then age 70, joined forces with Duckworth, then age 37, to run a roofing and sheet metal contractor business. Easterday contributed the assets of his former business in exchange for 51% of the new company's shares, while Duckworth contributed cash for his 49% interest. The two men also entered into a trust agreement that provided that each of them would place their shares in a trust. Upon the death of either man, the decedent's stock would be sold to the survivor at a price equal to "the par value of $10 per share unless modified by the parties by subsequent agreement." The parties could renegotiate the purchase price once a year.

When Easterday died seven years later, Duckworth attempted to buy Easterday's stock for $10 per share from Easterday's estate even though Duckworth readily admitted the fair market value of each share was $80. In attempting to cancel the trust agreement, Easterday's estate argued that Duckworth fraudulently misrepresented that he would consent to a periodic redetermination of the stock purchase price, when all along he knew that he would not. Moreover, Easterday was helpless to do anything about it. Indeed, the Court of Appeals noted that Easterday had boxed himself in. Pursuant to applicable law, he neither could dissolve the corporation nor sell all or substantially all of its assets without Duckworth's consent. Nor, of course, could he change the buyout price without Duckworth's consent.

Based on these facts, the Court refused to enforce the trust agreement's buyout provision. The Court emphasized that the agreement's periodic bargaining process relating to the price of shares required each party to participate in good faith. Negotiating in good faith required more than simply going through the motions of negotiating. Each party must negotiate "sincerely and in good faith" and without a secret intent of preventing agreement between the parties. Moreover, the Court went so far as to hold that stockholders in a closely-held corporation bear a fiduciary duty to deal fairly, honestly and openly with their fellow stockholders and to make disclosure of all essential information during negotiations.

## § 25.  VALUATION IN OPPRESSION PROCEEDINGS

### A.  Introduction

A common complaint from a disgruntled stockholder of a closely-held corporation is that the majority or controlling stockholders are engaged in oppressive conduct towards him. According to the Montana Supreme Court, the term *oppression* suggests "harsh, dishonest or wrongful conduct and a visible departure from the standards of fairdealing [sic] which inure to the benefit of [the] majority [stockholder(s)] and to the detriment of the minority [stockholder(s)]." *Whitehorn v. Whitehorn Farms, Inc.*, 195 P.3d 836 (Mont.2008). In an earlier case, the same court highlighted why stockholders of closely-held corporations—but not publicly-traded corporations—are vulnerable to oppressive tactics:

Oppression may be more easily found in a close-held, family corporation than in a larger, public corporation. The reason . . . is obvious. Shares in a closely held corporation are not offered for public sale. Without readily available recourse to the market place, a dissatisfied shareholder is left with severely limited alternatives if one group of shareholders chooses to exercise leverage and "squeeze" the dissenter out.

*Fox v. 7L Bar Ranch Co.*, 645 P.2d 929 (Mont.1982) (internal citations omitted).

A disgruntled stockholder may have been a salaried employee of the company, but now has been fired. If stockholders of the company earn a return on their investment primarily through salaries as opposed to dividends, the disgruntled stockholder can only recoup his investment by selling his shares. Sales to third parties, however, are often severely restricted by a shareholders' agreement. Even if this were not the case, most third parties would balk at paying good money to step into the shoes of the disgruntled stockholder.

## B.  Judicial Responses

A disgruntled stockholder often seeks judicial relief from oppressive tactics. *Donahue v. Draper*, 491 N.E.2d 260 (Mass.App.1986), is illustrative in this regard. The business in question (Donahue–Draper Corp. or "DDC") had been formed by two gentlemen, Thomas Draper and Douglas Donahue, and had been quite successful for many years. After the two men had a falling out, they mutually decided that the business should be liquidated. Sometime thereafter, but before the liquidation was completed, Draper restarted his old company (which had been in the same line of business as DDC) and began dealing with former customers of DDC. He also operated his business from DDC's old premises, using similar staff and the same telephone number.

As a result of the liquidation of DDC, Donahue received $321,000. However, he was dissatisfied with this amount as he believed it did not reflect any of DDC's corporate *goodwill*. According to the Massachusetts Appeals Court, "goodwill" is, "fundamentally, the value of an enterprise *over and above* the value of its net tangible assets [(total assets − intangible assets) − total liabilities], ... a value that may derive from the allegiance of customers, prolonged favorable relations with a source of financing, and the like." In other words, "goodwill" is essentially a company's value that is *not* reflected on its balance sheet.

Harold Peterson—Donahue's expert—determined the value of DDC by taking DDC's *normalized earnings* of $397,462 and applying a multiplier of 6.4 (which he believed was appropriate for the kind of business conducted by DDC) in order to reach the value of $2,543,757. By subtracting DDC's net tangible assets of $968,608 from $2,543,757, Peterson determined that DDC's goodwill was worth $1,574,000. In determining "normalized earnings," Peterson only treated $70,800 of the combined annual salaries of the partners as a business expense of the Company. He then considered the salary payments received by the partners in excess of that amount as a part of the company's earnings.

The jury, however, disagreed with Peterson's assessment of the goodwill figure, allowing instead a goodwill figure of around one third of what Peterson had determined. Apparently, the jury did not believe that Donahue and Draper could be replaced with executives that would accept combined pay of only $70,800 per year. Also, it can be inferred that the jury felt that the multiplier used by Peterson was too high.

Draper also was not happy with the jury's determination of goodwill. In attacking it, he argued that it was his personal skills, abilities, and attributes that created any goodwill in the first place. The Court, however, disagreed, holding that once a partner forms a joint enterprise with another and, in connection with its formation, contributes goodwill to the joint enterprise, he may not reappropriate it for his own use without paying for its value. Indeed, at that point the goodwill belongs to the corporation and not to any individual stockholder. Draper next pointed to the stock redemption agreement between the parties, which, if triggered, placed a maximum ceiling on goodwill of $437,049. Because the agreement was not drafted to cover liquidations, however, the Court held that the agreement was irrelevant to the case in question.

## C.  Statutory Responses

Oppression statutes provide disgruntled stockholders with a method to cash out of their investments by forcing a dissolution of the company. Most courts, however, are loathe to order the dissolution of a viable company. See *Alaska Plastics v. Coppock*, 621 P.2d 270 (Ak.1980). Thus, they allow the other stockholders and/or the company itself to buy out the disgruntled stockholder at "fair value." If the negotiation over what constitutes "fair value" collapses, only then will the court order a dissolution.

Such was the case in *Matter of Kemp & Beatley, Inc.*, 473 N.E.2d 1173 (N.Y.1984). The company in question had eight stockholders, all of whom worked for the company. The petitioners, two employee-stockholders who collectively owned 20.33% of the company's outstanding common stock, resigned after long terms of service. They previously received a return on their investment through the receipt of either dividends or extra compensation in the form of bonuses. After the petitioners left the employ of the company, its board of directors stopped paying dividends. The distribution of earnings to employee-stockholders in the form of bonuses, however, continued. Although the company had repurchased shares of other employee-stockholders in the past when they had left the company, the company did not offer to buy out the petitioners.

The petitioners brought suit claiming that the other stockholders had engaged in oppressive conduct that rendered their investments in the company worthless. They petitioned for dissolution of the company under Section 1104–a of the NYBCL, New York's oppression statute. The New York Court of Appeals defined "oppressive conduct" as conduct engaged in by the majority or controlling stockholder that "substantially defeats the 'reasonable expectations' held by minority stockholders in committing their capital to the particular enterprise." To determine a given minority stockholder's expectations, the trial court must determine what the majority stockholders knew, or should have known, to be that stockholder's expectations when that stockholder invested in a particular enterprise. For those expectations to be respected, however, they must be objectively reasonable under the circumstances and central to the stockholder's decision to invest.

Under the facts presented, the Court held that the majority stockholders had, indeed, substantially defeated the petitioners' reasonable expectations. Normally, the appropriate remedy for oppressive conduct is a court ordered dissolution of the corporation. However, the Court noted that it typically tries to find a less drastic remedy, particularly where the corporation is a viable business. In fact, the Court stated that "every order of dissolution must be conditioned upon permitting any stockholder of the corporation to elect to purchase the complaining stockholder's stock at fair value" under Section 1118 of the NYBCL.

Section 1118(b) of the NYBCL provides that if the parties cannot reach agreement on the fair value of the petitioner's shares, the court must make that determination. That determination must exclude any element of value arising out of the petition filed by the petitioner but may include a surcharge if the directors wilfully or recklessly dissipated or transferred assets or corporate property without just or adequate compensation therefor. The court may also award interest at its discretion from the date the petition was filed until the date of payment for the petitioner's shares.

In the case of *In the Matter of Pace Photographers, Ltd.*, 525 N.E.2d 713 (N.Y.1988), the New York Court of Appeals addressed the issue of whether stockholders can agree in advance to a valuation formula that a court should apply in an oppression proceeding. Here, after the plaintiff stockholder sought dissolution pursuant to Section 1104–a of the NYBCL, the corporation elected to repurchase his shares pursuant to Section 1118 of the NYBCL. The corporation, however, did not offer a fair price; rather, it offered a price based on a pricing formula contained in a shareholders' agreement that all stockholders, including the plaintiff, had signed. That pricing formula yielded a deeply discounted value for the plaintiff's shares.

The Court refused to apply this contractual pricing formula, because the shareholders' agreement did not specifically call for its use in a Section 1104–a dissolution proceeding. This formula was only to be used when the stockholder was engaging in a "voluntary sale," and not when the sale was the result of alleged majority oppression. The Court, however, indicated that "as an abstract matter, it may well be that shareholders can agree in advance that a predetermined formula be used in a 1104–a dissolution proceeding.... Participants in business ventures are free to express their understandings in written agreements, and such consensual arrangements are generally favored and upheld by the courts." The Court then went on to value the plaintiff's shares "based on the value of the business as a going concern."

## § 26.  VALUATION IN OTHER LEGAL CONTEXTS

Courts are required to value shares in the hands of stockholders in several other legal situations. These include, among others, divorce, tax and probate proceedings. For example, *Nardini v. Nardini*, 414 N.W.2d 184 (Minn.1987), addressed the valuation of a business in a divorce proceeding. The case involved the valuation of the family business—Nardini of Minnesota—in order to determine the amount to which Ralph Nardini's wife, Marguerite, was entitled. The trial court found that Ralph owned a one-half interest in the business as nonmarital property. Thus, the issue before the court related to what the *other* half interest in the business was worth, because that was what was going to be split in the divorce.

Under the Minnesota divorce statute, a Minnesota court may order a forced sale of a business interest by one spouse to the other. In doing so, the court will set a selling price and the terms of payment.

As part of the valuation process, the Minnesota Supreme Court in *Nardini* refused to apply a *minority discount* in determining the value to which Marguerite was entitled. See Nutshell Section

23D(4) for a discussion of a "minority discount." Even though shares in the business would be transferred from Marguerite to Ralph, the Court noted that no corporate asset or any fraction of the shares of the corporation would actually be sold to an outsider. The business would continue essentially unchanged. Accordingly, the Court first determined the value of the business as if the transaction or sale was of the *entire business* by a willing seller to a willing buyer, thus eschewing the application of a minority discount.

In valuing the business, the Court stated that the trial court must consider *all relevant facts* appropriate for use in valuing a closely-held corporation. According to the Court, specific consideration must be given to the following facts, which were taken from an Internal Revenue Service revenue ruling relating to estate and gift tax:

1. The nature of the business and the history of the enterprise from its inception.

2. The economic outlook in general and the condition and outlook of the specific industry in particular.

3. The book value of the stock and the financial condition of the business.

4. The earning capacity of the company.

5. The dividend paying capacity of the company.

6. Whether or not the enterprise has goodwill or other intangible value.

7. Sales of the stock and the size of the block of stock to be valued.

8. The market price of stocks of corporations engaged in the same or a similar line of business having their stocks traded in a free and open market.

Further, the Court held that the trial court, in weighing those factors, must apply "common sense, sound and informed judgment, and reasonableness to the process." The Court implied that this was something the trial court had failed to do.

# PART II

# RISK AND RETURN

## CHAPTER 9

## MEASURES OF RISK

### § 27. PORTFOLIO THEORY

*Portfolio theory* is a fancy term for the old adage, "don't put all your eggs in one basket." This theory provides that certain risks from owning a particular stock may be reduced by holding a portfolio of multiple stocks. Therefore, the key to portfolio theory is *diversification*. The risk associated with spreading your money over multiple stocks is less than investing it all in the stock of one company.

In order to understand portfolio theory, one must understand two types of risk: *unsystematic risk* and *systematic risk*. *Unsystematic risk* is the risk inherent in investing in a particular company. What if its products become obsolete? Its workers strike? Its management underperforms? Unsystematic risk, therefore, is *business-specific risk*.

*Systematic risk,* by contrast, is all non-business specific risk. Examples include the risk that the Federal Reserve will raise interest rates or new troubles in the Middle East will arise. If these events were to occur, they would affect markets as a whole, not just particular businesses and their stocks. Thus, systematic risk affects the "*system*" rather than just a given company.

Portfolio theory posits that an investor can reduce the *unsystematic* risk of a particular stock investment down to zero by holding a portfolio of multiple stocks. Because this type of diversification occurs within a single asset class (*i.e.,* common stocks), it is referred to as *vertical diversification*. Academic literature does not agree on the minimum number of stocks one must own to benefit from the full effect of diversification. Most studies point to between 20 and 30 stocks, although another suggests as many as 45 may be needed. What is clear, however, is that owning more than 20 stocks only marginally decreases risk, as the benefits of diversification begin to be offset by increased transaction costs. Individual investors with modest sums to invest can receive the benefits of diversification, professional investment management and transaction cost reduction by investing in a diversified stock mutual fund. The fund will spread out the collective investments of all its investors over multiple stocks for a modest advisory fee.

Reducing systematic risk is more difficult than reducing unsystematic risk. The best way to do so is by investing in asset classes other than just equities (*i.e.,* stocks). This type of diversification is referred to as *horizontal diversification*. For example, investing in gold is viewed as a hedge against downward movements in the stock market caused by negative world events. Large sums of money typically flow out of the stock market and into the gold market when a large-scale war is imminent.

Under portfolio theory, the market return received by an investor on a particular stock in a competitive market does not include any compensation for the investor shouldering *unsystematic* risk. Indeed, the market does not reward investors who fail to diversify this risk down to zero. Therefore, market returns on a given stock are solely a function of the systematic risk of that stock, as investors are rewarded for bearing that risk.

If portfolio theory were fully embraced, serious repercussions in the context of directorial fiduciary duties would follow. Some scholars have argued that the fiduciary duty of care is no longer needed, because an investor's exposure to incompetent actions by directors can be reduced down to zero. Therefore, the law should encourage stockholders to hold diversified portfolios by severely limiting their ability to sue directors who breach their duty of care. Judge Winter, in *Joy v. North*, 692 F.2d 880 (2d Cir.1982), supports this viewpoint: "Given mutual funds and similar forms of diversified investment, courts need not bend over backwards to give special protection to shareholders who refuse to reduce the volatility of risk by not diversifying."

## § 28.  BETA AND THE CAPITAL ASSET PRICING MODEL (CAPM)

### A.  Generally

Portfolio theory posits that the only risk for which issuing corporations will compensate investors is the sensitivity of their stock to systematic risk. It makes sense, therefore, that the correct or "intrinsic" value of a given stock must be a function of that sensitivity. The *Capital Asset Pricing Model* (CAPM (pronounced "cap-m")), which was first proposed by Lintner and Sharpe in the 1960s, reflects this.

The Greek letter *beta* (β) is the variable used to measure the relationship of the risk of an individual stock or portfolio of stocks to the risk of the stock market as a whole. The beta of the entire market is equal to 1.0, and the betas of individual stocks are measured against that. The beta of a stock that is more risky, from a systematic risk perspective, than the market as a whole will have a beta above 1.0. By contrast, the beta of a stock that is less risky will have a beta below 1.0. The beta of a security deemed to have no systematic risk (such as a short-term U.S. treasury security) would be zero.

Stocks with higher betas are viewed as more risky because their prices tend to swing more widely than the market as a whole as the market undulates up and down each trading day. In other words, they are more market sensitive. Assume, for example, that the Federal Reserve announces that inflation is becoming excessive and that interest rates need to rise to combat it. As a result, the stock market as a whole falls three percent. A stock like Coca–Cola with a beta of less than 1.0 should, *on average*, experience less than a three percent drop in price. The stock of a young Internet company with a beta well above 1.0, by contrast, should, *on average*, experience more than a three percent drop in price.

Beta can be used to determine the expected return of either an individual stock or a portfolio of stocks. Not surprisingly, a stock or portfolio with a beta less than 1.0 will have a lower expected return than the market as a whole, because it is less risky than the market as a whole. Conversely, a stock or portfolio with a beta greater than 1.0 will have a higher expected return than the market as a whole, because it is more risky than the market as a whole.

## B. The CAPM Formula

The expected return of a particular security is determined by using CAPM. The CAPM formula is:

$$E_i = [E_f] + [\beta_i \times (E_m - E_f)]$$

where:  $E_i$ is the expected return on the particular security (i).

$E_f$ is the expected return on a riskless security.

$\beta_i$ is the beta of the particular security (i) (sensitivity to the market as a whole).

$E_m$ is the expected return on the market portfolio.

The expected return on a "riskless security" needed for the CAPM formula can be gleaned by looking for the current yield on short-term U.S. treasury securities. These yields are available daily in papers like *The Wall Street Journal* and on various internet investment sites, such as Google Finance. The expected return for the market as a whole (the market portfolio) has been approximately 10% based on historical data.

The beta for a given publicly-traded stock over the preceding year is calculated by several financial services firms, such as Merrill Lynch and Value Line, and published in so-called "beta books." Betas can also be found on-line through Reuters and Google Finance.

Suppose you want to calculate the expected rate of return for a public company called Papa John's (ticker: PZZA). Assume that the "riskless" rate of return is 4.8%, the expected return on the market portfolio is 10% and Papa John's beta is 1.39. Simply plug this information into the CAPM formula to calculate the expected rate of return:

$$
\begin{aligned}
E_i &= [E_f] + [\beta_i \times (E_m - E_f)] \\
&= .048 + [1.39 \times (.10 - .048)] \\
&= .048 + [1.39 \times .052] \\
&= .048 + .07228 \\
&= \underline{.12028} \text{ or } \underline{12.028\%}
\end{aligned}
$$

Thus, Papa John's, because of its acute sensitivity to systematic risk, has an expected return higher than the expected market return of 10%. This makes sense, because the more risk you accept, the higher the expected return should be.

Once you calculate the expected return for a particular stock through CAPM, that return can be used to help determine the value of the stock. The expected return can be used as the discount rate in either the Dividend Discount or the Discounted Cash Flow valuation methods. See Nutshell Section 20. It also can be used as the capitalization rate in the Capitalization of Earnings valuation method. See Nutshell Section 19.

## C.  Alpha

While Beta measures a security's or portfolio's volatility in relation to the market as a whole, *alpha* measures risk-adjusted return. That is, it measures the actual return a security or portfolio provides in relation to the return one would expect it to provide based on its beta. Alpha is the *excess return* that a security or portfolio makes over and above what the capital asset pricing model estimates.

If a security's or portfolio's actual return is higher than its beta, the security has a positive alpha, and if the return is lower it has a negative alpha. For example, if a stock's beta is 1.5, and its benchmark gained 2%, it would be expected to gain 3% (2% x 1.5 = 0.03, or 3%). Thus, if the stock gained

4%, it would have a positive alpha. If it gained only 2.5%, however, it would have a negative alpha.

Alpha plays a significant role in the mutual fund industry in the context of actively managed stock funds as compared to passively managed index funds. In that context, alpha represents the value that an active portfolio manager adds to or subtracts from a fund's return in relation to the performance of the fund's benchmark index. A manager will have "added alpha" if her fund outperforms its benchmark index, while she will have "subtracted alpha" if her fund underperforms that index.

## D.  CAPM Assumptions and Empirical Evidence

Like any other theory, CAPM and its ability to determine expected returns is far from perfect. For example, the time period over which a given stock's beta is calculated can affect the value of beta. Has the stock's trading price fluctuated at some point during that time period due to extraordinary events? Such would be the case if the stock in question had been made the target of a hostile tender offer at some point during that time period. If so, then the trading value of that stock will have been inflated due to an extraordinary event. It would make sense, therefore, to calculate the beta for that stock over a period of time prior to the launch of that tender offer.

Such was the case in *Cede & Co. v. Technicolor*, 1990 WL 161084 (Del.Ch.). During an appraisal proceeding for Technicolor stock, Chancellor Allen noted that a beta figure used by one expert was "intuitively high for a company with relatively stable cash flows." He added, "[i]ntuition aside . . . [, the beta figure] plainly was affected to some extent by the striking volatility in Technicolor's stock during the period surrounding the announcement of [the] proposal to acquire Technicolor for $23 per share."

CAPM also rests on several assumptions, some of which are not only suspect but simply untrue. These assumptions include the following:

(A) *CAPM assumes that all investors are risk averse.* This results in investors diversifying their portfolios and demanding higher expected returns from riskier stocks. This is perhaps the most plausible of all the CAPM assumptions.

(B) *CAPM assumes that there is a security which provides a risk-free rate of return.* While certain securities may, at times, come close to this, in actuality no such security exists. Even short-term U.S. treasury securities are affected to some degree by inflationary pressures that cause interest rates to rise. Moreover, it is not completely implausible that the U.S. could default on some of its debt obligations, especially during those years when the president and Congress cannot agree on a budget.

(C) *CAPM assumes that all investors (1) seek to maximize their investment returns, (2) have identical investment time horizons and (3) have access to the same information.* Clearly, however, investors have different risk appetites, as more conservative investors seek the preservation of capital while more risk tolerant investors seek capital appreciation. Moreover, older investors clearly have different investment time horizons than younger investors. Certainly, all investors do not have access to the exact same information.

(D) *CAPM assumes that all assets can be broken down and divided into smaller parts and sold separately.* This, of course, is true at least with respect to stocks. This is particularly important for purposes of portfolio theory, as that theory depends on investors having access to shares of many different companies for diversification purposes.

(E) *CAPM assumes that investors can buy and sell securities without paying transaction fees, such as brokerage commissions.* This assumption, of course, is false, although transaction fees can be minimized by using discount brokerage houses.

(F) *CAPM assumes that all investors pay taxes at the same tax rate.* This is not even remotely true.

(G) *CAPM assumes that investors can lend their money and borrow another's money at the "risk free" rate of interest.* This is not even remotely true.

(H) *CAPM assumes that the buying and selling activities of individual investors are not significant enough to have a major impact on the market.* While true in most cases, large block trades that institutional investors make often do impact the trading prices of the individual stocks being sold or bought.

Overall, empirical evidence concerning CAPM has shown that beta is a useful measure of risk. In general, high beta stocks tend to be priced in a way that yields high rates of return. However, a number of types of stocks—referred to as "anomolies"—have higher returns than CAPM would predict. These include small capitalization stocks, high dividend stocks, low P/E ratio stocks, stocks trading below two-thirds of their net asset value and stocks followed by only a few stock analysts.

# CHAPTER 10

# DERIVATIVE INSTRUMENTS

## § 29.  DEFINITION

A *derivative instrument* is "derivative" in nature because its value is *derived* from the value of another asset or financial variable. Its value is linked to, or dependent on, the value of that other asset or financial or economic variable. Although the derivative instruments used by investors are varied, all instruments are comprised of one or more of the four building blocks of derivatives: options, forward contracts, futures contracts and swap contracts.

## § 30.  SPECULATION VERSUS RISK REDUCTION

Investors use derivative instruments either for speculation or risk reduction. The speculative use of derivatives typically entails an investor entering into a derivative transaction for betting purposes. The bet is on the direction the price of a particular asset will take in the future, or the movement of a particular financial variable over time.

For example, through the use of derivatives, an investor can bet that, over a specified period of time, the price of a particular stock will rise or fall, interest rates will decline or rise, or the U.S. dollar will appreciate or depreciate against the Euro. Investors who abused derivatives by using them for excessive speculation during the 1990s created instability in the world economy and led to urgent calls for regulation of the derivatives market. Derivatives were also abused prior to the economic meltdown of 2008. These abuses and the ensuing period of "derivaphobia" are explored in Nutshell Section 32A below.

Investors also use derivatives to reduce or *hedge* the risk of their investment portfolios. Hedging is the same concept referred to in the old adage, "hedging your bets." Simply put, it means engaging in a transaction that fully or partially *offsets* the risk associated with another transaction—*i.e.,* the transaction over which you are losing sleep. By using derivatives, investors can reduce their exposure to, among other things, drops in the price of particular stocks, changes in interest rates and fluctuations in the foreign currency and commodities markets.

## § 31.  THE BUILDING BLOCKS OF DERIVATIVES

Options, forward contracts, future contracts and swap contracts are the building blocks of derivative instruments. Each is considered below.

## A.  Options

### (1) Overview

Options are the most commonly used of all derivatives. An *option* gives its holder the right, but not the obligation, to buy from or sell to the *option writer* (also known as the *counterparty*) a specified asset on or before a specified expiration or maturity date at a specified price. The main emphasis is on the "right," and not the "obligation." As an option holder, you can choose to exercise the option or not. It is your prerogative. However, this right is not free. The option holder must pay a price for the option to the option writer. This fee is called the *option premium*.

Those seeking to acquire options can do so either in the private or public markets. The private market for options (referred to as the "over-the-counter" or "OTC" market) consists of individuals acquiring custom-tailored options that meet their particular needs, most typically risk reduction. The option holder's counterparty in these transactions is normally a brokerage house or investment bank. Before writing the option, this counterparty will negotiate over its terms with the prospective option holder.

The public market for options, by contrast, consists of individuals and institutions seeking to hedge positions or engage in speculation. Instead of the options being custom-tailored, they are written by investors in accordance with guidelines established by the Chicago Board Options Exchange (CBOE (pronounced "C–BO")). These options are listed on the CBOE for trading purposes, and can be bought and sold prior to their maturity based on the investment appetites of those who engage in options trading. A more complete discussion of the public market for options appears in Nutshell Section 31A(10).

Options are comprised of five key variables or terms. These are:

(a) The underlying asset upon which the option is written;

(b) Whether the option is a "put" or "call";

(c) The "strike" or "exercise" price of the option;

(d) The expiration or maturity date of the option; and

(e) The manner in which the option can be exercised.

(2) Underlying Assets

Almost any asset can serve as the *underlying asset* of an option, including goods, real estate, intellectual property, stocks and contractual rights. In the financial world, the assets upon which options are most commonly written are common stocks. Nevertheless, many other financial instruments, such as bonds and stock indices (*e.g.*, the S&P 500), can support options.

### (3) Types of Options

Options come in two types: calls and puts.

#### a.   Call Option

A *call option* gives its holder the right to buy (or "call away," hence the term "call") the underlying asset on which that option is written from the counterparty at a specified price, called the *strike* or *exercise price*, on or before a specified date. The *writer* of the call option must be prepared to sell the asset stated in the option contract at the stated strike price. To the extent the current market or *spot price* of the asset upon which a call option is written *rises above* the strike price, the call option becomes intrinsically valuable. The reason for this is simple. Having the right to buy a particular asset at a price below the current market price is valuable. By analogy, just think how valuable a 50% off coupon on something you really need to buy is to you.

Any option, including a call option, may have two components of value: *intrinsic value* and *time value*. *Intrinsic value* depends on the relationship between the current market or spot price of the underlying asset and the option's strike or exercise price. If, in the case of a call option, the spot price is above the strike price at any point during the option's term, the call option at that time is *in-the-money* (*i.e.,* it has intrinsic value at that moment). If exercised, you would receive the difference between the spot price and the strike price if the option is cash-settled. If, however, the spot price is below the strike price at any point during the option's term, the call option at that time is *out-of-the-money* (*i.e.,* it has no intrinsic value at that moment). If the spot price is exactly equal to the strike price at any point during the option's term, the call option is *at-the-money*, but unfortunately has no intrinsic value until the spot price rises above the strike price.

Any option, including a call option, also has *time value*. To the extent time remains until the option period expires, the spot price of the underlying asset could change. If, during the time remaining, the spot price rises from out-of-the-money to in-the-money, or, if currently in-the-money, rises even further into-the-money, intrinsic value or additional intrinsic value is created. Thus, the longer the period of time that a given call option has before expiration, the greater its time value. An option's time value, however, gradually declines to zero over its term.

*Call Option Example.* Suppose you think shares of Microsoft common stock, currently trading at $30 per share (the spot price), will increase in value over the next six months. Right now, however, you do not own shares of Microsoft. Nevertheless, you do not actually need to own shares of Microsoft (a "*long*" position) to speculate on a price increase in Microsoft stock. Instead, you can purchase a call option from a counterparty, most typically a brokerage firm. For a modest option premium, you can purchase a call option on 100 shares of Microsoft with a strike price of $33 per share that lasts six months. When initially written, therefore, your call option is out-of-the-money. In fact, the current market price (spot price) of Microsoft stock must rise above $33 per share before your option has any intrinsic value. Nevertheless, when issued, your option has some value, despite being out-of-the-money. Indeed, it has time value, as the current market price of Microsoft stock has the next six months to (hopefully) rise above $33 per share. The higher the rise in the Microsoft stock price above the $33 strike price, the more intrinsically valuable your Microsoft call option becomes.

### b. Put Option

The other type of option is the *put option*. A put option gives its holder the right to sell (or "put to," hence the term "put") the underlying asset on which that option is written to the counterparty at the strike or exercise price on or before a specified date. The *writer* of the put option must be prepared to buy the assets stated in the option contract at the stated strike price. As the value of the asset upon which a put option is written *falls below* the strike price, the put option becomes intrinsically valuable. The reason for this is simple. Having the right to sell a particular asset at above the current market price is valuable. By analogy, just think how valuable a contract to sell your home at top dollar is when home prices begin to fall.

Like the call option, the put option may have both intrinsic value and time value. If, in the case of a put option, the spot price is below the strike price at any point during the option's term, the put option is *in-the-money* (*i.e.,* it has intrinsic value at that moment). If, however, the spot price is above the strike price at any point during the option's term, the put option is *out-of-the-money* (*i.e.,* it has no intrinsic value at that moment). If the spot price is exactly equal to the strike price at any point during the option's term, the put option is *at-the-money*, but unfortunately has no intrinsic value until the spot price falls below the strike price.

Like the call option, the put option also has time value. To the extent time remains until the option period expires, the spot price of the underlying asset could change. If, during the time remaining, the spot price falls from out-of-the-money to in-the-money, or, if currently in-the-money, falls even further into-the-money, intrinsic value or additional intrinsic value is created. Thus, the longer the period of time before a given option has before expiration, the greater its time value. An option's time value, however, gradually declines to zero over its term.

*Put Option Example.* Suppose you think shares of Microsoft common stock, currently trading at $30 per share (the spot price), will decrease in value over the next six months. To capitalize on your belief, you can purchase a put option from a counterparty, most typically a brokerage firm. For a modest option premium, you can purchase a put option on 100 shares of Microsoft with a strike price of $26 per share that lasts six months. When initially written, therefore, your put option is out-of-the-money. In fact, the current market price (spot price) of Microsoft stock must fall below $26 per share before your option has any intrinsic value. Nevertheless, when issued your option has some value, despite being out-of-the-money. Indeed, it has time value, as the current market price of Microsoft stock has the next six months to (hopefully) decline below $26 per share. The greater the decline in the Microsoft stock price below the $26 strike price, the more intrinsically valuable your Microsoft put option becomes.

### (4) Expiration or Maturity Date

In the private options market, where counterparties negotiate over the duration or term of a particular option, the expiration or maturity date of a given option will be the time period upon which the parties agree. Options typically run for a period of less than one year. All other things being equal, the longer the option period, the higher the option premium. This is because a longer term option has more time to move into-the-money, thus making such a move more probable.

In the public options market, options are written to last for set periods of time, such as one month or three months. However, it is possible to purchase long-term options in the public market referred to as "LEAPs" (Long-term Equity AnticiPation Securities).

### (5) Manner of Exercise

All publicly-traded options have an *American Style* of exercise. An American Style option can be exercised by its holder at any time on or before its maturity date. Thus, if a given option moves quickly into-the-money, its holder theoretically could exercise the option and reap its intrinsic value. Rarely, however, does this occur. To do so would unnecessarily waste that option's remaining time value (*i.e.,* the chance that the spot price will move further into-the-money over the remaining term of the option). In cases where an option holder would like to exercise the option prior to its maturity, it is much more likely that the option holder will sell the option to another party and receive a price that reflects both the option's current intrinsic value and its remaining time value.

In the private options market, options can be written to be exercised in one of three ways. The first and most common form of exercise is *American Style*. However, options can also be written to have a *European Style* exercise or an *Asian Style* exercise. A European Style option can be exercised only on its maturity date. An Asian Style option, by contrast, can be exercised only on specified dates negotiated by the parties at the time the option is written.

All other things being equal, the option premium for an American Style option is higher than that for a European or Asian Style option. The reason for this is the tremendous flexibility that an American Style option provides its holder with respect to exercise. By contrast, the premium associated with a European Style option is typically the lowest, because exercise is only allowed at maturity. The premium associated with an Asian Style option will vary depending on the number of exercise dates for which an option holder has negotiated.

### (6) Physical Settlement and Cash Settlement

An option gives the option holder the right, but not the obligation, to sell or purchase the underlying asset upon which the option is written at the strike price. Exchange traded options, other than those written on stock indices, are normally settled physically. This means that the stock underlying an exchange traded option must be bought and sold if the option is in-the-money when exercised. By contrast, private options are almost always settled in cash. This means that, to the extent a private option is in-the-money upon exercise, the counterparty must pay the intrinsic value of the option to the option holder in cash.

*Example of Cash–Settled Option*: Assume you own privately-negotiated put options on 1,000 shares of Microsoft common stock with a strike price of $15. If, upon exercise, the spot price of Microsoft common stock is $12 per share, your counterparty owes you the difference between $15 and $12, or $3 per share. Because the options covered 1,000 shares, your counterparty must pay you, in cash, $3,000 [($15 – $12) x 1,000 shares]. To determine your profit, however, you must remember to net out the option premium you paid for the put options.

### (7) Setting Option Premiums

Brokerage firms typically price options for sale and purchase by their brokerage clientele. With respect to any given option, a brokerage firm will generate by computer the option premium it will charge a client for that option. Most firms use the *Black–Scholes option pricing model* as the starting point for building their own proprietary options pricing model. The Black–Scholes model is particularly useful because it does not depend on any assessment of the future or expected price of a security underlying an option or on any other non-observable facts related to the option being priced. The fact that it is independent of expectations and other subjective measures helps explain its popularity.

Option pricing models weigh multiple variables in order to generate an option premium. These variables include, among others:

- *The trading volatility of the underlying stock.* The more volatile the stock's trading price, the more likely an option written on that stock will move into-the-money. Thus, all other things being equal, an option writer will charge a larger option premium for an option on a more volatile stock than a less volatile stock.

- *The manner of exercise.* The greater the freedom an option holder has in exercising her option, the larger the option premium charged by the option writer. All other things being equal, premiums on American Style options are larger than those for European Style options. The option premium charged on an Asian Style option depends on the number of exercise dates for which the option holder has negotiated.

- *The proximity of the strike price to the current market price of the underlying stock.* All other things being equal, the closer the strike price is to the current market price of the underlying stock when an option is written, the larger the option premium. A strike price set in close proximity to the current market price of the underlying stock makes it more likely that the option will move into-the-money.

- *The duration of the option.* All other things being equal, an option with a longer term has a larger option premium, as that option has more time to move into-the-money.

- *The interest rate environment and other macroeconomic variables.* Interest rates affect the present value of any prospective cash settlement payable upon the exercise of an option. Other macroeconomic variables influence the market price of the underlying stock, thus impacting the likelihood that an option will move into-the-money.

- *For options on common stocks, cash dividends.* As of the ex-dividend date for a given stock (*i.e.,* the date on which the buyer of an equity security does not acquire the right to receive a recently declared dividend), the value of the stock should decline by an amount approximately equal to the amount of the cash dividend. Thus, the higher the dividends, the lower the value of a call option relative to the stock and the higher the value of a put option relative to the stock.

In sum, the greater the likelihood an option will move into-the-money, the greater the likelihood that the option writer will have to satisfy its obligations under the option. Accordingly, in return for accepting this greater risk, the option writer will charge a larger option premium.

### (8) Reducing Risk Through Options

Suppose you own 100,000 shares of IBM common stock that you acquired directly from IBM in a private placement four months ago at $55 per share. The current share price is $68 in the secondary market. Securities laws require you to hold your shares six months before you can resell them in the secondary market. See Securities Act Rule 144. Between now and the time you can resell, your IBM shares could decline in value, perhaps precipitously. Of course, they also could continue to rise in value. But assuming that the current share price of $68 is as high as you think it could go—or care to take a chance on—you are not overly concerned about continued appreciation in the IBM share price. Instead, you are worried about a decline.

One solution is for you to purchase put options on 100,000 shares of IBM common stock in order to hedge your position in that stock. Assume that each put option has a strike price of $64 and a maturity date two months from now. Between now and two months from now, you still will bear the risk of the per share price of IBM stock falling from $68 per share to $64 per share, because the put options are out-of-the-money between $68 and $64 per share. However, if the share price drops below $64 per share, your put options will have moved into-the-money. Excluding the option premium you paid, the rise in the value of your put options will offset the decline in value of the shares of IBM stock you own. In the meantime, you enjoy 100% of any appreciation in the IBM stock price between now and two months from now. In that event, your only out-of-pocket cost is the option premium you paid for the put options.

### (9) Using Options in Connection with Concentrated Equity Positions

Options are particularly useful for those investors whose net worth is primarily tied up in one large stock holding, better known as a *concentrated equity position*. This is simply a fancy term for having most of your eggs in one basket. The problem with having a concentrated equity position is a lack of diversification. If the value of that position declines, it could significantly reduce the investor's net worth.

An investor's concentrated equity position may be freely saleable, yet that investor may be unwilling to sell all or part of that position due to adverse tax consequences. Alternatively, that investor may not be able to sell any part of that position due to regulatory constraints. For example, if that investor received that stock in a transaction not involving a public offering, he will be deemed to own *restricted stock* under the Securities Act. Accordingly, he will have to satisfy the holding period requirement of Securities Act Rule 144. Under Rule 144, a person unaffiliated with the issuer who holds shares of restricted stock may sell those shares into the secondary market after holding them for a minimum of six months. Additional restrictions apply to those deemed "affiliates" of the issuer, as such term is defined in Rule 144.

An investor with a concentrated equity position can use privately-negotiated (*i.e.*, "over-the-counter" or "OTC") options to help diversify that position, monetize that position or enhance the yield of that position. Strategies that may be available include, among others, deep-in-the-money call options, cash-settled collars, and out-of-the-money call options. Whether a given strategy will work for a particular investor depends on a number of factors, including that investor's net worth, his relationship with the company that issued the shares and the number of shares involved.

### a. Deep-in-the-Money Call Options

*Deep-in-the-money call options* are useful for an investor with a concentrated equity position who would like to monetize (*i.e.,* convert into cash) a portion of her position or hedge the downside risk of her position without actually selling any of it. These call options work regardless of whether the position is freely tradeable or restricted. However, in the case of restricted stock, most brokerage firms require an investor to have held the stock for at least one month (or preferably longer) to demonstrate investment intent under the Securities Act.

This strategy requires the investor to sell deep-in-the-money call options to a brokerage firm. As the name suggests, a deep-in-the-money call option has a strike price *substantially below* the current market price of the stock in question. By selling call options that are already significantly in-the-money, the investor receives a cash amount from the brokerage firm approximately equal to the intrinsic value of the options. The investor's position will be protected down to the strike price of the calls during their term. The options are cash-settled with a European Style exercise.

*Example:* Suppose years ago an investor purchased 750,000 shares of PNH Corp. for $15 per share. Those shares are now trading at $30 per share in the secondary market. The investor would like to monetize a portion of her position and hedge the downside risk without actually selling her shares.

Utilizing the deep-in-the-money call option strategy, the investor would sell deep-in-the-money call options to a brokerage firm with a strike price equal to $20. The brokerage firm will pay the investor a premium equal to $10 per share [$30 − $20], thus providing the investor with substantial liquidity. The options are cash-settled with a European Style exercise. At expiration, if the options are "in-the-money" (*i.e.,* at the time the stock is selling above $20 per share), the investor will pay the intrinsic value of the options to the brokerage firm. If the options are either "out-of-the money" (*i.e.,* the stock is selling below $20 per share) or "at-the-money" (*i.e.,* the stock is selling exactly at $20 per share), the options expire worthless and the investor owes the brokerage firm nothing. Thus, the investor's position is hedged or protected down to the strike price of the calls.

If the stock price rose from $30 to $40 during the term of the options, the brokerage firm would exercise the options because they are "in-the-money."

Thus, the investor would have to pay the brokerage firm the difference between the current market price and the strike price per share [$40 − $20], or $20 per share. However, the investor gets to keep the $10 per share premium that the brokerage firm initially paid the investor. Moreover, the investor still owns stock worth $40 per share. The net effect to the investor of the transaction on a per share basis is $10 (initial premium) plus $40 (current market price) less $20 (intrinsic value of a call option), or $30 per share.

If the current market price of the stock fell to $25 per share, then the brokerage firm would exercise the options and the investor would have to pay the brokerage firm the difference between $25 and the strike price of $20, or $5 per share. However, the investor gets to keep the initial $10 per share premium and still owns stock worth $25 per share. The net effect of the transaction to the investor on a per share basis is $10 (initial premium) plus $25 (current market price) less $5 (intrinsic value of a call option), or $30 per share.

If the current market price of the stock fell to $20 per share, then the options, which are "at-the-money," would expire worthless. The investor nonetheless gets to keep the initial $10 per share premium and still owns stock worth $20 per share. The net effect of the transaction to the investor on a per share basis is $10 (initial premium) plus $20 (current market price), or $30 per share.

Finally, if the current market price of the stock dropped below the strike price to, say, $10, then the options, which are "out-of-the-money," would expire worthless. The investor nonetheless gets to keep the initial $10 per share premium and still owns stock worth $10 per share. The net effect of the transaction to the investor on a per share basis is $10 (initial premium) plus $10 (current market price), or $20 per share.

The benefits of the deep-in-the-money call option strategy to the investor include: (1) the monetization of the difference between the current market price of the stock at the time the options are written and the strike price of the options; (2) the hedging of the portfolio position down to the strike price of the options during their term; (3) the avoidance of the sale of shares due to the cash-settlement feature; and (4) the continued right to receive dividends and vote the shares.

The disadvantages of the deep-in-the-money call option strategy to the investor include: (1) the relinquishment of the upside appreciation of the stock for the life of the options; (2) the obligation to pay the brokerage firm the intrinsic value (if any) of the options upon expiration; (3) the lack of a secondary or public market in which to resell the options prior to their expiration; and (4) short-term capital gains tax treatment if the underlying stock has not been held for more than one year on the date the call options are written.

### b.    Cash–Settled Collars

*Cash-settled collars* are useful for an investor with a concentrated equity position who cannot or does not want to sell her position immediately for a variety of reasons. These could include adverse tax consequences or regulatory constraints relating to restricted stock. This investor, however, would like to hedge her position until such time as the stock can be sold free of those consequences or constraints.

The cash-settled collar strategy requires the investor to sell or write call options to a brokerage firm while simultaneously purchasing put options from that firm. Importantly, the cost of the puts are financed through the sale of the calls. The options are cash-settled with a European Style exercise.

The strike price of the put options is set below the current market price for the stock. Accordingly, the investor can suffer some price depreciation, but only down to the puts' strike price. The investor's position, however, would be protected from declines below the puts' strike price.

The strike price of the call options, by contrast, is set above the current market price for the stock. Thus, the investor benefits from any price appreciation up to the calls' strike price during the term of the call options. The investor, however, does not benefit from any increases above the strike price.

Because the current stock price is *surrounded* by the call options' strike price and the put options' strike price, this strategy is referred to as a *collar*.

*Example:* Suppose an investor owns restricted stock in PNH Corp. and has four months to wait until the stock can be sold under Securities Act Rule 144. The stock is trading near an all-time high of $50 per share. The investor would like to hedge her position but also continue to benefit from some of the potential price appreciation.

Utilizing the cash-settled collar strategy, the investor would purchase four month put options from a brokerage firm with a strike price of $45. To finance the puts, the investor would simultaneously sell or write four month call options to the same brokerage firm with a strike price of $58. All options are cash-settled with a European Style exercise. The investor's position is protected below the puts' strike price of $45. The investor enjoys any price appreciation up to and including the calls' strike price of $58.

If the stock price rose from $50 to $60 during the term of the options, the brokerage firm would exercise the call options because they are "in-the-money." Thus, the investor would have to pay the brokerage firm the difference between the current market price per share and the calls' strike price per share [$60 − $58], or $2 per share. However, the investor still owns stock worth $60 per share. Therefore, the net effect to the investor of the transaction on a per share basis is $60 (current market price) less $2 (intrinsic value of a call option), or $58 per share.

If the current market price of the stock stayed between $45 and $58 per share, then both the call and put options would expire worthless. The investor nevertheless still owns stock worth between $45 and $58 per share.

If the current market price of the stock fell to $40 per share, the investor would exercise the put options because they are "in-the-money." Thus, the brokerage firm would have to pay the investor the difference between the puts' strike price per share and the current market price per share [$45 − $40], or $5 per share. However, the investor still owns stock worth $40 per share. The net effect of the transaction to the investor on a per share basis is $40 (current market price) plus $5 (intrinsic value of a put option), or $45 per share.

The benefits of the cash-settled collar strategy to the investor include: (1) no out-of-pocket costs (as costs are typically built into the pricing of the collar); (2) price protection below the puts' strike price; (3) enjoyment of price appreciation up to and including the calls' strike price; (4) the avoidance of the sale of shares due to the cash settlement feature; and (5) the continued right to receive dividends and vote the shares.

The disadvantages of the cash-settled collar strategy to the investor include: (1) the relinquishment of the upside appreciation of the stock above the calls' strike price; (2) the lack of a secondary or public market in which to resell the options prior to their expiration; and (3) short-term capital gains tax treatment if the underlying stock has not been held for more than one year on the date the options are written.

### c.   Out-of-the-Money Call Options

*Out-of-the-money call options* are useful for an investor with a concentrated equity position who would like to enhance the yield on her position without triggering a taxable sale of that position. These call options work regardless if her stock position is freely tradeable or restricted.

To utilize this strategy, an investor would sell privately-negotiated, cash-settled out-of-the-money call options to a brokerage firm. (Listed options could also be used if their terms match the needs of the investor). The investor would receive the option premium from the sale of the options and continue to own the stock. In addition, she would benefit from any appreciation in the price of the stock up to and including the strike price of the calls during their term. The options would be cash-settled with a European Style exercise. The enhanced yield to the investor stems from her receipt of the option premium from the brokerage firm.

*Example:* Suppose an investor owns 100,000 shares in PNH Corp. which are currently trading at $50 per share. The investor would like to continue to own the stock but would also like to increase the yield. Listed options on the stock exist, but they are illiquid and have maturities extending out only six months.

Utilizing the out-of-the-money call option strategy, the investor would sell call options on PNH stock to a brokerage firm each with a strike price of $55 and a nine-month maturity. The brokerage firm pays the investor $5 per share for the options. The options are cash-settled with a European Style exercise. If the options are "in-the-money" at expiration, the investor pays their intrinsic value to the brokerage firm.

If the stock price rose from $50 to $65 during the term of the options, the brokerage firm would exercise them because they are "in-the-money." Thus, the investor would have to pay the brokerage firm the difference between the current market price and the strike price per share [$65 − $55], or $10 per share. However, the investor keeps the $5 per share option premium that the brokerage firm initially paid the investor. Moreover, the investor still owns stock worth $65 per share. The net effect to the investor of the transaction on a per share basis is $5 (initial premium) plus $65 (current market price) less $10 (intrinsic value of a call option), or $60 per share.

If the stock price rose from $50 to $55 per share during the term of the options, the options, which are "at-the-money," would expire worthless. The investor nonetheless gets to keep the initial $5 per share premium and still owns stock worth $55 per share. The net effect of the transaction to the investor on a per share basis is $5 (initial premium) plus $55 (current market price), or $60 per share.

Finally, if the current market price of the stock dropped from \$50 to, say, \$45 during the term of the options, the options, which are "out-of-the-money," would expire worthless. The investor nonetheless gets to keep the initial \$5 per share premium and still owns stock worth \$45 per share. The net effect of the transaction to the investor on a per share basis is \$5 (initial premium) plus \$45 (current market price), or \$50 per share.

The benefits of the out-of-the-money call option strategy to the investor include: (1) the receipt of an option premium from the sale of the call options; (2) enjoyment of price appreciation up to and including the calls' strike price; (3) the avoidance of the sale of shares due to the cash-settlement feature; (4) the ability to structure options for stock with no listed options; and (5) the continued right to receive dividends and vote the shares.

The disadvantages of the out-of-the-money call option strategy to the investor include: (1) the relinquishment of the upside appreciation of the stock above the calls' strike price; (2) the lack of a secondary or public market in which to resell the options prior to their expiration; and (3) short-term capital gains tax treatment if the underlying stock has not been held for more than one year on the date the call options are written.

### (10)  Exchange Traded Options

Options also trade on many different exchanges. *Exchange traded options* (also known as *"listed options"*) exist for assets such as stocks, currencies, futures and stock indices. Generally, exchange traded stock options have a unit of trade of 100 shares. This means that one option contract represents the right to buy or sell 100 shares of the underlying stock at the specified strike price. Thus, an investor who owns 1,000 shares of Microsoft common stock could protect herself from downside risk by purchasing 10 put contracts [10 contracts x 100 shares per contract] on Microsoft common stock.

Exchange traded options eliminate the need to actually draft, review and sign option contracts. Details of the contract, such as the expiration date, the strike price, what happens when dividends are declared, and other provisions, are specified by the exchange.

A stock option is referred to by the month in which its expiration date occurs and by its strike price. For any given stock, there may be many different option contracts trading. Table 1 below, for example, shows selected listed options quotations from June 11, 2010. In particular, it shows that there are two types of listed Microsoft options: call and put options. Moreover, there are three expiration dates and three different strike prices, for a total of nine different contracts. One would describe the third Microsoft call option listed in Table 1 as "Microsoft October–2010 Call @ $15.00."

Table 1 also illustrates how listed stock options appear in newspapers that carry options quotations.

(For more up to date quotations, many internet options—such as WSJ.com—are readily available.) The company on whose stock the option is written is listed in the first column along with its closing stock price (*i.e.,* on June 11, 2010, the price of Microsoft's common stock closed at $25.66). The strike price of the option and the month the contract expires appear in the second and third columns, respectively. If a call option was traded during the previous day, the next two columns will show the volume of trading and the price of the option contract based on the last trade. The final two columns show the same information for a put option.

## Table 1 Selected Options Data
(Source: *Wall Street Journal,* June 11, 2010)

| OPTION | STRIKE | EXP. | -CALL- | | -PUT- | |
|---|---|---|---|---|---|---|
| | | | VOL | LAST | VOL | LAST |
| **Bank of America** | 5.00 | Aug | . . . | . . . | 1 | .06 |
| 15.60 | 5.00 | Nov | 21 | 10.65 | . . . | . . . |
| 15.60 | 7.50 | Aug | 1 | 8.05 | . . . | . . . |
| **Microsoft** | 10.00 | Jan | 60 | 15.05 | 100 | .09 |
| 25.66 | 15.00 | Jul | 61 | 10.50 | . . . | . . . |
| 25.66 | 15.00 | Oct | 175 | 10.75 | 732 | .12 |
| 25.66 | 15.00 | Jan | 6 | 10.31 | 17 | .83 |
| 25.66 | 17.50 | Jul | 144 | 8.20 | 84 | .03 |
| 25.66 | 17.50 | Oct | . . . | . . . | 1422 | .21 |

### (11) Distinction From Warrants

Warrants are very similar to long-term call options. Both provide their holders with the right, but not the obligation, to purchase a specified number of shares of the issuer's common stock at a specified price for a specified period of time (usually a period of years). Normally, young companies that cannot afford to issue debt securities at prevailing market interest rates issue warrants in connection with a debt offering (a so-called "unit offering"). They issue warrants as a "sweetener" to induce prospective debt investors to purchase their below-market interest rate debt securities. Virtually all warrants issued in connection with debt securities are *detachable*, meaning that investors holding them can sell them separate and apart from the debt securities with which they were issued.

Unlike call options, which can be written by anyone, warrants can only be issued by the company whose stock underlies the warrants. Moreover, when call options are exercised, the stock provided to the option holder (assuming physical settlement) comes from the secondary market. By contrast, when a holder exercises a warrant, the company settles using newly-issued shares. Thus, the exercise of a warrant *dilutes* the value of shares held by existing stockholders.

## B.  Forward Contracts

### (1) Overview

The second building block of derivatives is the *forward contract*. A forward contract is a private agreement that *obligates* the purchaser to purchase, and the seller to sell, a specified asset at a specified price on a specified date in the future. The specified asset is typically a commodity, such as wheat or oil, but it also could be a financial instrument. A forward contract is a unique investment tool primarily designed to decrease the contracting parties' exposure to price fluctuations of the asset covered by the contract.

The asset being purchased and sold pursuant to a forward contract is referred to as the *underlying asset*. The *spot price* of the underlying asset is its current market price at any given time. The price at which the underlying asset is to be purchased and sold on the future date is referred to as the *forward price*. The date on which the contract will be settled in the future is called the *settlement* or *expiration date*. Thus, the purchaser of a forward contract commits to buy the underlying asset at the forward price on the settlement date. A seller of a forward contract commits to sell the underlying asset at the forward price on that date.

*Example:* Suppose that a group of corn farmers belong to a farmers' co-operative. In April, when corn is planted, the current price of corn is $3.50 a bushel. The farmers' co-operative would be pleased to receive the current price of $3.50 a bushel for its members' corn in October when the corn crop is harvested. Indeed, the farmers are worried that the Summer rains will be optimal, thus leading to a bountiful corn crop that will force prices lower. By contrast, Pillsbury needs corn meal for its corn muffin mix. Unlike the farmers, Pillsbury worries that the Summer weather will be hot and dry, thus reducing the amount of corn the farmers will harvest and raising its price.

The uncertainty of the Summer weather, and hence the ensuing corn crop, motivates the farmers' co-operative and Pillsbury to enter into a six-month forward contract for 10,000 bushels of corn with a forward price of $3.55 a bushel (see Nutshell Section 31B(2) below for how to determine the forward price). At the end of the six-month period, the co-operative must deliver the corn at a price of $3.55 a bushel regardless of what the spot price of corn is at that time. Pillsbury, in turn, must buy the corn at $3.55 a bushel regardless of what the spot price of corn is at that time. In other words, both parties have eliminated the risk associated with the rise and fall of corn prices, having been content to lock in a price in advance that worked for both of them.

### (2) Determining the Forward Price

Prospective parties to a forward contract negotiate over the underlying asset, the forward price and the settlement date. The forward price is typically based on three variables: (1) the spot price of the underlying asset on the contracting date; (2) the cost, if any, to carry the underlying asset between the contracting date and the settlement date; and (3) distributions (such as dividends or interest), if any, to be paid on the underlying asset. The formula for determining the forward price is thus:

$$FP = SP + CC - D$$

where: FP is the forward price.

SP is the spot price of the underlying asset on the contracting date.

CC is the cost, if any, to carry the underlying asset for the duration of the contract.

D is the distribution, if any, to be received on the underlying asset.

a. Cost to Carry

The *cost to carry* the underlying asset until the settlement date is determined by adding two variables: (1) the seller's opportunity cost and (2) the seller's cost of storage.

In a forward contract, the parties enter into the contract today, yet make payment and delivery at a future date. This delay imposes an opportunity cost on the seller. Theoretically, if the seller currently possesses the asset, the seller could sell it today and then reinvest the proceeds until the settlement date of the forward contract. The seller would earn interest on the proceeds during this time. The forward price, therefore, must reflect the seller's opportunity cost of waiting until the settlement date to be paid. For certain forward contracts, such as those covering crops that have yet to be harvested, the seller's opportunity cost is zero.

The cost to store the underlying asset until settlement is also a part of the seller's cost to carry. If the seller currently possesses the asset, the seller incurs transaction costs to hold it until the forward contract expires. The storage cost is typically a cost incorporated into the forward price for commodities such as wheat, oil and gold. However, in certain forward contracts, the storage cost is zero. A forward contract for financial assets, such as foreign exchange, is a prime example.

### b.   Distributions

In a forward contract, the buyer receives delayed delivery of the underlying asset. Accordingly, the seller rather than the buyer will receive any distribution on that asset made during the term of the forward contract. These distributions consist of dividends or interest, and thus are only applicable when the underlying asset is a financial instrument rather than a commodity. Anticipated distributions are deducted when calculating the forward price the buyer must pay the seller, because the seller is entitled to receive those distributions.

### (3) Distinction From Options

A forward contract differs from an option in three ways. First, performing a forward contract is obligatory, while exercising an option is discretionary. Second, no premium or other money is paid by either party upon execution of a forward contract, while options cost money to buy (the "option premium"). Lastly, forward contracts typically are physically-settled, not cash-settled, while options are often cash-settled. Physical settlement involves the actual transfer of the underlying asset from the seller to the purchaser on the settlement date.

### (4) Counterparty Credit Risk

Each party to a forward contract is exposed to *counterparty credit risk*. This is the risk that the other party to the contract will not be able to perform its contractual duties on the settlement date. The failure to perform may arise from internal factors, such as financial difficulties, or external factors, such as a natural disaster that affects a crop harvest. Counterparty credit risk remains a significant concern to both parties because forwards are private contracts. Accordingly, each party must assess the risk of conducting business with the other party prior to entering into a forward contract.

## C.   Futures Contracts

The third building block of derivatives is the *futures contract*. Futures contracts are essentially publicly-traded forward contracts. Thus, many of the fundamental characteristics of forward contracts directly apply to futures contracts. Nevertheless, several important differences exist.

### (1) Distinction From Forward Contracts

The following discusses the five primary operational differences between forward and futures contracts.

#### a.   Cash Settlement

Unlike a forward contract, where physical delivery is the norm, physical delivery of the underlying asset associated with a futures contract occurs less than two percent of the time. This is necessary to help establish a cash-based trading market in futures. Futures contracts are traded exclusively on regulated exchanges and are settled daily based on their current value in the marketplace.

#### b.   Standardized Contracts

Unlike a forward contract, the terms of which are privately-negotiated, most of the terms of a futures contract are standardized and non-negotiable. Thus, provisions including quantity, expiration date and underlying asset are fixed terms within the contract. This is necessary to create an organized trading market for futures.

The price of a futures contract (the *futures price*) is established by the buyer and seller on the floor of a commodity exchange, using the *open outcry* system. The term refers to the shouting exchanged between traders seeking to sell or buy at a particular price. When two traders connect on price, they have made a contract that will be recorded.

As Table 2 indicates, the contract size for each underlying asset is set and thus non-negotiable. Traders of futures specify how many contracts they would like to purchase or sell. Specific contracts are traded on specific exchanges, hence each exchange is a designated contract market. For instance, oil and natural gas derivative contracts (crude oil, heating oil, natural gas, etc.) are the only futures traded on the New York Mercantile Exchange (NYMEX).

## Table 2
## Examples of Actively Traded Futures Contracts

| Type of Asset | Underlying Instrument | Contract Size | Exchange Traded |
|---|---|---|---|
| Interest Earning | U.S. Treasury Bills | $1,000,000 | CME |
| Commodity (Energy) | Crude Oil | 1,000 Barrels | NYMEX |
| Commodity (Agriculture) | Wheat | 5,000 Bushels | CBOT |
| Commodity (Metal) | Copper | 25,000 lbs. | COMX |
| Foreign Currency | British Pound | £62,500 | CME |

### c. Elimination of Counterparty Credit Risk

Parties to forward contracts are exposed to counterparty credit risk. Futures markets eliminate counterparty credit risk. Futures transactions, which are executed on the floor of a given exchange, are settled through a separate entity from the exchange called a clearinghouse. A clearinghouse is the "financial sponsor" of all the participants who conduct daily trading on an exchange floor. Obligations of the parties to a futures contract are *guaranteed* by the clearinghouse.

### d. Daily Settlement

Futures traders settle their account balances on a daily basis. Any gains or losses resulting from the fluctuation of the spot price of the underlying asset in relation to the futures price are realized when trading ends each day. The daily settlement of these gains or losses is referred to as *marking-to-market*. Following each day's settlement, the futures price is "reset" to equal the closing spot price of the underlying asset on that day. In other words, at the end of each day, the market value of a futures contract is restored to zero. This daily gambling process continues until the contract expires. In a forward contract, by contrast, the forward price is fixed throughout the duration of the contract, and the contract is settled only on the settlement date.

### e.  Margin Requirements

Futures contracts are traded on margin. Trading on margin means that a trader is able to buy and sell contracts representing large amounts of money by putting down only a very small security deposit (as low as two percent of the contract price). The trading of futures contracts, therefore, represents a highly-leveraged form of investing. For example, a crude oil contract represents 1,000 barrels of oil (42,000 gallons). If the futures price of that contract is $75 per barrel, that contract represents a total value of $75,000. Yet, the typical *initial margin* required for trading crude oil futures on the NY-MEX is currently only $9,788 per contract. The initial margin requirement on a given type of futures contract varies depending upon the volatility of the price of the underlying asset.

Initial margin positions serve as collateral between the futures exchange and the trader. While an initial margin is the amount an exchange requires an investor to have available for each contract before the order to buy or sell can be executed, the *maintenance margin* is the amount that the trader must maintain in her margin account in order to remain in the market. If an investor incurs losses that cause his margin account balance to drop below the maintenance margin, he will be forced to deposit additional funds or liquidate her position. Depending on the type of contract, the maintenance margin is usually between $200 to $3,000 less than the initial margin per contract. For example, the maintenance margin required for trading crude oil futures on the NYMEX is currently $7,250 per contract.

### (2) Futures Markets

Futures contracts for agricultural commodities have been traded in the United States for more than 100 years and have been regulated since the early 1920s. Today, futures contracts are traded on many exchanges, including the Chicago Board of Trade (CBOT), the Chicago Mercantile Exchange (CME) and the New York Mercantile Exchange (NYMEX). All futures exchanges are open outcry. Trading of a particular contract takes place in specified locations on the trading floor referred to as *pits*. This distinguishes futures from forward contracts in that forward contracts are privately-negotiated ("over-the-counter") transactions.

The *Commodity Futures Trading Commission* (CFTC), which was created by the Commodity Exchange Act of 1922 (CEA), enforces the laws and makes the regulations that govern futures markets in the United States. Each individual exchange must gain permission from the CFTC to list and trade futures contracts on its trading floor. The rules and regulations that the CFTC promulgates are extremely detailed and specific, and thus the U.S. futures markets are highly-regulated.

## D. Swaps

### (1) Overview

The fourth building block of derivatives is the *swap contract* or *"swap."* A swap is essentially a forward contract that requires each party to satisfy a financial obligation of another party rather than physically deliver and pay for an underlying asset. Parties to a swap may exchange a variety of financial obligations, including those relating to debt securities, currencies and futures contracts.

The parties involved in a swap sign a contract specifying each party's obligations to the other just as in a forward contract. Moreover, the contract yields the same advantages as a forward (*e.g.,* customization, privacy, etc.), as well as its disadvantages (*e.g.,* counterparty credit risk, lack of liquidity, etc.). The following is an example of an *interest rate swap*, which is by far the most common type of swap.

One company, MRH, Inc., has $100 million in debt and pays interest annually based on an interest rate that fluctuates in line with the rate of a given government security. The interest rate on MRH's debt is currently at eight percent. MRH's management predicts that interest rates will rise in the coming quarters, resulting in an increase in the interest MRH must pay. MRH would like to convert its floating rate debt to fixed rate debt to guard against the risk of rising interest rates. Another company, PNH, Inc., has $100 million in debt outstanding and pays interest annually based on a fixed interest rate of nine percent. PNH's management believes that interest rates will decline in the following months and would like to convert its fixed rate debt into floating rate debt to reduce its interest payments in the future.

Each of these parties could attempt to refinance all their outstanding debt with new debt having the desired rate of interest (fixed or floating, as the case may be). However, their debt indentures must permit repurchases or redemptions and, if they do, these parties must incur related transaction costs. A swap would provide both companies with a cheap alternative to refinancing their outstanding debt. It would enable them to "swap" the interest payments they each pay on their debt, thereby achieving their respective interest rate objectives. Following the execution of the swap contract, PNH would pay MRH's interest payments based on the fluctuating rate described in MRH's indenture, while MRH would pay PNH's interest payments based on PNH's nine percent coupon.

In this swap, the principal amount of debt upon which interest is calculated is called the *notional amount* or *notional value* of the swap contract. There is no exchange of the principal amount due on the debt for either party. The swap only calls for the exchange of the periodic interest payments due on the notional value of the contract.

### (2) Types of Swaps

Besides the interest rate swap featured in the example above, many other types of swaps exist, including:

- *Currency Swaps*. These swaps are used in situations where one party has a comparative advantage in borrowing one currency over the second party, while the second party has a comparative advantage in borrowing a different currency over the first party. The fact that each party can borrow the currency that the other party desires at a cheaper rate of interest is the driving force behind the swap. Each party pays its counterparty the rate of interest that the other party incurs for the length of time that the funds are borrowed. Because each party's notional amount is denominated in different currencies in a currency swap, an exchange of the principal amounts at the beginning of the swap, and re-exchange at the end, are usually required.

- *Commodity Swaps*. These swaps are usually executed in order to hedge against price movements of specific commodities. The exchange of cash flows between two parties is dependent upon the price of the underlying commodity to the agreement. Through the swap, a manufacturer in need of the commodity will pay a fixed price to a producer of that commodity, thus locking in the maximum price the manufacturer will pay for the commodity for the duration of the swap. In return, the producer of the commodity will pay a price based on the average monthly spot price of the commodity to the manufacturer, thus hedging against adverse price movements. The majority of commodity swaps cover oil-based commodities.

- *Credit Default Swaps (CDSs).* These swaps are used to hedge against the credit or default risk inherent in the debt market. Insurance and asset management companies typically sell credit default swaps to investors in corporate debt. These allow investors to hedge against the risk that the corporate issuers of the debt they purchased may default on that debt. If a given corporate issuer does default, the buyers of these swaps may still receive 100 cents on each dollar of debt. Movements in the credit default swaps market often foretell impending corporate bankruptcies and liquidity crises. Of course, buyers of these swaps are subject to counterparty credit risk, as was made all too clear in 2008 when American International Group, Inc. ("AIG"), a leading issuer of credit default swaps, had to receive a government bailout in order to honor its CDS obligations. See Nutshell Section 32C(2).

### (3) ISDA and the Standardization of Swap Contracts

In 1984, representatives from the major banks dealing in swaps began the process of standardizing the forms for swap transactions. Soon after, the International Swaps and Derivatives Association (ISDA) was formed. ISDA is a trade association whose membership consists of representatives of institutions that deal in large volumes of swaps. ISDA released a set of standardized swap forms and a set of guidelines governing the execution of swaps. By standardizing the documentation of swaps and their execution, ISDA effectively decreased the time and cost of executing swaps. The forms issued by ISDA are essentially treated as "master" documents with respect to swap dealings between the same counterparties. Each additional swap entered into by those parties is treated as a supplement to that master agreement.

### (4) Credit Default Swaps and the Financial Crisis of 2008

Please see Nutshell Section 32C(2).

## § 32. DEVELOPMENTS IN THE DERIVATIVES MARKET

### A. Abusive Use of Derivatives

Beginning in the early 1990s, serious problems arose in the derivatives market when derivative instruments were used excessively for speculative purposes rather than as a tool for risk reduction. These excesses resulted in, among other debacles, the downfall of the hedge fund Long–Term Capital Management, the demise of Barings Bank, the bankruptcy filing of Orange County, California, and large losses at prominent companies such as Gibson Greeting Inc. and Procter & Gamble. Moreover, it led to an extended period of "derivaphobia" in the financial markets.

Long–Term Capital Management ("LTCM") was an arbitrage fund filled with luminaries from academia, including two individuals who won the Nobel Prize in economics. The firm's computer models that were used to help detect price discrepancies in the marketplace were predicated on the direction of past price movements of securities. (Of course, under the random walk model (see Nutshell Section 21), past price patterns are not reliable guides given the randomness of the future.) In early 1998, the firm viewed U.S. Treasury bonds as overpriced and other debt securities (including junk bonds, European government bonds, and mortgage-backed securities) as underpriced. Thus, the firm sold short U.S. Treasuries and purchased long positions in junk bonds, European government bonds, and mortgage-backed securities.

In mid–1998, a financial crisis broke out in Asia and the Russian government defaulted on its debt and devalued its currency. In a global "flight to quality," investors dumped the junk and European bonds of the type that LTCM held, buying instead U.S. Treasuries. This led the price of Treasuries to rise and their yield, which moves in the opposite direction, to fall. The decline in yields, in turn, lead to a decline in the interest rate on variable rate mortgages, depressing the value of the mortgage-backed securities LTCM owned. Ultimately, the debacle wiped out LTCM's equity, and the U.S. Federal Reserve had to organize a bailout of LTCM by 15 large financial institutions, mostly former lenders to LTCM.

In the case of Barings Bank, a 28 year-old trader named Nick Leeson began hedging on swings on the future direction of the Nikkei Index of Japanese stocks. Leeson claimed that he was executing purchase orders on behalf of a client, but he was actually trading with the bank's own money and hiding his losses in an error account. By December of 1994, Leeson's losses totaled $512 million. He attempted to cover his losses by speculating that the Nikkei Index would not fall below 19,000 points. After an earthquake shook Kobe, Japan in January 1995, the Nikkei Index plummeted 7% in one week. Ultimately, Barings' exposure was a staggering $1.3 billion. This amount represented more than the entire capital and reserves of the 233 year-old Barings, and forced the venerable institution into bankruptcy.

Gibson Greetings Inc. also had substantial problems with derivative instruments. Gibson had privately placed $50 million in senior notes with a fixed interest rate of 9.33%. Interest rates soon declined, but Gibson could not take advantage of that decline because its senior notes could not be prepaid for a number of years. Gibson, with the assistance of BT Securities Corp. (BT), entered into approximately 29 interest rate swap transactions between 1991 and 1994 to effectively reduce the interest rate paid on the notes.

The derivatives BT sold to Gibson were very complex. Many had leverage factors which caused Gibson's losses to increase dramatically with relatively small changes in interest rates. BT was solely responsible for determining the value of Gibson's derivatives, and Gibson personnel used BT's valuations to determine their propriety. Gibson also set forth those valuations in the footnotes to its financial statements. Gibson, a publicly-traded company, sent those statements both to its stockholders and to the SEC.

The SEC commenced a proceeding entitled *In the Matter of BT Securities Corporation* (58 S.E.C. Docket 1145 (Dec. 22, 1994)) charging that BT had engaged in a systematic pattern of deception about the true value of Gibson's derivatives. In particular, the SEC alleged that BT misled Gibson about the value of its derivatives, significantly understating Gibson's losses. As a result, Gibson was totally unaware of the extent of its losses and continued to purchase derivatives from BT. Those undervaluations caused Gibson to make material misrepresentations in the footnotes to its financial statements.

The SEC further alleged that BT's representatives were aware that they were understating Gibson's derivative losses. Those representatives had a plan to increase the disclosed losses gradually over time to their true figures by misrepresenting the size of any potential gains.

According to the SEC, BT violated the antifraud provisions of Section 17(a) of the Securities Act and Section 10(b) of the Exchange Act and Rule 10b–5 promulgated thereunder. The SEC further alleged that BT violated Section 15(b)(4)(E) of the Exchange Act by failing to supervise, with a view to preventing violations of the Federal securities laws, another person who commits such a violation, if such other person "is subject to his supervision." While Gibson's financial officers had a "pretty good understanding" of the derivatives, their understanding was "not perfect" and they put themselves into BT's hands "about 96%." Thus, according to the SEC, BT was required to properly supervise Gibson but failed to do so. Ultimately, BT settled with the SEC by, among other things, agreeing to pay a $10 million civil penalty.

The SEC, however, did not let Gibson completely off the hook. In October 1995, the SEC brought an administrative proceeding pursuant to Section 21(c) of the Exchange Act against Gibson, its CFO and its Treasurer. The SEC found that Gibson and its executive officers violated accounting and reporting standards and misrepresented information about the derivatives in Gibson's Form 10–Q filed with the SEC. Gibson and its two executives ultimately settled with the SEC and agreed to certain injunctive relief.

While concerns about derivative instruments settled down in the early 2000s, derivatives—particularly credit default swaps—once again helped to destabilize the financial markets in 2008. By that time, the CDS market had exploded to more than $45 trillion, according to the International Swaps and Derivatives Association. This was roughly twice the size of the U.S. stock market and far exceeded the $7.1 trillion mortgage market and $4.4 trillion U.S. treasuries market. A large portion of the CDSs at that time were linked to collateralized debt obligations supported by subprime mortgages. When the subprime mortgage market imploded, those holding CDSs linked to subprime mortgages feared their counterparties would not be able to honor them. At the end of the third quarter of 2007, the top 25 banks held more than $13 trillion in CDSs, where they acted as either the insured or insurer. Insurance companies and their affiliates were also in on the act, as exposure to CDSs would have brought down American International Group, Inc. (*a.k.a.* AIG), the world's largest insurance company, without extreme governmental intervention.

## B. Turf Wars

Historically, the SEC and the CFTC have been at odds about how to classify certain derivative transactions, especially privately-negotiated ("over-the-counter" or "OTC") derivatives. OTC derivative transactions, like those engaged in by Gibson Greetings Inc., posed a unique problem because they were not traded on any exchange. Because of this, they were exempt from SEC and CFTC regulation except for antifraud and antimanipulation provisions. As of 1994, neither the SEC nor the CFTC was willing to assert jurisdiction beyond this scope. Even when enforcing antifraud and antimanipulation provisions, these agencies found it difficult to classify these complex transactions. For example, some of the underlying assets in an OTC derivative may be deemed a "security," while others may be deemed "commodities" or may resemble a "future." These hybrid instruments have created legal uncertainty as to whether the CFTC or the SEC may assert jurisdiction over these transactions and, if so, to what extent.

Courts also grappled with this same question as illustrated by *Procter & Gamble v. Bankers Trust Co.*, 925 F.Supp. 1270 (S.D. Ohio1996). Procter & Gamble (P&G) entered into an interest rate swap transaction with BT in 1993. BT agreed to pay P&G a fixed interest rate of 5.30% for five years on a notional amount of $200 million. In return, P&G agreed to pay BT a floating interest rate based on the prevailing commercial paper rate minus 75 basis points for the first six months. Thereafter, P&G would have to pay BT an additional spread that was calculated at the end of the first six months. The calculation was based on a complex formula pegged to the yield on the five-year U.S. Treasury Note and the price of the 30–year U.S. Treasury Bond; thus, the transaction was known as the "5s/30s". The leverage factor in this transaction was highly sensitive to fluctuations in prevailing interest rates.

P&G and BT also entered into a currency swap transaction in January of 1994. This swap transaction (referred to as the "DM swap") was based on the value of the German Deutschmark and the U.S. dollar. BT was obligated to pay P&G a floating interest rate plus 233 basis points. P&G was obligated to pay the same floating interest rate plus 133 basis points. For the first year, therefore, P&G would receive a premium of 100 basis points. After the first year, P&G would have to add a spread to its payments to BT if the four-year DM swap rate dropped by more than 4.05% or rose higher than 6.01%. The spread was calculated using a complex formula pegged to the DM swap rate. Again, the leverage factor exposed P&G to grave losses.

P&G canceled both the "5s/30s" and the "DM" swaps before their set spread dates as interest rates in Germany and the U.S. rapidly increased. As a result of these transactions, BT claimed it was owed more than $200 million. P&G, in turn, filed suit against BT seeking a declaratory judgment and damages worth $200 million. In its complaint, P&G alleged fraud, misrepresentation, breach of fiduciary duty, negligent misrepresentation, and negligence for both transactions.

The District Court refused to classify the swaps as securities under the definitions set forth in the

Securities Act and the Exchange Act. The Court also rejected P&G's argument that the swap transactions could be defined as commodities. It stated that even if the swap transactions were commodities, they were exempt from the CEA other than its antifraud provisions. Moreover, P&G did not have standing to sue because only the CFTC could enforce the CEA's antifraud provisions.

The Court, however, did conclude that P&G had standing to sue on claims alleged under New York law. Specifically, the Court cited to Section 1–203 of the UCC which states: "Every contract or duty written in this Act imposes an obligation of good faith in its performance or enforcement." The Court also pointed to New York case law which imposed an implied contractual duty to disclose material information not readily available to the other party where the first party knows that the second is acting on the basis of mistaken knowledge.

## C. Regulatory Initiatives, the CFMA and Dodd–Frank

### (1) Events Leading Up to the Commodity Futures Modernization Act of 2000

In response to market developments and the high profile losses surrounding OTC derivative transactions, the SEC and the CFTC embarked on separate regulatory initiatives. The SEC adopted new rules governing the *disclosure* of derivatives early in

1997. The expanded disclosure rules were set up to keep investors informed about the risks public companies were taking through derivatives and what losses they could incur if interest rates, foreign currency exchange rates, or commodity prices fluctuated. This was the first time the SEC required reporting companies to quantify risks associated with derivative transactions.

The CFTC followed suit by issuing a concept release in mid–1998. In this concept release, the CFTC outlined possible reforms to the exemption policies concerning swap transactions and hybrid instruments. In particular, the CFTC sought to impose narrowly-defined exemptive conditions based on market developments. In doing so, OTC derivative transactions would have to comply with the new conditions or be subject to CFTC regulation. These sought after changes would impose a regulatory scheme on hybrid and swap transactions as a condition for exempting such products from CEA regulation.

The SEC later released a written statement regarding the regulation of OTC derivatives, largely in response to the CFTC's concept release. In this statement, the SEC challenged any assertion of jurisdiction by the CFTC over the OTC derivatives market. It also resisted the CFTC's proposal to change the scope of the exemption provided for hybrid instruments through its exemptive authority.

Congress attempted to resolve this turf war and the many problems surrounding OTC derivative transactions by passing the Commodity Futures Modernization Act of 2000 (CFMA), the year 2000 amendments to the CEA. The purpose of the CFMA was to eliminate the legal uncertainty surrounding derivative transactions by clarifying jurisdictional lines and statutory definitions of market instruments. The CFMA also sought to stimulate innovation and promote market efficiency for the U.S. derivatives market.

Among other things, the CFMA provided: (1) that OTC derivative transactions between "eligible contract participants" may not be voided as illegal off-exchange contracts; (2) that a transaction that is based on the price, yield or volatility of a security that (a) is not an option or forward on a security or (b) a swap between eligible participants will not be classified as a "security" under Federal securities laws; however, basic antifraud, antimanipulation and insider trading prohibitions will still apply; and (3) for the regulation of stock index futures by both the SEC and the CFTC.

Despite the CFMA, some courts continued to grapple with the definition of "security" for purposes of the Federal securities laws in the context of derivatives. For example, in *Caiola v. Citibank, N.A.*, New York, 295 F.3d 312 (2d Cir.2002), the plaintiff brought Federal securities fraud and state law claims against Citibank relating to a series of physical and synthetic investments. The plaintiff engaged in equity trades of Philip Morris stock and hedged his position in the options market through agreements with Citibank and various brokerage firms.

In 1994, Citibank and the plaintiff entered into a hedging strategy agreement involving synthetic trading. The Second Circuit described synthetic trading as a "contractual agreement between two counterparties usually an investor and a bank that seeks to economically replicate the ownership and physical trading of shares and options." In doing so, the counterparties create synthetic positions in shares or options which are in correlation to the market prices of the actual shares or options. The notional values that underlie the synthetic trades are treated as interest bearing loans to the investor. This type of hedging strategy protected the plaintiff's positions in the market while simultaneously reducing his risks.

The plaintiff and Citibank entered into two types of synthetic transactions. The first type involved equity swaps, whereby the plaintiff would make periodic interest payments on the notional value of a stock position and also payments equal to any decrease in value of the shares upon which the notional value was based. Citibank, in turn, paid any increase in the value of the shares and any dividends based on that same notional amount.

The second type involved cash-settled OTC options. These options were cash-settled based on the current market price of the underlying security when the option was exercised or upon expiration. Each transaction had its own terms.

Citibank used "delta hedging" to accommodate these trades and to minimize its own risks in the market. The Second Circuit described delta "as the ratio of the change in the price of the derivative to the change in the price of the underlying asset." Delta hedging meant that Citibank would continuously realign its hedge in response to changes in the market price of the underlying asset. It also allowed Citibank to make relatively small purchases in the physical market to offset its obligations to the plaintiff.

When Citibank merged with Traveler's Group Inc. in 1998, it assured the plaintiff that their relationship would not change. Despite this assurance, Citibank secretly stopped delta hedging and began making physical trades on the plaintiff's synthetic portfolio. These physical trades exposed the plaintiff to great market risks. On March 12, 1999, Citibank sought to exercise certain options early— something not done for synthetic trades. This led the plaintiff to investigate Citibank's activities.

The plaintiff's investigation revealed that Citibank had terminated synthetic trading in November 1998. As a result, the plaintiff lost tens of millions of dollars. In July 2000, he brought an action against Citibank alleging violations of Section 10(b) and Rule 10b–5 of the Exchange Act for misrepresentation as well as various state law claims. Citibank moved to dismiss the Exchange Act claims, arguing that the synthetic trades were not securities and therefore the Federal securities laws did not apply. Citibank further argued that a disclaimer found in the contract established that "neither party would rely on the representations of the other."

The lower court agreed with Citibank and, in dismissing the plaintiff's claims, held that the synthetic trades were not securities. The Second Circuit, however, reversed and remanded the case. Relying on the definition of securities found in Section 3(a)(10) of the Exchange Act, the Second Circuit held that the synthetic trades were indeed securities because they were options based on the value of actual securities. Furthermore, it held that Citibank's false assurances to the plaintiff were material misrepresentations that he reasonably relied on when he entered into the transactions. The Court also held that the disclaimer found in the contracts was too general and did not afford Citibank protection from liability for the type of misrepresentation involved in the case. In its reasoning, the Second Circuit rejected Citibank's argument that it owed no independent duty to disclose its hedging strategy. According to the Court, Citibank chose to discuss the strategy with the plaintiff and thus was obligated to "speak truthfully about material issues."

(2) Credit Default Swaps, the Financial Crisis of 2008 and Dodd–Frank's Regulation of the Swap Market

CDSs came under heightened scrutiny after playing a significant role in the financial crisis of 2008. Many insurance companies, such as American International Group, Inc. ("AIG"), were counterparties in a large number of CDS transactions. These insurers sold CDSs as insurance to cover financial instruments, including mortgage-backed securities and collateralized debt obligations. As the credit crisis ensued, investors became anxious about whether these insurers would be able to pay out in the event of a default. When the mortgage market collapsed, those holding CDSs (mainly financial institutions around the world) sought to collect on them. Not anticipating a complete collapse of the market, insurers like AIG were caught flat-footed and unable to pay out such massive amounts of money. AIG alone paid out over $100 billion to major global financial institutions after the U.S. Government agreed to bail it out.

As a result of the financial meltdown, Congress took another serious look at derivatives market regulation, particularly over-the-counter (OTC) derivatives (which include credit default swaps). The OTC derivative market, at $600 trillion, is the largest market for derivatives. It had been largely unregulated with respect to the disclosure of information between parties. Thus, it is not surprising that the Dodd–Frank Wall Street Reform and Consumer

Protection Act of 2010 ("Dodd–Frank") contains significant language aimed at reforming this market.

### a. Overview

Dodd–Frank comprehensively regulates most swap transactions formerly deregulated by the CFMA. In terms of dealing with the historical jurisdictional divisions between the CFTC and the SEC, the Act categorizes the swap transactions within its scope as either "*swaps*," which are subject to primary regulation by the CFTC, "*security-based swaps*," which are subject to primary regulation by the SEC, or "*mixed swaps*," which are subject to joint regulation by the CFTC and SEC. The most significant aspects of the derivatives section of the Act are (a) mandatory clearing through regulated central clearing organizations and mandatory trading through either regulated exchanges or swap execution facilities, in each case, subject to certain key exceptions, (b) new categories of regulated market participants, including "swap dealers" and "major swap participants" and (3) the requirement that banks "push-out" their swap activities into affiliates. As with other parts of the Act, regulators are required to flesh out through rule making the new regulatory regime relating to swaps.

The Act's jurisdictional grant of authority to the SEC was particularly intriguing, given that it represented a sea-change from previous congressional thinking. Indeed, in 2004 Congress had passed the

Graham–Leach–Bliley Act ("GBLA") to further restrict the SEC's authority over certain derivatives. Specifically, the GBLA had prohibited the SEC from regulating any swap agreement, whether "security-based" or otherwise, under both the Securities Act and Exchange Act. Dodd–Frank changed that.

### b. Swaps Covered

Dodd–Frank regulates, among other things, credit default swaps, interest rate swaps, and total return swaps on a broad range of asset categories. Swaps based on a single security or a narrow-based index of securities are generally considered *"security-based swaps"* and thus regulated by the SEC. Swaps based on broad-based securities indices, government securities and most other reference assets are considered regular *"swaps"* and thus regulated by the CFTC. *"Mixed swaps,"* which contain both swap and security-based swap characteristics, are regulated by both the CFTC and the SEC, in consultation with the Federal Reserve.

Options on equities and other securities, certain forward contracts and futures contracts are excluded from the definition of "swap," and their current regulatory status is generally not affected by the Act. Also excluded from the definition of "swap" are sales of a nonfinancial commodity or security for deferred shipment or delivery that are intended to be physically settled and any transaction providing for the purchase or sale of one or more securi-

ties on a fixed basis that is subject to the Securities
Act and the Exchange Act.

### c.   Other Jurisdictional Allocations

Dodd–Frank grants the CFTC jurisdiction over
puts, calls and options on securities exempted by
the SEC under Section 36(a)(1) of the Exchange
Act. The SEC, however, has jurisdiction over products exempted by the CFTC under Section 4(c)(1) of
the CEA. The two commissions may also cede authority to each other without giving up antifraud
authority in cases where jurisdiction is fuzzy. Importantly, the Financial Industry Regulatory Authority ("FINRA") and the National Futures Association are generally prohibited from regulating
swaps and security-based swaps, respectively.

### d.   Key Definitions and Definitional Mat- ters

Dodd–Frank contains several key definitions, including "swap dealer" and "major swap dealer."
The Act defines *"swap dealer"* as any person that
(i) holds itself out as a dealer in swaps, (ii) makes a
market in swaps, (iii) regularly enters into swaps as
an ordinary course of business for its own account,
or (iv) engages in any activity causing the person to
be commonly known in the trade as a dealer or
market maker in swaps. Specifically excluded from
the definition is a person that enters into swaps for
that person's own account, individually or in a

fiduciary capacity, "but not as part of a regular business." Also excluded is an entity that engages in *de minimis* swap dealing in connection with transactions with or for customers, as determined on the basis of factors to be established through CFTC and SEC rule making.

The Act defines "*major swap participant*" as any non-dealer: (A) that maintains a "substantial position" in swaps for any of the major swap categories as determined by the CFTC and SEC, excluding both positions (1) held for hedging or mitigating commercial risk and (2) maintained by an employee benefit plan under ERISA for the primary purpose of hedging or mitigating any risk directly associated with the operation of the plan; (B) whose outstanding swaps create *substantial counterparty exposure* that could have serious adverse effects on the financial stability of the U.S. banking system or financial markets; or (C) that is a financial entity that maintains a "substantial position" in outstanding swaps in any major swap category as determined by the CFTC and SEC, is highly leveraged relative to the amount of capital it holds and is not subject to capital requirements established by an appropriate Federal banking authority.

Of course, a key term in the "major swap participant" definition is "*substantial position.*" Dodd–Frank requires each of the CFTC and SEC to provide a definition of "substantial position" that is "prudent for the effective monitoring, management and oversight" of entities that are systemically important or can significantly impact the U.S. financial system.

The Act authorizes the CFTC and SEC to designate a person as a "swap dealer" or "major swap participant" for a single type, class or category of swap, but not others. It also alters the Exchange Act definition of "security" to include security-based swaps, but modifies the definition of "dealer" in the Exchange Act to clarify that a dealer in security-based swaps with eligible contract participants is not required to register as a broker-dealer. However, there is no similar exemption for persons who act as "brokers" of security-based swaps.

### e. Clearing, Trading and Reporting

Perhaps the most significant change Dodd–Frank imposes is the requirement that the CFTC or SEC determine which swaps should be cleared through clearinghouses. Indeed, the Act requires the CFTC and SEC, on an ongoing basis, to review swaps to determine if they should be required to be cleared through clearing organizations, and to provide a public comment period in that regard. In reviewing particular swaps, the CFTC and SEC must take into account, among other factors: notional exposures, trading liquidity and pricing data; the availability of operational expertise and relevant infrastructure; the effect on the mitigation of systemic risk and on competition; and the existence of reasonable legal certainty, in the event of the insolvency of the relevant clearinghouse or its clearing members, with regard to the treatment of customer and swap counterparty positions, funds and property.

Clearinghouses must submit to the CFTC or SEC any swaps they plan to accept for clearing and provide notice to its members of the submission. The CFTC and SEC are required to publish any submission for comment and, in general, make a determination within 90 days of receipt of the submission.

The Act provides an optional exemption from clearing to any swap counterparty that (1) is *not* a financial entity, (2) is using the swap to hedge or mitigate commercial risk and (3) notifies the CFTC or SEC how it generally meets its financial obligations associated with entering into uncleared swaps. In this regard, the term *"financial entity"* means a swap dealer, a major swap participant, a commodity pool, a private fund, an employee benefit plan or a person predominantly engaged in the business of banking, or in activities that are financial in nature. The Act requires any reporting company under the Exchange Act to obtain approval to enter into swaps that are subject to an exemption from the clearing requirement from an appropriate committee of its board of directors.

### f.  Mandatory Trade Execution Requirements for Swaps

Dodd–Frank requires that all swaps that are subject to the clearing requirement be traded on a board of trade designated as a contract market or a securities exchange or through a "swap execution facility," unless no such entity accepts the swap for trading. Trades may be executed other than on an exchange or through a swap execution facility if the clearing requirement does not apply. Thus, for example, trades with a non-financial entity that are exempt from clearing need not be executed on an exchange.

The Act defines "*swap execution facility*" as a trading system or platform in which multiple participants have the ability to execute or trade swaps by accepting bids and offers made by multiple participants in the facility or system, through any means of interstate commerce. This would include any trading facility that (1) facilitates the execution of swaps between persons and (2) is not a designated contract market or national securities exchange.

Importantly, the Act requires the CFTC and SEC to promulgate rules for real-time public data reporting of swap transactions, including price and volume. Both cleared and uncleared swaps must be reported to a registered swap data repository. Reporting responsibility is primarily allocated to swap dealers.

### g. Business Conduct Requirements

Dodd–Frank requires registered swap dealers and major swap participants to conform with business conduct standards that the CFTC and SEC prescribe relating to fraud, diligent supervision of the business of the swap dealer or major swap participant, adherence to position limits and any other matter that the commissions determine to be appropriate. Specifically, these business conduct standards must require swap dealers and major swap participants to (i) verify that any counterparty meets the eligibility standards for an eligible contract participant, (ii) disclose the material risks of a swap, any material incentives or conflicts of interest the swap dealer or major swap participant may have and the daily mark for each swap, in each case to any counterparty that is *not* a swap dealer or major swap participant, and (iii) communicate in a fair and balanced manner based on principles of fair dealing and good faith. Special conduct requirements apply when swap dealers and major swap participants deal with "special entities," which include pension funds, endowments, retirement plans and government agencies and entities, including municipalities.

### h.    Capital and Margin Requirements

Dodd–Frank imposes capital and, for uncleared swaps, initial and variation margin requirements on dealers and major swap participants. The purpose behind the capital and margin requirements is twofold. First, they will help ensure the safety and soundness of swap dealers and major swap participants. Second, they will address the risk associated with the uncleared swaps of swap dealers and major swap participants. While cash certainly can be used to meet margin requirements, non-cash collateral may also be used if doing so is consistent with preserving the financial integrity of markets trading swaps and the stability of the U.S. financial system. Although not specifically addressed in the Act, it appears that swap counterparties that are exempt from the clearing requirement will also be exempt from the margin requirements.

### i.   Position Limits and Large Swap Trader Reporting

Dodd–Frank requires the CFTC, with respect to physical commodities other than excluded commodities as defined by the CFTC, to establish *limits on the amount of positions*, other than bona fide hedge positions, that may be held by any person in futures contracts, options on futures contracts or on commodities traded on or subject to the rules of a designated contract market, or any swaps that are economically equivalent to such contracts or options. In addition, the Act requires the CFTC to establish *limits for each month*, including related hedge exemption provisions, on the aggregate number or amount of positions in contracts based upon the same underlying commodity, as defined by the CFTC, that may be held by any person, including any group or class of traders. The Act also requires the SEC to establish limits, including related hedge exemption provisions, on the size of positions in any security-based swap that may be held by any person.

In terms of reporting, the Act requires traders who *exceed* CFTC or SEC-prescribed thresholds in (1) CFTC regulated swaps performing a significant price discovery function or (2) security-based swaps and related instruments to file reports with the CFTC or SEC. These "large swap traders" in CFTC-regulated swaps must keep specified books and records.

### j.   The Swaps Pushout Rule and Federal Assistance

One of the most contentious aspects of the U.S. government's response to the financial crisis was the eventual Federal guarantee of derivative dealer's trading books. Many dealers assumed that, in the event of a systemic collapse of the markets, the Federal government would underwrite the risk inherent in a derivatives portfolio to avoid an even larger economic meltdown. They were right.

A key measure of Dodd–Frank is the removal of this implicit Federal guarantee. The "Swaps Pushout Rule" *prohibits* the provision of "Federal assistance" to depository institutions that qualify as "*swap entities*." "*Federal assistance*" means the use of any advances from any Federal Reserve credit facility or discount window that is not part of a program or facility with broad-based eligibility, or any Federal Deposit Insurance Corporation (FDIC) insurance or guarantees, for the purpose of: (a) making any loan to, or purchasing any stock, equity interest, or debt obligation of, any swaps entity; (b) purchasing assets of any swaps entity; (c) guaranteeing any loan or debt issuance of any swaps entity; or (d) entering into any assistance arrangement, loss sharing, or profit sharing with any swaps entity. A *"swap entity"* is any swap dealer or major swap participant that is registered with the CFTC or SEC, but does not include any major swap participant that is also an insured depository institution.

The Act does allow for Federal assistance to be provided to an FDIC-insured depository institution so long as its swap activities are limited to (1) hedging and other similar risk-mitigating activities directly related to the insured depository institution's activities, (2) acting as a swaps entity for swaps involving rates or reference assets permissible for investment by a national bank under applicable banking law, and (3) acting as a swaps entity for credit default swaps that are cleared by a derivatives clearing organization or clearing agency.

## D.  Interpreting the Derivatives Contract

The courts have had to confront the complexity of derivative instruments directly on a number of different levels. The most basic level involves the *contractual interpretation* of the terms of derivatives. In this regard, and in a foretaste of things to come, the Second Circuit grappled with a dispute over a credit default swap in *Eternity Global Master Fund Ltd. v. Morgan Guaranty Trust Co.*, 375 F.3d 168 (2d Cir.2004).

In *Eternity Global Master Fund*, the plaintiff fund had purchased credit default swaps from two banks in October 2001. The Second Circuit noted that CDSs were simply contracts that transfer *credit risk* from the "protection buyer" to a "credit protection seller." The protection buyer makes periodic payments to the protection seller in return for a contingent payment if a predefined *"credit event"* occurs in the reference credit. The risk against which the plaintiff fund was trying to hedge was the country risk associated with the Argentine bonds owned by the plaintiff fund.

The specific CDSs in question protected the plaintiff fund from four specific credit events: (1) Argentina's failure to pay on the bonds; (2) an acceleration of payment obligations under the contracts evidencing the Argentine bonds; (3) Argentina's repudiation of the bonds or its imposition of a moratorium on their payment; and (4) a restructuring of the obligations evidenced by the bonds.

On November 19, 2001, the Argentine Government announced that a "voluntary debt exchange" would be offered to sovereign bondholders. Willing bondholders could exchange their obligations for secured loans that would pay a lower rate of interest over a longer term, but that would be secured by certain Argentine federal tax revenues. If the Government defaulted on the secured loans, bondholders would have recourse to the original obligations, which were to "remain effective" for their duration. The plaintiff fund believed that the voluntary debt exchange constituted a credit event under the CDSs, but the defendant banks disagreed. Later, on December 24, 2001, the new Argentine interim president announced a public debt moratorium, which both the plaintiff fund and the defendant banks agreed was a credit event under the CDSs.

The Second Circuit was asked to decide whether, purely as a matter of procedure, the lower court had properly dismissed the plaintiff fund's action based on the lower court's determination that the CDS contracts were not "ambiguous" based on the pleadings alone. The Second Circuit, however, held that certain material terms of the contracts could not be found unambiguous on the basis of the pleadings alone, and thus remanded the case back to the lower court.

By contrast, *Brane v. Roth*, 590 N.E.2d 587 (Ind. Ct.App.1992), involved a farmers' co-operative that lost significant sums of money in the grain market by failing to adequately hedge its exposure to that market. The defendant directors were warned about the need to hedge the co-op's grain position to protect the co-op from future losses. Therefore, they authorized the co-op's manager to engage in hedging transactions. However, the manager never followed through and the co-op experienced significant losses.

Shareholders alleged that the co-op's directors breached their fiduciary duty of care by not properly overseeing the manager, and they argued that the business judgment rule should not shield the directors from liability. Both the trial court and the Indiana Court of Appeals agreed. The evidence showed that the directors made no meaningful attempt to be informed of the hedging activities they had authorized and the effects of those activities on the co-op's financial position. Thus, the directors' failure to provide adequate supervision of the manager's actions was a breach of their duty of care to protect the co-op's interests in a reasonable manner.

# PART III

# CLAIMANTS ON THE ENTERPRISE

## CHAPTER 11

## DEBT HOLDERS

### § 33. THE USE OF LEVERAGE (DEBT) AND ITS IMPACT ON CAPITAL STRUCTURE

#### A. Overview

In its most basic sense, *leverage* is the financial impact on a company when it borrows money (*i.e.*, takes on debt). In fact, those operating in finance use the terms "leverage" and "debt" interchangeably. The greater a company's debt load in relation to its shareholders' equity, the greater its leverage.

Like a lever resting on a fulcrum, debt financing increases the potential for greater gains or losses on a company's common stock. This potential is often referred to as the *leverage effect,* and it occurs for two reasons. First, a lender of capital (*e.g.*, a commercial bank or a bondholder) has a fixed contractual claim on a corporate borrower. That claim is limited to the payment of interest and the repayment of principal in accordance with the contract evidencing the debt. Thus, the return to the lender is *capped* at the rate of interest associated with the debt. Second, the return that a company earns on its use of borrowed funds is not limited. It may be more than, less than, or equal to the rate of interest associated with the debt. Because stockholders of a company have a residual claim to whatever monies are left after the lender's claim is satisfied, any return on borrowed funds that *exceeds* the cost of those funds accrues solely to the stockholders. The following example will clarify the leverage effect.

Assume that DBR Corp. has the chance to pursue a new project that requires a $100,000 investment. DBR expects the new project to earn $14,000 per year, a return of 14% [$14,000 ÷ $100,000]. DBR invests $50,000 in the new project using the proceeds from the sale of common stock. It finances the other $50,000 by borrowing those funds from a commercial bank at an interest rate of 12% per annum. Thus, DBR will be required to make an annual interest payment of $6,000 on the loan [$50,000 x .12]. *For purposes of the following examples, assume that DBR faces no transaction costs or allowances and that the tax effects of incurring debt are ignored.*

If DBR's expectation is realized, leveraging the investment will increase DBR's pre-tax cashflow more than if it had financed the investment solely from the sale of equity. As seen below, DBR will receive a 16% annual return on its $50,000 equity investment by borrowing the other $50,000 at a 12% interest rate and reinvesting it in a project that returns 14%:

$$\text{Return on Equity (\%)} = \frac{\text{(investment return} - \text{interest payment)}}{\text{equity}}$$

$$= \frac{\$14,000 - \$6,000}{\$50,000}$$

$$= \frac{\$\ 8,000}{\$50,000}$$

$$= .16 \text{ or } 16\%$$

This result compares favorably to the 14% return on equity achieved when DBR uses 100% equity to finance the same new project:

$$\text{Return on Equity (\%)} = \frac{\text{(investment return} - \text{interest payment)}}{\text{equity}}$$

$$= \frac{\$14,000 - \$0}{\$100,000}$$

$$= \frac{\$\ 14,000}{\$100,000}$$

$$= .14 \text{ or } 14\%$$

Importantly, DBR must receive an annual investment return from the new project of at least 12% for the leverage to benefit the company. If the project were to earn less than that, leveraging would work against DBR. As indicated in Table 3 below, if, for example, the project were to earn only 10%, then DBR's return on equity would fall to 8% because the project is earning less than the cost of borrowed funds. At the 12% "breakeven" point, there will be no gain or loss from the use of leverage (assuming, once again, no transaction costs or allowances).

## Table 3
## Leverage Effect on DBR Corp.
## Based on Various Returns on Investment (%)
### (Debt-to-Equity Ratio = 1:1)

Assumptions:

| | |
|---|---|
| Investment in New Project | $100,000 |
| Debt Financing | $ 50,000 |
| Equity Financing | $ 50,000 |
| Interest on Debt | 12% |

| Return on Investment (%) | 8% | 10% | 12% | 14% | 16% |
|---|---|---|---|---|---|
| Return on Investment ($) | $8,000 | $10,000 | $12,000 | $14,000 | $16,000 |
| Interest Payment ($) | $6,000 | $ 6,000 | $ 6,000 | $ 6,000 | $ 6,000 |
| Return on Equity ($) | $2,000 | $ 4,000 | $ 6,000 | $ 8,000 | $10,000 |
| Return on Equity (%) | 4% | 8% | 12% | 16% | 20% |

## B. Pure Leverage Effect

Taking the lessons just learned, the next step in understanding leverage is to apply those lessons to multiple investment projects. Assume that DBR Corp. knows of four investment opportunities that have identical characteristics (cost, risk, expected return, etc.). Each investment costs $100,000 and is expected to earn $10,000 per year, a return of 10% [$10,000 ÷ $100,000]. Assume that DBR has $100,000 in equity capital to invest and has no other assets or debts. Furthermore, assume that a commercial bank will lend DBR up to $75,000 for each investment opportunity at an annual interest rate of 6%.

At one end of the financing continuum, DBR could choose to take its own $100,000 in equity capital and invest in only one of the four opportunities. In other words, DBR will not use leverage and, therefore, can only invest in one of the four projects. DBR's expected return on equity will be $10,000 per year, or 10% [$10,000 ÷ $100,000].

At the other end of the financing continuum, DBR could use the maximum available leverage by borrowing $75,000 for each of the four projects (total borrowing of $300,000), and use its own $100,000 in equity capital to pay the remaining cost. In this scenario, DBR will have an expected return each year of $40,000 before interest payments ($10,000 from each investment). Its interest payments will total $18,000 per year [$300,000 of borrowed funds x .06].

DBR's net expected return per year will be $22,000 [$40,000 − $18,000]. By utilizing available leverage to help finance its investments, DBR has increased its net expected return on equity from 10% up to 22%. DBR essentially borrowed funds at 6% to help finance investments in four projects, each of which is expected to yield 10%. Table 4 illustrates the leverage effect on DBR based on the assumptions set forth therein.

## Table 4
## Leverage Effect on DBR Corp. Based on
## Various Returns on Investment (%)
(Debt-to-Equity Ratio = 3:1)

Assumptions:

| | |
|---|---|
| Investment in New Projects | $400,000 |
| Debt Financing | $300,000 |
| Equity Financing | $100,000 |
| Interest on Debt | 6% |

| Return on Investment (%) | 4% | 6% | 8% | 10% | 12% |
|---|---|---|---|---|---|
| Return on Investment ($) | $16,000 | $24,000 | $32,000 | $40,000 | $48,000 |
| Interest Payment ($) | $18,000 | $18,000 | $18,000 | $18,000 | $18,000 |
| Return on Equity ($) | ($2,000) | $ 6,000 | $14,000 | $22,000 | $30,000 |
| Return on Equity (%) | −2% | 6% | 14% | 22% | 30% |

Theoretically, DBR could borrow all the money for as many projects as are available to it, thus maximizing the leverage effect. However, in reality this would never happen because of the default risk associated with such substantial leverage. Indeed, projected future cash flows associated with the projects may not materialize if the assumptions on which those projections are based prove to be erroneous. Lenders of capital are well aware of this.

As the debt-to-equity ratio of a company increases, its default risk increases because the likelihood that it can service its debt obligations decreases. In addition, the more highly-leveraged a company is, the more it *depends* on its underlying assumptions coming true. Indeed, highly-leveraged companies depend on the realization of "best case scenarios," a risky proposition that can lead them down the road towards bankruptcy.

## C. Optimal Level of Debt

Debt-to-equity mixes vary from industry to industry and from company to company. CFOs of companies continually conduct analyses to determine the optimal mix of debt and equity for their companies. The return on equity—the stockholders' rate of return—is an important consideration to a CFO contemplating the use of leverage in financing investment opportunities, but so too is default risk. In theory, a company should only incur debt to finance a given opportunity if, after factoring in the default risk related to the additional debt, a higher rate of return on its common stock will result.

Much academic attention has been paid to the issue of whether there is an "optimal" debt-to-equity ratio—*i.e.*, a *balance* between a corporation's equity and debt that actually *enhances* shareholder value. The two primary schools of thought are the "entity" or "irrelevance" approach and the "optimal" approach.

The *entity approach* states that, except for any *positive tax impact* associated with leverage, a company's capital structure has *no effect* on the aggregate market valuation of the company's securities. As espoused by David Durand, this approach argues that "the totality of risk incurred by all security holders of a given company *cannot be altered* by merely changing the capitalization proportions. Such a change could only alter the *proportion* of the total risk borne by *each class* of security holder." Of course, Modigliani and Miller, in their book *The Cost of Capital*, were the first to theorize that leverage *does not* increase shareholder wealth. Their theory, known as the *"irrelevance theory,"* rested on the so-called *"arbitrage effect."* According to Modigliani and Miller, no investor will pay a corporation to incur debt at the entity level that investors themselves can create by borrowing money directly. That is, rather than invest in a leveraged company, investors themselves can incur their own debt and invest it in unleveraged firms that require a lower capital investment for the same return. As investors recognize this opportunity, they will sell stock of leveraged companies and buy stock of unleveraged companies, thus driving the values of the two types of companies towards equilibrium.

The *optimal approach*, by contrast, argues that *conservative increases* in debt do not increase the risk borne by the common stockholders, as security analysts need not adjust their earnings and dividend multipliers downward so long as the debt load remains *conservative*. That is, there is no need to *increase the discount rate* to any significant degree when discounting future net cash flows when conducting valuations. Given the *tax savings* relating to the deductibility of interest payments on debt, the value of a company incurring leverage should, therefore, *increase*.

Moreover, the optimal approach recognizes the normative role that leverage can play in firm management. Specifically, the incurrence of debt can potentially decrease *agency costs*—the costs associated with having agents rather than owners manage the firm. Because banks, debt security holders and other significant lenders demand contracts containing, among other things, affirmative and negative covenants which prescribe and proscribe certain firm behaviors, a reduction in agency costs could occur when senior firm management must live up to the terms of the firm's debt contracts as opposed to running the firm according to their whim. For more on affirmative and negative covenants, see Nutshell Section 36C.

## § 34.  CHARACTERISTICS OF DEBT

### A.  Types of Debt Instruments

Three main types of corporate debt securities exist: bonds, debentures and notes. All three represent contractual claims against the corporate borrower. Each is evidenced by a promissory note which incorporates the terms of a lengthy contract, typically called an indenture. Each security represents a promise by the borrower to pay the amount borrowed on a specified maturity date, together with interest at specified times until that date.

An *indenture* is a contract between the issuer of debt securities and an indenture trustee. The trustee typically is an commercial bank that acts as the agent for the actual holders of the debt securities and serves to protect their rights. The use of a trustee also provides the issuer with the convenience of dealing with a centralized representative rather than with a potentially dispersed group of debt holders. See Nutshell Section 35 for a discussion of indenture trustees and the Trust Indenture Act of 1939.

In practice, no clear-cut definition of bonds, debentures or notes exists. The term "bond," in fact, is sometimes used to describe a debenture or a note, as well as a bond. Accordingly, the description of each of these three debt securities set forth below is a generalization only.

### (1) Bonds

*Bonds* are long-term promissory notes with maturities of 30 years or longer that are generally secured by specified assets of the corporate issuer (*i.e.*, "collateral"). Corporate bonds are normally issued in denominations of $1,000. The denomination is also known as the bond's *face value* or *par value*. An investor pays the face value when she purchases a bond from its issuer upon issuance. During the life of the bond, its issuer pays *interest-only*. When the issuer makes the final interest payment upon the bond's maturity, it also repays the principal (the bond's $1,000 face value) in one lump-sum.

The rate of interest on a bond is referred to as its *coupon rate*. This refers back to the time when each bond was represented by a certificate. Each certificate, in turn, included a series of actual coupons (similar to a sheet of postage stamps), each of which represented the right to receive one interest payment from the corporate issuer. Bondholders thus "clipped coupons" and turned them in to receive interest payments. Today, issuers primarily sell bonds in "uncertificated form" to facilitate bond trading in the secondary market. However, so-called *"bearer bonds"* still include coupons. These bonds are still used in many parts of the world and are favored by those investors who wish to remain anonymous. The only evidence of a bearer bond is the bond itself.

Terms of a particular issuance of bonds are set forth in a contract called the *bond indenture*. The corporate issuer and the indenture trustee are signatories to the bond indenture and, thus, stand in privity of contract. The bondholders themselves are technically third-party beneficiaries of that contract.

### (2) Debentures

A *debenture* is a long-term *unsecured* promissory note. Thus, the main difference between a debenture and a bond is that the former is an unsecured obligation of the corporate issuer while the latter is a secured obligation. Debentures often have shorter maturities than bonds, such as ten to 20 years as opposed to 30 years, but this is not always the case. Terms of a particular issuance of debentures are set forth in a contract called a *debenture indenture* entered into between the corporate issuer and the debenture trustee. Other than its name, a debenture indenture is substantially similar to a bond indenture.

### (3) Notes

*Notes* are shorter-term promissory notes with maturities generally ranging from one to ten years. Notes may be either secured or unsecured obligations of the corporate issuer. Terms of the notes are set forth in a contract called a *note agreement*. Other than its name, a note agreement is substantially similar to a bond indenture except in one respect. Because notes are often issued to only a handful of investors, each note holder is often a direct signatory to the note agreement. Thus, the corporate issuer may stand in privity of contract with the note holders directly rather than with a trustee.

## B.  Credit Rating Agencies

### (1) Generally

Presently, there are two primary credit rating agencies operating within the securities industry: Moody's Investors Service Inc. and Standard & Poor's Corp. (S&P). These agencies, sometimes referred to as *nationally recognized statistical rating organizations* (NRSROs), attempt to assess the likelihood that an issuer (whether a company or a government) will *both promptly and fully pay* its outstanding debt. Approximately 98% of all large corporate bond issues are rated by at least one rating agency, with the issuers themselves paying the rating agencies for their services in almost all cases. Due to the debt-like characteristics of preferred stock (see Nutshell Section 41), publicly offered preferred stock is generally rated by a rating agency as well.

Given that a higher credit rating leads to a lower cost of capital, one would expect issuers to seek out the highest possible credit rating available for their debt securities. However, the facts do not support this hypothesis. Indeed, the number of triple-A rated American companies has declined substantially since 1979. In 1979, there were 61 such companies, while today that number has dwindled below five. While many reasons have been proffered to explain the decline, it should be pointed out that many companies may have simply concluded that their optimal *debt-to-equity ratio* is *not* one that yields a triple-A rating. See Nutshell Section 33C.

Debt security ratings are not permanent. Rating agencies review their ratings periodically throughout the course of a debt security's life. If the financial circumstances of the issuer of that security change, a rating agency may change the rating for that security. The most current rating is reflective of the present investment quality of the debt security. Moreover, different rating agencies may disagree on the appropriate rating for a given debt security. When this occurs, the debt security is said to have a *split rating*.

Table 5 sets forth the ratings used by Moody's and S&P. These ratings are primarily based on the ability of the issuer to meet the principal and interest payments on its debt on a timely basis. Some debt securities are not rated (NR) because their quality is lower than that of the lowest grade. Debt securities also may not be rated if the issue is very small, if there is a lack of information pertaining to the issuer, or if the issue is privately placed solely to a limited group of institutional investors.

### Table 5

|  |  | Moody's | Standard & Poor's |
|---|---|---|---|
| Investment Grade Debt Securities | High Grade | Aaa<br>Aa | AAA<br>AA |
|  | Medium Grade | A<br>Baa | A<br>BBB |
| "Junk" Securities | Low Grade | Ba<br>B | BB<br>B |
|  | Very Low Grade | Caa<br>Ca<br>C | CCC<br>CC<br>C<br>D |

Debt rated Aaa by Moody's or AAA by S&P has the highest rating because it carries the least amount of investment risk. The issuer's capacity to meet its principal and interest payments on its debt is extremely strong. Changes in the business, financial and economic environments of this issuer are unlikely to impair its capacity to repay its debt.

Debt rated Aa by Moody's or AA by S&P is considered high quality. The issuer has a very strong capacity to make principal and interest payments. Debt falling within this group and the highest rated group comprises the *high grade debt security class*.

Debt rated A by Moody's or S&P is considered upper-medium grade. It possesses many favorable investment attributes. Principal and interest payments are adequately secured, but factors may be present which suggest a susceptibility to impairment some time in the future.

Debt rated Baa by Moody's or BBB by S&P is considered medium grade. The issuer of this debt is regarded as having adequate capacity to make principal and interest payments. Adverse economic conditions or changing circumstances, however, are more likely to lead to a weakened capacity to make principal and interest payments in the future. Debt falling within this group and the upper-medium grade group comprises the *medium grade debt security class*.

Debt rated Ba by Moody's or BB by S&P is referred to as *"junk."* It is considered speculative because of its vulnerability to payment defaults. Debt rated Ba/BB, however, is less vulnerable to nonpayment than lower rated junk. Junk securities face major ongoing uncertainties or exposure to adverse business, financial or economic conditions that could leave the issuer unable to service its debt. Due to their speculative nature, junk securities offer a much higher yield (or stated interest rate) than investment grade debt.

Debt rated B by Moody's or S&P is considered highly-speculative. Receipt of principal and interest payments or compliance with other terms of the debt contract over any extended period of time may be limited. Although the issuer may currently have the capacity to meet its financial commitments on its debt, adverse business, financial or economic conditions may impair the issuer's capacity or willingness to meet those commitments in the future. Debt falling within this group and the Ba/BB group comprises the *low grade debt security class*.

Debt rated Caa or Ca by Moody's or CCC or CC by S&P is considered in poor standing and extremely speculative. Although this debt will likely have an extremely high yield, this is outweighed by major risk exposure to adverse economic conditions. Some of the issuers of this debt may be in default. Hence, this class of debt, and any lower rated debt, is referred to as *distressed debt*.

Debt rated C by Moody's or C or D by S&P is considered to be in default. This debt is the lowest rated class of debt, and these issues are regarded as having extremely poor prospects of ever attaining any real investment standing. Debt rated lower than Caa by Moody's or CCC by S&P comprises the *very low grade debt security class*.

## (2) Regulation of Credit Rating Agencies

### a.  Introduction

During the financial crisis of the early 2000s, many investors appropriately asked why the credit rating agencies had not ferreted out problems at scandal-ridden companies like Enron, WorldCom, Tyco and other financially troubled companies. After all, that *is the job* of the credit rating agencies. Commentators expressed still more astonishment during the financial meltdown of 2008, as the credit rating agencies failed to appreciate and highlight the risk associated with mortgage-backed securities, especially those backed by subprime mortgages.

As a possible explanation, some commentators pointed to what they perceived as a debilitating conflict of interest inherent in the ratings process. This conflict arises from the fact that a prospective issuer generally pays for an agency's services (the "issuer pays" model). Over the years, both the SEC and Congress have contemplated regulating credit rating agencies due to this conflict of interest and the perceived difficulty of competitors to enter the ratings business.

Prior to the Fall of 2006, the SEC did not have the explicit authority to regulate credit rating agencies. However, it built into its *broker-dealer net capital rule* (Exchange Act Rule 15c3–1) the concept of a market-recognized credible rating agency (which the SEC designated as a *"nationally recognized statistical rating organization"* or NRSRO).

The net capital rule is used as an indicator of a broker-dealer's liquidity. NRSRO-rated securities could be used to satisfy the SEC's net capital rule for broker-dealers, and thus credit rating agencies *desired* to become NRSROs. Unfortunately, of the approximately 130 rating agencies in existence, the SEC only recognized five as NRSROs at that time.

### b.  Credit Rating Agency Reform Act of 2006

In the Fall of 2006, Congress passed the Credit Rating Agency Reform Act. This Act allows a rating agency to become *registered* as a NRSRO if it provides certain specified data to the SEC. This data must include the performance measurement statistics, procedures, and methodologies for rating companies, possible conflicts of interest, and confidential lists of the largest issuers that use the agency. Importantly, the Act allows the SEC to *oversee* NRSROs through *examinations* and *enforcement actions*. It also allows the SEC to issue rules regarding NRSRO conflicts of interest and the misuse of non-public information. Through the Act, Congress hoped that most credit rating agencies would choose to become NRSROs and thus become subjected to SEC regulation and scrutiny. It was hoped that this would lead to increased transparency in the ratings process, fewer conflicts of interest, and a reduction in abusive and anti-competitive practices.

Since 2006, the SEC has added several rules to the existing rules under the Exchange Act that specifically address credit rating agencies. See Exchange Act Rules 17g–1 through 17g–5. Under those rules, agencies seeking to become NRSROs must file a registration statement with the SEC on Form NRSRO. Once they become NRSROs, they must make and retain specific records that relate to their business as credit rating agencies. They must file financial reports with the SEC on an annual basis. They must take steps to prevent insider trading and the abuse of material nonpublic information. Finally, the rules define "conflict of interest" and prohibit NRSROs from having certain specified conflicts of interest outright, while allowing other conflicts to exist providing, among other things, full disclosure is made. For example, an NRSRO is prohibited from issuing or maintaining a credit rating that is solicited by a person that, in the most recently ended fiscal year, provided the NRSRO with net revenue equaling or exceeding 10% of its total net revenue for that year. See Exchange Act Rule 17g–5(c)(1).

### c.  Dodd–Frank

One of the causes of the financial crisis of 2008 was the overly rosy ratings that credit rating agencies gave to mortgage-backed securities. When these agencies ultimately downgraded these securities, it led to a pricing collapse that left the market for structured products virtually extinct. In light of this, Congress took another hard look at credit rating agencies and addressed them in the Dodd–

Frank Wall Street Reform and Consumer Protection Act of 2010 ("Dodd–Frank"). This time Congress was intent on regulating NRSROs from soup to nuts.

Dodd–Frank covers nine primary areas with regard to credit rating agencies. The first area relates to SEC oversight. The SEC is required to establish a new Office of Credit Ratings. This Office will administer SEC rules relating to NRSRO practices in determining ratings. It will also conduct annual examinations of each NRSRO and issue a public annual report summarizing essential findings of examinations, NRSRO responses to identified material deficiencies and whether the NRSROs have implemented previous SEC recommendations.

The second area is governance and compliance. The Act requires each NRSRO to have a board of directors with at least one-half, but not less than two, independent members, a portion of which must be actual users of NRSRO ratings. In addition, each NRSRO must have a chief compliance officer (CCO) who will establish procedures for the receipt, retention and treatment of complaints, both anonymous and otherwise, regarding credit ratings, models, methodologies and compliance with the securities laws. The CCO must submit an annual report to the NRSRO and SEC addressing compliance related matters. Importantly, the CCO's compensation cannot be linked to the NRSRO's financial performance; nor can she perform any credit rating, marketing or sales functions.

The third area involves management of conflicts of interest. The Act requires the SEC to issue rules to prevent sales and marketing considerations from influencing a NRSRO's production of ratings. Each NRSRO must establish a conflicts of interest policy with respect to former NRSRO employees who participated in a particular issuer's ratings going to work for that issuer. The SEC will review that policy annually and upon the policy's material modification or amendment.

The fourth area covers accountability for ratings procedures. Each NRSRO must establish, maintain, enforce and document an internal control structure to govern its implementation of and adherence to policies, procedures and methodologies for determining ratings. Each NRSRO must submit an annual internal controls report to the SEC which includes an attestation from its chief executive officer.

The fifth area covers rules relating to ratings procedures and methodologies. The Act tasks the SEC with implementing rules addressing the procedures and methodologies (including qualitative and quantitative data and models) used by NRSROs. These rules must, among other things: (a) ensure that ratings are determined in accordance with procedures and methodologies that a NRSRO's board of directors approves; (b) ensure that when material changes to rating procedures and methodologies occur, they are applied consistently to all ratings to which they apply, including current ratings (to the extent surveillance procedures and methodologies are impacted), (c) require public disclosure of any changes to ratings procedures and methodologies; and (d) require a NRSRO to notify ratings users: (i) of the version of a procedure or methodology used with respect to ratings; (ii) when a material change is made to a procedure or methodology and the likelihood of this resulting in a change to current ratings; and (iii) when a significant error is identified in a procedure or methodology that may result in credit rating actions. In addition, when producing a rating, each NRSRO must consider information about an issuer that it has or receives from persons other than from the issuer or underwriter if it finds the information credible and potentially significant to the rating decision.

In terms of *ratings symbols*, the SEC must adopt rules that require each NRSRO to establish, maintain and enforce policies and procedures that clearly define and disclose the meaning of any ratings symbol and that apply this symbol consistently for all instruments for which the symbol is used. However, a NRSRO may use distinct sets of symbols to denote credit ratings for different types of instruments. The SEC must also issue rules requiring each NRSRO to establish, maintain and enforce policies and procedures that assess the probability that an issuer will default, fail to make timely payments, or otherwise not make payments in accordance with the terms of a rated instrument. In terms of *ratings analysts*, the SEC must issue rules to ensure persons employed to perform ratings are tested for knowledge of the rating process and meet standards of training, experience and competence necessary to produce accurate ratings. In terms of *ratings performance*, the SEC must issue rules to require each NRSRO to publicly disclose performance information on initial ratings and any subsequent changes to allow assessment of ratings accuracy and establish comparability across NRSROs.

The sixth area covers the use of ratings in statutes and regulations. Dodd–Frank requires the removal of certain statutory references to credit ratings within two years of the Act's enactment. Moreover, all Federal agencies must review and modify their rules and regulations to remove references to or reliance upon credit ratings and substitute an alternative standard of creditworthiness. The agencies must complete this within one year of the Act's enactment.

The seventh area covers SEC penalties for NRSROs. Dodd–Frank establishes penalties that the SEC may impose (in addition to those already available) on persons associated with a NRSRO for specified misconduct, including the failure to reasonably supervise an individual who commits a violation of the securities laws. The SEC may suspend or revoke a NRSRO's registration with respect to a particular class or subclass of securities upon a determination, after notice and hearing, that the NRSRO lacks adequate financial or managerial resources to consistently produce ratings with integrity. Moreover, each NRSRO must act as a whistle blower if it receives any credible information from a third party that alleges that an issuer of securities rated by the NRSRO committed or is committing a material violation of law.

The eighth area relates to Securities Act registration statements. A company registering its securities under the Securities Act must, in order to include a NRSRO credit rating in its registration statement, file the NRSRO's consent along with its registration statement. A NRSRO that so consents opens itself up to liability as an expert under Section 11 of the Securities Act for material misstatements or omissions in its rating.

The last area relates to a private right of action. Dodd–Frank establishes that the enforcement and penalty provisions of the Exchange Act apply to statements made by credit rating agencies in the same manner and to the same extent as they apply to statements made by registered public accounting firms or securities analysts under the securities laws. Moreover, the Act modifies the requisite "state of mind" requirement for private securities fraud actions for monetary damages against a credit rating agency or controlling person. It is now sufficient for a plaintiff to state with particularity that the credit rating agency knowingly or recklessly failed to conduct a reasonable investigation of a rated security with respect to the factual elements relied upon by its own methodology for evaluating credit risk or to obtain reasonable verification of such factual elements from sources independent of the issuer and underwriter that the credit rating agency considered competent.

The current "issuer pays" model of picking a credit rating agency was not abandoned by the Act. However, the Act requires the SEC to study the feasibility of establishing an independent entity or self-regulatory organization to assign NRSROs to determine credit ratings for structured finance products, such as mortgaged-backed securities. Such a system would prevent an issuer, underwriter or sponsor from selecting a NRSRO to rate securities which it is issuing or involved with, thus avoiding the conflicts of interest associated with the current "issuer pays" model.

## § 35.  THE TRUST INDENTURE ACT OF 1939

### A.  Introduction

The Trust Indenture Act of 1939 (TIA) evolved from the Securities Act and the Exchange Act, and represented yet another congressional attempt to exercise control over the securities industry after the stock market collapse of 1929. The primary purposes of the TIA are: (1) to provide full and fair disclosure to debt holders, not only at the time when corporate issuers originally issue debt securities, but also throughout the life of those securities; (2) to provide a tool whereby debt holders may organize for the protection of their own interests; and (3) to ensure that debt holders will have the services of a disinterested indenture trustee which conforms to the high standards of conduct observed by trust institutions.

Since the TIA's enactment, significant changes have occurred in the U.S. and international debt markets. The types of securities offered have changed along with the method of their distribution. As market developments rendered aspects of the original TIA outdated, the SEC submitted a proposal to Congress in the late 1980s to modernize the TIA to enable it to adapt to current practices and future developments in the public market for debt securities. Congress passed the first extensive revision of the TIA in 1990. This revision, which is known as the Trust Indenture Reform Act of 1990 (TIRA), not only modernized the fifty-year old TIA going forward, but it also applied retroactively to all existing indentures.

## B. Summary of the TIA

The TIA generally applies to the sale by issuers of debt securities and interests in debt securities to the public. The TIA does not apply to debt securities issued in private placements, because transactions which are exempt from the registration requirements of the Securities Act are also exempt from the TIA. Absent an exemption, any security subject to the TIA must be distributed under an indenture that complies with the TIA.

In limited instances, certain debt securities not required to be registered under the Securities Act nevertheless remain subject to the TIA. For example, an issuer reorganizing under Chapter 11 of the Bankruptcy Code may issue debt securities as part of its new capital structure. While those securities are exempt from registration under the Securities Act (pursuant to Section 3(a)(7) of that Act), the indenture related to those securities must be qualified under the TIA.

The TIA sets forth the eligibility requirements for indenture trustees and prohibits conflicts of interest involving trustees at any time. However, TIRA changed this so that the trustee conflict provisions are only triggered when an issuer is in default on its debt securities. The TIA also sets forth certain statutory duties and obligations of the trustee, such as the issuance of periodic reports to debt holders. Additionally, it grants trustees certain powers such as the right to bring suit against the issuer on behalf of debt holders in the event of a default by the issuer.

### (1) Exemptions

The TIA contains several exemptions that limit its applicability, three of which are particularly important. First, Section 304(a)(9) exempts those securities covered by an indenture where the total amount of debt issued does not exceed $10 million within a thirty-six (36) month period. The 36–month period is a "rolling period," commencing with the initial offering under the indenture. Second, exempt securities under the Securities Act are generally exempt under Section 304(a)(4) of the TIA. Thus, this provision exempts securities listed as exempt under most of the provisions of Section 3 of the Securities Act, including those issued by the Federal government and not-for-profit organizations. Third, debt securities issued pursuant to a transactional exemption under the Securities Act are generally exempt under Section 304(b) of the TIA. Debt securities issued in a private placement under Section 4(2) of the Securities Act (which would include debt securities sold in Securities Act Rule 144A offerings as well) are a prime example. Additional exemptions are listed in TIA Section 304.

### (2) Qualification of the Indenture

Under TIA Section 305, an issuer is required to file the indenture for its debt offering as an exhibit to its Securities Act registration statement. Also filed as an exhibit to that registration statement is an eligibility statement of the trustee on Form T–1. In instances when an individual is designated to act as indenture trustee, Form T–2 is used instead. The TIA requires each registration statement to contain the information necessary for the SEC to determine accurately whether the associated indenture qualifies under the TIA and whether the trustee thereunder is eligible to act as such under the TIA.

If an issuer files a shelf registration statement under Securities Act Rule 415 in order to register the offer and sale of debt securities on a delayed or continuous basis, or the issuer subsequently adds debt to a shelf registration statement by post-effective amendment, the determination of when the trustee must be named and qualified under the TIA depends on whether the offering is made on a delayed basis in accordance with Securities Act Rule 415(a)(1)(x). If the offering is made on such a delayed basis, TIA Section 305(b)(2) permits the issuer to designate the trustee on a delayed basis as well. In that instance, the Form T–1 would become effective ten calendar days after filing unless effectiveness is accelerated by the SEC. If the offering is not made on a delayed basis, the issuer must file the Form T–1 as an exhibit to the shelf registration statement or as a post-effective amendment to the shelf registration statement, and qualification would occur upon effectiveness of those filings.

### (3) Trustee Eligibility Requirements

Throughout the duration of an indenture, one or more qualified trustees must serve as indenture trustee. The TIA has specific eligibility requirements for those seeking to be trustees under qualified indentures. See TIA Section 310. Prior to 1990, at least one trustee must have been either a corporation organized and doing business under U.S. or state law or a corporation or other person permitted to act as trustee by the SEC. However, a U.S. subsidiary of a foreign company could serve as trustee if it was organized and doing business under the laws of the U.S. or any state. After the passage of TIRA, a foreign entity may now apply to the SEC (on Form T–6) to serve as sole trustee so long as it is authorized under the laws of its jurisdiction to exercise corporate trust powers and is subject to supervision or examination by its foreign government that is substantially equivalent to that given to U.S. trustees. Additional trustees may be appointed by the issuer in the event the indenture should require or permit it.

The TIA requires each trustee to be authorized under law to exercise trust powers and be subject to supervision or examination by government authorities such as the SEC. It also requires trustees to have capital and surplus of no less than $150,000 throughout the life of the indenture. While easily met by corporate trustees, this last requirement makes it difficult for a natural person to qualify as a trustee under the TIA.

### (4) Conflicts of Interest

In passing the TIA, Congress declared that the national public interest and the interest of investors were adversely affected when an indenture trustee had any relationship with the issuer that involved a material conflict with the interests of investors. Section 310(b) of the TIA directly addresses the problem of conflicts.

Historically, Section 310(b) proscribed nine relationships. If one or more existed, a trustee would be disqualified under the TIA. For example, when a trustee owned in excess of a specified percentage of the securities it is obligated to represent, the conflict of interest that resulted from that ownership precluded the trustee from serving as trustee.

The TIA mandates that if a trustee has a conflict of interest, the trustee must remove the conflicting interest within 90 days or resign as indenture trustee. If the trustee does not resign its post, the trustee must notify all debt holders within 10 days after the 90–day period has elapsed. Upon such notice, any bona fide debt holder who has been a holder of the indenture securities for at least six months may seek the removal of the conflicted trustee and the appointment of a successor trustee.

TIRA modified the TIA's conflict of interest provisions in two ways. First, it proscribed a new relationship: a trustee may not become a creditor of the issuer or its affiliates except in certain specified instances set forth in Section 310(b). To the extent a creditor relationship is allowed, however, Section 311 of the TIA regulates it. Among other things, Section 311(a) requires the creditor-trustee to *share* any amounts collected from the issuer with all the debt holders under the indenture except for payments or property received by the trustee in its capacity as a creditor within three months of the issuer's bankruptcy. Those payments and property must be set aside for the benefit of the security holders, as Section 311 is intended to reach preferential transfers. See Nutshell Section 38D(2).

Second, TIRA created an additional requirement before a conflicting interest would disqualify a trustee: the forbidden relationship must exist at the same time the indenture securities are in default. In this event, the trustee has 90 days to cure the default. If the default is not cured, the trustee must eliminate the conflict of interest or resign. The trustee need not resign, however, if it can show that resignation would be inconsistent with the interests of the debt holders or that the default can be cured within a reasonable period of time. Thus, TIRA allows a trustee to continue to serve as trustee even if it is conflicted so long as there is no default.

In the event a trustee seeks to resign its post, the issuer must take prompt steps to have a successor trustee appointed in the manner provided in the indenture. Additionally, TIRA provides that any resignation is effective only upon the appointment of a successor trustee. Nothing in the original TIA had prevented the trustee from resigning without a successor trustee being appointed.

### (5) Mandatory and Permissive Indenture Provisions

The TIA requires qualified indentures to set forth certain mandatory provisions to safeguard investors of debt securities. For example, an indenture must contain reporting requirements, a list of the duties and responsibilities of the trustee, and a guarantee of the debt holders' right to receive payment. All other indenture provisions are deemed to be "permissive provisions," pursuant to Section 318(b) of the TIA.

Prior to TIRA, if a mandatory provision were omitted from an indenture or contradicted by a permissive provision, the SEC could not intervene on behalf of debt holders after qualification of the indenture. TIRA corrected this problem. Now, Section 318(c) of the TIA automatically includes all mandatory provisions within every indenture whether or not they are physically contained within it. Moreover, such inclusion is both retroactive and prospective in its application.

### (6) Legal Actions by Debt Holders

Debt holders are protected from payment defaults by Section 316(b) of the TIA. That section provides that the right of any debt holder to receive payment of principal and interest when due shall not be impaired or affected without the consent of such holder. Thus, provisions in the indenture to the contrary are ineffective. Likewise, a debt holder may institute suit for the enforcement of such payment on or after the due date.

With regard to non-payment defaults, indentures themselves typically provide that no holder may institute any action under the indenture unless: (1) the holder gives notice to the issuer and the trustee of the occurrence of a default; (2) holders of 25 percent in principal amount of the outstanding debt securities agree to bring a cause of action; and (3) the trustee refuses to act to alleviate and cure the default. See Nutshell Section 37C(1)b.

Courts have generally held that debt holders have a private cause of action against any trustee who has violated a trustee's standard of conduct under the TIA or who has violated any terms of the indenture and failed to cure the default. See, e.g., *Bluebird Partners, L.P. v. First Fid. Bank, N.A., New Jersey*, 85 F.3d 970 (2d Cir.1996); *Zeffiro v. First Penn. Banking & Trust Co.*, 623 F.2d 290 (3rd Cir.1980).

## C. Duties and Obligations of a Trustee Under the TIA

### (1) Pre–Default Versus Post–Default

The TIA specifies certain duties and obligations which a trustee must fulfill when performing its role as indenture trustee. However, a given duty may depend on whether a default (as defined in the indenture) has occurred.

Prior to default, the duties of an indenture trustee are limited to those expressly set forth in the indenture. As a result, the trustee's duties prior to default are essentially ministerial and controlled by contract. Following this theory, the trustee does not have broad fiduciary duties running toward debt holders prior to an event of default. See, e.g., *Elliott Assoc. v. J. Henry Schroder Bank & Trust Co.*, 838 F.2d 66 (2d Cir.1988); *Harriet & Henderson Yarns, Inc. v. Castle*, 75 F.Supp. 2d 818 (W.D. Tenn.1999); *AG Capital Funding Partners, L.P. v. State St. Bank & Trust Co.*, 896 N.E.2d 61 (N.Y.2008).

Pursuant to Section 315(b) of the TIA, the trustee must normally give notice to the debt holders of all defaults known to the trustee within 90 days after the occurrence of each default. Thereafter, the trustee must exercise the rights and powers vested in it by the indenture. Under Section 315(c) of the TIA, the standard of care in the case of default is the same degree of care and skill as a prudent man would exercise in the conduct of his own affairs. This "prudent man" standard requires the trustee to try to prevent injury to the debt holders' interests as would a prudent man under similar circumstances. Failure to comply with this standard may result in the trustee incurring liability to the debt holders under the TIA.

While the TIA imposes special duties on the trustee when a default occurs, it simultaneously grants the trustee special powers. For example, the indenture trustee is authorized to recover judgment in its own name and as trustee of an express trust against the issuer for any amount due. It also can file a proof of claim on behalf of the debt holders it represents when the issuer has filed for bankruptcy. Additionally, it may sit on the unsecured creditors' committee relating to that bankruptcy. Indenture provisions that interfere with a trustee's powers to act upon default are ineffective under the TIA.

## (2) Limitations on a Trustee's Liability

Under Section 315(d) of the TIA, an indenture generally may not contain any provision relieving the indenture trustee from liability for its own negligent action, its own negligent failure to act, or for its own willful misconduct. Still, the TIA permits certain limited provisions to be included in an indenture regarding the extent of the trustee's liability so long as the provisions do not contradict any provision of the TIA.

The TIA protects trustees who make errors in good faith unless the indenture specifically provides otherwise. For example, the trustee may rely, in good faith, upon certificates or opinions conforming to the requirements of the indenture so long as the trustee examines the certificates or opinions to see if they conform to the indenture's terms. The trustee also will not be liable except for the performance of those duties expressly stated in the indenture. Moreover, the trustee will be protected from liability for actions taken at the debt holders' request.

If a trustee willfully makes a statement which is false or misleading with respect to any material fact throughout the duration of the indenture, it may be subject to criminal penalties under Section 325 of the TIA. Penalties for willful violations of the TIA may include up to a $10,000 fine, imprisonment for not more than five (5) years, or both. Section 323(a) of the TIA, by contrast, provides those who relied on false statements with a private cause of action for damages. Trustees, however, will not be held liable with respect to misstatements made in good faith and without knowledge that they were false or misleading. Any such action must be brought within the statute of limitations period specified in Section 323(a).

# § 36.  KEY CONTRACTUAL TERMS AND PROTECTIVE PROVISIONS

## A.  The Promise to Pay and Provisions Designed to Support It

Every debt indenture contains a detailed set of contractual provisions relating to the debt securities in question. Two excellent resources that address key indenture terms have been published by the American Bar Association. The first is the Revised Model Simplified Indenture ("RMSI") published in 2000, which covers all the standard provisions typically contained in an indenture. The second is the Model Negotiated Covenants and Related Definitions ("MNCRD") published in 2006, which discusses debt covenants in detail and provides alternative formulations for many.

At its most basic, an indenture sets forth the issuer's promise to repay debt holders the borrowed funds along with interest. This promise is fully enforceable in contract by those debt holders, as it was given by the issuer in a bargained for exchange in return for the loaned funds.

Besides relying on the issuer's naked promise to repay its debt, many investors insist on additional indenture provisions designed to reduce the risk or impact of a payment default. One way to reduce risk is to secure or "collateralize" the debt securities with the assets of the issuer. Whether debt is collateralized is the subject of negotiations between the issuer and prospective debt holders (or their agent). If the issuer defaults, and that default is not cured in a timely fashion, debt holders, through the indenture trustee, can seize the collateral supporting the issuer's payment obligation, sell it, and pay themselves back with the proceeds. Any excess proceeds must be returned to the issuer.

Almost any of an issuer's assets can secure its debt, including land, accounts receivable, inventory and equipment. An exception would be assets that require governmental approval to own, such as a casino gaming license. In order to ensure the ability to seize collateral, debt holders, through the indenture trustee, must "perfect" a security interest in that collateral in accordance with Article 9 of the UCC.

A second way investors can protect themselves against non-payment is by demanding a *guarantee* from a third party. Guarantees take many forms. Most typical is a payment guarantee, whereby the guarantor must pay if the issuer does not. More unusual guarantees include an equity infusion guarantee, whereby a third party commits to infusing equity capital into the issuer in the event the issuer's debt-to-equity ratio becomes dangerously unbalanced.

Parties closely affiliated with issuers commonly provide guarantees. They do so because of the indirect benefits they receive when the issuer gains access to the loaned funds. Most typical is a guarantee from a controlling stockholder, whether an individual or a parent company. However, when the issuer is a holding company, debt holders typically demand guarantees from the holding company's operating subsidiaries. In that situation, the holding company is almost entirely dependent on those subsidiaries up-streaming cash to pay off the holding company's debt.

A third way investors can protect themselves is through the creation of a *sinking fund.* A sinking fund indenture provision requires the issuer to periodically deposit a percentage of its cash flow into a custodial account (the "sinking fund") typically maintained by the indenture trustee. The goal of this provision is to assure investors that the issuer will have the funds necessary to repay the principal on the debt securities when those securities mature.

Sinking funds, however, are often a mixed blessing. On the one hand, debt securities supported by a sinking fund are less risky than those without. On the other hand, an issuer that is required to make sinking fund payments cannot use those funds to grow its business.

## B.  Subordination

### (1) Generally

When an issuer has multiple classes of debt securities outstanding (*e.g.*, bonds and debentures), the priority in which debt holders of different classes are repaid is crucial. Ranking among classes is particularly important when the issuer declares bankruptcy or seeks to liquidate. See Nutshell Section 38D(3).

The concept of *subordination* refers to one class of debt holders standing behind another in order of payment. A given issuer, for example, may have senior debt securities, senior subordinated debt securities, and subordinated debt securities outstanding at any given time. Holders of the senior debt securities rank ahead of the holders of the other two classes of debt securities. Holders of the senior subordinated debt securities rank ahead of the holders of the subordinated debt securities. Thus, in terms of the repayment "food chain," holders of subordinated debt securities are at the bottom of the list of creditors. Nevertheless, all creditors, including holders of subordinated debt securities, stand ahead of preferred stockholders and common stockholders on the repayment food chain.

Where a given issue of debt securities ranks vis-á-vis another issue is purely a matter of contract law. For a given issue to be subordinated, its indenture must so provide. Thus, subordination is a topic of negotiation. In return for accepting the additional risk relating to subordination, investors in subordinated debt demand a higher rate of interest.

### (2) "Junk" Bonds

Subordinated debt securities are referred to as both *high-yield debt securities* and *junk bonds*. These bonds are considered high in yield because they yield about three to five percent more than regular investment grade bonds on average. Michael Milken, of the now defunct Drexel Burnham Lambert, Inc. investment banking firm, is credited with having the insight that led to the creation of the junk bond market in the 1980s. His insight was that a significant demand existed for higher-yielding, non-investment grade debt instruments, the value of which was linked more to the prospects of the issuers than the ratings given to those instruments by the credit rating agencies.

Most junk bonds fall into one of three categories. The first category consists of bonds that are contractually subordinated to the issuer's other debt obligations at the time of their issuance. Thus, they were "born" junk bonds. An example would include junk bonds issued in connection with corporate takeover transactions, such as leveraged buy-outs (LBOs), which were particularly plentiful during the go-go LBO period of the late–1980s.

The second category consists of bonds that were not contractually subordinated when issued. Rather, they were investment grade bonds when issued but have been subsequently downgraded to junk status due to increased default risk associated with the issuer. A vivid example of this is found in *Metropolitan Life Ins. Co. v. RJR Nabisco, Inc.*, 716 F.Supp. 1504 (S.D.N.Y.1989). Here, plaintiff bondholders sued when the "investment grade" rating of their bonds was changed to a "speculative grade" rating (*i.e.*, junk status) as a result of an LBO of the issuer. Because the issuer was responsible for servicing the enormous amount of debt incurred in connection with buying out the issuer's common stockholders, its default risk increased exponentially.

The third category of junk bonds consists of debt securities originally issued as junk for reasons other than contractual subordination. This category includes junk bonds issued by low-rated companies simply as a means of financing their on-going operations. In other words, these are bonds issued by companies that simply do not qualify for an "investment grade" credit rating in the first place.

Many investment bankers and commentators refer to junk bonds as "equity in drag" because those bonds are only one step away from being equity. This stems from the fact that junk bonds—especially those that are contractually subordinated—are typically valued based on the issuer's fundamentals and are somewhat less sensitive to interest rate changes. Moreover, due to their riskiness, a distinct possibility exists that an issuer will never pay them off. Indeed, if need be, the issuer could swap out some or all of the junk bonds for equity as part of a reorganization either inside or outside of bankruptcy.

## C.   Covenants

A debt indenture typically contains two types of covenants: affirmative and negative. Covenants are designed to ensure that the issuer operates in a way most conducive to fulfilling its promise to repay the debt holders.

### (1)   Affirmative Covenants

Affirmative covenants are promises that an issuer makes to perform specified, affirmative acts. For example, an issuer may promise to: (1) maintain its properties and corporate existence; (2) pay its taxes; (3) deliver its financial information to the indenture trustee whether or not the issuer is a reporting company under the Exchange Act; (4) obtain and maintain insurance on its properties; (5) deliver a compliance certificate to the trustee annually stating that the issuer is in compliance with all indenture covenants and conditions; and (6) give prompt notice to the trustee of the occurrence of certain specified events, such as a default. Most indentures contain standard affirmative covenants regardless of the type of debt securities being issued or the credit quality of the issuer.

### (2)   Negative Covenants

Negative covenants, by contrast, are issuer promises *not* to engage in specified acts. They often are referred to as "thou shalt nots." Negative covenants include those discussed below.

> ### a.   Limitation on the Incurrence of Indebtedness

This covenant prevents the issuer from increasing its indebtedness *unless* it passes a ratio test, which indicates that the issuer is generating enough cash flow to easily satisfy its payments on the debt securities in question as well as the new indebtedness, or the incurrence of the new indebtedness falls into one of several negotiated exceptions. Debt holders worry about the issuer's ability to incur additional indebtedness before they have been repaid for three reasons. First, additional debt increases the issuer's leverage, thus raising the issuer's default risk. Second, additional debt increases the number of creditors vying for the issuer's assets in the event of a bankruptcy or liquidation. Third, the increase in risk associated with additional debt often diminishes the value of the existing debt securities, as the market applies a higher discount rate when valuing those securities due to the increase in the issuer's default risk. See Nutshell Section 14C(2).

In terms of the ratio test, the covenant typically allows the issuer to incur additional indebtedness if, on the date of such incurrence and after giving effect to the new indebtedness on a pro forma basis, (a) no default under the indenture has occurred and is continuing and (b) the consolidated coverage ratio exceeds 2 to 1 (or higher). The consolidated coverage ratio is the ratio between the issuer's cash flow and fixed charges over a given period of time. Although cash flow can be measured in different ways, typically it equates to an issuer's earnings before interest, taxes, depreciation and amortization (EBITDA), plus any extraordinary loss deducted when computing the issuer's net income. Fixed charges typically include the issuer's interest expense plus any preferred stock dividend payments.

In terms of the negotiated exceptions list, the main exception is for bank debt. The issuer will be allowed to enter into a credit agreement with a local bank or other lending institution and borrow the greater of (i) a certain specified amount (*e.g.,* $5 million) and (ii) the sum of a certain specified percentage of the book value of the issuer's inventory and accounts receivables. Additional exceptions will include, among others, (a) one for the issuer's debt that existed at the time the debt securities in question are issued, (b) intercompany debt (so long as the right to payment is not transferred to a third party) and (c) debt incurred to refinance existing debt. In terms of refinancing existing debt, however, the issuer is generally not allowed to increase the principal amount (except to the extent needed to pay related costs, such as accrued interest, premium and other retirement costs), shorten the average life of the debt that is being refinanced, or refinance the debt with more senior or structurally superior debt.

"Indebtedness" as used in this covenant is broadly defined. The definition brings within it both conventional and unorthodox leverage. Conventional leverage covers, among other things, new debt securities or bank loans. Unorthodox leverage, by contrast, would include an issuance of stock (often referred to as *disqualified stock*) that is redeemable by the issuer prior to the maturity of the debt securities in question. Redeemable preferred stock is a prime example. Disqualified stock is included within the indebtedness definition because debt holders do not want cash leaving the issuer to pay contract claimants lower down the repayment food chain unless the issuer is in good financial health. See generally MNCRD § 4.04.

### b. Restricted Payments

This covenant is designed to keep money within the issuer for use in servicing the debt securities in question. The covenant prohibits the issuer from making so-called "restricted payments," subject to certain exceptions. A restricted payment occurs when the issuer (a) distributes its cash to its equity holders either through the payment of dividends or through repurchases or redemptions of stock, (b) purchases or redeems prior to maturity any indebtedness of the issuer that is subordinated to the debt securities in question or (c) makes an investment in any company that would not result in that company becoming subject to the covenants of the indenture.

The covenant, however, typically allows the issuer to make some restricted payments if certain conditions are met. These conditions typically include the following:

(a) no default or event of default must exist;

(b) the issuer must be able to incur at least $1.00 of additional indebtedness under the "Limitation on the Incurrence of Indebtedness" covenant (see Nutshell Section 36C(2)(a)) at the time the restricted payment is made, having given pro-forma effect to that payment; and

(c) the restricted payment, together with all previous restricted payments, is less than the sum of (1) a percentage (typically 50%) of the issuer's net income for the period from the date the debt securities in question were issued until its most recently ended fiscal quarter and (2) a percentage (typically 100%) of the aggregate net cash proceeds received during that same period from the issuance of equity securities or the conversion of convertible debt securities into equity securities.

In essence, the covenant would allow the issuer to make a restricted payment if the issuer is in good financial health and the payment in question is reasonable in amount.

Certain restricted payments are always allowed even if the conditions above are not met. For example, the issuer is allowed to make a restricted payment with the net proceeds from a common stock offering, so long as the two events occur substantially concurrently. Additionally, the issuer is allowed to pay a dividend within 60 days of its declaration date even if, at the time of payment, the issuer no longer complies with the conditions above (due to, for example, an intervening net loss). See generally MNCRD § 4.05.

### c.   Asset Sales

This covenant prohibits an issuer from selling substantial assets unless (a) no default or event of default exists, (b) the issuer receives consideration for the assets at least equal to the fair market value (as determined in good faith by the issuer's board) of the assets sold, and (c) a high percentage (typically 70 to 90%) of the consideration received is cash or cash equivalents. To the extent the asset purchaser assumes liabilities of the issuer as part of the transaction, the amount assumed is typically deemed to be "cash" for purposes of clause (c) above.

The covenant captures sales of assets outside the ordinary course of business, and thus covers the issuer's sale of any shares of capital stock of a restricted subsidiary or all or substantially all of the assets of any *division* or *line of business* of the issuer or any restricted subsidiary. Sales of assets less than a specified de minimus amount ($500,000 is typical) are usually carved-out from the covenant altogether. Any asset sale that constitutes a sale of "all or substantially all" of the issuer's assets (as opposed to a division or line of business) is covered by the "Merger, Consolidation or Sale of All or Substantially All of the Issuer's Assets" covenant described below in Nutshell Section 36C(2)d.

Importantly, while the covenant does place restrictions on how assets are sold, its main purpose is to actually specify *how* the issuer is to *use the proceeds* in the event the issuer does sell assets. The covenant typically prohibits the issuer from selling income producing assets unless the proceeds are either reinvested in revenue-producing assets or used to permanently repay senior indebtedness. If the issuer fails to redeploy all the proceeds for those purposes within a specified period of time (usually one year after the later of the sale of the assets or the receipt of the proceeds), then the issuer must offer to buy back a portion of the debt securities in question (sometimes at a small premium) with the remaining proceeds. See generally MNCRD § 4.06.

### d.   Merger, Consolidation or Sale of All or Substantially All of the Issuer's Assets

This covenant prevents the issuer from consolidating, merging or selling all or substantially all of its assets to any other person unless certain conditions are met. These conditions may include: (1) the issuer must be the surviving entity or, if not, the surviving entity must be a company existing under the laws of the United States or any of its states; (2) the surviving entity (if not the issuer) must assume all of the issuer's obligations under the indenture pursuant to a supplemental indenture or otherwise; (3) the net worth of the issuer or, if the issuer is not the surviving entity, the surviving entity after the transaction must not be less than the issuer's net worth prior to the transaction; (4) immediately after the transaction no default or event of default must exist; and (5) the issuer or, if the issuer is not the surviving entity, the surviving entity must, at the time of the transaction and after giving pro forma effect thereto, be permitted to incur at least $1.00 of additional indebtedness under the "Limitation on the Incurrence of Indebtedness" covenant. See Nutshell Section 36C(2)a.

The main purpose of this covenant is to restrict the issuer from engaging in a reorganization in which either the issuer does not survive or the surviving entity is financially weaker than the issuer. Additionally, this covenant prevents the surviving entity from purchasing the issuer's assets without also assuming the indebtedness related to the debt securities in question. Because of this covenant, the debt securities must follow the assets that produce the revenue needed to service them. See generally MNCRD § 4.14.

*Sharon Steel Corp. v. Chase Manhattan Bank*, 691 F.2d 1039 (2d Cir.1982), involved the interpretation of a "successors provision" found in various indentures of UV Industries. Each provision provided that UV Industries could merge or consolidate with, or sell all or substantially all of its assets to, another company so long as that company promised to pay principal, interest and any premium on the debt, agreed to adhere to all covenants, and entered into a supplemental indenture with the indenture trustee.

The Second Circuit viewed the successors provision as "boilerplate." That is, interpretation of that provision did not depend on the particularized intentions of the parties. Accordingly, whether the transaction being litigated satisfied the "successors provisions" of the various indentures was an issue of law for the court to decide rather than an issue of fact for a jury. According to the Court, an important policy goal in this regard is uniformity of interpretation of standard provisions found in virtually all indentures. Uniform interpretation is essential to the efficiency of the capital markets.

### e.　Dividend and Other Payment Restrictions on Subsidiaries

This covenant typically appears when a holding company is the issuer of debt securities. In this event, the holding company is dependent on its subsidiaries up-streaming the cash necessary for it to service those securities. Thus, this covenant prohibits the issuer (holding company) and its subsidiaries from entering into any contract or arrangement that could impede the subsidiaries from up-streaming cash or other assets to the holding company, whether in the form of dividends, loans or other property transfers. Encumbrances that are contained in refinancing agreements and that are not more restrictive than those in the debt being refinanced are typically carved-out from this covenant. See generally MNCRD § 4.12.

### f.　Limitation on the Sale or Issuance of Stock of Subsidiaries

This covenant is important when the issuer of the debt securities owns one or more wholly-owned subsidiaries. In that case, the issuer has complete control over the flow of cash between those subsidiaries and itself. The debt security holders under-

standably are concerned about the issuer losing its
flexibility in this regard, as would be the case were
the issuer to sell a portion of the stock of those
subsidiaries to newly-created minority shareholders.
Indeed, corporate law dictates that the boards of the
subsidiaries would then owe fiduciary duties to
those minority shareholders, thus impeding the issuer's ability to make investments into and take
dividends out of those subsidiaries. Thus, the covenant generally prohibits the issuer from selling
stock it owns in its wholly-owned subsidiaries and
those subsidiaries from issuing stock to third parties. Often, the covenant will only apply to wholly-
owned subsidiaries owned by the issuer on the date
the debt securities in question were sold. See generally MNCRD § 4.10.

### g.  Transactions with Affiliates

This covenant is designed to ensure that the
issuer does not circumvent the "Restricted Payments" covenant (see Nutshell Section 36C(2)b) by
disguising dividend-like transactions with affiliates
as legitimate business transactions. Thus, the covenant requires that the issuer bargain on an arms'-
length basis with its affiliates. In essence, this covenant prevents sweetheart deals between the issuer
and affiliates—such as a controlling stockholder—
which siphon off funds of the issuer that otherwise
could be used to service the debt securities in question. Often, this covenant contains transactional
dollar thresholds which can only be surpassed with

the explicit good faith approval of the issuer's disinterested directors and/or upon receipt of an opinion of an investment banking, appraisal or accounting firm that the terms of the transaction are fair to the issuer. See generally MNCRD § 4.09.

### h.    Restrictions on Liens

This covenant typically appears when the issuer has issued secured (collateralized) debt securities. The covenant prohibits the issuer from placing additional liens on its assets unless certain conditions are met. It protects the holders of the secured debt securities by minimizing the likelihood that other creditors will have liens on the same assets as those holders. Additionally, this covenant controls whether any additional indebtedness that the issuer is allowed to incur pursuant to the "Limitation on the Incurrence of Indebtedness" covenant (see Nutshell Section 36C(2)a) may itself be secured.

Certain exceptions to this covenant (so-called *permitted liens*) are typically negotiated. These may include: (1) liens in favor of the issuer; (2) liens on the assets of companies that are merged into the issuer that were in existence prior to the merger, so long as those liens do not automatically attach to the issuer's assets; (3) pledges and deposits under worker's compensation and unemployment insurance laws; (4) liens imposed by statutory law (*e.g.*, carriers', warehousemen's and mechanics' liens, etc.); (5) liens securing the debt securities in question; (6) liens securing additional indebtedness allowed to be incurred under the "Limitation on the Incurrence of Indebtedness" covenant (see Nutshell Section 36C(2)a); (7) liens for taxes; and (8) other liens of the issuer in existence on the issuance date of the debt securities in question. See generally MNCRD § 4.08.

### i. Limitation on Sale–Leaseback Transactions

This covenant generally only appears in debt offerings involving senior notes. A sale-leaseback transaction is very similar to a secured financing. In such a transaction, the issuer sells a significant asset (*e.g.,* the issuer's headquarters) and immediately leases it back. Because the issuer will receive sale proceeds (similar to loan proceeds) and will make rental payments over the life of the lease (similar to loan repayments), the resemblance to secured financing is spot on. This covenant, therefore, generally permits an issuer to enter into a sale-leaseback transaction so long as (a) the issuer has the ability to incur the related indebtedness represented by the lease obligation pursuant to the "Limitation on the Incurrence of Indebtedness" covenant (see Nutshell Section 36C(2)a), (b) the proceeds received equal the fair market value of the asset being sold, as determined by the issuer's board of directors, (c) the issuer would be able to incur the lien on the asset securing the lease under the "Restrictions on Liens" covenant (see Nutshell Section 36C(2)h), and (d) the proceeds are used in accordance with the "Asset Sales" covenant (see Nutshell Section 36C(2)c), since as a technical matter the asset is being sold and will no longer be part of the issuer's consolidated assets following the sale (unlike in the case of a secured financing). See generally MNCRD § 4.11.

### j. SEC Reports

This covenant requires the issuer, whether or not it is a reporting company under the Exchange Act, to make regular SEC reports to ensure the steady flow of readily accessible information for current debt security holders and prospective holders. It requires timely filing of SEC reports as opposed to providing those reports to debt security holders once the reports have been filed. Issuers that find it necessary to restate earnings and thus are unable to make their filings on a timely basis are in technical default of this covenant. See generally MNCRD § 4.13.

### k. Line of Business

An indenture may include a covenant that prohibits the issuer from engaging in any business activity other than those specified in the indenture. Thus, this covenant is of the "devil you know is better than the one you don't know" variety.

## D. Redemption

The indenture relating to a particular issuance of debt securities may provide for optional and/or mandatory redemption of those securities by the issuer prior to their maturity date. Debt securities called for redemption no longer earn interest beyond the date the issuer fixes for redemption. After that date, debt holders are only entitled to receive the redemption price from the issuer. Therefore, debt holders have an incentive to turn in their debt securities on or before any redemption date. See *Rudbart v. North Jersey District Water Supply Commission*, 605 A.2d 681 (N.J. 1992).

### (1) Optional Redemption

The contractual right to pay off debt securities prior to their maturity is something most issuers seek, and against which most investors fight. When interest rates fall, an issuer may seek to refinance existing debt with lower interest rate debt. Doing so, however, prevents existing debt holders from continuing to receive their now above-market return. Indeed, if existing debt holders are paid off early, any newly-issued debt securities they purchase with the proceeds will be lower yielding than their previous investment.

Indentures ordinarily contain a compromise. The issuer receives the ability to redeem its debt securities early, but only after a period of years transpires during which redemption is prohibited. This period of years is referred to as the debt holders' *call protection*, because the issuer is prohibited from "calling away" the debt securities from the debt holders during this period. Thereafter, the issuer has the option of redeeming some or all of the securities at a *premium* (the "redemption premium") that declines to zero over subsequent years, plus accrued and unpaid interest (if any) to the date of redemption. Importantly, an issuer cannot voluntarily trigger a default under the indenture in an attempt to avoid paying the redemption premium. See *Sharon Steel Corp. v. Chase Manhattan Bank*, 691 F.2d 1039 (2d Cir. 1982).

For example, the indenture for 20–year debentures might provide the issuer with the ability to redeem those debentures in accordance with the following schedule and at the following prices:

| | |
|---|---|
| Years 1–3 . . . . . . | Call Protection (no redemption allowed) |
| Years 4–7 . . . . . . | 103% of principal (3% premium) |
| Years 8–11 . . . . . | 102% of principal (2% premium) |
| Years 12–14 . . . | 101% of principal (1% premium) |
| Years 15–20 . . . | 100% of principal (no premium) |

Another type of call protection arises when an indenture allows for optional redemption, but specifies that debt securities cannot be redeemed with the proceeds from the issuer's incurrence of new, *lower* interest rate debt. Such was the case in *Morgan Stanley v. Archer Daniels Midland Co.*, 570 F.Supp. 1529 (S.D.N.Y.1983). Archer Daniels Midland Co. (ADM) had issued sinking fund debentures that could be redeemed early at the redemption prices specified in the debenture indenture. A restrictive proviso, however, provided that during an initial ten-year period, ADM could not redeem the debentures if the proceeds used for redemption came from its incurrence of cheaper debt (*i.e.,* debt with a lower interest rate than that of the debentures). Thus, if interest rates fell during this period, ADM could not refinance the debentures. However, it could redeem the debentures during this time with the proceeds from the sale of equity securities.

During this period, ADM raised substantial amounts of capital through two additional debt offerings, as well as through two offerings of common stock. The cost of the debt in both offerings was below that of the debentures. ADM then announced it was redeeming the debentures. Morgan Stanley had purchased debentures in the secondary market at a substantial premium just before the announcement. The prices it paid were substantially above the redemption price that ADM would be paying.

Morgan Stanley brought suit against ADM claiming that ADM was redeeming the debentures with the proceeds of cheaper debt in violation of the debenture indenture. It argued that ADM's two common stock offerings were an "irrelevant juggling of funds" used to circumvent the indenture provision. ADM countered by arguing the "source" rule. So long as it could point to a non-debt source of funds for the repayment of the debentures, the fact that it also raised funds through the incurrence of cheap debt was irrelevant.

The District Court agreed with ADM. Case law and the Model Debenture Indenture Provisions (MDIP) of the American Bar Foundation supported ADM's position. The language of the indenture's redemption provision also supported ADM's position, because the restrictive proviso relating to cheap debt followed a broad provision permitting redemption. Importantly, ADM had established a system whereby the proceeds of its two stock offerings could be *traced directly* to the repayment of the debentures.

### (2) Mandatory Redemption

Many indentures require an issuer to redeem some or all of the debt securities prior to their maturity upon the incurrence of certain events. For example, an indenture may require the issuer to offer to repurchase debt securities if the issuer's cash flow from operations is greater than a predetermined benchmark. Early redemption of some of the debt securities reduces the on-going risk associated with owning the debt securities by decreasing their average life.

Another mandatory redemption trigger stems from the "Asset Sales" covenant. If the issuer has not redeployed excess proceeds from asset sales within a specified period of time, it must offer to buy back debt securities with those excess proceeds. Holders of the debt securities need not accept that offer. See Nutshell Section 36C(2)c.

Another mandatory redemption trigger is a *change in control*. If a change in control (as discussed below) occurs, the issuer has to *offer to purchase* all the outstanding debt securities at a purchase price usually equal to 101% of their aggregate principal amount (*i.e.*, at a 1% premium), plus accrued and unpaid interest (if any) to the date of purchase. This change in control *"put,"* as it is often referred to, effectively forces a potential acquiror to either negotiate with the debt holders over how the debt securities will be treated in the overall transaction or face having to buy back all those securities at a small premium after acquiring control of the issuer.

Of course, a change in control put does not entitle the issuer to redeem the debt securities at its election. Indeed, if the issuer is required to make a change in control offer, the holders of the debt securities do not have to accept it. A big factor in their decision is the identity and creditworthiness of the prospective acquiror. If the acquiror is a larger, established and more creditworthy company than the issuer itself, then the acquiror's acquisition of the issuer is a "credit positive" event from the debt security holders' perspective. It is likely that they will ignore a change in control offer as their debt securities may likely be trading at a price higher than the change of control price of 101% of principal amount. This stems from the fact that traders in the secondary market will view the debt securities as less risky and thus discount their cash flow streams at a lower discount rate. See Nutshell Section 14C(2). If the debt security holders do not tender, then their securities will remain outstanding post-change in control unless the issuer makes a another tender offer for the debt securities (obviously at a higher price than 101% of principal amount) and all the debt security holders choose to tender. See generally MNCRD § 4.07.

"Change in control" is a carefully defined term. Ordinarily, several events qualify. They typically include:

(a) The sale of all or substantially all of the assets of the issuer (determined on a consolidated basis);

(b) Any person becomes the beneficial owner of a specified percentage (typically 25% to 35%) of the issuer's voting stock through a tender offer made to the issuer's public stockholders;

(c) The adoption of a plan relating to the liquidation or dissolution of the issuer;

(d) Any time that a majority of the issuer's board of directors is not comprised of *continuing directors*. Continuing directors are members of the board on the issuance date of the debt securities and any subsequent members of the board who can trace their nominations back to those members. Thus, a director nominated by a third party (*e.g.*, a hostile party engaging in a proxy fight) would *not* qualify as a continuing director; and

(e) The merger or consolidation of the issuer with or into another person, or the merger of another person with or into the issuer. Excluded is a transaction following which holders of securities that represented 100% of the voting stock of the issuer immediately prior to such transaction own directly or indirectly at least a majority of the voting power of the voting stock of the surviving person immediately after such transaction and in substantially the same proportion as before the transaction.

In situations where a controlling stockholder exists on the issuance date of the debt securities (as is often the case when the issuer is a privately-held company), the "change in control" definition often includes the consummation of any transaction resulting in any person or group holding more of the issuer's voting stock than is owned by the controlling stockholder. See generally MNCRD § 1.01.

### E. Events of Default

(1) Generally

All debt indentures specify *events of default* and discuss the consequences of the occurrence of such an event. See generally RMSI § 6.01. The following events typically fall within that definition:

### a. Default in the Payment of Interest or Principal

The failure of an issuer to make a scheduled interest or principal payment (referred to as a *payment default*) is the most fundamental event of default. A grace period may attach to a default on an interest payment (typically 30 days), but not on a principal payment.

### b. Breach of a Covenant, Warranty or Representation

An issuer's breach of any of its covenants, warranties or representations (a *non-payment default*) qualifies as an event of default. The issuer is usually given a grace period (typically 30 days) to state in writing that it will cure the breach.

A non-payment default, however, does not constitute a true event of default until the trustee gives notice to the issuer. Alternatively, the holders of a significant percentage (typically at least 25%) in principal amount of the debt securities may notify both the issuer and the trustee, of the default and the issuer does not cure the default, or it is not waived, within a specified number of days (typically 60) after receipt of the notice.

### c. Bankruptcy/Insolvency

An involuntary order or decree resulting in an issuer's bankruptcy or insolvency and a voluntary filing of a bankruptcy petition by the issuer both constitute an event of default. The same is true when the issuer consents to the appointment of a custodian or makes a general assignment of its assets for the benefit of creditors. Also, an event of default occurs when a court orders the liquidation of the issuer and that order remains unstayed and in effect for 60 days.

When the issuer is involved in an involuntary insolvency (*i.e.,* one commenced by the issuer's creditors), the issuer typically has a grace period (normally 60 consecutive days) before this event becomes an event of default. This gives the issuer time to attempt to have the proceeding dismissed. If the issuer voluntarily engages in an insolvency proceeding, however, the issuer is immediately in default under the terms of the indenture.

### d.   Cross–Default

An indenture may contain a *cross-default provision*. This provision provides that any default by the issuer under any *other* agreement evidencing indebtedness generally constitutes an event of default under the indenture for the debt securities in question. If an issuer triggers the cross-default provision, the indenture trustee can take action even if those debt securities are not otherwise in default.

### (2)   Acceleration

If an event of default occurs and is continuing, the indenture trustee, by notice to the issuer, or the holders of a significant percentage (typically at least 25%) in principal amount of the debt securities, by notice to both the issuer and the indenture trustee, may declare the principal of, and accrued and unpaid interest on, all the debt securities to be *immediately due and payable.* This is known as the *acceleration* of the debt. See generally RMSI § 6.02.

<h1 style="text-align:center">§ 37.  LEGAL TREATMENT<br>OF DEBT HOLDERS</h1>

## A.  Fiduciary Duties

### (1) Generally

Corporate directors owe common stockholders fiduciary duties because stockholders generally have no "contract" with the corporation protecting their rights. Thus, they must rely on their agents—the directors—to protect their interests. Corporate debt holders, by contrast, do have a contract with the corporate issuer. Under the so-called *bond doctrine,* the rights of debt holders are determined by their indenture. Accordingly, corporate directors normally do not owe fiduciary duties to debt holders, even those holding debt securities convertible into common stock of the corporation. This was made amply clear in *Simons v. Cogan,* 549 A.2d 300 (Del.1988).

In *Simons,* a convertible debenture holder sued for the loss of her ability to convert her debentures into the stock of the issuer. Due to a merger between the issuer and another company, the terms of the debentures were changed so that each debenture thereafter could only be converted into a designated cash amount. The plaintiff brought suit against the issuer's directors and its controlling stockholder. Her main allegation was that the defendants breached their fiduciary duty to the debenture holders by terminating their right to convert the debentures into the common stock of the issuer.

The Delaware Supreme Court, however, disagreed with the plaintiff. Picking up on the Delaware Chancery Court's reasoning in *Harff v. Kerkorian*, 324 A.2d 215 (Del.Ch.1974), the Court held that the debenture holders stand as "creditors" of the corporation with their rights determined by their indenture. The fact that the debentures in question were convertible into equity of the issuer does not change this conclusion. According to the Court, until the convertible debentures are converted into equity, the convertibility feature itself does not impart an equity element to the debentures. The convertibility feature is a mere "expectancy interest" which does not create the type of trust relationship that can support the imposition of fiduciary duties. See also *Anadarko Petroleum Corp. v. Panhandle Eastern Corp.*, 545 A.2d 1171 (Del.1988).

The Court, however, noted that the Delaware Chancery Court in *Harff* had created an exception to the bond doctrine. The *Harff* court held that debenture holders could seek recovery apart from the debenture provisions whenever "special circumstances" are found. These special circumstances include fraud, insolvency or violation of a statute. When those circumstances are present, a court can look "beyond the four corners" of the indenture when granting relief.

But the Delaware Supreme Court in *Simons* took issue with *Green v. Hamilton Int'l Corp.*, 76 Civ. 5433 (S.D.N.Y., July 31, 1981), an unreported case in which the District Court interpreted the "special circumstances" language of *Harff* very broadly. The *Green* court held that a cause of action for breach of fiduciary duty could lie apart from the terms of the debenture indenture. Furthermore, it stated that convertible debenture holders were part of the entire community of interests in a corporation—creditors as well as stockholders—to whom the fiduciary duties of directors and controlling stockholders ran. However, the Delaware Supreme Court in *Simons* stated that the *Green* court "misperceive[d] the type of interest required for the imposition of fiduciary duties" due to that court's reliance on the expectancy interest created by the conversion feature of the debenture in question.

    (2) Actual Insolvency and the "Zone" of Insolvency

       a.  History

Insolvency, one of the "special circumstances" referred to in *Harff v. Kerkorian*, 324 A.2d 215 (Del.Ch.1974), "can do curious things to incentives, exposing creditors to opportunistic behavior and creating complexities for [corporate] directors," stated Chancellor Allen in *Credit Lyonnais Bank Nederland, N.V. v. Pathe Communications Corp.*, 1991 WL 277613 (Del.Ch.). In this famous opinion, Chancellor Allen continued:

> [W]here a corporation is operating in the *vicinity of insolvency*, a board of directors is not merely the agent of the residual risk bearers, but owes a duty to the corporate enterprise.... [The management] had an obligation to the community of interests that sustained the corporation, to exercise judgment in an informed, good faith effort to maximize the corporation's long-term wealth creating capacity. (Emphasis added.)

See also *Pepper v. Litton*, 308 U.S. 295 (1939) (discussed in Nutshell Section 38D(6)); *Geyer v. Ingersoll Publications Company*, 621 A.2d 784 (Del.Ch. 1992).

Chancellor Allen's apparent extension of fiduciary duties to creditors when a corporation is operating in the "vicinity of insolvency" (referred to subsequently as the "*zone of insolvency*") was never fully addressed by the Delaware Supreme Court until 2007. Thus, great uncertainty existed in this area until 2007.

### b. Insolvency Entitles Creditors to Sue Derivatively

In *North American Catholic Educational Programming Foundation v. Gheewalla*, 930 A.2d 92

(Del.2007), the Delaware Supreme Court weighed in on the "zone of insolvency" debate. The case involved the North American Catholic Educational Programming Foundation (the "Foundation"). In March 2001, the Foundation, along with certain other independent networks and foundations, entered into a contract with Clearwire, a company primarily financed by Goldman Sachs. The contract called for the Foundation and the others to sell their FCC-approved licenses for microwave signal transmission ("spectrum") to Clearwire for approximately $24.3 million. Clearwire's stated goal was to create a "national system of wireless connections to the internet." However, after the agreement was entered into, Worldcom announced its dire accounting problems, and it soon became clear that there would be a "surplus of spectrum" available to purchase from Worldcom. Having ultimately paid only $2 million to the Foundation and the others, Clearwire sought to end its obligations under the contract.

While the others settled with Clearwire, the Foundation held out and sued Clearwire. Among other things, the Foundation alleged that Clearwire was at all relevant times either *insolvent* or in the *zone of insolvency*. According to the Delaware Chancery Court, "*insolvency*" could be demonstrated in at least the following two ways:

> (1) Show a "deficiency of assets below liabilities with no reasonable prospect that the

> business can be successfully continued in the face thereof''; or
>
> (2) Show "an inability to meet maturing obligations as they fall due in the ordinary course of business."

The Chancery Court determined that the Foundation had alleged facts satisfactory to create a reasonable inference that Clearwire had operated within the "zone of insolvency" during at least a portion of the relevant time periods and had actually been "insolvent" during at least another portion of the relevant time periods.

The Foundation also alleged that, in light of the insolvency determination, the directors of Clearwire owed the Foundation, as a substantial creditor of Clearwire, *fiduciary duties.* These directors breached these allegedly owed fiduciary duties, according to the Foundation, by: (a) failing to preserve the assets of Clearwire for its benefit and that of its creditors when it became apparent that Clearwire was not able to continue as a going-concern and would need to be liquidated; and (b) holding on to the Foundation's spectrum licenses when Clearwire would not be using them, solely to keep Goldman Sach's investment "in play."

Before weighing in on the "zone of insolvency" issue, the Delaware Supreme Court noted the litany of ways in which creditors are already protected under the law. Indeed, creditors are protected most notably through their agreement. Moreover, they benefit from a variety of creditor-oriented law, including fraud and fraudulent conveyance law, bankruptcy law, general commercial law and other sources of creditor rights. Because of this, the Delaware Supreme Court noted that Delaware courts have generally been reluctant to expand existing fiduciary duties to cover creditors.

Not surprisingly, therefore, the Delaware Supreme Court held that directors *do not owe fiduciary duties* to creditors when the corporation in question is operating in the "zone of insolvency." Affirming the Chancery Court's ruling, the Delaware Supreme Court reasoned that "an otherwise solvent corporation operating in the zone of insolvency is one in most need of effective and proactive leadership—as well as the *ability to negotiate* in good faith with its creditors—goals which would likely be significantly undermined by the prospect of individual [director] liability arising from the pursuit of direct claims by creditors." (Emphasis added). The Court added that "[w]hen a solvent corporation is navigating in the zone of insolvency, *the focus for Delaware directors does not change*: directors must discharge their fiduciary duties to the corporation and its shareholders by exercising their business judgment in the best interests of the corporation *for the benefit of its shareholder owners*." (Emphasis added.)

Things change, however, when the corporation actually becomes insolvent. The Court noted that when a corporation is insolvent, creditors take the place of shareholders as the residual beneficiaries of any increase in value in the corporation. Thus, *creditors* are the principal constituency injured by any fiduciary breaches that diminish a corporation's value at that time. Accordingly, the Court held that creditors of an *insolvent corporation* have standing to maintain *derivative claims* against directors *on behalf of the corporation* for breaches of fiduciary duty. However, the Court refused to allow creditors to sue *directly* for fiduciary breaches. Allowing a *direct claim*, according to the Court, would conflict with a director's duty to maximize the value of the insolvent corporation for the benefit of all those having an interest in it. "Directors of insolvent corporations must retain the freedom to engage in vigorous, good faith negotiations with individual creditors for the benefit of the corporation."

Other states have begun to follow the reasoning in *Gheewalla*, and have rejected claims made by creditors of corporations operating in the "zone of insolvency." In *RSL Communications PLC v. Bildirici*, 649 F.Supp. 2d 184 (S.D.N.Y.2009), the District Court, applying New York law, rejected a creditor's claim that the defendant corporate directors breached a fiduciary duty to creditors while operating within the "zone of insolvency." The Court followed the reasoning of *Gheewalla*, and concluded that allowing creditor claims based on a duty of care in a pre-insolvency context would provide redundant protections to creditors, and confuse directors' allocation of their duties during that time. In particular, the Court agreed with the Delaware Supreme Court that creditors can protect themselves contractually and take advantage of laws designed to protect creditors, including fraudulent transfer law.

The Court also highlighted the problem with deciding *when* a given corporation entered the "zone of insolvency" (as opposed to becoming insolvent). If corporate directors were to owe fiduciary duties to creditors when the corporation entered that zone, then the zone itself must be properly defined.

### c. Exculpatory Charter Provision Works Against Creditors

Although creditors can now bring derivative lawsuits when the company in question is insolvent, this does not mean that they are afforded any additional rights in this regard as compared to stockholders bringing those suits. In *Production Resources Group, L.L.C. v. NCT Group, Inc.*, 863 A.2d 772 (Del.Ch.2004), a case which predates *Gheewalla*, the creditor plaintiffs alleged, among other claims, that the defendant directors breached their fiduciary duties to the insolvent corporation, and, by extension, owed fiduciary duties to the corporation's creditors. They further argued that these alleged breaches should not be exculpated by virtue of the exculpatory charter provision contained in the corporation's charter (adopted pursuant to Section 102(b)(7) of the DGCL).

The Delaware Chancery Court held that "insolvency does not change the primary object of the director's duties, which is the firm itself." While insolvency expands the standing of those who can sue derivatively on a corporation's behalf to include creditors, "the claim against the director is still one belonging to the corporation." The Court held that the exculpatory protections of Section 102(b)(7) work against *all* derivative claims for breaches of the duty of care, even if brought by creditors of an insolvent corporation. According to the Court, "[a]lthough § 102(b)(7) itself does not mention creditors specifically, its plain terms apply to all claims belonging to the corporation itself, regardless of whether those claims are asserted derivatively by stockholders or by creditors."

## B.  Implied Covenant of Good Faith and Fair Dealing

Absent special circumstances (see Nutshell Section 37A), corporate directors do not have fiduciary duties running in favor of debt holders. The rights of debt holders are contractual and are set forth in their indentures. Courts, of course, are called upon to interpret language in indentures from time to time. They also are called upon to resolve issues that arise but are not covered by contractual language. Indeed, a given indenture cannot possibly cover all contingencies that may arise during the life of the securities to which it relates.

When a dispute arises that is not covered by a debt indenture, a disgruntled debt holder often invokes the "implied covenant of good faith and fair dealing" to get her way. The goal behind this covenant, however, is solely to preserve the benefit of the parties' bargain. Indeed, the covenant, according to the Delaware Supreme Court, "requires a party in a contractual relationship to refrain from arbitrary or unreasonable conduct which has the effect of preventing the other party to the contract from receiving the fruits of the bargain." *Dunlap v. State Farm Fire & Cas. Co.*, 878 A.2d 434 (Del. 2005) (internal quotation omitted). Thus, a court attempts to determine how the parties negotiating at "arms'-length" would have resolved the issue in question had they thought about it in the first place. Judicial clarification of this covenant is found in *Katz v. Oak Industries*, 508 A.2d 873 (Del.Ch. 1986), and *Metropolitan Life Insurance Co. v. RJR Nabisco, Inc.*, 716 F.Supp. 1504 (S.D.N.Y.1989).

*Katz* involved Oak Industries ("Oak"), a company experiencing severe financial problems. Oak ultimately located Allied–Signal as a prospective strategic partner. The two companies entered into an acquisition agreement, whereby Oak would sell its materials business to Allied–Signal for much needed cash. They also entered into a stock purchase agreement, whereby Allied–Signal would infuse needed capital into Oak in exchange for common stock and warrants to purchase common stock. The stock purchase agreement, however, was conditioned on holders of at least 85% of the aggregate principal amount of all of Oak's six classes of debt securities tendering into and accepting Oak's exchange offers. In other words, Allied–Signal would not invest in Oak unless Oak first restructured its balance sheet.

One of Oak's exchange offers—a payment certificate exchange offer—was open to holders of all six classes of Oak's debt securities. Tendering debt holders would receive a payment certificate redeemable for cash five days after the closing of the sale of Oak's materials business to Allied–Signal. Although the value of the payment certificate varied depending on the type of debt held by a given debt holder, the value of each certificate was less (sometimes substantially less) than the $1,000 principal amount of each of the six classes of debt securities.

The payment certificate exchange offer was conditional. One of those conditions was that a specified minimum amount of each class of debt securities had to be tendered into the offer. In addition, each tender had to be accompanied by the debt holder's consent to amendments to the indenture underlying his debt security. These amendments had the effect of (1) removing from each indenture significant negotiated debt holder protections, including the deletion of all financial covenants, and (2) circumventing the provisions in the indentures that prohibited exchange offers outright.

The plaintiff debt holder believed Oak's "tender and consent" requirement was coercive. If he did not tender and consent with respect to his securities, he would be left holding unsaleable, unsecured debt obligations of Oak governed by an indenture without any protective financial covenants. While the linkage between the exchange offer and the consent solicitation did not violate any explicit provision in Oak's debt indentures, the plaintiff argued that the linkage violated Oak's implied covenant to act fairly and in good faith towards its debt holders.

In deciding this issue, the Delaware Chancery Court spelled out the appropriate legal test:

> [I]s it clear from what was expressly agreed upon that the parties who negotiated the express terms of the contract would have agreed to proscribe the act later complained of as a breach of the implied covenant of good faith— had they thought to negotiate with respect to that matter. If the answer is yes, then ... a court is justified in concluding that such act constitutes a breach [of the indenture].

Applying this test to the facts of the case, the Court determined that the linkage of the exchange offer to the consent solicitation did not breach the implied covenant of good faith for three reasons. First, it found nothing in Oak's conduct that would violate the reasonable expectations of those who negotiated the indentures on behalf of the debt holders. Second, it determined that nothing in the indentures implied that Oak could not offer an "inducement" to debt holders to give their consent to the amendments in question. Fashioning the exchange offer and consent solicitation in a way designed to encourage consents is not illegal per se, according to the Court. Finally, the Court did not see any conflict of interest in having tendering debt holders consent to amendments to the indentures even though those holders would no longer have a continuing interest in the debt securities. According to the Court, consents will be granted or withheld only by those with a "current" financial interest in the debt securities.

*Metropolitan Life Insurance Co. v. RJR Nabisco, Inc.*, 716 F.Supp. 1504 (S.D.N.Y.1989), involved the leveraged buy-out (LBO) of RJR Nabisco by the leveraged buy-out firm of Kohlberg Kravis Roberts & Co., better known as KKR. KKR's winning bid for the company was approximately $25 billion, or about $109 per share. This represented about a 100% premium over the per share price at which the company's stock had been trading before the company's announcement that it was for sale.

When news of the proposed LBO became public, the value of RJR Nabisco's public bonds, of which several classes were outstanding, plummeted in value. The additional debt that the company would incur as part of the LBO would make its financial viability questionable. Thus, the outstanding bonds became much more risky. This was underscored by the fact that two of the major bond rating agencies—S&P and Moody's—both downgraded those bonds from "investment grade" (which is the highest grade) to "speculative" or "junk" (which is the lowest grade). The price of the outstanding bonds, therefore, fell dramatically as the market began applying a much higher discount rate when valuing them. See Nutshell Section 14C(2).

Along with the significant ratings downgrade came a change in the identity of those who could own the RJR Nabisco bonds. Many institutional investors are prohibited by their governance documents from investing in "junk bonds." Therefore, when RJR Nabisco's bonds were downgraded, these institutional investors were forced to dump them, leading to additional downward pressure on the price of the bonds in the secondary market.

The plaintiff bondholders—two insurance companies—brought suit against RJR Nabisco alleging that its actions relating to the LBO drastically impaired the value of their bonds. According to the plaintiffs, RJR Nabisco had, in effect, "misappropriated" the value of those bonds to help finance the LBO and provide an enormous windfall to the company's stockholders. They argued that RJR Nabisco could not incur the new debt needed to buy out the stockholders at such a large premium unless it was willing to surrender its "investment grade" credit rating. By willingly doing so, therefore, RJR Nabisco consciously impaired the value of its bonds.

Although the plaintiffs' amended complaint contained nine counts, the District Court considered only two on competing motions for summary judgment and to dismiss the complaint. One of those counts alleged a breach of an implied covenant of good faith and fair dealing. Plaintiffs argued that RJR Nabisco had breached this covenant because it took actions which deprived them of the intended object of the indentures relating to their bonds, namely the purchase of "investment grade" securities.

The Court began its analysis with the explicit terms found within the four corners of the indentures. It did so because the implied covenant will only aid and further the explicit terms of the agreement. The covenant will never impose an obligation inconsistent with other terms of the contractual relationship.

According to the Court, the implied covenant is breached only when one party seeks to prevent the contract's performance or to withhold its benefit. The covenant ensures that parties to a contract perform the substantive, bargained-for terms of their agreement. Importantly, the covenant does not give a contracting party any rights inconsistent with those set out in the contract.

The plaintiffs did not persuade the Court, as it found that the main purpose of the indentures—the payment of interest and principal on the bonds—remained intact after the LBO. Accordingly, the plaintiffs were attempting to have the Court create additional benefits for which they did not bargain. While the Court would stand ready to enforce an implied covenant of good faith to ensure that the bargained-for rights of the parties were performed and upheld, it would not permit an implied covenant "to shoehorn into an indenture additional terms plaintiffs now wish they had included."

Supporting the Court's determination was the fact that the indentures did not prohibit RJR Nabisco from completing an LBO or otherwise incurring additional debt. Nor was there any restriction on the ability of the company to engage in a merger, consolidation, sale or conveyance, so long as any acquiror was a U.S. company and agreed to assume all of RJR Nabisco's debt. While the Court took notice of the fact that certain RJR Nabisco predecessor indentures did contain restrictive covenants that would have prevented the LBO, it highlighted the fact that the plaintiffs gave away these protections in exchange for other benefits when negotiating the successor indentures implicated in the case.

## C.  Right to Sue

### (1)  Direct Actions

Direct actions by debt holders against issuers for breach of the debt indenture can be broken down into two categories: (1) actions alleging payment defaults; and (2) actions alleging all other defaults (*i.e.*, non-payment defaults).

#### a.  Payment Defaults

In the context of *payment defaults*, any debt holder can bring a direct action against the issuer seeking payment of interest and/or principal. This right is protected by Section 316(b) of the Trust Indenture Act of 1939. (See Nutshell Section 35B(6)). Section 316(b) provides that the right of any debt holder to receive payment of principal and interest when due shall not be impaired or affected without the consent of such holder. Thus, provisions in the indenture to the contrary are ineffective. Accordingly, Section 508 of the MDIP and Section 6.07 of the RMSI allow for direct suits in the event of a payment default.

### b. Non-payment Defaults

With respect to *non-payment defaults*, the ability of a debt holder to bring a direct action against the issuer is severely limited by the *no-action rule*. While actual indenture provisions may vary, Section 507 of the MDIP and Section 6.06 of the RMSI set forth the standard no-action rule. Before a disgruntled debenture holder may bring an independent lawsuit under the indenture against the issuer, five things must occur:

(1) The debenture holder must give written notice to the indenture trustee of a continuing Event of Default (as defined in the indenture);

(2) Holders of at least 25% in principal amount of the outstanding debentures must make a written request to the trustee to institute proceedings in respect of such Event of Default;

(3) In its request to the trustee, the debenture holder must have offered to indemnify the trustee for costs and expenses;

(4) The trustee either (a) gives notice that it will not follow the debenture holder's request or (b) must have failed to institute any proceeding for 60 days [the RMSI re-

duces this to 15 to 30 days] after its receipt of such request; and

(5) Prior to the earlier of the date, if ever, on which the trustee delivers a notice denying the debenture holder's request or the expiration of the 60–day period, holders of a majority in principal amount of the debentures must not have given any inconsistent direction to the trustee.

The no-action rule serves two important purposes. First, it deters individual debenture holders from bringing lawsuits for unworthy or unjustifiable reasons, and thus minimizes issuer outlays to defend against such lawsuits. If a given lawsuit is indeed worthy, the disgruntled debenture holder will be able to entice holders of 25% of the principal amount of debentures to join in. This, of course, largely ignores the difficulty a widely-dispersed group of claimants has in communicating with each other and taking action collectively (referred to as a *collective action* problem).

Second, the no-action rule supports the "all for one, one for all" principle that seeks to promote equal, ratable treatment of all debenture holders. It also recognizes that the first line of defense for debenture holders is their agent—the trustee. As mentioned above, the "all for one, one for all" principle *does not apply* with respect to *payment defaults*. Individual debenture holders can always sue the issuer directly for missed interest and principal payments, even though a debenture holder who succeeds in securing a judgment against the issuer places other debenture holders at a disadvantage.

Case law amply underscores the efficacy of the no-action rule. In *Simons v. Cogan*, 549 A.2d 300 (Del.1988), a convertible debenture holder sued for the loss of her ability to convert her debentures into the stock of the issuer. Due to a merger between the issuer and another company, the terms of the debentures were changed so that each debenture thereafter could only be converted into a designated cash amount. Because no payment default had occurred, the Delaware Supreme Court held that the plaintiff had to satisfy the no-action provision of the indenture. Among other things, this provision required holders of 35% (not just 25% as in the MDIP) in principal amount of the debentures then outstanding to request the trustee to take action before a holder could bring an independent action.

In an attempt to side step the no-action provision, the plaintiff pointed to the indenture's provision on cumulative remedies. That provision stated that "no remedy in the indenture ... is intended to be exclusive of any other remedy...." The Court, however, rejected this argument. It held that the cumulative remedies provision was designed to allow debenture holders to seek relief for statutory violations or fraud apart from the indenture, not as a means of getting around the 35% no-action threshold.

Debenture holders may attempt to circumvent a no-action provision by demonstrating that the indenture trustee has a conflict of interest which would prevent it from properly representing their interests. In *Rabinowitz v. Kaiser–Frazer Corp.*, 111 N.Y.S.2d 539 (N.Y.Sup.Ct.1952), a plaintiff convertible debenture holder directly sued the issuer for a non-payment default despite the fact that he held less than one-eighth of 1% of the outstanding debentures. The plaintiff argued that the indenture trustee, a commercial bank, was not capable of protecting the debenture holders' interests. Therefore, similar to the *demand futility* concept in stockholder derivative actions, the plaintiff argued that making a demand on the trustee would be entirely "useless and futile."

The plaintiff highlighted that the trustee knew that the issuer was planning on selling substantially all of its assets to a third party. The indenture required the third party to enter into a supplemental indenture providing for the third party to assume the performance of all of the indenture provisions. The trustee failed to push for this. In addition, the plaintiff provided evidence that the trustee had made several loans both to the issuer and the third party, and thus had a conflict of interest. The trustee did not want to bite the hand that fed it by requiring the third party to do something the third party strongly preferred not to do.

In agreeing with the plaintiff that demand on the trustee was pointless, the New York Supreme Court pointed to the following language in *Campbell v. Hudson & Manhattan Railroad Co.*, 277 A.D. 731 (N.Y.App.Div.1951): "[If a trustee] acts in bad faith, or, abdicating its function with respect to the particular point in question, declines to act at all, bond holders for themselves and others similarly situated may bring a derivative action *in the right of the trustee*, rather than in their own individual rights as bondholders." (Emphasis added.) The Court found that the trustee had abdicated its functions as trustee due to its extensive conflicts of interest, and thus the no-action provision in the indenture was inoperative and inapplicable. Quoting *Farmers' Loan & Trust Co. v. Northern Pacific Railroad Co.*, 66 F. 169 (C.C.D. Wis.1895), the Court emphasized that "[a] trustee cannot be permitted to assume a position inconsistent with or in opposition to his trust. His duty is single, and he cannot serve two masters with antagonistic interests."

A similar situation arose in *Cypress Assoc., LLC v. Sunnyside Cogeneration Assoc. Project*, 2006 WL 4762880 (Del.Ch.). Here, under the loan agreement the debtor was contractually prohibited from amending any ancillary agreement to the loan agreement unless "[b]ondholders of eighty percent (80%) or more in aggregate principal amount of the Outstanding Bonds" consented, such consent not to be unreasonably withheld. The debtor sought to amend an ancillary agreement in a way that would adversely affect the plaintiff bondholder. That bondholder owned enough bonds to thwart the 80% approval requirement unilaterally. When it was clear that that bondholder would not consent to the amendment, the debtor attempted to do an end-around. Specifically, the debtor believed that the trustee in its own right could approve the amendment once the debtor proposed it. The debtor then secured letters of support from a majority, but not 80%, of the bondholders and promised to indemnify the trustee if the trustee agreed to the amendment, which the trustee did.

When the plaintiff bondholder brought suit to stop the implementation of the amendment, the debtor argued that the plaintiff could not proceed because it had failed to comply with the no-action provision in the bond indenture. The Delaware Chancery Court, however, disagreed. The Court highlighted that the plaintiff was not bringing a claim that would inure to the benefit of all bond-holders pro rata to their ownership, but rather seeking to vindicate rights essentially personal to it. It held:

> [T]he law is clear that no-action clauses ... do not present an insuperable barrier to all suits not brought in strict conformity with their terms. Rather, the law has read no-action claus-es as an important, but surmountable, barrier to suits. They may be overcome when it is plain that procession under the suit would be futile, a line of reasoning that draws on the law of [shareholder] derivative suits.

In light of this, the Court found that it would be futile for the plaintiff bondholder to ask a majority of the bondholders who disagree with it to join in a suit to declare an amendment that they supported invalid. While the Court noted that Utah law applied to the dispute, it asserted that a Utah court would likely follow Delaware precedent on this issue.

### (2) Derivative Actions

A debt holder's right to sue the corporate issuer of debt securities is primarily defined by the contract between that issuer and the debt holders. However, should debt holders and other creditors be entitled to bring a *derivative action* naming the issuer's directors as defendants? A derivative action is a legal action in which a *stockholder* sues in the corporation's name when its directors refuse to protect the corporation from harm or assert a claim belonging to the corporation. Generally, debt holders—even those holding debt securities convertible into the common stock of the issuer—do not have the legal right to bring a derivative action. Exceptions, however, exist.

The seminal case denying debt holders the right to bring a derivative action in Delaware is *Harff v. Kerkorian*, 324 A.2d 215 (Del.Ch.1974). Cf. *Brooks v. Weiser*, 57 F.R.D. 491 (S.D.N.Y.1972). In *Harff*, the plaintiff convertible subordinated debenture holders brought a purported derivative suit against the issuer and its controlling stockholder (who was also a director). The plaintiffs alleged that the controlling stockholder caused the issuer to declare and pay a large cash dividend to the issuer's common stockholders. This, according to the plaintiffs, depleted the issuer's cash reserves and thus impaired the value of the plaintiffs' conversion feature.

Section 327 of the DGCL addresses derivative suits. The Delaware Chancery Court interpreted it to say that stockholders alone may bring derivative actions. It pointed to long standing Delaware law providing that a plaintiff in a derivative action must be both an actual stockholder of the corporation and maintain his or her stock ownership throughout the litigation. Moreover, the Court highlighted that the plaintiffs in this case were creditors—*i.e.,* contract claimants. In this regard, the Court rejected the plaintiffs' argument that they were simply one step away from being stockholders (*i.e.,* they need only convert their debentures). According to the Court, "That a bond is convertible at the sole option of its holder into stock should no more affect its essential quality of being a bond than should the fact that cash is convertible into stock affect the nature of cash."

Delaware, however, does allow creditors to bring derivative claims on behalf of the corporation when that corporation is *insolvent.* In *North American Catholic Educational Programming Foundation v. Gheewalla,* 930 A.2d 92 (Del.2007), the Delaware Supreme Court held that when a corporation is insolvent, creditors take the place of shareholders as the residual beneficiaries of any increase in value in the corporation. Thus, creditors are the principal constituency injured by any directorial fiduciary breaches that diminish a corporation's value at that time. Accordingly, the Court held that creditors of an insolvent corporation have standing to maintain derivative claims against directors on behalf of the corporation for breaches of fiduciary duty. However, the Court refused to allow creditors to sue *directly* for fiduciary breaches. For more on *Gheewalla*, see Nutshell Section 37A(2).

In stark contrast with *Harff* is *Hoff v. Sprayregan*, 52 F.R.D. 243 (S.D.N.Y.1971). Here, the plaintiff convertible subordinated debenture holders of a publicly-traded corporate issuer brought a purported derivative action against two directors and senior officers of that issuer. The plaintiffs alleged the issuer entered into a "sweetheart" arrangement with a company affiliated with the two defendants. The arrangement granted the company warrants to purchase the issuer's stock at below market prices in exchange for the company arranging private financing for the issuer. The plaintiffs argued that this arrangement constituted fraud under the Exchange Act and represented "an unlawful diversion, gift and waste of the assets" of the issuer under state law.

Despite the fact that the plaintiffs had not yet converted their debentures into stock of the issuer when the arrangement was consummated, the District Court held that the plaintiffs had standing to sue derivatively. Plaintiffs had alleged a violation of the Exchange Act. Because Section 3(a)(11) of the

Exchange Act defines "equity security" to include convertible bonds, plaintiffs had standing to sue because their interest in the issuer's common stock was sufficient to satisfy the derivative suit requirements of the Federal Rules of Civil Procedure.

The Court, however, did not appear completely comfortable with its decision, and its holding has been viewed as an exception to the general rule. See, e.g., *Garbayo v. Chrome Data Corp.*, 2001 WL 34039495 (D.Or.). The Exchange Act defines "equity securities" broadly to further its policy of disclosure. Convertible debt securities are included within that definition to force issuers to provide investors with earnings and other information on a "fully diluted" basis (*i.e.*, as if all convertible securities had been converted into common stock). The definition was not designed to allow convertible debt holders to bootstrap their way into bringing derivative suits. Despite this, the Court notes that the plaintiffs had a "substantial investment" at stake in the issuer which was worth more than the 100 shares normally needed to bring a derivative claim.

Like the court in *Hoff*, the ALI's Principles of Corporate Governance is sympathetic to the convertible debt holders' plight. Section 7.02 of the ALI–PCG allows convertible debt holders to bring derivative actions, as a convertible security is included within the ALI's definition of "equity security." However, a convertible debt holder bringing a derivative suit "must be able to represent fairly and adequately the interests of the shareholders."

## § 38.  INSOLVENCY REORGANIZATION

### A.  Fraudulent Conveyance

A *fraudulent conveyance* occurs when a debtor conveys or transfers funds or assets for the purpose of defrauding its creditors. The third party that receives the funds or assets from the debtor typically provides little or no consideration in return. Both the Bankruptcy Code and state law invalidate these conveyances or transfers.

Section 548(a) of the Bankruptcy Code covers fraudulent conveyances that are made or incurred on or within two years before the date of the filing of the bankruptcy petition, whether they are either intentionally fraudulent or constructively fraudulent. Actual fraudulent intent is usually established through evidence that demonstrates a close relationship between the transferor and the transferee. When determining whether a transfer was constructively fraudulent, courts examine the adequacy of consideration for the transfer and the financial position of the debtor. A rebuttable presumption arises that a transfer is constructively fraudulent if certain indicia are found to exist. A bankruptcy trustee or the debtor itself (referred to as a *debtor-in-possession* or *DIP*) has the power under the Bankruptcy Code to recover for the benefit of the debtor's creditors any property fraudulently conveyed to third parties.

Section 544(b) of the Bankruptcy Code permits a bankruptcy trustee or DIP to attack a pre-bankruptcy transfer as fraudulent under *state law* as well. In pertinent part, Section 544(b) allows a trustee or DIP to void any transfer of the debtor's property or any obligation incurred by the debtor that is voidable under applicable state law by a creditor holding an unsecured claim. Acting as an unsecured creditor, a trustee or DIP who makes a successful claim through Section 544(b) can pursue remedies under applicable state law or the Bankruptcy Code.

State fraudulent transfer laws are modeled after either the Uniform Fraudulent Conveyance Act (1918) (UFCA) or the newer Uniform Fraudulent Transfer Act (1984) (UFTA). Section 5 of the UFCA is broad in scope and applies to all transfers of any property by any debtor for any purpose, provided that the debtor makes the transfer without fair consideration and is engaged or is about to engage in a business or transaction for which the property remaining in the debtor's hands after the transfer is an unreasonably small capital. Actual intent to defraud is not important to the inquiry.

The UFTA provides both an actual intent test and a constructive intent test. Section 4(a)(1) of the UFTA finds "actual intent" if there is intent to hinder, delay or defraud creditors. Section 4(a)(2) of the UFTA finds constructive intent when the seller does not receive reasonably equivalent value for the transferred assets and either (1) the seller's remaining assets are unreasonably small in relation to its business or (2) the seller intended to incur, or believed or reasonably should have believed that the seller would incur, debts beyond its ability to pay as those debts became due. Courts look to the balance sheet of a debtor corporation when determining whether a given transfer was intended to leave the corporation insolvent. The standards under Section 548(a)(1)(B) of the Bankruptcy Code are more embellished than those under the UFTA for determining whether a transfer is constructively fraudulent. Consideration must be given as to which law is best suited to invalidate a particular transfer.

## B. Overview of a Chapter 11 Proceeding

Chapter 11 of the Bankruptcy Code governs corporate reorganizations conducted through bankruptcy proceedings. During a Chapter 11 proceeding, the debtor, as DIP, generally continues to operate its business while it restructures its financial obligations. The debtor must file with the bankruptcy court a *plan of reorganization* within a specified period of time. The plan, if approved by the bankruptcy court, would enable a debtor to settle all of the claims and interests of its creditors and stockholders.

A Chapter 11 case is commenced when a petition is filed by the debtor or its creditors in the bankruptcy court. If the debtor files the petition (a *voluntary petition*), no formal adjudication is necessary. If creditors seek to force the debtor into bankruptcy against its will (an *involuntary petition*), Section 303(b)(1) requires three creditors holding noncontingent, undisputed claims of at least $13,475 in the aggregate to file the involuntary petition. This dollar amount is adjusted upwards every three years based on the Consumer Price Index for All Urban Consumers. See Bankruptcy Code § 104(b)(1). Upon commencement of a bankruptcy case, Sections 362 (automatic stay) and 541 (property of the estate) of the Bankruptcy Code are triggered. Section 362(a) imposes an automatic stay against creditors' attempts to collect monies from, or attach assets of, the debtor. Section 541 subjects all the debtor's property, wherever located and by whomever held, to the jurisdiction of the bankruptcy court.

Furthermore, upon commencement of a Chapter 11 case, Section 521 of the Bankruptcy Code requires that the debtor, among other things, file a list of creditors so that creditors may be notified of its bankruptcy filing. Section 342(a) then requires that appropriate notice of the bankruptcy filing be given to creditors.

Section 1102(a)(1) directs that the Office of the United States Trustee, a division of the United States Department of Justice, appoint a committee of unsecured creditors as soon as practicable after the commencement of the case. This committee represents the interests of all unsecured creditors. Among other things, it seeks to safeguard the assets of the debtor's estate and negotiates with the debtor regarding its Chapter 11 plan of reorganization. The committee serves an important role in Chapter

11 cases, as it is often impracticable for the debtor to negotiate with each unsecured creditor in a large case. Finally, Section 1102(b)(1) indicates that the committee will ordinarily consist of creditors holding the seven largest claims, so long as the committee is representative of the claims held by different types of unsecured creditors (*e.g.,* bondholders versus trade creditors) of the debtor's estate. If the committee cannot properly represent different types of unsecured creditors, then more than one committee will be formed.

Even after a bankruptcy proceeding is commenced, a strong presumption exists that the debtor's existing management should continue to run the business. A bankruptcy court will displace management and appoint a trustee only for cause (including fraud, dishonesty, mismanagement or incompetence) or if the court determines that the appointment of a trustee is in the best interest of creditors, equity security holders or other interested parties. See Bankruptcy Code § 1104(a).

During the first 120 days of a Chapter 11 case, the debtor normally has the exclusive right to file a plan of reorganization. The exclusive period may be extended or reduced "for cause." Thereafter, any creditor may file a competing plan. See Bankruptcy Code § 1121(b), (c) & (d).

A plan of reorganization generally designates classes of claims or interests, specifies which classes of claims and interests remain unaffected (*i.e.,* "*unimpaired*") by the plan, and explains the proposed treatment of any class of claims that is affected (*i.e.*, "*impaired*") by the plan. In Chapter 11, the debtor has 180 days from the date that its bankruptcy case was commenced to obtain the approval of its plan from the bankruptcy court and holders of each class of claims or interests that is impaired under the plan. If a trustee is appointed, the exclusive period is automatically terminated, and the trustee, debtor, creditors, the creditors' committee or other interested parties may file a plan of reorganization. See Bankruptcy Code § 1121(c).

In Chapter 11 cases, creditors and stockholders may vote to accept or reject a plan of reorganization, unless their claim or interest is subject to a bona fide dispute. Under Section 1126 of the Bankruptcy Code, if a class of creditors or equity holders is to receive nothing under the plan, it is deemed to have rejected the plan. If, however, a class is not "impaired" under the plan (*i.e.,* its legal rights remain unaltered (see Bankruptcy Code § 1124)), the class is deemed to have accepted it. An impaired class of creditors is deemed to have accepted the plan when, within such class, the holders of at least two-thirds in amount and a majority in number that actually vote approve the plan. An impaired class of equity holders is deemed to have accepted the plan when holders of at least two-thirds in amount of interests that actually vote approve the plan. Under certain circumstances, a bankruptcy court can confirm a plan over the objections of one or more impaired classes of creditors or stockholders. See Nutshell Section 38D(3) below.

Even if the plan is accepted by the requisite number and amount of creditors and stockholders, the bankruptcy court must nevertheless find that the plan meets the requirements of the Bankruptcy Code and applicable non-bankruptcy law before it can be confirmed.

## C. Pre–Packaged Bankruptcies

Many bankruptcies these days are *"pre-packaged"* in nature. Those holding interests or claims against a debtor company that will likely survive bankruptcy agree in advance to a reorganization plan. Once this has occurred, the debtor company files for Chapter 11 reorganization and proposes that the plan be approved by the court. Like a traditional bankruptcy, a pre-packaged bankruptcy still results in the extinguishment of the interests or claims that will not survive bankruptcy. However, by developing the bankruptcy plan in advance of the filing, the costs and expenses associated with the bankruptcy process are minimized.

Pre-packaged bankruptcies can and do come under fire by those who will receive nothing under the plan. *In re Zenith Electronics Corp.*, 241 B.R. 92 (Bankr. D. Del.1999), involved Zenith, an electronics company whose financial condition deteriorated substantially during the 1990s. In 1998, LGE, which was Zenith's controlling shareholder and also a major creditor, proposed a possible restructuring of Zenith's capital structure.

LGE first negotiated the plan with a special committee of Zenith's board of directors. After an agreement was reached with the special committee, LGE then negotiated it with a committee of Zenith's bondholders. After the bondholders' blessed the plan, a disclosure statement and proxy statement-prospectus were prepared and filed with the SEC. This disclosure statement was needed in order to solicit votes on the plan prior to Zenith's bankruptcy filing. After 11 months of discussions with the SEC, and after numerous amendments had been made to the disclosure statement, the SEC approved it. After the bondholders and certain other creditors had overwhelmingly voted in favor of the plan, Zenith filed its Chapter 11 petition for bankruptcy reorganization.

Zenith's common stockholders (other than LGE), through the equity committee, attempted to block the Bankruptcy Court's confirmation of the plan on two grounds. First, the committee believed that the disclosure statement did not provide adequate information to those receiving it. However, under Section 1126(b) of the Bankruptcy Code, any holder of a claim or interest that has accepted or rejected the plan *before* the commencement of the bankruptcy case is deemed to have accepted or rejected the plan *for purposes of the case* if either: (1) the solicitation was in compliance with any applicable *non-bankruptcy* law, rule, or regulation governing the adequacy of disclosure in connection with such solicitation; or (2) if no such law, rule, or regulation exists, such acceptance or rejection was solicited after disclosure to such holder of adequate information as defined in the Bankruptcy Code. In light of the fact that the SEC had reviewed the disclosure statement based on the Federal securities laws, the Bankruptcy Court held that the disclosure statement did, in fact, provide adequate information.

Second, the equity committee challenged the bankruptcy plan on the grounds that it was not fair and equitable. See Nutshell Section 38D(3). In this regard, the equity committee challenged the plan in several respects. It alleged that the plan discriminated unfairly against stockholders because, in a true cramdown scenario, the bondholders would have received *nothing*. However, the plan offered bondholders $50 million of 8.19% Senior Debentures but only if they voted in favor of it. Because the stockholders were not offered a similar deal, the equity committee complained that the plan was not fair and equitable. The Bankruptcy Court, however, highlighted that the Bankruptcy Code does not prohibit a plan's proponents from offering *different treatment* to a class depending on whether it votes to accept or reject the plan. Because a cramdown fight is expensive and fraught with uncertainty, the Court believed it was not irrational for a plan's proponents to make such an offer in order to induce the plan's acceptance.

The equity committee also argued that the plan violated the absolute priority rule by allowing LGE under the plan to obtain the stock of Zenith without subjecting the stock to a sale on the open market. However, the Bankruptcy Court disagreed, noting that the opportunity to purchase new equity interests in Zenith were presented only to those with priority over the stockholders. This was entirely consistent with the absolute priority rule. Of course, LGE was also a stockholder as well as a creditor. Nevertheless, the Court made it clear that LGE was obtaining the equity in Zenith because of its *status as a creditor*, senior in right to the minority stockholders, and *not* because of its stockholder status.

The equity committee further asserted that LGE's *creditor claims* should be disallowed and instead recharacterized as equity based on the doctrine of *equitable subordination*. See Nutshell Section 38D(6). However, as the Bankruptcy Court pointed out, a creditor's claim may only be equitably subordinated when the creditor in question has done something *inequitable*. Here, the equity committee presented no evidence that LGE engaged in any inequitable conduct.

Lastly, the equity committee argued that the plan must not only comply with the provisions of the Bankruptcy Code, but also must meet the standards for approval of a *controlling stockholder acquisition* under Delaware corporate law. The Bankruptcy Court agreed that Section 1129(a)(3) of the Bankruptcy Code does, indeed, incorporate Delaware law (as well as any other applicable non-bankruptcy law). When reviewing the propriety of a controlling stockholder acquisition, the Delaware courts apply the "entire" or "intrinsic" fairness test. See Nutshell Section 60A(1).

The first part of that test is *"fair dealing,"* and the Bankruptcy Court held that it was satisfied. Indeed, all sides that negotiated the plan had separate counsel and other professionals representing them. Zenith properly appointed a special committee (which *did not* include any LGE appointees) to negotiate with LGE. LGE neither objected to nor impeded Zenith's efforts to find a different strategic investor or purchaser and, in fact, introduced Zenith to some potential purchasers.

The second part of the test is *"fair price,"* and the Bankruptcy Court also held that it was satisfied. It pointed out that Zenith's net equity was worth $193 million. Under the plan, LGE relinquished $200 million of debt claims, invested up to an additional $60 million in capital funds, and exchanged certain other claims for other assets. This, in the Court's mind, was a fair bargain.

Because the Bankruptcy Court found that the *process* and the *price* involved in the plan met the entire fairness standard under Delaware law, and that the equity committee's other allegations were unfounded, the Court found that the plan was both *fair and equitable* under the Bankruptcy Code and therefore the plan should be confirmed.

## D.  Key Concepts in Bankruptcy

### (1) Automatic Stay

Upon the filing of a bankruptcy petition, an *automatic stay* is triggered under Section 362 of the Bankruptcy Code. During the pendency of the stay, virtually all collection activities that creditors normally pursue are prohibited. Thus, creditors cannot take action against the debtor or its property to satisfy pre-bankruptcy debts; nor can they take action to harass and pressure the debtor, such as telephoning the debtor. The automatic stay, however, also protects creditors by preventing a race to the courthouse to obtain or enforce judgments against the debtor. The stay is not dependent upon receipt of notice by creditors. See generally *In re Bunting Bearings*, 302 B.R. 210 (Bankr. N.D. Ohio 2003).

The automatic stay generally remains in effect in a Chapter 11 case until the earlier of (1) the confirmation of the reorganization plan when the debtor receives a discharge, (2) the dismissal of the case or the closing of the case, or (3) the issuance of a court order granting relief from the stay. With respect to the latter, a bankruptcy court can grant relief from the stay "for cause" upon the request of a creditor. Such cause may exist, for example, when a secured creditor lacks *adequate protection* for property of the debtor's estate on which that creditor has a lien. See Bankruptcy Code § 362(d)(1). Other exceptions to the automatic stay (27 to be exact) are found in Section 362(b) of the Code. These include, among others, an action by a governmental unit to effectuate public policy or protect public safety (362(b)(4)) and an action by a lessor to evict the debtor from non-residential premises where the lease was terminated prior to the filing of the Chapter 11 petition (362(b)(10)).

### (2) Preference

A *preference* is a transfer of the debtor's property made within 90 days before the filing of a bankruptcy petition to satisfy an existing debt. Section 547 of the Bankruptcy Code makes preferences avoidable due to the perceived inequity of allowing a debtor with limited funds to pay back some but not all creditors when its bankruptcy filing is imminent.

Section 547(b) of the Bankruptcy Code defines a preference as:

- Any transfer of an interest of the debtor in property to or for the benefit of a creditor;

- For or on account of an antecedent debt owed by the debtor before such transfer was made;

- While the debtor was insolvent;

- Made on or within 90 days before the date of the filing of a bankruptcy petition, or within one year of the filing if the creditor is an insider; and

- That enables the creditor to receive more than it would receive in a Chapter 7 liquidation distribution of the bankruptcy estate had the transfer not been made.

For example, suppose that Peter's debts vastly exceed the value of his property. He decides to pay his last $5,000 in cash to Sammie, one of his existing creditors, to satisfy an old debt. Two weeks later, Peter files for bankruptcy. If Peter was insolvent at the time he paid Sammie, the Bankruptcy Code creates a presumption that the "transfer" to Sammie was preferential. This enables the debtor or a party in interest to unwind the payment by filing a lawsuit in the bankruptcy court for that purpose. Thus, by making the $5,000 payment to Sammie, Peter paid Sammie in full, but left the debts of his remaining creditors unsatisfied at a time when he had insufficient funds to pay off all his creditors in full.

### (3) Absolute Priority Rule and "Cram Down"

Under normal circumstances, holders of impaired claims and interests in the debtor must approve a plan of reorganization under Chapter 11 of the Bankruptcy Code. Nevertheless, the bankruptcy court can approve a plan over the objections of an impaired class of creditors or interest holders if the *absolute priority rule* embodied in Section 1129 of the Bankruptcy Code is met.

The absolute priority rule provides that a Chapter 11 plan of reorganization is fair and equitable as to the holders of claims or interests that are not repaid in full, so long as the holders of *junior* claims or interests do not receive or retain property under the plan on account of such junior claim or interest. In other words, if a plan allows those lower down the repayment food chain to receive something of value when senior claimants or interest holders are not being made whole, then those senior claimants or interest holders should not be forced to accept that plan.

There are two conditions that must be met under Section 1129 before a court can approve the plan over a dissenting class—otherwise known as *"cram-down."* First, the bankruptcy court must determine that the requirements of Section 1129(a) have been met. Second, the bankruptcy court must determine that the plan is fair and equitable with respect to each class of claims or interests that is impaired under the plan and has not accepted it.

Section 308 of the Sarbanes–Oxley Act of 2002 (SOX), the "Fair Funds for Investors" provision, may have thrown a wrench into the workings of the absolute priority rule. Pursuant to that provision, the SEC may level penalties on reporting companies that commit fraud. The estate of a bankrupt reporting company may be obligated to pay these penalties. The SEC, in turn, would allocate the money to a stockholder fund under Section 308 of SOX. Thus, assets which would otherwise flow to creditors are now reserved to common stockholders. To the extent creditors are not being paid back in full, the provision of such funds would represent an exception to the absolute priority rule, in general, and Section 510(b) of the Bankruptcy Code, in particular. Section 510(b) states that a claim for damages arising from the purchase or sale of common stock has the same priority as common stock—*i.e.,* such a claim is subordinated to the claims of all other creditors.

The SEC invoked this provision in proposing a settlement of its civil action against WorldCom, Inc. The SEC alleged that WorldCom misled investors by overstating its income from 1999 through the first quarter of 2002 due to undisclosed accounting improprieties. The SEC's proposed $2.25 billion civil penalty would be discharged in Worldcom's bankruptcy through the payment of $750 million, with $500 million payable in cash and the remainder in shares of the reorganized company's common stock. In discussing the conflict between Section 308 of SOX and Section 510(b) of the Bankruptcy Code, the District Court in *SEC v. Worldcom, Inc.*, 273 F. Supp. 2d 431 (S.D.N.Y.2003), stated:

> As a general rule, defrauded shareholders cannot expect to recover one penny in bankruptcy; and nothing in section 308(a) [of SOX] suggests that Congress intended to give shareholders a greater priority in bankruptcy than they previously enjoyed.

> This is not to say, however, that the [SEC] cannot give its penalty recovery to the shareholders, as section 308(a) [of SOX] so laudably prescribes, or that it cannot take some account

of shareholder loss in formulating the size and nature of its penalty: for while the securities laws limit the size of the penalty to the amount that the company has gained from its fraud (an amount here estimated at between ten and seventeen billion dollars), that does not mean that the [SEC] cannot rationally take account of shareholder loss as a relevant factor in determining the size of the penalty up to that limit. What the [SEC] may not do, at least in a case in which the company is in bankruptcy, is determine the size of the penalty primarily on the basis of how much shareholder loss will thereby be recompensed, for this would not only be adverse to the priorities established under the bankruptcy laws but would also run contrary to the primary purposes of S.E.C. fraud penalties themselves.

### (4) New Value Exception

Although not officially recognized by the U.S. Supreme Court, some circuits have embraced a *"new value exception"* to the absolute priority rule. The exception is based on dicta contained in several U.S. Supreme Court cases decided under the old Bankruptcy Act of 1898. See, e.g., *Case v. Los Angeles Lumber Products Co.*, 308 U.S. 106 (1939) and *Kansas City Terminal Ry. v. Central Union Trust Co.*, 271 U.S. 445 (1926). The exception allows interest holders to retain their interests in the debtor, even when senior claimants are not made whole under a plan of reorganization. In order to do so, these interest holders must provide "new value" to the debtor in an amount that is equal to or greater in value than the amount of their retained interests. In essence, these interest holders are paying to retain their old interests with additional or new consideration. See *Kham & Nate's Shoes No. 2, Inc. v. First Bank of Whiting*, 908 F.2d 1351 (7th Cir.1990).

The new value exception has not been uniformly embraced in each Federal judicial circuit. However, "new value" has been determined to mean money or money's worth. See *Case v. Los Angeles Lumber Products Co.*, 308 U.S. 106 (1939). For instance, a farmer's promise to provide "sweat equity" by operating and managing a farm could not, as a matter of law, qualify as a new value contribution. See *Norwest Bank Worthington v. Ahlers*, 485 U.S. 197 (1988). A personal or corporate guaranty has also been held insufficient to constitute new value, as such consideration does not appear as an asset on the debtor's balance sheet. See *Kham & Nate's Shoes No. 2.*, 908 F.2d 1351 (7th Cir.1990).

The U.S. Supreme Court has yet to decide whether a new value exception exists under the newer Bankruptcy Code. In *Bank of America Nat'l Trust v. 203 North LaSalle Street Partnership*, 526 U.S. 434 (1999), the Court skirted the issue by holding that the plan of reorganization in question was not fair and equitable on other grounds. In this case, the debtor submitted a plan of reorganization during the period of time when it had the exclusive right to do so. That plan allowed for the debtor's existing partners—but not other claimants or interest holders—to contribute new capital over a period of five years in exchange for their retention of 100% of the ownership in the reorganized debtor. The Court held that a reorganization plan that affords junior interest holders an exclusive opportunity to retain all the equity without competition or the benefit of a market valuation was not "fair and equitable." Thus, the bankruptcy court could not approve the debtor's plan of reorganization.

Importantly, the Court recognized that the Bankruptcy Code, when adopted in 1978, did not expressly abolish the new value exception. Moreover, the Court created an inference that a new value plan may pass the fair and equitable test if the new value is made subject to a market test. Thus, a new value plan proponent may secure a bankruptcy court's confirmation of that plan if the proponent first exposes the original offer for the equity interests to the market and then implements a separate open marketing and bidding process for the equity interests that coincides with the plan's confirmation. See, e.g., *In re Situation Mgt. Systems, Inc.*, 252 B.R. 859 (Bankr. D. Mass. 2000).

### (5) Treatment of Secured Creditors

A secured creditor holds a claim against the debtor that is secured by a lien on specific property or assets of the debtor. Secured creditors receive priority above all other creditors as to the collateral that secures their claim. Under Section 362(d)(1) of the Bankruptcy Code, these creditors may file a demand that the automatic stay be lifted unless their collateral is *"adequately protected."* A prime example of when adequate protection is needed is when the collateral is declining in value causing an erosion in the secured creditor's claim. See *In re Elmira Litho, Inc.*, 174 B.R. 892 (Bankr. S.D.N.Y.1994). When collateral depreciates in value below the amount of the secured claim, adequate protection may be granted in many forms, such as requiring the debtor to make periodic cash payments to the secured creditor or the provision of a replacement lien. It may also include the provision of replacement collateral of "indubitably equivalent" value to that of the property that currently secures the lien.

### (6) Equitable Subordination

Section 510(c) of the Bankruptcy Code allows a bankruptcy court to subordinate certain claims and interests to other claims and interests when it would be inequitable to permit a pro rata sharing. *Equitable subordination* allows a court to punish inequitable conduct by reducing the payment priority of an offending creditor to a lesser status than the payment priority of non-offending creditors. Equitable subordination is sometimes referred to as the "Deep Rock" doctrine, "Deep Rock" being the name of a subsidiary in the seminal case of *Taylor v. Standard Gas & Elec. Co.*, 306 U.S. 307 (1939), discussing the doctrine. The doctrine's purpose is to eliminate unfairness or injustice to innocent creditors in a bankruptcy proceeding.

In bankruptcy cases, creditor claims may be subordinated to other creditors' claims, but not to stockholders' interests. However, when a controlling stockholder engages in inequitable conduct at a time when she also is asserting a creditor claim, a court may subordinate all or part of her creditor claim below the claims of other creditors and preferred stockholders. In other words, the subordinated creditor claim is essentially treated as an equity claim. See *Costello v. Fazio*, 256 F.2d 903 (9th Cir.1958); *Arnolds v. Phillips*, 117 F.2d 497 (5th Cir.1941).

According to *Benjamin v. Diamond*, 563 F.2d 692 (5th Cir.1977), bankruptcy courts must consider the following factors when deciding whether to equitably subordinate a claim:

- The claimant must have engaged in some type of inequitable conduct;
- The misconduct must have resulted in injury to the creditors of the debtor or conferred an unfair advantage on the claimant; and
- Equitable subordination of the claim must not be inconsistent with the provisions of the Bankruptcy Code.

Inequitable conduct is largely an undefined concept. However, conduct of a claimant that is unjust or unfair to other creditors generally qualifies.

Thus, fraud, illegality, breach of fiduciary duties and undercapitalization have been found to be inequitable. Another typical situation involves a director, shareholder or other insider engaging in deceptive conduct that injures other creditors following the insider's extension of credit to the debtor. See, e.g., *Stoumbos v. Kilimnik*, 988 F.2d 949 (9th Cir.1993). Invariably, the insider has attempted to dress up like a creditor after the debtor's business has taken a turn for the worse, under the belief that receiving something as a creditor beats getting nothing as a shareholder or other insider.

For example, in *Pepper v. Litton*, 308 U.S. 295 (1939), the U.S. Supreme Court equitably subordinated the claim of a judgment creditor in an action brought by an unsecured creditor of the debtor's estate. The debtor's sole stockholder had caused the debtor to confess to a judgment to him relating to a fraudulent claim for back salary. The sole stockholder then placed the debtor in bankruptcy and sought to have the confessed judgment paid ahead of the debtor's other creditors as a senior claim. An unsecured creditor of the debtor's estate challenged the sole stockholder's judgment claim, and sought to equitably subordinate the claim to those held by the debtor's other creditors for having been fraudulently procured. The Court granted equitable relief to the unsecured creditor and subordinated the stockholder's judgment to the claims of the debtor's other creditors.

While courts normally apply equitable subordination in cases involving corporate insiders, they have, on occasion, applied it to claims held by non-insiders. However, these courts also apply a higher standard in these situations. Typically, a court needs to find gross or egregious misconduct on the part of the non-insider before equitably subordinating its claim. See *In the Matter of Teltronics Services, Inc.*, 29 B.R. 139 (Bankr. E.D.N.Y.1983).

## § 39. ASSET–BACKED SECURITIZATION

### A. Introduction

Securitization is a multi-trillion dollar industry. However, its origins are quite humble. Indeed, securitization is simply a more modern and sophisticated version of *factoring*—a financial transaction that has been around for centuries. In a typical factoring transaction, a financial services company (referred to as a *"factor"*) will purchase accounts receivable from a selling company at a discount. The selling company generated those receivables by selling goods and providing services to its customers on credit. The sale to the factor is *without recourse.* Thus, if the factor cannot collect on some of the receivables, it cannot seek payment from the selling company. The factors's profit is the difference between the amount ultimately collected on the receivables (hopefully 100 cents on the dollar) and the discounted amount it paid to the selling company to purchase the receivables (*e.g.,* 90 cents on the dollar) in the first place. Companies selling their accounts receivable do so because they receive money from the factor today—in one lump sum—and do not have to wait around until their customers pay off the receivables.

Securitization is like factoring in that companies sell assets at a slight discount to an entity willing to pay for them in one lump sum. The entity raises the money necessary to make the purchase by selling securities that are secured (*i.e.,* collateralized) by the assets in question. This process is described in more detail below in Nutshell Section 39C.

The key to securitization is recognizing that only certain classes of assets can be securitized effectively. These include, among others, accounts receivable, home mortgages, car loans, credit card debts, student loans and, depending on the artist, music royalties (David Bowie's in particular). All these assets have one primary feature in common: they are all *income producing assets*. They generate a stream of future cash flows payable to the owner of the assets in question.

## B. Mortgage–Backed Securities and the Financial Meltdown of 2008

Mortgage-backed securities are a type of asset-backed securities. Two government sponsored enterprises—the Federal National Mortgage Association ("Fannie Mae") and the Federal Home Loan Mortgage Company ("Freddie Mac")—purchase "packages" of promissory notes and mortgages from banks and other home mortgage lenders. These notes and mortgages have similar characteristics as to quality, term and interest rate (so-called *"conforming loans"*). Banks and mortgage lenders create these notes and mortgages by lending money to prospective home buyers—a process known as loan *"origination."* After selling packages of notes and mortgages to Fannie Mae or Freddie Mac, the banks and mortgage lenders—flush with cash—can then originate *more* mortgage loans. Thus, Fannie Mae and Freddie Mac increase the supply of money available for mortgage lending.

But where did Fannie Mae and Freddie Mac get the money to purchase the packages of notes and mortgages—*i.e.,* the assets being securitized? Fannie Mae and Freddie Mac issued debt securities (mortgage-backed securities, in the case of Fannie Mae, and participation certificates, in the case of Freddie Mac) to investors that are secured by the packages of notes and mortgages. They then collect interest and principal from homeowners (*i.e.,* "service" the loans) and use the proceeds to repay the debt securities they issued.

Unfortunately, the securitization of home mortgages went into overdrive during the housing bubble of the mid–2000s. Because banks and other mortgage lenders did not hold most of the home loans they originated on their own books, they became less and less concerned about the credit quality of home buyers. Indeed, the lenders made most of their money charging origination and other processing fees to those seeking to purchase homes. Thus, the race was on to make the most loans because it led to the highest amount of fee income. Prospective homeowners were delighted to play their part, as home values only seemed to rise during the early to mid–2000s. Another important facilitator was Alan Greenspan and the Federal Reserve who maintained an easy money policy by keeping interest rates at historic lows. Greenspan had initiated this policy soon after the "dot.com" bubble burst in the early 2000s in an attempt to revitalize the economy.

Adding to the credit quality problem was the Community Reinvestment Act of 1977. This Act requires lenders to help meet the credit needs of the communities in which they operate, including low- and moderate-income neighborhoods, consistent with safe and sound operations. During the 1990s, the Clinton Administration pressured lenders to expand mortgage loans to low- and moderate-income borrowers by increasing the ratio of their loan portfolios in distressed inner city areas designated by the Act. These lenders, in turn, pressured Fannie Mae and Freddie Mac to ease credit requirements on the mortgages they were willing to purchase.

Ultimately, the wheels came off beginning in 2008 as home prices began to fall and many homeowners discovered their homes were worth less than their home mortgages. Defaults on home mortgages rose, leading to a severe credit downgrade of mortgage-backed securities. Moreover, the secondary market for these securities froze as ready and willing buyers became scarce. A great many financial institutions, including Lehman Brothers, held millions of dollars worth of these securities. The result was almost cataclysmic. Given that Fannie Mae and Freddie Mac owned or guaranteed about half of the U.S.'s $12 trillion mortgage market, the Federal Housing Finance Agency was forced to place both Fannie Mae and Freddie Mac under its conservatorship.

In mid–2010, President Obama signed the Dodd–Frank Wall Street Reform and Consumer Protection Act ("Dodd–Frank") into law. Part of that Act addressed securitization. See Nutshell Section 39E for a discussion of how Dodd–Frank impacts securitization.

## C.  The Securitization Process

Companies that securitize their income producing assets (*e.g.,* credit card receivables) do so in large part to borrow money at a cost (*i.e.,* interest rate) that is *less* than traditional financing. Securitization separates the cash flow associated with the company's income producing assets from the *company itself.* For securitization to work, the creditworthiness of the *income stream* associated with the assets (*i.e.,* the likelihood that it will be received) must be higher than the creditworthiness of the *company as a whole.* In other words, the risk associated with receiving the income stream must be less than the risk associated with the entire company. If a given company can isolate its income producing assets from the company itself without too much cost and expense and, as a result, receive higher credit rated financing, then securitization makes sense for that company. If not, then it does not.

The securitization process involves six steps. The *first step* is the company's origination/creation of the income producing assets. It does this by, among other things, selling goods and providing services on credit to its customers. In the *second step*, the originating company will sell the income producing assets to a "Special Purpose Entity" (SPE) or "Special Purpose Vehicle" (SPV) at a slight discount to their face value. It then can use the sale proceeds to finance its operations going forward. Through this sale, the company isolates the income producing assets from the rest of the company in order to achieve higher credit rated financing. The SPE purchaser is also referred to as a *"bankruptcy remote vehicle."* This means that a bankruptcy involving the originating company should, in theory, not result in the income producing assets (now held by the SPE) being considered assets of the bankrupt estate. The *third step* involves the SPE reselling the income producing assets to a *second* SPE. This makes the assets even more bankruptcy remote.

But where did the first and second SPEs obtain the money necessary to purchase the income producing assets from the originating company? The money is obtained from investors who purchase debt securities (typically notes) securitized by the income producing assets. Thus, in the *fourth step*, the second SPE will have the debt securities it is planning on issuing to investors rated by one or more credit rating agencies, such as Moody's and Standard & Poor's. Of course, everything will be for naught if the credit rating given to the debt securities is not higher than that associated with the originating company as a whole. The rating agencies will review all the deal documentation. Additionally, they will try to determine whether customer payments on the income producing assets will continue to flow to the debt security holders even if the originating company experiences financial difficulties or goes into bankruptcy. In other words, they will analyze whether the two SPEs utilized in the transaction are, in their opinion, truly bankruptcy remote. Finally, the rating agencies will look at the substantive economics of the deal. In this regard, they will analyze the "cushion" that exists between what is paid for the income producing assets and the historical payment performance of the originating companies' customers in paying their bills.

The *fifth step* is the second SPE's sale of the debt securities collateralized by the income producing assets to investors. The second SPE uses the proceeds to purchase the income producing assets from the first SPE. The first SPE, in turn, uses the proceeds to purchase the income producing assets from the originating company.

The *sixth* and final step is the servicing of the income producing assets. Because the second SPE will have few if any employees, a sophisticated organization is needed to ensure *maximum collection* on the income producing assets. Indeed, the key to securitization is the willingness of the customers to pay the amounts they owe in respect of the income producing assets. In this regard, it makes sense for the originating company itself to service the assets. After all, the originating company has the greatest interest in ensuring that its customers are happy. Of course, the originating company is not willing to service assets it no longer owns for free. Thus, the second SPE will pay a very small percentage of the monies collected on the assets to the originating company for servicing the assets going forward.

## D.  Risks Associated with Securitization

Securitization suffers from not only the risk that customers will default on their payments relating to the income producing assets that have been securitized, but also from the risks associated with the *structure of the transaction itself*. These risks include, among others: (1) the risk that the SPEs will not be bankruptcy remote after all; (2) the risk that a court will not respect the originating company's sale of the income producing assets as a "true sale"; (3) the risk that a court will view the originating company's sale of the assets as a fraudulent conveyance; and (4) the risk that a court will substantively consolidate the SPEs with the originating company.

### (1) Bankruptcy Remoteness

It is vital to securitization that the income producing assets be isolated from the business of the originating company. If the originating company owns or controls the SPE holding the income producing assets, the originating company may have the power to cause the SPE to file a voluntary petition for bankruptcy. If that were to happen, all payments to the debt security holders would be *stayed* during bankruptcy. Moreover, a chance exists that the income producing assets—the assets securing the debt securities—could be vulnerable to the originating company's creditors.

While having not one but two SPEs involved in the transaction helps with bankruptcy remoteness (as the income producing assets are further removed from the originating company), securitization lawyers do not stop there. Indeed, they put a structural bar in the SPE's charter that limits the SPE's board of directors from voting to approve a voluntary bankruptcy filing. Typically, the charter will prohibit the SPE from filing a voluntary petition for bankruptcy unless a requisite number of independent directors of the board votes for bankruptcy. An "independent director" is normally defined as a person who is not a director, officer, employee or holder of five percent or more of the voting securities of the originating company or any of that company's affiliates. In theory, someone who qualifies as being "independent" under this standard would be less influenced by the originating company and more likely to consider her fiduciary obligations when required to vote for or against the SPE's bankruptcy.

### (2) "True Sale" Objections

Another concern when the originating company files for bankruptcy is whether the bankruptcy court will uphold the originating company's sale of the income producing assets to the SPE as a *"true sale."* If a "true sale" *has* occurred and later the originating company files for bankruptcy, the SPE would be deemed the "owner" of the assets rather than the originating company. Indeed, in that case all of the originating company's property rights in the assets will have passed to the SPE, leaving nothing in the originating company that could be labeled as *"property of the estate"* if the originating company later files for bankruptcy.

If, however, a "true sale" has not occurred, then a bankruptcy court will treat the securitization financing as a *simple loan or other advance of funds* by the SPE to the originating company which is secured by the income producing assets. Thus, the SPE would be treated as a *secured creditor* of the originating company and not the owner of the assets. Because of this, the finding of a "true sale" is important even *outside* of bankruptcy. The originating company wants the financing transaction reflected on its balance sheet as a *sale of assets* and not as a *secured loan*. Indeed, a secured loan *increases* the amount of debt on the originating company's balance sheet, *increases* its debt-to-equity ratio, and thus *limits* its ability to borrow from other sources.

When a "true sale" is not found, the bankruptcy court would treat the SPE as a secured creditor and, under Section 362 of the Bankruptcy Code, the SPE would be *automatically stayed* from foreclosing on the income producing assets. Until the stay is modified by the court, the SPE will be unable to collect payments relating to the assets. While secured creditors are entitled to "adequate protection" of their collateral, adequate protection does not necessarily mean the SPE would receive an alternative cash source of the same quality or type as that provided by the income producing assets. See Nutshell Section 38D(5).

When determining whether a "true sale" has occurred, a bankruptcy court is not bound by the labels attached to a transaction by the parties. Instead, it will look at the substance behind the transaction to determine if the assets have truly been sold. Perhaps oddly, a bankruptcy court normally looks to state law, not bankruptcy law, when making the "true sale" determination. The court normally looks at five factors—mostly gleaned from *factoring* cases—when determining whether the originating company truly parted with the future economic risks and benefits of ownership of the assets purported to be sold. These factors, which are discussed below, include: (a) recourse; (b) retained rights and right to surplus; (c) pricing mechanism;

(d) administration and collection of accounts; and (e) miscellaneous factors. Importantly, it is rare for a securitization transaction to have all of the "true sale" factors working in its favor.

### a.   Recourse

The nature and extent of the *recourse* that the SPE has against the originating company is the most important true sale factor. "Recourse" means the ability, if any, of the SPE to seek repayment against the originating company if the cash flows from the securitized assets are insufficient to pay off the debt securities held by investors. As the degree of recourse increases, the likelihood of a court finding a "true sale" decreases. Indeed, having greater recourse makes the SPE look like a secured creditor of the originating company.

*Major's Furniture Mart, Inc. v. Castle Credit Corp.*, 602 F.2d 538 (3d Cir.1979), involved a factoring transaction between Major's Furniture Mart (the originating company) and Castle Credit Corp. (the factor). Pursuant to the transaction, Major's sold its accounts receivable to Castle. In the contract Major's made several representations and warranties running in favor of Castle. These included: (1) that Major's customers met the credit criteria set forth by Castle; (2) that Major's performed a credit check to verify that these credit criteria were met by each customer; and (3) that Major's accounts were fully enforceable as a legal matter and were fully and timely collectible. The reps and warranties, particularly the third, impacted on the issue of recourse.

Additionally, Major's had a contractual obligation to indemnify Castle for losses relating to a customer's failure to pay. Major's also had an obligation to repurchase any account after the customer was in default for more than 60 days. Both of these obligations directly impacted on the issue of recourse.

In deciding whether Major's sale of the receivables to Castle was a "true sale," the Third Circuit easily held that such a sale had not happened. It highlighted Major's reps and warranties running in favor of Castle and Major's indemnification and repurchase obligations. It concluded that a true sale had not occurred because "Castle attempted to shift all risks to Major's, and incur none of the risks or obligations of ownership."

### b.   Retained Rights and Right to Surplus

A second important "true sale" factor is whether the originating company has the right to redeem or repurchase the transferred assets. Obviously, the absence of this right works in favor of a "true sale." Additionally, some courts have concluded that the existence of a transferor's right to any surplus collections, once the transferee has collected its investment plus agreed yield, works against a "true sale." Because asset-backed securitization transactions are normally set up that way, this works against a finding of a "true sale" in that context.

### c.  Pricing Mechanism

How the assets are priced for sale has bearing on the "true sale" determination. For example, pricing based on a fluctuating interest rate, such as one based on the prime rate or LIBOR, works against a "true sale" determination. Indeed, it makes the transaction look more like a loan. In addition, purchase price adjustments made retroactively to reflect *actual* rather than *expected collections* on the assets work against a "true sale" determination.

### d.  Administration and Collection of Accounts

For a court to find a "true sale," the SPE should have the authority to *control the collection of monies* paid on the income producing assets. However, in most securitizations, the *originating company* or its affiliate acts as the collection agent. Nonetheless, this is generally permissible so long as the contractual agency relationship that is established between the SPE and the collection agent provides for two things. First, it must require the SPE to pay the collection agent an *arms'-length fee*. Second, it must give the SPE the option to appoint itself or a third party as collection agent in place of the originating company.

### e.  Miscellaneous Factors

Courts sometimes view certain additional factors as indicative of a secured loan rather than a "true sale." For example, if the SPE's right to the assets can be extinguished by payments made by the originating company to the SPE, the transaction looks more like a secured loan. Also, if the originating company is required to pay the SPE's costs (including attorney's fees) incurred in collecting delinquent or uncollectible receivables, the transaction looks more like a secured loan.

### (3) Fraudulent Transfer Concerns

A third major risk relating to securitization is that a court will deem the transaction to be a fraudulent conveyance or transfer, regardless of whether the originating company has filed for bankruptcy protection. If the originating company is in bankruptcy, then, under Section 548 of the Bankruptcy Code, transfers of assets made by that company within two years before the filing of a bankruptcy petition can be voided if, among other things, (a) the transfer was done with the intent to delay, hinder or defraud its creditors, (b) the company received less than reasonably equivalent value in exchange for the assets and (c) the company was insolvent at the time or was rendered insolvent as a result of the transfer.

In terms of a securitization, if an SPE pays a purchase price that is less than the "reasonably equivalent value" of the income producing assets it is purchasing, a bankruptcy court could set aside the sale as a fraudulent transfer. The same is true if the sale is actually structured to hinder, delay or defraud the originating company's creditors. Of course, the risk that a creditor will level a fraudulent transfer accusation against an originating company is much greater when the originating company engages in a securitization at a time when it is in financial distress.

### (4) Substantive Consolidation

The fourth and final major risk in a securitization is that the assets of the originating company and the SPE will be *"substantively consolidated."* Substantive consolidation is an equitable bankruptcy doctrine. It allows a bankruptcy court to consolidate the assets and liabilities of the originating company and the SPE. This is true even if only the originating company—and *not* the SPE—has filed for bankruptcy.

Bankruptcy courts will look at several factors when making a substantive consolidation determination. These include: (a) the commingling of assets and business functions; (b) a unity of ownership and interests between the two entities; (c) the degree of difficulty in segregating and ascertaining individual liabilities and assets; (d) a parental guarantee of a loan to its subsidiary; (e) the presence or absence of consolidated financial statements; and (f) the transfer of assets without observing corporate formalities.

# E.  Dodd–Frank's Credit Retention Requirements

Congress rightfully believed that certain aspects of securitization were to blame for the financial crisis that began in 2008. In passing the Dodd–Frank Wall Street Reform and Consumer Protection Act of 2010 ("Dodd–Frank"), Congress attempted to better align the interests of those who securitize assets with those who purchase asset-backed securities. Specifically, and as further described below, so-called "securitizers" (as defined below) will be required to retain a portion of the credit risk with regard to the asset-backed securities they sell. They will, indeed, have to eat some of their own cooking.

Although many of the key details relating to securitization will only emerge in regulations yet to be written, the Act itself requires the Federal banking agencies and SEC to jointly prescribe regulations that require securitizers to maintain *five percent* of the credit risk in assets transferred, sold or conveyed through the issuance of asset-backed securities. A lower risk retention requirement will apply in the case of deals where the underwriting and diligence efforts meet high underwriting standards specific to the class of the securitized asset. Moreover, the Act requires regulators to allocate the risk retention obligation between securitizers and "originators" (as defined below). A party subject to the risk retention obligation may not hedge the required retained credit risk.

Importantly, retention obligations will not require a securitizer to retain any part of the credit risk if *all* of the assets that collateralize the asset-backed security in question are *qualified residential mortgages*. The Federal banking agencies, the SEC, the U.S. Department of Housing and Urban Development (HUD) and the Federal Housing Finance Agency (FHFA) will define the criteria for "qualified residential mortgages," taking into account underwriting and product features indicating a lower risk of default. In addition, the SEC must require an issuer to certify, for each issuance of an asset-backed security collateralized exclusively by qualified residential mortgages, that the issuer has evaluated the effectiveness of its internal supervisory controls designed to ensure that all assets are, indeed, qualified residential mortgages.

The Act defines an *"asset-backed security"* as a "fixed-income or other security collateralized by any type of self-liquidating financial asset, including a loan, a lease, a mortgage, or a secured or unsecured receivable, that allows the holder of the security to receive payments that depend primarily on cash flow from the asset." The definition specifically includes collateralized mortgage obligations, collateralized debt obligations ("CDOs"), collateralized bond obligations, CDOs of asset-backed securities, CDOs of CDOs and any security that the SEC determines to be an asset-backed security for purposes of the credit retention obligation. However, the Act excludes from the definition any security "issued by a finance subsidiary held by the parent company or a company controlled by the parent company, if none of the securities issued by the finance subsidiary are held by an entity that is not controlled by the parent company."

The Act defines *"securitizer"* as "(i) an issuer of an asset-backed security; or (ii) a person who organizes and initiates an asset-backed securities transaction by selling or transferring assets, either directly or indirectly, including through an affiliate, to the issuer." The Act defines *"originator"* as "a person who: (a) through the extension of credit or otherwise, creates a financial asset that collateralizes an asset-backed security; and (b) sells an asset to a securitizer."

In light of the SEC's $550 million settlement with Goldman Sachs & Co. in the Summer of 2010, Congress also inserted a conflicts of interest prohibition into the Act. According to the SEC's complaint, Goldman structured and marketed a synthetic CDO tied to the performance of subprime residential mortgage-backed securities just as the housing market was beginning its downward spiral. The marketing materials for the product allegedly did not disclose that Paulson & Co., one of the world's largest hedge funds, played a key role in selecting the residential mortgaged-backed securities (RMBSs) for the portfolio underlying the CDO, and that Paulson would reap gains if the RMBSs defaulted. Rather, the materials represented that ACA Management LLC, an expert in analyzing credit risks for RMBSs, would select the portfolio.

Paulson, meanwhile, effectively shorted the RMBS portfolio by entering into credit default swaps with Goldman on the CDO.

The Act, therefore, prohibits an underwriter, placement agent, initial purchaser, or sponsor, or any affiliate or subsidiary of any such entity, of an asset-backed security (as defined in the Exchange Act, and including a synthetic asset-backed security) from engaging in any transaction for one year after the first closing of the sale of the asset-backed security that would involve or result in any material conflict of interest with respect to any investor in a transaction arising out of such activity. However, this prohibition is inapplicable to: (a) any risk-mitigating hedging activity in connection with positions or holdings arising out of the underwriting, placement, initial purchase or sponsorship of an asset-backed security, provided that such activity is designed to reduce the specific risks to the underwriter, placement agent, initial purchaser, or sponsor associated with positions or holdings arising out of such underwriting, placement, initial purchase, or sponsorship; or (b) any purchase or sale of asset-backed securities made (i) pursuant to and consistent with commitments of the underwriter, placement agent, initial purchaser, or sponsor, or any affiliate or subsidiary of any such entity, (ii) to provide liquidity for the asset-backed security, or (iii) in connection with bona fide market-making in the asset-backed security.

Finally, the Act modifies the Securities Act in certain respects. For example, it eliminates the exemption from registration for certain specific categories of mortgage-backed securities provided by Section 4 of the Securities Act. It also requires the SEC to adopt rules requiring an issuer of an asset-backed security to perform a review of the assets underlying the asset-backed security and to disclose the nature of the review.

# CHAPTER 12

# PREFERRED STOCKHOLDERS

## § 40. OVERVIEW

Preferred stock is a *hybrid security* featuring characteristics of both debt and equity. Preferred stock is called "preferred" because its holders have a *dividend preference* and a *liquidation preference* over common stockholders. Generally, the preferred stockholders' dividend preference requires the issuer to pay preferred stockholders their dividend before it can pay any dividend to the common stockholders. Their liquidation preference means that, in a liquidation context, the issuer must pay preferred stockholders their contractual liquidation preference (a specified dollar amount), plus any accrued but unpaid dividends, prior to distributing any assets to the common stockholders. Because of these preferences, preferred stock is a less risky investment than common stock.

In terms of other rights, preferred stockholders generally have very limited voting rights. Their stock may be callable or redeemable at the company's discretion or otherwise. Their stock may also be convertible into shares of the company's common stock or exchangeable into debt securities with similar attributes. Most of these other rights are the subject of negotiation between an issuer and prospective preferred stockholders (or their agent).

## § 41.  SIMILARITY TO DEBT AND EQUITY

A given series of preferred stock may have the following debt-like characteristics: (1) a high par value (often as high as $100 a share) similar to the face value of a bond; (2) regular, defined dividends similar to interest payments; (3) conversion rights; (4) redemption rights; (5) restricted voting rights; (6) a ranking "senior" to common stock in liquidation; and (7) rights spelled out primarily in a contract.

In many ways, preferred stock is similar to subordinated debt. However, preferred stock dividends are payable at the discretion of the company's board of directors and then only out of funds legally available for the payment of dividends. By contrast, a company with debt outstanding must make interest payments "come hell or highwater" or suffer the consequences of a default. Additionally, unlike debt holders, preferred stockholders cannot force the company involuntarily into bankruptcy.

A given series of preferred stock may have the following equity-like characteristics: (1) dividends payable at the board's discretion and subject to the legal capital rule of the state of the company's formation; (2) limited board fiduciary duties running towards the preferred stockholders; (3) nondeductibility of preferred stock dividends for tax purposes; (4) indefinite duration unless subject to redemption; (5) a ranking "junior" to the company's creditors in liquidation; and (6) rights, although contractual, are set forth in the company's certificate of incorporation or an amendment thereto.

While preferred stock has characteristics of both debt and equity, it is important to understand that the courts clearly treat preferred stock as *equity* for legal purposes. See *HB Korenvaes Investments, L.P. v. Marriott Corp.*, 1993 WL 205040 (Del.Ch.). This, however, has not stopped preferred stockholders from arguing the contrary, especially when the company in question is in financial difficulty and thus order of repayment becomes a pressing issue. *Harbinger Capital Partners Master Fund I, Ltd. v. Granite Broadcasting Corp.*, 906 A.2d 218 (Del.Ch. 2006), addressed one such challenge.

In *Harbinger Capital*, the plaintiff preferred stockholder sought to enjoin Granite Broadcasting Corp. from selling assets based on the plaintiff's belief that the sale breached the terms of Granite's indenture governing Granite's senior notes and constituted a fraudulent conveyance in respect of Granite's current and future creditors. Granite defended on the basis that the plaintiff, as a preferred stockholder, had no standing to sue as only creditors could pursue the claims that the plaintiff had brought. The plaintiff countered by highlighting that the preferred stock it held was "mandatorily redeemable" preferred stock. Recent changes in GAAP (particularly Financial Accounting Standard

(FAS) 150) required that this type of stock be treated as long-term debt for financial statement purposes, and Granite in fact had complied.

The Delaware Chancery Court, however, disagreed with the plaintiff. Although the Court noted that the certificate of designation for the preferred stock required Granite to "redeem, to the extent of funds legally available therefore[,]" all shares at a fixed price plus accumulated dividends on April 1, 2009, redemption would only occur if Granite had sufficient legally available funds to make payment. If Granite defaulted on its obligation, the certificate of designation provided that the preferred stockholders would receive certain voting rights entitling the preferred stockholders to elect the lesser of two directors or that number of directors constituting 25% of the members of the board. That remedy was the exclusive remedy provided to the preferred stockholders. Because of this, the Court held that the redemption feature of the preferred stock "has not and never will give rise to a right of payment against the corporation. . . ." In addition, after reviewing cases with similar facts, the Court noted that "the touchtone of 'equity' under these cases is whether the security holder has a legally enforceable right to payment." If he does, then his claim is debt rather than equity.

Moreover, the Court took issue with the argument that *accounting standards* could dictate the law in this area. According to the Court:

FAS 150 is not so determinative as the plaintiff asserts. To believe that it decides this case would grant [the Financial Accounting Standards Board (FASB)], which is neither lawmaker nor judge, the power to fundamentally alter the law's understanding of the role of preferred shares. Thus, if the plaintiff is correct, the remedies of a preferred stockholder of a Delaware corporation are no longer contract and (sometimes) fiduciary duty. Because the court would be required by FAS 150 to treat preferred stock as debt, preferred stockholders would have lost the latter right entirely, and gained creditors' remedies instead. . . .

Nor would FASB's power over Delaware law be constrained to the treatment of preferred shares. The court can imagine any number of other financial instruments whose accounting treatment might, in the future, be changed by FASB, and would thus require some concomitant, and major, innovation in Delaware precedent. Further, if FASB ever shifted its view again, under this theory ... Delaware ... would have to shift with it.

## § 42.  THE PREFERRED
## STOCK CONTRACT

The "contract" for a given series of preferred stock does not take the form of a traditional contract. Rather, the rights, preferences and other terms of that series are set forth in the company's charter. They typically enter the charter through a charter amendment.

The preferred stock amendment could take the form of a traditional charter amendment that common stockholders must approve. This, however, is seldom done. The reason relates to the debt-like characteristics of preferred stock. Companies attempt to issue preferred stock in a way that takes advantage of dips in market interest rates. Because windows of opportunity in this regard can open and close quickly, most companies simply do not have the time to secure stockholder approval of a charter amendment that creates a new series of preferred stock. This is particularly true of publicly-traded companies which must comply with the Federal proxy rules contained in the Exchange Act when seeking stockholder approval. See Nutshell Section 56B.

Most companies, therefore, insert into their charter and thereafter utilize a *blank check preferred stock provision*. This provision grants the board the authority to issue a new series of preferred stock when the board believes doing so is desirable. Common stockholders will have approved a charter amendment providing for a blank check provision in advance of its need. Thereafter, the provision provides the necessary authority to the board of directors to issue one or more series of preferred stock from the company's authorized but unissued shares of preferred stock.

When utilizing the power of a blank check provision, the board will set forth the rights, preferences and other terms of a new series of preferred stock in board resolutions. Those resolutions will then be folded into a *certificate of designation* or *certificate of amendment*, depending on the jurisdiction in which the company was formed. Once that certificate is filed with the state, it becomes part of the company's charter. Thus, the rights, preferences and other terms of a given series of preferred stock will be negotiated at the time the company seeks to issue shares of that series. They then will be quickly inserted into the company's charter through a certificate of designation or amendment. The necessity of obtaining stockholder approval at that time is, therefore, avoided. See, e.g., DGCL §§ 102(a)(4) and 151(g).

## § 43.  CHARACTERISTICS OF PREFERRED STOCK

### A.  Preference Rights

Preferred stockholders have a dividend and liquidation preference over common stockholders. Each of these preferences is described below.

### (1) Dividend Preference

Dividends, whether on preferred or common stock, are payable at the discretion of the company's board of directors. They are also subject to any restrictive charter provision and the legal capital rule of the company's state of incorporation. However, in the event dividends are paid, preferred stockholders must receive their fixed dividend before the company can pay any dividends to its common stockholders. Importantly, if the preferred stock in question is *cumulative,* then the preferred stock dividend preference extends to any previous dividends—known as a *dividend arrearage*—the board did not declare.

For example, assume that NAH Corp. has a series of cumulative preferred stock outstanding that has a stated dividend of $2.80 per share per year, payable in equal quarterly installments of $0.70. NAH must pay each quarterly installment to the preferred stockholders before any dividends can be paid to its common stockholders. Therefore, assuming NAH has not paid its preferred stockholders their last three quarterly dividends ($2.10 [$0.70 x 3 quarters]), it must pay that arrearage ($2.10) *in addition* to the quarterly dividend for the current quarter ($0.70) to the preferred stockholders *before* paying any dividends to the common stockholders.

### (2) Liquidation Preference

The preferred stockholders' dividend preference benefits them if the company succeeds. Their liquidation preference, by contrast, helps protect them if the company fails. In the event of any voluntary or involuntary liquidation, dissolution or winding up of the company, the company must pay preferred stockholders their stated (*i.e.*, contractual) *liquidation preference*, plus any accrued and unpaid dividends, prior to distributing any assets to its common stockholders.

The liquidation preference is a dollar amount usually equal to the par value of a given series of preferred stock. Therefore, paying the preferred stockholders their liquidation preference is akin to paying back bondholders the face value of their bonds. In the event the company has insufficient funds to pay the preferred stockholders their full liquidation preference, then the company will divide its available assets among them on a pro rata basis.

While preferred stockholders stand ahead of common stockholders when the company liquidates, they contractually stand behind creditors. Therefore, the value of the preferred stockholders' liquidation preference may be illusory if the company is highly-leveraged when it liquidates. Indeed, such a company usually does not have sufficient funds remaining to distribute to any of its stockholders after first attempting to fully satisfy creditor claims.

The preferred stock contract usually defines what constitutes a liquidation, winding up or dissolution and the procedures a company must take if such an event occurs. Beyond the obvious events such as bankruptcy or receivership, the contract may provide that any substantial change in the company's business, such as a merger, consolidation or sale of all or substantially all of the company's assets, also constitutes a liquidation. Such a broad definition protects preferred stockholders because it forces the company to negotiate with them over a proposed change or risk having to pay the aggregate liquidation preference to the preferred stockholders at perhaps an inopportune time.

## B.   Noncumulative and Cumulative Preferred Stock

### (1) Noncumulative Dividend Rights

When preferred stock is *noncumulative*, its contract states that preferred stock dividends that the board does not declare and pay in any quarterly period *will not accrue*. The declaration of dividends, including preferred stock dividends, is within the discretion of the company's board of directors. Therefore, its decision not to pay a quarterly noncumulative dividend means, in almost all jurisdictions, that the dividend cannot legally be paid at a later date. Even if the board is willing to do so and the company has the available funds, as a matter of law the board cannot declare the dividend. However, if a quarterly noncumulative dividend is not paid on the preferred stock, the company cannot pay a dividend on its common stock or any other stock "junior" to the preferred stock in question.

The extinguishment of undeclared, noncumulative preferred stock dividends was amply demonstrated in *Guttmann v. Illinois Central Railroad*, 189 F.2d 927 (2d Cir.1951). Here, the directors of Illinois Central Railroad (ICR) failed to declare divi-

dends on ICR's outstanding shares of preferred
stock over a ten-year period. They then declared a
dividend on ICR's common stock without first paying the preferred stockholders the arrearage these
stockholders believed they were owed. According to
the plaintiff preferred stockholder, this constituted
an "abuse of the directors' discretion." The preferred stock in question, however, was noncumulative.

In deciding the case, the Second Circuit looked to
*Wabash Railway Co. v. Barclay*, 280 U.S. 197
(1930), a case presenting similar facts. In *Wabash*,
holders of noncumulative preferred stock sought an
injunction to prevent the company from paying
dividends on common stock unless it first paid
dividends on the preferred stock to the extent the
company had, in previous years, net earnings available for that payment. The U.S. Supreme Court,
interpreting Indiana law, ruled against the preferred stockholders. It held that if profits from
those earlier years "are justifiably applied by the
directors to 'Capital Improvements' and no dividend
is declared within the year, then the claim for that
year is gone and cannot be asserted at a later date."

The plaintiff in *Guttmann* interpreted *Wabash* as
saying a corporation's profits had to be used either
(a) for capital improvements or (b) for dividends
payable to the preferred stockholders. Apparently,
ICR's board had not used ICR's net profits for
"capital improvements." Instead, the board "legiti-

mately retained [them] for any one of a variety of other corporate purposes."

The Second Circuit, however, disagreed with the plaintiff's interpretation of *Wabash*. It found untenable the plaintiff's forced distinction between using profits for capital improvements versus other legitimate corporate purposes. According to the Court, "there is no sensible ground for singling out legitimate capital outlays, once made, as the sole cause of the irrevocable destruction of the claims of the preferred."

The Court held that once a dividend on noncumulative preferred stock has gone undeclared and unpaid, the directors have no discretion whatsoever to declare that dividend subsequently. Thus, the plaintiff and the other preferred stockholders were not entitled to accrued dividends at a later date, even if the directors wanted to pay those dividends and the company had the funds to do so. Indeed, given that preferred stockholders have no contractual right to the missed dividends, directors who declare and pay those dividends open themselves up to common stockholder allegations of gift or corporate waste.

While most jurisdictions follow the *Guttmann* interpretation of the term "noncumulative," exceptions exist. New Jersey, for example, follows the so-called *dividend credit rule*. This rule says that preferred stockholders are entitled to accrued dividends on noncumulative preferred stock for years in which the corporation has net earnings. In other words, undeclared, noncumulative preferred stock dividends do accrue in years when the company is profitable. Nevertheless, dividends would only accrue when the preferred stock contract was silent on the issue or so general as to leave adequate room for the rule's application. See *Sanders v. Cuba Railroad Co.*, 120 A.2d 849 (N.J.1956); *Leeds & Lippincott Co. v. Nevius*, 144 A.2d 4 (N.J.Super.1958).

The policy underpinnings for New Jersey's dividend credit rule are twofold. First, it prevents common stockholders, who control the corporation through the board of directors, from taking advantage of the holders of noncumulative preferred stock by pressuring the directors to forgo declaring and paying dividends on that stock. Second, without the dividend credit rule, only ignorant investors would purchase noncumulative preferred stock. Thus, having that rule keeps noncumulative preferred stock a financing option for New Jersey companies.

New Jersey, however, might be surprised to learn that *venture capitalists* typically purchase noncumulative convertible preferred stock in young companies that have not yet gone public. They do so for a number of reasons. First, they are well aware that dividends that are not declared on noncumulative preferred stock are gone for good. However, they also know that potential creditors (*e.g.,* a local bank) are more likely to lend money to a young company if the preferred stock that has been issued is noncumulative. Because young companies in any event almost never pay a dividend on their stock, whether common or preferred, venture capitalists really are not giving up anything by purchasing preferred stock that is noncumulative. Indeed, the dividend preference on preferred stock that young companies issue is often worthless.

Second, while venture capitalists could purchase the company's common stock directly, they often choose to invest in preferred stock because of its liquidation preference over common stock. Unlike the dividend preference, this preference does have some value in the context of a young company. If that company goes bankrupt, the venture capitalists are likely to receive more if they hold preferred stock rather than common stock.

Third, venture capitalists insist on preferred stock that is convertible so they can convert their shares into the company's common stock if the company succeeds. In fact, selling shares of common stock that they receive upon conversion at an enormous profit is one of several "exit strategies" venture capitalists hope for when they make their initial investment in a young company. Noncumulative convertible preferred stock, therefore, provides venture capitalists with the downside protection of preferred stock and the upside potential of common stock.

Finally, venture capitalists generally have the clout to insist on real voting rights. In fact, they normally receive the contractual right to elect one or more directors to the board through their own voting power. Thus, they do not give up the control they desire merely by investing in noncumulative preferred stock.

### (2) Cumulative Dividend Rights

When preferred stock is *cumulative*, its contract states that preferred stock dividends that the board does not declare and pay in any quarterly period are not extinguished but rather *accrue*. Importantly, accrual occurs regardless of the financial condition of the company. Before the company can pay any dividends on its common stock or any other stock "junior" to the preferred stock in question, the company must pay all cumulative preferred stock dividends, both the current quarterly dividend and the entire arrearage. The vast majority of preferred stock that companies issue today is cumulative.

## C.  General Terms of a Preferred Stock Contract

The preferred stock contract will specify whether a given series of preferred stock is cumulative or noncumulative and will set forth that stock's dividend and liquidation preferences. Additionally, it will address some or all of the following, depending on the negotiations between the company and the prospective preferred stockholders (or their agent): (1) number of shares offered and price per share; (2) dividend yield; (3) rank among other classes of securities; (4) voting rights; (5) redemption rights; (6) conversion rights; (7) exchange rights; (8) participation rights; and (9) certain affirmative and negative covenants.

### (1) Number of Shares and Price Per Share

With respect to an offering of shares of a new series of preferred stock, the number of shares offered along with the price per share depends on the amount of capital the company is seeking to raise. Because preferred stock is typically sold at its par value, the number of shares offered is determined by dividing the amount of capital being raised by the proposed par value of the preferred stock. Par value for preferred stock is significantly higher than it is for common stock as it is more reflective of the face value of debt securities. Typical preferred stock par values range from $20 to $100 per share.

### (2) Yield

The annual dividend or "yield" on a new series of preferred stock is reflective of current market interest rates due to the debt-like characteristics of preferred stock. Preferred stock, however, has equity-like characteristics as well, most notably that preferred stockholders stand behind creditors in a liquidation and that preferred dividends are payable at the discretion of the board of directors. Because of this, preferred stock is a riskier investment than debt. Its yield, therefore, is typically higher than the interest rate for an equivalent debt instrument.

Although issuing variable rate preferred stock is possible, issuers generally issue preferred stock with a fixed yield. The yield on a given series of preferred stock is often stated in the name for that series. For example, "6% Convertible Series B Preferred Stock, par value $25 per share," will provide investors with a 6% annual yield (assuming the board of directors declares and pays dividends). The annual per share dividend (typically paid out in quarterly installments) for this preferred stock would be $1.50 [6% × $25 per share par value].

Sometimes the yield on a given series of preferred stock is not expressly given in its name, while the annual cash dividend amount is. For example, "$2.25 Convertible Series C Preferred Stock, par value $50 per share," pays an annual dividend per share of $2.25 (typically paid out in quarterly installments). Its yield is 4.5%, which is calculated by dividing the dividend amount by the preferred stock's par value [($2.25 ÷ $50 per share par value) × 100].

### (3) Subordination

When a company has more than one series of preferred stock outstanding at any given time, it typically labels them "Series A," "Series B," "Series C," etc. in order to tell them apart. When shares of multiple series of preferred stock are outstanding, where each series ranks in terms of its dividend and liquidation preferences—*i.e.*, its "seniority"—becomes important. Subordination is strictly a matter of contract law. Thus, it is a subject of negotiation between the company and prospective preferred stockholders (or their agent). Prospective preferred stockholders willing to subordinate their interests to holders of another series of preferred stock receive concessions from the issuer, such as a higher dividend yield.

"Senior" preferred stockholders stand in front of all holders of classes of "junior" preferred stock and, of course, common stockholders. "Junior" preferred stockholders are "junior" to "senior" preferred stockholders, but are "senior" to all common stockholders. Importantly, when the preferred stock contract does not specify seniority or rank, holders of multiple series of preferred stock will stand *pari passu* (on the same level) with the holders of all other series. Thus, when a company liquidates at a time when it is unable to pay the aggregate liquidation preference to holders of different series of pari passu preferred stock, the company will distribute the funds that are available on a pro rata basis to all holders of those series. For a case providing an extensive discussion of ranking and its consequences, see *Burton v. Exxon Corp.*, 583 F.Supp. 405 (S.D.N.Y.1984).

### (4) Voting Rights

#### a.  Generally

Preferred stockholders typically receive very limited voting rights. Some of these rights are statutory while others are contractual. In terms of statutory rights, preferred stockholders and common stockholders, voting together as a single class, generally must approve any proposed amendment to the company's charter. See, e.g., DGCL § 242(b)(1) and NYBCL § 803(a). In addition, if the proposed charter amendment would affect or change, *in an adverse way*, the powers, preferences or other special rights of a series of preferred stock, then holders of that series also are entitled to vote on the amendment as a separate class. See, e.g., DGCL § 242(b)(2) and NYBCL § 804(a). This, of course, gives them *veto power* over that amendment.

### b.   Contractual Right to Elect Directors

In terms of contractual voting rights, the preferred stock contract for cumulative preferred stock typically provides preferred stockholders with the right to elect a specified number of members (typically two) to the company's board of directors if the company misses a specified number of quarterly cumulative dividends (typically six). A pro-preferred stockholder version of this provision will provide that the missed dividends do not need to be consecutive. A pro-company version will provide otherwise. The directors that the preferred stockholders elect are normally in addition to the board's existing directors. Thus, the board expands to accommodate the new directors. Once the dividend arrearage has been paid, the contingent voting rights of the preferred stockholders cease and the board members elected by them must resign from office.

This was illustrated in *Baron v. Allied Artists Pictures Corp.*, 337 A.2d 653 (Del.Ch.1975). In *Baron*, preferred stockholders had contingent voting rights which were triggered when Allied Artists Picture Corporation (Allied) missed paying preferred stock dividends in six or more quarters. The holders of preferred stock, voting as a separate class, had the right to elect a majority of Allied's directors until the preferred stock arrearage had been paid.

A common stockholder later sued to take back control of the board from the preferred stockholders. The plaintiff argued that one or more years had gone by since the preferred stockholders took control and, even though Allied had sufficient funds to pay off the preferred stock arrearage, the board refused to do so. The plaintiff, therefore, sought to void the contractual right of the preferred stockholders to elect a majority of the board and to have a new election that would allow the common stockholders to elect all the directors.

The plaintiff also argued that the "sole purpose" of allowing the preferred stockholders to elect a majority of the board in the first place was to enable them to elect directors who would immediately pay off the preferred stock arrearage as soon as the directors could do so legally. The Delaware Chancery Court, however, disagreed. It held that the main purpose of the voting provision was to bring in "new management" that could hopefully turn Allied around in such a way as to make possible the payment of the preferred stock arrearage in the future. Until that time came and the directors elected by the preferred stockholders stepped down, those directors—like all directors—had fiduciary duties to the corporation and all its stockholders, not just the preferred stockholders.

The Court highlighted that the determination as to when and in what amounts a corporation may prudently distribute its assets by way of dividends rests in the honest discretion of the directors in the performance of their fiduciary duties. Because the board had not engaged in fraud or abused its discretion, the Court determined that the board had not improperly failed to pay dividends to the preferred stockholders. Nor was the board guilty of perpetuating itself in office. Indeed, due to the "hit and miss" financial history of Allied, the Court believed the directors were merely being prudent in not paying off the preferred stock arrearage.

In situations where preferred stockholders have the contractual right to elect one or more directors to a company's board, the issue of timing arises. Specifically, *when* are preferred stockholders entitled to elect these directors—immediately or at the next regularly scheduled annual meeting of stockholders? This issue arose in *FGC Holdings Ltd. v. Teltronics Inc.*, 2005 WL 2334357 (Del.Ch.). Teltronics's Certificate of Designation provided holders of Teltronics' Series B preferred stock with the right to elect one director to Teltronics' board. Although the original owner of all the shares of

Series B preferred stock had chosen not to exercise this right for five years, the new owner sought to exercise it immediately upon purchasing the shares. Teltronics refused, and the new owner, as plaintiff, sued.

In ruling in favor of the plaintiff, the Delaware Chancery Court noted that the Certificate of Designation controlled the situation. Pursuant to it, the Series B shareholders, voting as a separate class, had "the exclusive and special right at all times to elect one (1) director ..." to Teltronics' five member board. Teltronics had argued that the plaintiff must wait until the next annual election because the board already had a full complement of directors. But that argument was flawed, according to the Court, because embracing it would allow the common stockholders to eliminate the plaintiff's right to elect a director for up to a whole year. The Court also rejected Teltronics' argument that the plaintiff had waived its right to elect a director by failing to do so at the annual meeting held immediately after the plaintiff purchased the shares, but before the plaintiff had notified Teltronics of its status. Indeed, the Court highlighted that the Certificate of Designation unambiguously granted the plaintiff the right to elect a director "at all times."

Nevertheless, in order not to overly disrupt Teltronics' corporate governance, the Court did not force the board to accept the plaintiff's representative as a full board member immediately. Instead, the Court ordered the board to provide the plaintiff's representative with board materials and to allow him to attend meetings (but not to vote) until such time as Teltronics held an annual meeting, which the Court ordered to be held within the next month and a half. In a subsequent proceeding, the Court awarded the plaintiff 50% of its attorneys fees and all of its court costs because the defendants' conduct in the latter part of the litigation constituted an improper attempt to delay or render more burdensome than necessary the plaintiff's effort to secure its clear and established right to a seat on the board. See *FGC Holdings Ltd. v. Teltronics, Inc.*, 2007 WL 241384 (Del.Ch.).

### c.  Contractual Right to Approve Mergers and Related Transactions

The preferred stock contract may also provide that preferred stockholders must vote to approve a merger, consolidation, or similar transaction. Such was the case in *Pasternak v. Glazer*, 1996 WL 549960 (Del.Ch.), where plaintiff preferred stockholders sought to enjoin a proposed merger between Houlihan's and Zapata Acquisition Corp., a wholly-owned subsidiary of Zapata created for the purpose of effecting the merger. As merger consideration, Houlihan's stockholders would receive shares of Zapata common stock in exchange for their shares of Houlihan's stock. According to Zapata's charter, a supermajority vote of its stockholders (with preferred and common stockholders voting together as a single class) was required to approve a "merger or consolidation with or into any other corporation." The merger agreement, however, only called for a majority vote of the holders of Zapata's outstanding shares of common stock in order to approve the merger.

Plaintiffs sued to enjoin the merger, arguing that the language in Zapata's charter did not limit the applicability of the merger voting provision to mergers involving only Zapata itself. They believed that the language was broad enough to include mergers with or into Zapata's subsidiaries as well. The defendant directors of Zapata claimed that the voting provision did not explicitly include mergers with Zapata's subsidiaries; therefore, the merger in question did not trigger the merger voting provision.

The Delaware Chancery Court reasoned that the provisions of Zapata's charter that immediately followed the merger voting provision included language specifically limiting those provisions to Zapata itself. Therefore, the Court opined that the drafters of the merger voting provision intended it to be broader in scope because they excluded that limiting language. The Court also highlighted language in a relevant Zapata proxy statement that supported the conclusion that the voting provision was intended to include Zapata and the subsidiaries it owned or controlled. Accordingly, the Court held for the plaintiffs and granted a permanent injunction against the merger.

The precedential value of *Pasternak* is unclear. Zapata appealed the Chancery Court's decision, but the Delaware Supreme Court ruled that Zapata's appeal was moot because Zapata had ultimately abandoned its merger with Houlihan's. Given that Zapata was now prevented from obtaining appellate review, the Delaware Supreme Court remanded the case to the Chancery Court for the purpose of vacating the Chancery Court's judgment. Under the circumstances, the Delaware Supreme Court held that Zapata should not be bound by the precedential effect of the Chancery Court's decision concerning Zapata's charter. See *Glazer v. Pasternak*, 693 A.2d 319 (Del.1997).

In another case, *Elliott Associates, L.P. v. Avatex*, 715 A.2d 843 (Del.1998), plaintiff preferred stockholders commenced an action to enjoin Avatex Corporation from merging with Xetava Corporation. Avatex formed Xetava (conveniently "Avatex" spelled backwards) for the purpose of effecting a merger designed to eliminate Avatex's outstanding preferred stock. Plaintiffs, however, alleged that the proposed merger triggered a voting provision in Avatex's charter requiring the consent of the holders of two-thirds of the preferred shares.

The proposed merger would convert the preferred stock of Avatex into the common stock of Xetava and eliminate Avatex's charter. Xetava would then be renamed Avatex. Plaintiffs alleged that Avatex's weak financial condition made the preferred stock more valuable than the common stock. Thus, the conversion would adversely affect the preferred stockholders by placing them on equal ground with common stockholders.

The merger agreement did not call for a separate class vote of Avatex's preferred stockholders. It only called for a vote of Avatex's common stockholders. The terms of the certificate of incorporation for Avatex stated that a two-thirds vote of the preferred stock was necessary to amend, whether by merger, consolidation or otherwise, any provision in Avatex's certificate of incorporation that would materially and adversely affect any right, preference or privilege or voting power of the preferred stock or its holders.

The Delaware Supreme Court held that the conversion of the Avatex preferred stock into Xetava common stock coupled with the elimination "by merger" of the preferred stock provisions of Avatex's charter triggered the merger voting provision. Indeed, "the merger does cause an adverse effect because [it] is the corporate act that renders the Avatex certificate that protects the preferred stockholders a 'legal nullity'...." The Court acknowledged that *Warner Communications, Inc. v. Chris–Craft Indus.*, 583 A.2d 962 (Del.Ch.1989) (see Nutshell Section 54F(1)), a case involving similar facts, was distinguishable from *Elliot Associates*. The Court highlighted that the preferred stock voting provision in *Warner Communications* did not include the language "by merger, consolidation or otherwise."

### (5) Redemption Provisions

The preferred stock contract may require or allow the company to redeem some or all of the outstanding shares of a given series of preferred stock. Preferred stockholders whose shares have been redeemed no longer are stockholders of the company once the redemption date has passed. The shares of those preferred stockholders who have not turned them in by that date merely represent the right to receive the redemption price, without interest, from the company once that date has passed.

#### a. Optional Redemption

Preferred stock is "callable" (*i.e.*, redeemable) if the preferred stock contract grants the company the option to redeem it, in whole or in part, at specified redemption prices. The redemption price is usually the liquidation value of the preferred stock plus a small premium. That premium typically declines over the years in a way similar to the premium paid on redeemable bonds. See Nutshell Section 36D(1). When the preferred stock in question is cumulative, the redemption price will also include any accrued and unpaid dividends.

Optional redemption rights are meaningful because they allow companies to refinance their existing preferred stock when interest rates decline through the issuance of a new series of preferred stock with a lower dividend yield. Because redemption prevents current preferred stockholders from receiving their now above-market dividend yield, they demand that the redemption price include a premium. Additionally, they typically demand (and receive) a period of years following the issuance of the preferred stock during which the preferred stock is not redeemable (so-called *call protection*). Of course, debt securities subject to optional redemption are treated similarly. See Nutshell Section 36D(1) (particularly the schedule set forth therein).

### b. Mandatory Redemption

A mandatory redemption provision obligates the company to redeem some or all of its preferred stock at a specified price upon the occurrence of certain events or on specified dates. Multiple redemption dates and redemption prices may be set forth in the preferred stock contract. For example, the preferred stock contract may require the company to redeem all of its preferred shares on the last day of a particular month of a specified year at a specified redemption price plus any accrued and unpaid dividends.

Another mandatory redemption provision often found in the preferred stock contract obligates the company to repurchase preferred stock upon a "change in control" of the company. A company contemplating a transaction constituting a change in control (as defined in the preferred stock contract), therefore, must negotiate with the preferred stockholders over how the preferred stock will be treated in that transaction or face having to re-purchase each holder's shares of preferred stock, typically at a small premium to its liquidation preference, together with any accrued and unpaid dividends. Hand-in-hand with a change in control provision will be an affirmative covenant requiring the company to give notice to all preferred stockholders if a change in control occurs. Events falling within the definition of a "change in control" are similar to those applicable to redeemable debt securities. See Nutshell Section 36D(2).

### (6) Conversion Rights

The preferred stock contract may grant conversion rights to the preferred stockholders. These rights allow them to convert their shares of preferred stock into shares of the company's common stock at a specified *conversion price*. In most cases, conversion is at the option of each preferred stockholder. Until the preferred stockholder converts (if at all), he enjoys a liquidation and dividend preference over common stockholders. Thus, a convertible preferred stockholder has the downside protection of preferred stock and the upside potential of common stock. The preferred stock contract, however, may also provide for automatic conversion upon the occurrence of specified favorable corporate developments (*e.g.,* an initial public offering of the company's common stock).

The conversion price is initially set around 20 to 30% above the current trading price of the company's common stock and is subject to certain future adjustments. Preferred shares are usually convertible into the nearest whole number of common shares. Any fractional shares are payable in cash based on the per share trading price of the company's common stock at the time of conversion.

The economics of convertible preferred stock are substantially similar to those of a convertible bond. The conversion right of convertible preferred stock, however, is coupled with preferred stock rather than a straight bond. See Nutshell Section 45A.

A preferred stock contract will contain provisions protecting the conversion rights of preferred stockholders against specific actions that the company may take in the future that affect its common stock. These provisions protect the conversion rights by adjusting the conversion price to counteract the effects of these actions. These actions include, among others, stock splits, reverse stock splits and stock dividends. They also protect against actions, such as recapitalizations and mergers, which may result in the elimination of the company's common stock. See Nutshell Chapter 13.

The preferred stockholder's conversion right typically allows conversion at any time (similar to an American-style call option). However, conversion rights may be subject to the company's right of optional redemption. Thus, by indicating that it intends to exercise its right of redemption, the company will "force" preferred stockholders to convert if the aggregate value of the company's common stock that the preferred stockholders will receive upon conversion is greater than the aggregate redemption price payable by the company. When this is the case, the company often seeks to force conversion in order to eliminate the need to pay preferred stock dividends going forward. The company, however, must properly notify convertible preferred stockholders of any redemption in advance so that preferred stockholders can convert their shares prior to redemption if they choose to do so. See *Van Gemert v. Boeing Co.*, 520 F.2d 1373 (2d Cir.1975).

Most conversions are "downstream" conversions, whereby holders of preferred stock convert their shares into lower ranking securities such as common stock. Some states permit "upstream" conversions, whereby holders of "junior" preferred stock can convert their shares into higher ranking securities such as "senior" preferred stock or debt securities. As a policy matter, "upstream" conversions are problematic when a company is operating within the vicinity of insolvency, as they allow security holders with subordinated securities to move up the repayment food chain at the expense of existing senior security holders.

### (7) Exchange Rights

The preferred stock contract may provide the company with the ability to exchange shares of an existing series of preferred stock for debt securities (typically debentures) of the company featuring comparable attributes. If the company chooses to exercise its exchange rights, each holder of preferred stock will receive debentures (referred to as *exchange debentures*). The principal amount of the exchange debentures will equal the aggregate par value of the shares of preferred stock held by the holder at the time of the exchange. A company typically cannot force an exchange if dividends on cumulative preferred stock are in arrears. The interest rate payable on the exchange debentures will mirror the dividend yield on the preferred stock. Other negotiated rights of the preferred stockholders, such as conversion, will also be included in the indenture for the exchange debentures.

A company may choose to exchange new debt securities for preferred stock because, unlike preferred stock dividends, interest payments on debt securities are tax deductible. However, unlike preferred stock dividends, which are payable at the board's discretion, interest payments must be paid "come hell or highwater." Accordingly, a company would not exchange new debt securities for preferred stock unless the company is profitable (and thus can utilize the tax deduction).

### (8) Participation Rights

The preferred stockholders' dividend preference is normally "nonparticipating." This means preferred stockholders only receive dividends at the fixed rate specified in the preferred stock contract regardless of the company's earnings. However, preferred stockholders can negotiate for *participation rights*. These rights entitle them to receive, in addition to their preferred stock dividends, dividends payable on common stock as if each share of preferred stock they held were a share of common stock.

The preferred stockholders' liquidation preference does not normally allow preferred stockholders to share in the company's remaining assets beyond the liquidation preference set forth in the preferred stock contract. However, preferred stockholders may negotiate for a share of those assets on top of their stated liquidation preference. When this is done, participating preferred stockholders would receive, in addition to their liquidation preference, some of the company's remaining assets either on a pro rata basis with the common stockholders or according to a specified formula.

### (9) Affirmative and Negative Covenants

A preferred stock contract may contain affirmative and negative covenants. These covenants require (in the case of affirmative covenants) and prohibit (in the case of negative covenants) certain actions by the company. These covenants are substantially similar to those traditionally found in debt indentures, and thus represent another debt-like characteristic of preferred stock. See Nutshell Section 36C.

An affirmative covenant, for example, may require the company to provide holders of convertible preferred stock with a written statement setting forth any adjustment to their conversion price. A negative covenant, by contrast, may prevent the company from merging, consolidating, or selling all or substantially all of its assets without an affirmative vote of the preferred stockholders, voting as a separate class.

*In re Sunstates Corp. Shareholder Litigation*, 788 A.2d 530 (Del.Ch.2001), required the Delaware Chancery Court to interpret a negative covenant contained in Sunstates Corp.'s certificate of incorporation. That covenant prohibited the "Corporation" (defined as Sunstates) from repurchasing shares of its common stock or preferred stock while preferred stock dividends were in arrears. After Sunstates fell into arrears, subsidiary corporations owned or controlled by Sunstates repurchased nearly 70% of Sunstates' outstanding common stock and nearly 30% of Sunstates' outstanding preferred stock.

Plaintiff preferred stockholders brought suit against Sunstates and others arguing that because the purchases were made by subsidiaries controlled or owned by Sunstates or its chairman, those purchases violated Sunstates' certificate of incorporation. Pointing to the doctrine of good faith and fair dealing, they asked the Court to interpret the definition of "Corporation" found in the certificate broadly enough to include Sunstates' subsidiaries. The defendants countered by arguing that the certificate of incorporation had not been violated because Sunstates itself did not purchase any of the stock in question.

The Court agreed with the defendants. It held that the limitation in the certificate was unambiguous and, therefore, must be construed strictly. The Court reasoned that special rights of preferred stockholders must be expressed clearly. Nothing in the certificate barred the subsidiaries from purchasing Sunstates' outstanding common and preferred stocks. According to the Court, "If the special limitation had been meant to apply to the actions of Sunstates' subsidiaries, the certificate of incorporation could have easily said so."

The Court specifically rejected plaintiffs' argument that the duty of good faith and fair dealing prohibited Sunstates from doing indirectly through its subsidiaries that which it could not do directly. The Court stated that the duty of good faith was not implicated because the issue before it was expressly addressed in the certificate of incorporation. Indeed, those who negotiated its terms "knew and understood the scope of the limitations contained therein."

## § 44.  FIDUCIARY AND GOOD FAITH DUTIES

In private transactions, prospective preferred stockholders and their legal and financial representatives bargain over the terms of the preferred stock they purchase. In the context of a public offering of preferred stock, the managing underwriter and its legal representative will negotiate those terms on behalf of prospective public preferred stockholders. In any event, the terms of the preferred stock—whether it is issued privately or publicly—are folded into the issuer's corporate charter typically through a certificate of designation or amendment that becomes part of that charter. Preferred stockholders, therefore, are contract claimants of the corporate issuer.

Yet, preferred stockholders are still "stockholders." This implies they are more than mere contract claimants. But what, if any, are their extra-contractual rights and how do those rights mesh with the fiduciary duties a board of directors owes to common stockholders? The two leading cases in this area are *Dalton v. American Investment Co.*, 490 A.2d 574 (Del.Ch.1985), and *Jedwab v. MGM Grand Hotels, Inc.*, 509 A.2d 584 (Del.Ch.1986).

In *Dalton*, plaintiff preferred stockholders alleged that the American Investment Co. (AIC) board of directors breached its fiduciary duty to them in structuring a merger with Leucadia, Inc. The merger would cash out the common stockholders at $13.00 per share but leave the preferred stockholders "frozen" in the new company.

As a consolation prize, Leucadia had agreed to increase the dividend yield on the preferred stock and to redeem 5% of the outstanding preferred shares at $25 per share each year over a twenty-year period. This, however, paled in comparison to the consideration offered by Household Finance

Corp. (HFC) in a previously proposed deal that was never consummated. HFC would have cashed out the preferred stockholders at $25 per share (equal to the preferred stockholders' liquidation preference).

Plaintiffs argued that the defendant directors breached their fiduciary duty to deal fairly with them. Specifically, they claimed that the Leucadia transaction unfairly promoted the interests of the common stockholders at the expense of the preferred stockholders. Plaintiffs' argument centered on their allegation that the president of AIC (who was also an AIC board member) engaged in misconduct by soliciting the pro-common stockholder offer that Leucadia presented.

Defendants argued that the AIC board had no fiduciary duty to bargain on the preferred stockholders' behalf because the preferred stockholders were only contract claimants of AIC. Moreover, AIC's certificate of incorporation did not contain a provision requiring the board to bargain for the preferred stockholders in the context of a merger. Thus, according to the defendants, the preferred stockholders had only themselves to blame for failing to bargain for redemption or other rights in the event of a merger or sale of substantial assets. Defendants also denied any allegations of misconduct by the president in his negotiations with Leucadia. They claimed that the offer Leucadia presented was unsolicited and that Leucadia had its own economic reasons for presenting it.

Based on the record, the Delaware Chancery Court determined that the offer from Leucadia was unsolicited. Accordingly, the defendants could not have breached any duty because their actions did not cause the loss about which plaintiffs complained. Importantly, the Court refused to clarify whether the defendants owed fiduciary duties to the preferred stockholders, as clarification was not necessary due to the Court's findings on causation.

A year later the Delaware Chancery Court confronted the legal question of whether a board owes fiduciary duties to preferred stockholders in *Jedwab v. MGM Grand Hotels, Inc.*, 509 A.2d 584 (Del.Ch. 1986). The plaintiff owned shares of MGM preferred stock and brought a class action suit seeking to enjoin MGM from consummating a merger with Bally Manufacturing. The plaintiff alleged that the terms of the proposed merger constituted a breach of the duty of MGM's directors to deal fairly with all stockholders (an extension of the duty of loyalty).

The merger would cash out the common stockholders at a price of $18 per share and the preferred stockholders at only $14 per share. Importantly, Kirk Kerkorian, the majority stockholder of MGM and also a defendant, had taken an active role in negotiating the terms of the merger and agreed to vote his shares in favor of it.

The plaintiff argued that the merger was unfair to her because the two classes of stock were essentially equivalent and therefore should have been cashed out at the same price. According to the plaintiff, the circumstances surrounding the issuance of the preferred stock were highly-relevant because they bolstered her equivalency argument.

Bally believed that all the equity in MGM was worth $440 million, but, unlike Leucadia in *Dalton,* made no determination as to how the consideration should be divided amongst the two classes of stockholders. Ultimately, Kerkorian decided that the common stock should be cashed out for $18 per share and the preferred stock for $14 per share. Kerkorian felt compelled to allocate $18 per share for the common stock because that was the price one of his companies had previously offered in a scuttled transaction to purchase all of MGM. To make the deal work given Bally's offer of only $440 million, Kerkorian agreed to sell his common stock for only $12.44 in cash plus certain other property of MGM.

The Court held that under these circumstances directorial fiduciary duties did run in favor of the preferred stockholders. The Court reasoned that while the contract between the preferred stockholders and MGM specified their rights or preferences as against the common stockholders, the rights of preferred stockholders not associated with preferences are shared equally with the common stockholders. The Court stated:

> Thus, with respect to matters relating to preferences or limitations that distinguish preferred stock from common, the duty of the

corporation and its directors is essentially contractual and the scope of duty is appropriately defined by reference to the specific words evidencing that contract; where however, the right asserted is not a preference as against the common stock but rather a right shared equally with the common, the existence of such a right and the scope of the correlative duty may be measured by equitable as well as legal standards.

According to the Court, the plaintiff's claim to a "fair allocation" of merger consideration implicated fiduciary duties rather than a contractual analysis. This was because the appropriate split of merger consideration was not spelled out in the preferred stock contract.

The Court then applied the heightened judicial standard of "entire" or "intrinsic" fairness to the board's allocation of merger consideration. It did so because the plaintiff had pled facts with particularity indicating that Kerkorian may have engaged in self-dealing, thus disabling the business judgment rule. The triggering event was Kerkorian's receipt as a common stockholder of different consideration than that received by the other common stockholders.

Under the intrinsic fairness test, the defendants have the burden of showing that the transaction in question was intrinsically fair. According to the Court, two analyses were warranted in this case. The first was an analysis of the fairness of the allocation of merger consideration between common stockholders and preferred stockholders. The second was an analysis of the fairness of the allocation of merger consideration between Kerkorian as a common stockholder and all other common stockholders.

With respect to the first analysis—the one relating to the plaintiff's complaint—the Court underscored that "fair" does not necessarily mean "equal." Instead of looking at what the public common stockholders were receiving on a per share basis versus what the public preferred stockholders were receiving on a per share basis, the Court examined what all stockholders—both common and preferred—were receiving on a per share basis. This was determined by taking the total merger consideration and dividing it by the combined number of outstanding common and preferred shares. Viewed in this way, the allocation did not appear to be unfair to the Court.

With respect to the second analysis, the Court examined the different consideration Kerkorian was receiving as a common stockholder and viewed it as less valuable than what the other common stockholders were to receive. According to the Court, the other common stockholders were receiving more on a per share basis than Kerkorian because Kerkorian chose to accept less for his shares of common stock in order to make the deal work. The Court highlighted that this was Kerkorian's prerogative. The Court believed, therefore, that the defendants would be able to demonstrate the intrinsic fairness of the merger. Accordingly, it dismissed the plaintiff's motion for a preliminary injunction.

In the subsequent decision *HB Korenvaes Investments, L.P. v. Marriott Corp.*, 1993 WL 205040 (Del.Ch.), the Delaware Chancery Court expanded on its fiduciary duty analysis with respect to preferred stock. It first noted that, in most instances, a review of the preferred stock contract "will exhaust the judicial review of corporate action challenged as a wrong to preferred stock." It added:

> In fact, it is often not analytically helpful to ask the global question whether ... the board of directors does or does not owe fiduciary duties of loyalty to the holders of preferred stock. The question ... may be too broad to be meaningful. In some instances (for example, when the question involves adequacy of disclosures to holders of preferred who have a right to vote) such a duty will exist. In others (for example, the declaration of a dividend designed to eliminate the preferred's right to vote) a duty to act for the good of the preferred does not. Thus, the question whether duties of loyalties are implicated by corporate action affecting preferred stock is a question that demands reference to the particularities of context to fashion a sound reply.

Cases involving the split of merger consideration appear to be the ones most likely to implicate directorial fiduciary duties to preferred stockholders. In *In re FLS Holdings Inc. Shareholders Litigation*, 1993 WL 104562 (Del.Ch.), the plaintiff preferred stockholders asserted that the price negotiated with respect to the cash merger between FLS and Kyoei Steel Ltd., an unrelated third party, was not fairly allocated between the preferred stockholders and the common stockholders of FLS. While most of the preferred stockholders agreed to settle the case, holders of a significant percentage challenged the proposed settlement in court.

With respect to the merger negotiations with Kyoei, FLS was represented exclusively by directors who either owned large amounts of common stock or were affiliated with financial companies that did. No independent advisor or independent directors' committee was appointed to represent the preferred stockholders who were in a conflict of interest situation with the common stockholders. The preferred stockholders did not have a right to vote on the merger or on the allocation. The only protection for the preferred was an ex post facto investment banking fairness opinion indicating that the allocation to the preferred was "fair from a financial point of view." Later, as part of the settlement, the settling preferred stockholders also obtained an expert opinion that the allocation was fair. The Delaware Chancery Court, in refusing to approve the settlement, held that the two fairness opinions, while of some weight, would not substantially assist in satisfying the defendants' burden of showing that the allocation was fair.

A more recent case involving the allocation of merger consideration is *LC Capital Master Fund, Ltd. v. James*, 990 A.2d 435 (Del.Ch.2010). Here, the plaintiff preferred stockholders of QuadraMed Corp. sought to enjoin the acquisition of Quadra-Med by Francisco Partners II, L.P. The preferred stock in question was convertible into shares of common stock. In the event of a merger, the preferred stockholders were contractually entitled to receive the "as if converted value." That value was based on a formula in the certificate of designation governing the preferred stock, and gave the preferred the bottom line right to convert into common at a specified ratio and then receive the same consideration as the common in the merger.

Ignoring their contractual right, the preferred stockholders sought merger consideration above and beyond their "as if converted value" because of their belief that that value understated the value of their shares. They contended that the preferred stock had a strong liquidation preference and certain non-mandatory rights to dividends to which the board of QuadraMed failed to accord adequate value. As a result of these "contractual rights," the preferred stockholders alleged that the board owed the preferred a "fiduciary duty" to accord them more than they were contractually entitled to receive by right in a merger.

The Delaware Chancery Court, however, disagreed. It held that when a certificate of designation does not provide the preferred with any right to vote upon a merger, does not afford the preferred a right to claim a liquidation preference in a merger, but does provide the preferred with a contractual right to certain treatment in a merger, a board of directors that allocates consideration in a manner fully consistent with the bottom-line contractual rights of the preferred need not, as an ordinary matter, do more. According to the Court, "When, by contract, the rights of the preferred in a particular transactional context are articulated, it is those rights that the board must honor. To the extent that the board does so, it need not go further and extend some unspecified fiduciary beneficence on the preferred at the expense of the common." Thus, once the QuadraMed board honored the special contractual rights of the preferred, it was entitled to favor the interests of the common stockholders.

Importantly, the Court distinguished this case from *FLS Holdings* and *Jedwab*, two cases where there was no *objective contractual basis* for determining the allocation of merger consideration. In the absence of such a basis, the only protection for the preferred is if the directors, as the backstop fiduciaries managing the corporation that sold them their shares, figure out a fair way to fill the gap left by incomplete contracting. Otherwise, the preferred would be subject to entirely arbitrary treatment in the context of a merger.

Although unusual, occasions do arise where it is the *common stockholders* rather than the preferred stockholders who complain about an unfair allocation of merger consideration. For example, in *In re Trados Inc. Shareholder Litigation*, 2009 WL 2225958 (Del.Ch.), the merger between Trados Inc. and SDL, plc triggered the $57.9 million liquidation preference of the Trados' preferred stockholders. Of the $60 million in merger consideration offered by SDL, approximately $52 million flowed to the preferred stockholders in partial satisfaction of their liquidation preference. Trados' executive officers received the remaining amount pursuant to a management incentive plan (MIP) which set a graduated compensation scale for the officers based on the price obtained for Trados in an acquisition. Unfortunately, the common stockholders received nothing.

The plaintiff common stockholder brought suit alleging that the directors of Trados breached their duty of loyalty to the common stockholders by approving the merger with full knowledge of the deleterious impact the merger would have on those stockholders. The plaintiff believed that, given the up-swing in Trados' business and its ability to obtain financing, there was no need to sell the company. The plaintiff asserted that the reason the directors never considered the interest of the common stockholders in continuing Trados as a going-concern was that a majority of them were all interested in the transaction.

In supporting its assertion, the plaintiff noted that preferred stockholders consisting of venture capital firms and similar entities contractually appointed four of the seven directors on Trados' board. The plaintiff alleged that the preferred stockholders desired to exit their investment in Trados, and thus these directors had a reason to seek a sale. Two of the three remaining directors were to receive (and did receive) sizable amounts of cash and stock in SDL pursuant to the MIP.

The Delaware Chancery Court, in refusing to dismiss the plaintiff's complaint, held:

> [I]n circumstances where the interests of the common stockholders diverge from those of the preferred stockholders, it is *possible* that a director could breach her duty by improperly favoring the interests of the preferred stockholders over those of the common stockholders.... [T]he factual allegations in the Complaint support a reasonable inference that the interests of the preferred and common stockholders diverged with respect to the decision of whether to pursue the merger.

# CHAPTER 13

# CONVERTIBLE SECURITY HOLDERS

## § 45. ECONOMICS OF CONVERTIBLE SECURITIES

### A. Generally

A convertible security, such as a convertible bond or share of convertible preferred stock, is a hybrid security that allows its holder to exchange it for a given number of shares of the company's common stock any time up to and including the maturity date or earlier redemption of that security. A convertible security is the combination of two distinct financial instruments. In terms of a convertible bond, it is the combination of: (1) a straight bond (*i.e.,* a nonconvertible bond) with the same coupon rate and maturity as the convertible bond; and (2) a conversion right, similar in many respects to a warrant, to purchase shares of the issuer's common stock. The conversion right is not a stand-alone instrument that can be separated from the straight bond and traded, but rather is embedded within the bond. Similarly, convertible preferred stock is the combination of straight preferred stock and a conversion right. While the characteristics of bonds and

preferred stock are addressed elsewhere (see Nutshell Sections 34A(1) and 43, respectively), the conversion right is deserving of its own discussion.

The conversion right is similar to a warrant (see
Nutshell Section 31A(11)) in that it allows its holder to convert the convertible security into shares of
the company's common stock at a preset *conversion
price*. Thus, like a warrant it provides the convertible security holder with the upside potential of
owning common stock in the company. Moreover,
the conversion right, when exercised, increases the
number of outstanding shares of the company's
common stock, thus diluting existing common
stockholders. While the exercise of a warrant has a
similar dilutive effect, a warrantholder normally
pays the exercise price of the warrant in cash. To
exercise the conversion right, by contrast, the convertible security holder does not pay cash but rather surrenders his convertible security.

The initial conversion price is typically set somewhere between 20% and 30% above the issuer's per
share trading price of its common stock at the time
the convertible security is issued. This price is subject to adjustment in the future based on certain
actions an issuer may take that affect its common
stock. These events include, among others, the declaration of forward and reverse stock splits. See
Nutshell Section 49D(3).

To illustrate, assume that a given convertible
bond has a face value of $1,000 and a conversion
price of $36 per share. If a bondholder turns in one

bond for conversion, she will receive 27 shares of the issuer's common stock [$1,000 face value ÷ $36 per share conversion price = 27.77 shares]. The 0.77 of a share in the calculation is called a *fractional share*. Convertible bond indentures typically provide that fractional shares are cashed out by the issuer based on the current trading price of the issuer's common stock. See RMSI § 10.03.

Due to the conversion right, the deal between the convertible bondholders and the issuer differs from that between nonconvertible bondholders and the issuer in three significant ways. First and foremost, convertible bonds typically pay a rate of interest lower (anywhere from 250 to 350 basis points) than that paid on nonconvertible bonds. This lower rate reflects the fact that the conversion right has value. Convertible bondholders "pay" for that right by accepting a lower rate of interest. Second, convertible bondholders customarily accept "subordinated" status. Third, the indenture for convertible bonds typically contains less restrictive financial covenants than does an indenture for nonconvertible bonds.

All three of these differences provide the issuer with operational flexibility which, in turn, could enhance the intrinsic value of the conversion right. The lower interest rate makes it easier for the issuer to service the interest obligations relating to the convertible bond. The subordinated status of the convertible bond means that the issuer is in a position to incur additional indebtedness at a senior level. The less restrictive financial covenants allow the issuer to operate more freely and with less concern of triggering a covenant default under the convertible bond's indenture.

## B. Investment Value and Conversion Value

As seen in Figure 1 below, when a convertible bond is issued, the present value of the straight bond component (the *investment* or *straight* value) is worth less than the convertible bond's face value of $1,000 ($850 in the case of Figure 1). This stems from the below market coupon rate associated with the convertible bond. When the interest payments and the principal to be received in the future are discounted by the interest rate payable on comparable, *nonconvertible* bonds (which rate is higher than that associated with the convertible bond), the resulting present value is less than $1,000. (This is the same notion as a nonconvertible bond with a 5% coupon trading in the secondary market at a discount when interest rates rise above 5%). As the convertible bond's maturity approaches, however, the value of the straight bond component quickly rises to $1,000 (assuming interest rates and issuer credit quality are held constant), as the issuer is contractually obligated to pay $1,000 to the convertible bondholder at maturity. See Figure 1. (The investment value of convertible preferred stock is discussed below.)

The difference between the convertible bond's $1,000 face value and its present value at issuance is the cost of the conversion right to the convertible bondholder. The value of the conversion right (the *stock* or *conversion value*) upon issuance of the convertible bond is substantially less than the bond's $1,000 face value, as the conversion right is similar to an "out-of-the-money" call option. For a discussion of call options, see Nutshell Section 31A(3)a.

To illustrate, Figure 1 provides an example of a convertible bond with a $1,000 face value and a conversion price of $18.20 per share. At issuance, the issuer's common stock was trading at $14.00 per share; therefore, at that time the conversion value of the convertible bond was only $770. This is calculated by first determining how many shares the bondholder would receive when she converts. The answer (rounded) is 55 shares [$1,000 face value ÷ $18.20 conversion price]. However, if she converted immediately, she would receive 55 shares with a market value of only $14.00 per share. Thus, the conversion value of her convertible bond is only $770 [50 shares x $14.00 per share].

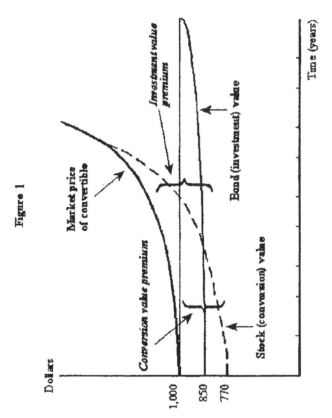

Figure 1

As seen in Figure 1 above, converting a convertible bond before the issuer's stock price rises up to the conversion price makes no sense. To do so would be to over pay for shares of the issuer's common stock. In the preceding example, why give up your convertible bond to buy stock at $18.20 per share when you can use cash and buy shares in the secondary market for only $14.00 per share? More-

over, converting when the issuer's common stock
trading price reaches the conversion price also does
not make sense. This is because a convertible bondholder gives up her right to receive the present
value of the expected bond payments once she converts, and these payments are valuable. Furthermore, a bondholder who converts gives up her senior status as she is now only a common stockholder.
However, the decision whether to convert could be
influenced if the issuer pays dividends (particularly
large dividends) on its common stock, as convertible
bondholders are not entitled to common stock dividends until such time as they convert.

As highlighted in Figure 2 below, the value of a
convertible bond will always be the *greater* of its
investment value and its conversion (stock) value.
At issuance both the investment value and conversion value are less than the convertible bond's
$1,000 face value. The difference between the mar-
ket price of the convertible and the investment
value is called the *investment value premium*. The
difference between the market price of the convertible and the conversion value is called the *conversion value premium*. See Figure 1 above. Until the
conversion value premium is eliminated, it makes
no sense to convert. Because the value of the
straight bond component is unlikely to rise in any
significant way due to its below-market coupon
rate, the main way the conversion value premium is
eliminated (if at all) is through an increase in the
conversion value related to the conversion right.
Conversion value, in turn, depends on the value of

the issuer's common stock. Increases in the value of the issuer's common stock whittle away at the conversion premium. At some point after the common stock price rises above the conversion price, the conversion value premium will be eliminated. Convertible bondholders should not convert until this occurs.

Figure 2

The investment value of convertible preferred stock is determined in a similar manner. Because preferred stock is a form of ownership, its life is assumed to be infinite and therefore the present value factor used to find its value is not readily available. The investment value of convertible preferred stock is assumed to equal the present value of the preferred dividends over an infinite life (an annuity) discounted at the higher yield associated with *straight* preferred stock. The present value factor for an infinite-lived annuity is, therefore:

$$V = \frac{D}{r}$$

where:     $D$ = dividend on the preferred stock
           $r$ = appropriate discount rate or current yield on nonconvertible preferred stock

For example, assume that The P&S Company has just issued 6% convertible preferred stock with a $100 par value. If the company had issued nonconvertible preferred stock, the annual dividend (paid in quarterly installments) would likely have been around 8%. Dividing the annual dividend of $6 (6% of $100) by the yield on nonconvertible preferreds, or 8%, results in an investment value for the preferred stock of $75 ($6/.08) per share.

## C. Calling the Security

A company typically issues convertible securities expecting that its common stock price will rise above the conversion price, thus resulting in investors exercising their conversion rights. Investors, however, would prefer to continue holding convertible securities even after the conversion right is significantly "in-the-money." Indeed, a convertible security's price will continue to rise as the price of the underlying stock increases. Additionally, investors will continue to receive interest or dividend payments along the way while maintaining their seniority over common stock. However, if the company pays a common stock dividend, investors must factor this into their decision on whether to convert or to continue to hold.

An issuer, however, seeks the optional right to redeem (or "call in") convertible securities, and the desire for this right is why issuers generally prefer to issue convertible bonds rather than straight debt with warrants attached. Indeed, it is generally in the issuer's interest, on behalf of *existing stockholders*, to force conversion as soon as the conversion value of the securities exceeds the redemption or call price for two reasons. First, whenever stock is sold at a price below the current market price, existing stockholders suffer value dilution; higher current market prices lead to more substantial dilution. Because management is suppose to act in the best interests of existing stockholders and not prospective stockholders, management has a built in incentive to minimize the wealth transfer that results from value dilution. Second, calling the securities eliminates the issuer's obligation to pay interest or dividends on those securities. However, an issuer typically pays a call price that includes a small premium when it redeems its convertible securities.

In order to ensure that investors convert, most issuers wait for the conversion value to rise at least 15% over the redemption or call price. This provides a sufficient cushion for possible declines in the market price of an issuer's common stock between the date the call is announced and the actual redemption date. If a company calls in its convertible securities at a time when their conversion value is not favorable in relation to the redemption or call price, investors could choose to have their securities redeemed for cash (at the call price), thus forcing the company to make a cash outlay at possibly an inopportune time. (If a company finds itself in a gray area, it could simply "encourage" rather than "force" investors to convert simply by raising its common stock dividend to an attractive level.)

Faced with choosing between a higher conversion value or a lower redemption or call price (even one representing a small premium), convertible security holders opt for the former and convert their convertible securities into shares of the issuer's common stock. Those who forget to do so may pay a very high price for their mistake, as seen in Nutshell Section 46C(1). One study has shown that the median delay before an issuer calls in its convertible securities, once the conversion value of those securities exceeds the redemption or call price, is only 77 days. However, the median delay is only 20 days when the conversion value rises 20% above the redemption or call price.

## D. Justifications for Convertible Securities

What motivates investors to purchase convertible securities and issuers to issue them? Why wouldn't an investor interested in capital gains and an appetite for risk simply buy shares of common stock outright? Why wouldn't an investor seeking current income and the relative safety of principal buy a higher yielding straight bond?

Investors buying convertible securities apparently are seeking a compromise vehicle. This vehicle blends current income, safety of principal and capital gain potential. Thus, for example, those who buy convertible bonds receive interest on the straight bond component while having the upside potential of common stock. Furthermore, they retain senior security holder status until they convert their convertible bonds into common stock. Even if the issuer's common stock falls in price, the worst-case scenario for a convertible security holder seeking to sell her convertible security in the secondary market is that the price of that security will only have declined to the point where its yield matches that of a comparable straight bond. See Figure 2 above.

An issuer, by contrast, is often driven to issue convertible securities for two reasons. First, it may view the issuance of convertible securities as deferred common stock financing. In other words, the issuer may desire to raise capital through the sale of common stock rather than straight debt or preferred stock. However, if its management believes its common stock is currently undervalued by the market, then issuing additional shares of common stock today is unappealing. By issuing convertible securities instead, the issuer reasons that it is essentially selling its common stock today at a price 20% to 30% higher than the current trading price of its stock. In return for doing so, it must pay interest or dividends to investors until the time, if ever, that it makes economic sense for them to convert their securities.

Second, the issuer may prefer to issue straight bonds or preferred stock but finds it cannot sell them at a reasonable interest or dividend rate due to the issuer's creditworthiness or other factors. In this regard, issuing convertible securities may be better tailored to the issuer's cash flow pattern. The lower coupon or dividend rate associated with convertibles makes it more likely that the company can meet its interest or dividend obligations.

These issuer rationales, however, have been challenged with respect to convertible bonds (although these challenges would apply equally to convertible preferred stock). Thomas Copeland, Fred Weston and Kuldeep Shastri have analyzed the true cost of capital associated with both the straight bond component and the associated conversion right of a convertible bond. They have concluded that, while convertible bonds may represent a deferred sale of the company's common stock, that sale is not at an attractive, above-market price. Moreover, based on the convertibles' true cost of capital, they argue that convertible bonds do not represent a form of "cheap debt." Thus, they encourage companies to reexamine why they issue convertible debt securities.

## § 46. PROTECTING THE CONVERSION RIGHT

### A. Introduction

Holders of convertible securities, such as convertible bonds and convertible preferred stock, typically receive a lower yield on those securities in exchange for receiving conversion rights. These rights allow the holder to convert his convertible securities into shares of the company's common stock at a conversion price specified in his contract. If the company succeeds going forward, the trading price of its common shares will eventually rise above the conversion price. This makes conversion attractive because convertible security holders can convert their securities into common stock at a below-market price per share (*i.e.,* at the conversion price). It is crucial, therefore, to protect the benefits conversion rights confer.

## B.  Fiduciary Duties

Delaware law is clear that convertible security holders' rights are not protected by fiduciary duties. In *Simons v. Cogan*, 549 A.2d 300 (Del.1988), the Delaware Supreme Court ruled that the conversion rights of a holder of convertible subordinated debentures did not create the type of expectancy interest that would support the imposition of fiduciary duties on officers and directors. Rather, the security holder would have to depend on her contract for protection. Cf. *Anadarko Petroleum Corp. v. Panhandle Eastern Corp.*, 545 A.2d 1171 (Del.1988) (holding that a corporate parent and the directors of its wholly-owned subsidiary owed no fiduciary duties to prospective stockholders of the subsidiary after the parent declared its intention to spin-off the subsidiary.)

## C.  Contractual Rights

Given the holding of *Simons v. Cogan* above, special provisions must be inserted into the convertible security contract (be it an indenture or a certificate of designation) to protect the value of conversion rights when the company engages in certain actions that affect its common stock. The goal of these protective provisions is to preserve the benefit of the convertible security holders' bargain as reflected in their contract.

## (1) Notice of Redemption

The convertible security contract often grants the company an optional right of redemption. If the company exercises this right, convertible security holders cannot convert their securities once the conversion deadline (typically a specified number of days prior to the date of redemption) arrives. If the conversion value of a convertible security holder's conversion rights exceeds the redemption price payable by the company, that convertible security holder will forfeit the difference between the two if he fails to convert prior to the conversion deadline. Therefore, it is crucial that the company notify the convertible security holders of its intention to redeem the convertible securities.

This notice requirement was underscored in *Van Gemert v. Boeing Co.*, 520 F.2d 1373 (2d Cir.1975). Appellants owned convertible redeemable debentures of the Boeing Company that were listed for trading on the NYSE. After Boeing redeemed the debentures, appellants sued Boeing alleging that Boeing gave them "inadequate and unreasonable notice" of Boeing's intention to redeem the debentures. Because of Boeing's actions, appellants were unable to exercise their right to convert their debentures into Boeing common stock before the conversion deadline. This resulted in a tremendous forfeiture of value by the appellants.

While the debentures themselves stated that a holder could convert up to and including the tenth day prior to the redemption date, they did not say how Boeing should provide notice of redemption. The debenture indenture, however, required Boeing to publish prior to the date fixed for redemption a notice of redemption at least twice in an authorized newspaper, the first such publication to be not less than 30 days and not more than 90 days before the date fixed for redemption. The NYSE required Boeing to notify immediately, typically via a general news release, the holders of any listed securities of any action taken by the company with regard to any rights or benefits pertaining to the ownership of its securities. Furthermore, the NYSE required Boeing to afford holders a "proper period" within which to exercise their rights.

Boeing issued a news release that mentioned, among other things, that the company's management was authorized to call for redemption at a future date all of the debentures. The dates for redemption and the expiration of conversion rights, however, were not mentioned. Boeing did, however, thereafter comply with the requirements of the debentures and the indenture by publishing formal "notices" in the requisite newspapers. As for the NYSE's requirements, Boeing did not issue a general publicity release until three days before the expiration of conversion rights.

Boeing's main defense was that the debenture holders had accepted the risk that they might not receive notice of redemption at the time they subscribed for the debentures. The Second Circuit, however, disagreed, finding two deficiencies with

Boeing's notice. First, Boeing failed to tell debenture holders what notice would be given in the event of redemption. According to the Second Circuit, a "duty of reasonable notice" arose out of the contract between Boeing and the debenture holders. Although debenture holders could have reviewed the indenture, the Court held that burying notice mechanics in a 113 page indenture was "no notice at all." Second, the newspaper notice given by Boeing itself was inadequate. Boeing could have ran more than two advertisements and put the information in the proxy statement it mailed off to stockholders (many of whom were debenture holders as well) during that time.

Thus, the Court stepped in to protect the conversion rights of convertible debenture holders. Today, security lawyers are careful to draft documents that clearly specify how an issuer will provide a notice of redemption. Thus, the blame for failing to convert on time in the face of an impending redemption will fall squarely on the shoulders of the convertible security holders.

### (2) Antidilution

Convertible security contracts, as well as a contract for a warrant, will typically include antidilution provisions. These provisions protect security holders against actions which companies voluntarily take that dilute the common stock these holders receive upon conversion or exercise. Thus, antidilution provisions cover stock splits (both forward and reverse), stock dividends and the issuance of so-called "cheap stock." They also cover situations where companies distribute assets or evidences of indebtedness to their common stockholders.

### a.    Cash Dividends

Convertible security contracts often do not protect convertible security holders from cash dividends that companies pay out to their common stockholders. The ones that do, however, typically differentiate between ordinary cash dividends and extraordinary cash dividends, and call for a conversion price adjustment in the case of the latter. For example, Section 10.08 of the RMSI requires a conversion price adjustment with respect to cash dividends or distributions, unless such dividends or distributions are paid in any fiscal year out of the company's consolidated net income for the current fiscal year or the prior fiscal year, as shown on the books of the company prepared in accordance with GAAP.

In *Corporate Property Associates 14 Inc. v. CHR Holding Corp.*, 2008 WL 963048 (Del.Ch.), the plaintiffs held warrants to purchase common stock in the defendant company, CHR. The warrant contract did not require CHR to provide warrantholders with advanced notice of cash dividends; nor did it protect the warrantholders from dilution from cash dividends. In two successive years, CHR was recapitalized through two large debt issuances.

CHR paid out the proceeds of those issuances to common stockholders as cash dividends.

Several weeks before the second dividend was issued, the plaintiffs sent CHR a questionnaire for the purpose of valuing their warrants, asking about "any significant changes/developments related to the business over the course of the past six months." Rather than remaining silent, a CHR officer replied but omitted any reference to the second debt issuance or cash dividend that CHR alleged was still in the process of being finalized at the time of the reply, but was in fact issued within the next three weeks. CHR supported the decision not to discuss the upcoming dividend because the questionnaire related to the past activities of the company. But the plaintiffs contended that if the pending dividend had been fully disclosed at that time, they would have exercised their warrants to obtain shares in CHR in order to participate in the dividend.

The warrantholders alleged that the defendants breached their fiduciary duties to them. They also alleged a breach of the implied covenant of good faith and fair dealing, in addition to separate claims of fraud and negligent misrepresentation. Citing long-standing Delaware case law, the Delaware Chancery Court held that warrantholders are not owed fiduciary duties until their warrants are converted into shares of the company. It therefore approved the defendants' motion to dismiss the claim for breach of fiduciary duties. The Court also refused to find that the defendants had breached the implied duty of good faith and fair dealing, noting that the parties were sophisticated and knew that the payment of cash dividends has a dilutive effect and, therefore, the only protection from that duty is contractual. Thus, the Court was not about to "fill the gap" using the implied covenant of good faith and fair dealing.

The Court, however, denied the defendants' motion to dismiss the fraud and misrepresentation tort claims with respect to the second dividend. CHR's voluntary response to the question of whether there had been "any significant changes/developments" was misleadingly incomplete. Although one can choose to remain silent, according to the Court, the choice to speak exposes the speaker to liability if his words are materially misleading. Quoting Section 529 of the Restatement (Second) of Torts, the Court held that once a party chooses to speak, he can be held liable if he makes "[a] representation stating the truth so far as it goes but which the maker knows or believes to be materially misleading because of his failure to state additional or qualifying matter."

### b.  Forward and Reverse Stock Splits and Stock Dividends

A company may, for many reasons, declare a forward stock split or stock dividend. See Nutshell Section 49D. A convertible security contract, including contracts for warrants, will typically include antidilution provisions which protect security holders against these actions as well as others that dilute the common stock they receive upon conversion or exercise. Also included in an antidilution provision are adjustments for reverse stock splits, although these adjustments protect the company rather than the convertible security holders. See RMSI § 10.06.

Antidilution provisions typically seek to adjust the conversion price based on a proportional formula. The conversion price must be adjusted so that a convertible security holder receives that number of shares of common stock for each convertible security *after* the action in question had he converted *immediately prior* to that action.

For example, in the event of a 2–for–1 forward stock split, the conversion price is simply divided by 2. Thus, a convertible security holder receives twice as many shares of common stock when he converts following the split. This is needed because, after the split, shares of the company's common stock are only half as valuable. (See Nutshell Section 49D(3)a). A similar adjustment is made to offset a stock dividend, which essentially is a stock split of 1.2–to–1 or less. (See Nutshell Section 49D(2)).

In the event of a 1–for–2 *reverse* stock split, the conversion price is doubled. Thus, a convertible security holder receives half as many shares of common stock when he converts following the reverse split. This is needed because, after the reverse split, shares of the company's common stock are twice as valuable. (See Nutshell Section 49D(3)b).

In *Reiss v. Financial Performance Corp.*, 764 N.E.2d 958 (N.Y.2001), the defendant Financial Performance Corporation (FPC) issued warrants to the plaintiffs in partial repayment of a loan. The warrants allowed the plaintiffs to purchase shares of FPC's common stock for 10 cents per share until specified dates. Before the warrants expired, FPC effected a 1–for–5 reverse stock split. As a result, FPC stockholders were deemed to own one-fifth the number of shares they held before the split. Their shares, however, increased five times in value due to the split. When the plaintiffs thereafter attempted to exercise their warrants, they sought to purchase all the stock specified in the warrants at 10 cents per share without taking into account that the reverse stock split had made FPC's shares five times as valuable.

The warrants in question did not address what should be done in the case of forward or reverse stock splits. Therefore, the plaintiffs argued that FPC assumed the risk of a reverse stock split and the warrants should be enforced on their own terms. FPC countered that the plaintiffs' interpretation would result in a "windfall" to the plaintiffs. It asked the court to imply an adjustment provision into the warrants, because splits were not contemplated at the time the warrants were issued.

The New York Court of Appeals determined that FPC could have foreseen the occurrence of a reverse stock split at the time it issued the warrants to the plaintiffs. One month prior to the issuance of the warrants in question, FPC had issued a warrant to a third party that covered the contingency of a reverse stock split. The Court also determined that the warrant contract was drafted by sophisticated parties who may have intentionally omitted a provision addressing reverse stock splits. Because the Court believed all material provisions of the contract were present, it held that the warrants were enforceable on their own terms.

Importantly, the Court distinguished the case of *Cofman v. Acton Corp.*, 958 F.2d 494 (1st Cir.1992). *Cofman* involved a forward stock split but its facts were otherwise similar to those in *Reiss*. However, the parties in *Cofman*, unlike the parties in *Reiss*, had not given any thought at all to stock splits. Therefore, according to the *Cofman* court, an *essential term* of the contract was missing. The *Cofman* court therefore *inferred* a contract term to deal with a forward stock split. In doing so, the *Cofman* court stated that, without such a provision, a forward stock split would *"eviscerate"* the warrants involved in the case. It underscored the necessity of inferring a contract term, noting that the plaintiff certainly "[did] not intend to acquire nothing."

In *Lohnes v. Level 3 Comm., Inc.*, 272 F.3d 49 (1st Cir.2001), the plaintiff's warrant contained a two-paragraph antidilution provision which, upon the occurrence of certain described events, automatically adjusted the number of shares to which the plaintiff would be entitled upon exercise of the warrant. Share adjustments were triggered by the following five separate contingencies, *none of which were defined*: capital reorganization; reclassification of common stock; merger; consolidation; and sale of all or substantially all the capital stock or assets of Level 3 Communications, the issuer of the warrant. Conspicuously missing, however, was language covering stock splits.

Later, Level 3 conducted a two-for-one stock split which was effected in the form of a stock dividend granting shareholders one new share of stock for each share held. After Level 3 had answered the plaintiff's inquiry as to whether the share adjustment provision in the warrant had been triggered in the negative, the plaintiff exercised his warrant and sued for breach of the warrant contract. The plaintiff's contention was that the stock split implemented as a stock dividend constituted either a "capital reorganization" or a "reclassification of stock."

The First Circuit, however, disagreed with the plaintiff's position. In doing so, it pointed out that the accounting mechanics that accompany a stock split are mere window dressing that has no effect on the total shareholders' equity or on any other substantive aspect of Level 3's balance sheet. Because a stock split does not entail a substantial change in a corporation's capital structure, the unelaborated term "capital reorganization," according to the First Circuit, cannot plausibly include a stock split effected as a stock dividend.

The First Circuit further held that the stock split effected as a stock dividend did not result in the "reclassification of stock." According to the Court, "the sine qua non of a reclassification of stock is the modification of existing shares into something fundamentally different. [There are] two ways in which a security can be altered fundamentally: (a) by changing the class of stock, or (b) by modifying important rights or preferences linked to stock." The Court highlighted that stock splits effected by stock dividends do not entail any such fundamental alteration of the character of an existing security. For example, Level 3's stock split in no way altered its shareholders' proportionate ownership interest, varied the class of securities held, or revised any of the attributes associated with the stock. Moreover, the stock split did not have a meaningful impact on either the corporation's balance sheet or capital structure.

### c.    "Cheap Stock"

Antidilution provisions also cover a company's issuance of common stock at prices below the current market price of its common stock (so-called *cheap stock*). Exceptions, however, are made for employee stock options and the conversion of existing securities. One example of a cheap stock issuance is a "rights offering." Here, existing shareholders are given the right to purchase additional shares of common stock in the issuer at a slight discount to the current market price of the issuer's common stock. Companies experiencing severe financial difficulties often conduct rights offerings in order to raise capital at a time when a public offering is infeasible. However, because the issuance of cheap stock dilutes the value of the company's existing common stock (see Nutshell Section 50A), convertible security holders deserve to receive more shares of the now diluted common stock to make them whole. Thus, a downward adjustment to the conversion price is in order. See RMSI §§ 10.07 & 10.09.

The following formula illustrates the adjustment made to the conversion price when the company issues cheap stock.

$$ACP = CP \times \frac{OCS + \dfrac{(NCS \times \mathbf{OP})}{\mathbf{CMP}}}{OCS + NCS}$$

where:

| | | |
|---|---|---|
| ACP | = | adjusted conversion price |
| CP | = | conversion price in effect at the time the adjustment is calculated |
| OCS | = | number of outstanding shares of common stock |
| NCS | = | number of new shares (*i.e.,* the cheap stock) of common stock being issued |
| OP | = | offering price per share of new shares (*i.e.,* the cheap stock) of common stock being issued |
| CMP | = | current market price per share of common stock (typically based on a 30–day average) |

The key to the formula above (see bold) is the below-market offering price (OP) of the cheap stock essentially being divided by the current market price of the company's common stock (CMP). This results in a number less than one. When this is multiplied by the conversion price (CP), it results in an adjusted conversion price (ACP) that is lower than that conversion price. A lower conversion price, in turn, provides the convertible security holders with more shares of common stock upon conversion. No adjustment to the conversion price is typically made until a one percent change occurs. Changes affecting the conversion price by an amount less than one percent are carried forward and added to future adjustments when determining whether the one percent threshold has been met.

### d.  Distribution of Evidences of Indebtedness and Assets

Adjustments to the conversion price are typically made when the company distributes evidences of indebtedness or assets (*e.g.*, shares of a subsidiary distributed as part of a "spin-off") to its common stockholders. Excluded, however, are cash dividends and warrants or rights covered by other protective provisions typically contained in the convertible security holders' contract. See RMSI § 10.08.

In the event of a distribution, the existing conversion price (CP) is adjusted as follows:

$$\text{ACP} = \text{CP} \times \frac{\text{CMP} - \mathbf{D}}{\text{CMP}}$$

where:  
ACP = adjusted conversion price  
CP = conversion price in effect at the time the adjustment is calculated  
CMP = current market price per share of common stock (typically based on a 30–day average)  
D = per share value of the distribution being received by common stockholders

The key to the formula above (see bold) is the subtraction of the per share distribution (D) that common stockholders will receive from the current market price per share of the common stock (CMP). When the difference is then divided by the current market price per share of the company's common stock (CMP), it results in a number less than one. When this is multiplied by the conversion price (CP), it results in an adjusted conversion price (ACP) that is lower than that conversion price. A lower conversion price, in turn, provides the convertible security holders with more shares of common stock upon conversion. No adjustment to the conversion price is typically made until a one percent change occurs. Changes affecting the conversion price by an amount less than one percent are carried forward and added to future adjustments when determining whether the one percent threshold has been met.

*HB Korenvaes Investments v. Marriott Corp.*, 1993 WL 257422 (Del.Ch.) discusses adjustments to the conversion price of convertible preferred stock in the face of a spin-off (*i.e.*, a distribution of assets). Marriott Corp. (Marriott) decided to place all of its "growth businesses" into a new subsidiary, "Marriott International," and distribute all the shares of that new subsidiary to Marriott's common stockholders in a spin-off. Marriott would retain all of its other businesses and change its name to "Host Marriott." See Nutshell Section 54G.

For various reasons, plaintiff convertible preferred stockholders of Marriott sought a preliminary injunction to enjoin the spin-off. One of their many allegations was that Marriott undervalued the subsidiary it was spinning off. The value of the subsidiary was crucial because it was the main determinant of the adjustment to be made to the preferred stockholders' conversion price. (On a per share basis, it is the "D" in the formula above). A higher value would result in a lower conversion price; thus, the preferred stockholders would receive more shares of Host Marriott after the spin-off when they converted.

The plaintiffs argued that the value of the distribution was easily determined, because Marriott International's shares of common stock, although not yet issued, had begun trading on the NYSE on a "when issued" basis. ("D," therefore, should equal the "when issued" per share price). Marriott, however, essentially determined the intrinsic value of

Marriott International without reference to its "when issued" stock price. The Delaware Chancery Court sided with Marriott. Because both valuation methods made sense to the Court, it simply deferred to the business judgment of Marriott's directors.

### (3) Antidestruction

Conversion rights are typically drafted to provide the convertible security holders with a substitute for the company's common stock in the event its common stock is eliminated. A typical *antidestruction* provision will allow a convertible security holder to convert into the same consideration paid to the company's common stockholders as part of the transaction leading to the elimination of the company's common stock. See RMSI § 10.17.

For example, suppose SGH Company has shares of convertible preferred stock outstanding that are protected by an antidestruction provision. Currently, each share of preferred stock is convertible into four shares of SGH's common stock based on the current conversion price. Suppose SGH Company agrees to merge with JJH Corp., a subsidiary formed by RHR Co. to effect the merger. SGH will be the surviving company in this reverse triangular merger (see Nutshell Section 54C(3)). Therefore, SGH's convertible preferred stock will remain outstanding. Its common stock, however, will not remain outstanding, as its sole share of common stock will be owned by RHR after the merger. As merger consideration, common stockholders of SGH will receive 1.5 shares of RHR common stock. Accordingly, based on the antidestruction provision, SGH's convertible preferred stockholders will be able to convert each share of their preferred stock into six shares of RHR common stock after the merger [4 x 1.5].

The Delaware Supreme Court in *Wood v. Coastal States Gas Corp.*, 401 A.2d 932 (Del.1979), interpreted an antidestruction provision. Coastal States Gas Corp. (Coastal) had issued two series of cumulative convertible preferred stock, both with identical dividend and liquidation preferences. After the business of Coastal and its subsidiaries took a dramatic turn for the worse, Coastal decided to spin-off its most valuable subsidiary to its common stockholders in the form of a "special dividend." Plaintiff preferred stockholders sued Coastal to enjoin the spin-off.

The plaintiffs argued that the spin-off violated their contractual rights because they would not receive any of the subsidiary's shares. They further argued that the spin-off was a "recapitalization" which, by virtue of an antidestruction provision, entitled them to a portion of the spun-off shares. Plaintiffs believed a "recapitalization" was occurring because Coastal's capital structure would be significantly changed as a result of the spin-off.

The Court, however, looked at the antidestruction clause and noticed the key phrase *"in lieu of."* The antidestruction clause in Coastal's two certificates of designation only covered transactions resulting in the elimination of Coastal's common stock. If the provision was triggered, preferred stockholders would receive something "in lieu of" common stock upon conversion of their preferred stock. That "something" was the consideration received by the common stockholders as part of the transaction.

The Court looked at the "in lieu of" phrase and held that no recapitalization was occurring as a result of the spin-off. Indeed, the antidestruction clause could not be triggered if, after the consummation of the transaction in question, Coastal's common stock remained outstanding. The Court thus held that the distribution of subsidiary stock in the spin-off could go forward because it did not constitute a "recapitalization." Coastal common stock would still exist after the transaction, and thus it was still possible for the preferred stockholders to convert their preferred shares into shares of Coastal common stock. Of course, as the plaintiffs noted, the Coastal common stock they would receive upon conversion would be substantially less valuable following the spin-off, as that stock no longer represented an indirect ownership interest in the spun-off subsidiary.

### (4) Appraisal Rights

The courts have also been asked whether convertible security holders receive appraisal rights if a proposed merger entitles common stockholders to those rights. In *Aspen Advisors LLC v. United Art-*

*ists Theatre Co.*, 861 A.2d 1251 (Del.2004), the Delaware Supreme Court answered in the negative. The plaintiff warrantholders believed the common stock of United Artists was worth more than the merger consideration being offered. Because the common stockholders were entitled to appraisal rights, the plaintiffs sued for those rights hoping to receive the "fair value" of the stock underlying their warrants rather than the merger consideration to which they were entitled due to an antidestruction clause in their warrants.

In denying the plaintiff's request for appraisal rights, the Delaware Supreme Court underscored that a "[w]arrantholder is not a stockholder. Warrantholders have paid for an option. They have a choice: whether to take an investment risk or not. A warrantholder only becomes a shareholder by investing something of value that meets the exercise terms of the warrant." It further added that "[a] warrantholder is only entitled to the rights of a shareholder—including statutory appraisal rights— *after* they [sic] make an investment in the corporation in accordance with the terms of the warrant and thereby expose themselves to the risks that are incident to stock ownership." The Court also highlighted that warrantholders are not entitled to vote on the merger, and therefore are not in a position to vote against it and eschew the merger consideration—both key components to the statutory appraisal remedy found in Section 262 of the DGCL. For more on common stockholder appraisal rights, see Nutshell Section 23.

# CHAPTER 14

# COMMON STOCKHOLDERS

## § 47.  CHARACTERISTICS
## OF COMMON STOCK

Unlike creditors and preferred stockholders, common stockholders generally are not contract claimants of the corporation. Indeed, very few rights of common stockholders are typically spelled out in a corporation's charter, with an exception being made for certain hybrid forms of common stock. Rather, common stockholders, as the equity owners of a corporation, are *residual claimants*. In an earnings context, they have a claim on the corporation's earnings subject to the dividend preference of preferred stockholders. In a liquidation context, they are entitled to any assets of the corporation that remain after the corporation pays off all its contract claimants.

Dividend payments to common stockholders are not guaranteed. They are payable at the discretion of the board of directors. Moreover, they are subject to any restrictions in the corporation's charter and to the legal capital rule of the state in which the corporation was formed. See Nutshell Section 49B.

Common stockholders elect the board of directors and vote on many fundamental corporate transactions. Each share of stock typically entitles its holder to one vote, although stock with multiple votes per share or even no votes per share is permissible under the corporate codes of most states. See, e.g., DGCL § 212(a) and NYBCL § 501(a).

Most corporations typically have shares of only one class of common stock outstanding. Outstanding shares are issued shares in the hands of investors other than the company itself. Therefore, they represent the entire equity interest in the corporation, and those who own them own the corporation. Shares that are authorized under the corporate charter but not yet issued are not considered when determining the ownership percentage of each shareholder—only outstanding shares are considered. Moreover, a corporation can repurchase previously outstanding shares and hold them in its treasury. Such shares—referred to as "treasury shares"—are not considered outstanding when determining ownership percentages, although they are still considered to have been issued. See Nutshell Section 5C.

Corporations can issue shares of more than one class of common stock. Doing so recognizes that many investors have little or no interest in controlling the corporation by exercising voting rights. Instead, they only seek the financial benefits of an investment in the corporation. The typical situation involves a corporation currently owned by a single stockholder or group of stockholders (often family members). In order to raise equity financing while at the same time keeping control in the hands of those who currently hold it, the corporation will convert the shares of the controlling stockholders into shares of a class of common stock that has multiple votes per share (often as high as 10)—so called "supervoting stock." The corporation will then sell to new investors (often through an IPO) shares of another class of common stock that only has one vote per share. Other than voting rights, the only other substantive difference between the two classes is that those who hold the supervoting stock typically have conversion rights enabling them to convert their supervoting stock into shares of the other class of stock. Conversion rights thus allow the controlling stockholders to "unwind" the dual class structure and go back to a single class structure. Other than voting and conversion rights, shares of each class of stock in a dual class structure are otherwise substantively equivalent. The variance in voting rights between the dual classes as well as the conversion rights associated with the supervoting stock will be spelled out contractually in the corporation's charter.

## § 48. CORPORATE GOVERNANCE AND FIDUCIARY PROTECTIONS

### A. Corporate Governance

Corporate governance refers to the allocation of decisionmaking power between directors, officers and stockholders of a corporation. The corporate code of a given state specifies the governance structure for corporations incorporated within that state. Within the parameters of the applicable corporate code, a corporation's charter and by-laws will further delineate the allocation of power among stockholders, directors and officers.

## (1) Stockholders

A fundamental concept in corporate governance is the separation between ownership and control. While stockholders are the equity owners of the corporation, they generally do not manage the business and affairs of the corporation. (Closely-held corporations are typically an exception, as stockholders often are also directors and officers of those corporations). Managerial control is statutorily provided to the directors, although a corporation's charter can modify this. See DGCL § 141(a). Directors are agents of the stockholders and are charged with representing their interests. Directors, in turn, often delegate the day-to-day managerial responsibilities to the corporation's senior officers. This is especially true when the corporation in question is publicly-traded.

Part of the power of the stockholders lies in their ability to elect directors. Stockholders typically elect directors at the annual meeting of stockholders. Each stockholder's voting power is directly tied to the amount of her capital contribution, as votes are allocated on a per share basis. Under Section 141(k) of the DGCL, stockholders may also remove directors "with or without cause" at any meeting called for the specific purpose of removing a director or directors. The corporate charter, however, can be modified so that stockholders can remove a director only for "cause." Under Delaware law, directors must have a "compelling justification" for taking unilateral action which impinges on the stockholders' voting franchise. See *Blasius Industries, Inc. v. Atlas Corp.*, 564 A.2d 651 (Del.Ch.1988).

Another part of the stockholders' power lies in their ability to approve certain fundamental changes and corporate transactions, including the following: (1) an amendment to the corporate charter (DGCL § 242(b)); (2) most mergers or consolidations (DGCL § 251, et al.); (3) a sale of all or substantially all of the assets of the corporation (DGCL § 271); and (4) the dissolution of the corporation (DGCL § 275). Additionally, stockholders always retain the power to amend the corporation's by-laws, although this power can be shared with the directors (DGCL § 109(a)). Lastly, stockholders have the ability to "cleanse" an interested director transaction through a stockholder vote (DGCL § 144) (see Nutshell Section 48B(2)a).

### (2) Directors

Under Section 141(a) of the DGCL, the business and affairs of a Delaware corporation are managed by or under the direction of the board of directors, except as otherwise provided in the corporation's charter. The board of a publicly-traded company, however, generally operates only in an oversight capacity, while senior officers run the day-to-day affairs of the corporation. Directors have fiduciary duties running to the corporation and its stockholders.

The board of a publicly-traded company typically meets six to eight times a year to deal with two primary responsibilities: decisionmaking and oversight. Directors review and approve corporate strategy, policy and direction based on recommendations proffered by senior officers. They also debate and approve specific corporate actions, such as a proposed merger and the hiring of key officers. Directors also are responsible for overseeing those to whom they delegated day-to-day managerial authority.

### (3) Officers

Corporations typically have a chief executive officer (CEO), a president, one or more vice presidents, a corporate secretary and a treasurer. These officers are charged by the board with the responsibility of managing the day-to-day operations of the corporation. Like directors, corporate officers have fiduciary duties running to the corporation and its stockholders.

The general authority of corporate officers to act as agents of the corporation is typically set forth in a state's corporate code and the corporation's charter or by-laws. However, more explicit authority for a given officer to take specific actions on behalf of the corporation is often set forth in resolutions that the board of directors adopts either at a meeting or through unanimous written consent.

## B. Fiduciary Duties

The rights of common stockholders are not contractual in most instances. Because of this, the law imposes fiduciary duties on the stockholders' agents—a company's directors and officers—in order to protect their interests. Very limited fiduciary duties also run to preferred stockholders. See Nutshell Section 44.

Directors and officers must satisfy their fiduciary duties of care, good faith and loyalty. These duties are embodied in Section 4.01(a) of the ALI–PCG. Under this section, a director or officer has a duty to the corporation to perform her functions in good faith, in a manner that she reasonably believes to be in the best interest of the corporation, and with the care that an ordinarily prudent person would reasonably be expected to exercise in a like position and under similar circumstances.

### (1) The Duty of Care

Corporate directors and officers owe the corporation and its stockholders a duty of care. They must perform their duties with the care that an ordinarily prudent person in a like position would exercise under similar circumstances. At a minimum, the duty requires directors and officers to have a general understanding of their corporation's business. See *Francis v. United Jersey Bank*, 432 A.2d 814 (N.J.1981); *Brane v. Roth*, 590 N.E.2d 587 (Ind.Ct. App.1992). Directors, especially those of publicly-traded companies, must also have attempted to install a reasonable reporting system designed to upstream information from the corporation's ranks to the directors. See *In re Caremark Int'l Inc. Derivative Litigation*, 698 A.2d 959 (Del.Ch.1996).

Duty of care jurisprudence, however, mostly relates to allegations of directorial negligence in the context of business decisionmaking. In Delaware, the standard against which directorial decisionmaking is measured is gross negligence, rather than simple or "mere" negligence. See *Smith v. Van Gorkom*, 488 A.2d 858 (Del.1985). This stems from the public policy of encouraging directors to be business risk takers, something a simple negligence standard would deter. Further supporting this policy is the duty of care's focus on the *process* followed by fiduciaries when they make decisions, rather than on the actual decisions they make. For example, in *Joy v. North*, 692 F.2d 880 (2d Cir.1982), the Second Circuit, applying Connecticut law, held that business decisions made upon reasonable information with some rationality do not give rise to directorial liability even if they turn out poorly or even disastrously from the standpoint of the corporation.

Judicial reluctance to impose liability on directors after the fact has been doctrinally labeled the *busi-*

*ness judgment rule.* The business judgment rule is a rebuttable legal presumption that, in making a business decision, directors of a corporation acted on an informed basis, in good faith and in the honest belief that the action taken was in the best interests of the corporation. See *Unocal Corp. v. Mesa Petroleum Co.*, 493 A.2d 946 (Del.1985). In other words, the business judgment rule is a rebuttable legal presumption that directors satisfied their fiduciary duties when making a business decision.

In *Smith v. Van Gorkom*, 488 A.2d 858 (Del. 1985), for example, the Delaware Supreme Court held that the directors of Trans Union Corp. did not adequately inform themselves about the value of their corporation in connection with its sale to another corporation. The Court concluded that under the business judgment rule, there is no protection for directors who have made an unintelligent or ill-advised judgment if their decisionmaking process is grossly negligent.

The burden is on the party challenging a board action to establish facts rebutting the presumption. See *Unitrin, Inc. v. American General Corp.*, 651 A.2d 1361 (Del.1995). If the presumption is not rebutted, "a court will not substitute its judgment for that of the board if the [board's] decision can be 'attributed to any rational business purpose.'" *Unocal.* The plaintiff has both the initial burden of proving that the act complained of cannot be attributed to any rational business purpose, as well as the ultimate burden of persuasion. See *Simon Property Group, Inc. v. Taubman*, 2003 WL 430485 (E.D. Mich.2003).

A director's duty of care in the context of a decision to sell her company or purchase another company is discussed in Nutshell Section 59.

### (2) The Duty of Loyalty

In addition to the duty of care, directors and officers also owe a duty of loyalty to the corporation and its stockholders. The duty of loyalty requires a director or officer to put the interests of the corporation and its stockholders ahead of her own personal interests or those of another person or organization with which she is affiliated.

The duty of loyalty is implicated primarily in three situations. First, it is implicated when a director transacts business with her corporation, either directly or through another entity in which that director has a personal financial interest (a *self-interested* or *self-dealing* transaction). Second, it is implicated when a director personally pursues a business opportunity belonging to the corporation (a *corporate opportunity* problem). Lastly, this duty is implicated whenever a director approves an action, such as the adoption of a takeover defense, which has as a byproduct the protection of the director's job (an *entrenchment* problem). Each of these situations is considered below.

### a.   Self–Interested Transactions

When a fiduciary and her corporation transact business, a conflict of interest arises. The fiduciary stands to gain from a transaction which, as a director, she is also responsible for approving on behalf of the corporation. The self-interested transaction is "direct" when the corporation and the director are both parties to the transaction. The self-interested transaction is "indirect" when the director has a personal financial interest in and/or sits on the governing board of an entity that is directly involved in the transaction with the corporation.

Historically, self-interested transactions were voidable by the corporation or a stockholder. However, many of these transactions provide net benefits to the corporation and thus should be pursued. Therefore, while duty of loyalty concerns are triggered by self-dealing transactions, those transactions can be cleansed under so-called "interested director" statutes.

For example, Section 144 of the DGCL states, in pertinent part, that a transaction shall not be void or voidable solely for the reason that a director or officer, or an entity in which the director or officer has an interest, is a party to a transaction with the corporation in question if:

> (1) the material facts as to the director's or officer's relationship or interest and as to the transaction itself are disclosed or known to the board, and a majority of disin-

terested directors authorizes the transaction;

(2) the material facts as to the director's or officer's relationship or interest and as to the transaction itself are disclosed or known to the stockholders, and the stockholders vote to approve the transaction; or

(3) the transaction is fair to the corporation.

The interested director or officer has the burden of proof under DGCL Section 144. If she satisfies her burden, then the business judgment rule attaches to the board's decision to approve the transaction. A plaintiff stockholder challenging the transaction would then have the burden of demonstrating that it amounted to waste or a gift (*i.e.*, it was "unfair"). See *Fliegler v. Lawrence*, 361 A.2d 218 (Del.1976).

### b.  Corporate Opportunities

Duty of loyalty concerns also arise when a fiduciary takes (*"usurps"*) a business opportunity that the corporation could have pursued. The corporate opportunity doctrine is based upon the principle that corporate directors and officers are bound by their duty of loyalty to subordinate their self-interest to the well-being of the corporation.

The corporate opportunity doctrine does not prohibit corporate managers from taking outside business opportunities. However, the doctrine requires that the corporation reject the opportunity following complete disclosure before the fiduciary can pursue it. See *Northeast Harbor Golf Club, Inc. v. Harris*, 661 A.2d 1146 (Me.1995). The party challenging a given transaction, rather than the fiduciary, has the burden of proving that the opportunity in question is a "corporate opportunity" in the first place.

The courts have articulated a variety of tests to determine whether a given opportunity is a "corporate opportunity" or not. For example, in *Guth v. Loft*, 5 A.2d 503 (Del.1939), the Delaware Supreme Court embraced the "line of business" test. In holding that the corporate officer violated his fiduciary duty to his corporation in this case, the Court reasoned that the business opportunity presented to the officer was one that the corporation was financially able to undertake and was in the corporation's line of business. In other words, by seizing the opportunity and pursuing it the officer literally became a *competitor* of the corporation. Therefore, the officer could not seize that opportunity unless, after full disclosure, the corporation chose not to pursue it.

By contrast, the Maine Supreme Court in *Northeast Harbor Golf Club* rejected the "line of business" test employed by Delaware. It believed that it was too difficult to answer whether or not a particular opportunity was within the corporation's line of business. Moreover, in the Court's view, the "line of business" test placed too much emphasis on the corporation's financial ability to pursue an opportunity, as excellent opportunities very often open up financing that would not otherwise be available.

Instead, the Maine Supreme Court embraced Section 5.05 of the ALI–PCG. That model provision states that a corporate officer or director cannot take a "*corporate opportunity*" (as defined) *unless*: (1) she offered it to the corporation after *full disclosure* of the conflict of interest and the opportunity; (2) the corporation has rejected the opportunity; and (3) either (a) the taking of the opportunity was "fair" to the corporation, (b) disinterested directors rejected the opportunity in advance in a manner that met the standards of the business judgment rule; or (c) disinterested shareholders rejected the opportunity in advance (or ratified it after-the-fact) and the rejection was not a waste of corporate assets. Importantly, the official comment to Section 5.05 underscores that the rejection of the opportunity by the corporation may be based on a number of factors, including its *financial inability* to pursue the opportunity.

Under Section 5.05, a "corporate opportunity" means one of two things. First, it is *any opportunity* to engage in a *business activity* of which a director or officer becomes aware either (a) in connection with the performance of his or her job, or under circumstances that should reasonably lead the director or officer to believe that the person offering the opportunity expects it to be offered to the corporation, or (b) through the use of corporate information or property, if the resulting opportunity is one that the director or officer should reasonably be expected to believe would be of interest to the corporation. Thus, opportunities learned while "on the job" or through corporation information or property are "corporate opportunities." Second, it is any opportunity to engage in a business activity of which an *officer* (but not a director) becomes aware essentially while off the job (*i.e.*, from a source other than those listed in clauses (a) and (b) above) and *knows* is *closely related* to a business in which a corporation is engaged *or* expects to engage.

In terms of the burden of proof, if a given opportunity's rejection was not properly authorized by disinterested directors or ratified by disinterested shareholders, then the director or officer has the burden of proving that her taking of the opportunity was *fair* to the corporation. Otherwise, the person challenging the taking of the opportunity has the burden of proving that its taking was unfair.

### c. Entrenchment

See discussion in Nutshell Section 60D(2).

### (3) The Duty of Good Faith

The duty of good faith has a fairly short yet tortured history, at least when it comes to Delaware law. Most commentators and practitioners had viewed the duty of good faith simply as a subset of the duty of loyalty. Indeed, if a director acts in bad faith, then she is being disloyal to the corporation.

Nonetheless, in the watershed opinion *In re Walt Disney Derivative Litigation*, 906 A.2d 27 (Del. 2006), the Delaware Supreme Court *strongly implied* that the duty of good faith is, indeed, a separate and distinct fiduciary duty. However, it quickly clarified its decision in two subsequent cases.

The *Disney* case involved Walt Disney Co.'s ill-fated employment of famed super agent Michael Ovitz for about a one-year period beginning in October 1995 and ending ignominiously in December 1996. Ovitz was a founding partner of Creative Artist Agency ("CAA") when the CEO of Disney, Michael Eisner, came courting. Ovitz's main concern in leaving CAA was that Disney would terminate him prematurely "without cause," and therefore he wanted a contract containing a termination payment that reflected the fact that he was giving up his sizeable ownership in CAA to join Disney. Ultimately, Ovitz's contract contained, among other things, a no-fault termination (or "NFT") payment provision.

Once on board, Ovitz clashed with Eisner, leading Eisner to fire Ovitz *without cause*. As a result, Disney was forced to write Ovitz a check for approximately $130 million in accordance with the NFT payment provision of his employment contract. This did not sit well with Disney's shareholders, and they brought suit challenging the payment.

While the appellant shareholders alleged that the Disney directors breached their duty of care and wasted corporate assets, the case is primarily known for the shareholders' allegation that the directors engaged in "bad faith" conduct—that is, they breached their duty of good faith. Of course, the appellant shareholders have the burden of proving bad faith in order to rebut the business judgment rule's presumption of good faith conduct.

The Delaware Chancery Court had defined bad faith as follows:

> [Bad faith is the] *intentional* dereliction of duty, a *conscious* disregard for one's responsibilities. *Deliberate* indifference and inaction in the face of a duty to act is … conduct that is clearly disloyal to the corporation. It is the epitome of faithless conduct. (emphasis added)

The appellant shareholders challenged this definition, arguing, among other things, that it was not properly tied to board decisionmaking under the *duty of care*. In reviewing this allegation, the Delaware Supreme Court noted that there are three *potential* categories of "bad faith" conduct. The first potential category involved *subjective bad faith*, which consists of fiduciary conduct motivated by an *actual intent to do harm*. This is the clearest example of "bad faith" conduct. However, the appellant shareholders had not alleged that the Disney directors engaged in this type of bad faith conduct.

The second potential category of bad faith conduct—one proffered by the appellant shareholders—was grossly negligent directorial conduct without any malevolent intent. In this regard, the appellants asserted that claims of gross negligence establish breaches of not only the duty of care but also the duty of good faith. In other words, appellants sought to *conflate* the duty of care with the duty of good faith by making a violation of the former an automatic violation of the latter.

The Delaware Supreme Court, however, disagreed. In doing so, the Court pointed to two acts of the Delaware General Assembly that clearly indicated that the Assembly had viewed the duties of good faith and due care as distinct duties from a legal standpoint. First, DGCL Section 102(b)(7) allows a Delaware corporation to insert a provision in its charter that exculpates directors from monetary damage liability for most breaches of the *duty of care*. However, specifically carved out are "acts or omissions *not* in good faith." Viewing due care and good faith as the same thing would eviscerate the impact of DGCL Section 102(b)(7). Second, pursuant to DGCL Section 145, a Delaware corporation may *indemnify* any person who is or was a director, officer, employee or agent of the corporation against certain expenses where (i) that person is, was, or is threatened to be made a party to that action, suit or proceeding, and (ii) that person "acted in *good faith* and in a manner the person reasonably believed to be in or not opposed to the best interests of the corporation." Thus, a Delaware corporation can indemnify a director for liability incurred by reason of her violation of the duty of care, but *not* for a violation of the duty to act in good faith. Thus, according to the Court, the second potential category of bad faith conduct *is not*, in fact, a true category of bad faith conduct.

The third and final potential category of bad faith conduct covers the *intentional* dereliction of duty, a *conscious* disregard of one's responsibilities. This is the type of conduct covered by the lower court's definition of "bad faith." According to the Delaware Supreme Court, this type of fiduciary misconduct is *more culpable* than gross negligence. This stems from the fact that grossly negligent conduct is at least *affirmative* conduct engaged in by the fiduciary who is taking the action *believing* it will benefit the corporation. An intentional dereliction of duty, by contrast, is intentional conduct *not* taken for the benefit of the corporation.

The Delaware Supreme Court further noted that intentional dereliction of duty does not involve traditional disloyalty. Indeed, traditional disloyalty involves a fiduciary putting her own needs ahead of those of the corporation and its shareholders. See Nutshell Section 48B(2). Situations where the fiduciary acts with a purpose *other than* advancing the interests of the corporation, but *not* in her own self-interest, are *not covered* by the traditional duty of loyalty. Instead, they are covered by the duty to act in good faith. In other words, disloyal conduct without self-interest amounts to bad faith conduct.

Finding that the defendant directors had not engaged in an intentional dereliction of duty, the Delaware Supreme Court upheld the lower court's determination that the Disney directors had not engaged in bad faith conduct. It disavowed any attempt to provide a comprehensive or exclusive definition of "bad faith." However, it was quick to note that the lower court's definition of "bad faith" was sufficient to decide the case.

As a result of the *Disney* decision, many plaintiffs' attorneys became giddy with the idea that the Delaware Supreme Court had held that the duty of good faith was an independent fiduciary duty and, by extension, formed the basis for an independent cause of action for breach of it. The Delaware Supreme Court, however, quickly dashed their hopes in this regard through two subsequent decisions.

The first case, *Stone v. Ritter*, 911 A.2d 362 (Del.2006), involved a derivative shareholder suit against the directors of a bank holding company. Plaintiff shareholders alleged that the defendant directors had improperly discharged their "oversight" duties by failing to detect that bank employees had, in some cases, failed to file Suspicious Activities Reports with respect to money laundering monitoring duties under the Federal Bank Secrecy Act. The Delaware Supreme Court reaffirmed that the following "oversight" standard taken from *In re Caremark Int'l Deriv. Litig.*, 698 A.2d 959 (Del.Ch. 1996), continued to apply in this situation:

> Generally, where a claim of directorial liability for corporate loss is predicated upon ignorance of liability creating activities within the corporation[,] ... only a sustained or systematic

failure of the board to exercise oversight—such as an utter failure to attempt to assure a reasonable information and reporting system exists—will establish the *lack of good faith* that is a necessary condition to liability. (Emphasis added).

The Delaware Supreme Court went on to state that, in *Disney*, it had deliberately left open the issue of whether a violation of the duty of good faith created an independent cause of action. It then held that a failure to act in good faith is not conduct that results, *ipso facto*, in the direct imposition of fiduciary liability. Instead, the failure to act in good faith *may* result in liability because a lack of good faith is a "subsidiary element," *i.e.*, a condition, of the *fundamental duty of loyalty*. Therefore, a demonstration of bad faith conduct is essential to establish director oversight liability, and the fiduciary duty violated by that conduct is the duty of loyalty.

The Delaware Supreme Court in *Stone* also stated that its view on the issue of good faith has two consequences. The first consequence is that, although the duty of good faith may be "colloquially described" as one of a "triad" of fiduciary duties, including the duties of care and loyalty, only violations of the duties of care and loyalty may result in *direct* liability. Violations of the duty of good faith may only result in *indirect* liability. The second consequence is that the duty of loyalty is not limited to issues regarding "financial or other cognizable fiduciary conflict of interest," but also includes actions involving good faith. Indeed, a director cannot act loyally towards the corporation unless she acts in the good faith belief that her actions are in the corporation's best interest.

In the second case, *Lyondell Chem. Co. v. Ryan*, 970 A.2d 235 (Del.2009), shareholders alleged that the defendant directors breached their fiduciary duties, including the duty of good faith, in connection with the sale of their company. The company's charter contained an exculpatory charter provision which exonerated directors for breaches of the duty of care. However, such a provision is impotent against breaches of the duty of loyalty through a failure to act in good faith. The lower court had denied the directors' motion for summary judgment on the issue of bad faith due to their "two months of slothful indifference despite knowing that the Company was in play," as well as the fact that they "languidly awaited overtures from potential suitors. . . ."

In finding that the lower court had erred in not granting summary judgment in favor of the directors, the Delaware Supreme Court stated that, in a transactional context like the one involved in this case, an extreme set of facts is required to sustain a disloyalty claim premised on the notion that disinterested directors were intentionally disregarding their duties. The lower court asserted that the defendant directors' "unexplained inaction" had prevented it from determining that the directors had acted in good faith (and thus granting their motion for summary judgment). But, according to the Delaware Supreme Court, if the directors failed to do all that they should have done under the circumstances, then they breached their *duty of care*. According to the Court, "[o]nly if they knowingly and completely failed to undertake their responsibilities would they breach their duty of loyalty." The Court determined that the lower court had approached the record from the wrong perspective. Indeed, according to the Court: "Instead of questioning whether disinterested, independent directors did everything that they (arguably) should have done to obtain the best sale price, the inquiry should have been whether those directors utterly failed to attempt to obtain the best sale price."

## § 49.　DECLARATION AND PAYMENT OF DIVIDENDS AND DISTRIBUTIONS

### A.　Introduction

While the cash dividend remains the foremost method by which a corporation allocates its earnings to its stockholders, it is not the only way, and many times, not the most beneficial way. Indeed, Section 173 of the DGCL states that "dividends may be paid in cash, in property, or in shares of the corporation's capital stock."

Dividends are payable at the discretion of the board of directors. The board, however, must exercise its discretion in accordance with its fiduciary duties to the corporation and all of its stockholders.

See Nutshell Section 49E. Moreover, the board's discretion is subject to any restrictions in the corporation's charter and the legal capital rule of the jurisdiction in which the corporation was formed.

A contractual right of the stockholders to a cash dividend arises when the board *declares* a dividend. Upon a valid declaration of a cash dividend, the corporation becomes indebted to the stockholders, and the stockholders may recover the declared amount in an action, *ex contractu*, against the corporation. The same rule, however, does not apply to non-cash dividends, such as stock dividends. See *Anadarko Petroleum Corp. v. Panhandle Eastern Corp.*, 545 A.2d 1171 (Del.1988).

## B.  Legal Capital Rules

### (1) Basic Theory

Each state's corporate code has a legal capital rule. *Legal capital* is the amount of capital that stockholders contribute to the company that, by statute, must remain permanently in the company to satisfy the claims of creditors. Thus, a state's legal capital rule is designed to protect a company's creditors by ensuring that a minimal capital cushion always exists from which their claims may be satisfied.

A legal capital rule will prohibit the company's directors from either (a) declaring and paying dividends to common or preferred stockholders or (b) redeeming shares of stock, in each case out of the amount determined to be legal capital. Thus, before directors pay a dividend or redeem stock, they must assure themselves that the payment or redemption will not violate the legal capital rule of the state of their company's formation.

Older legal capital rules, such as Delaware's, are based primarily on the concept of "par value." More modern statutes depend on insolvency rules that are not linked to that concept. Both are discussed in Nutshell Sections 49B(3) and (4).

### (2) Par Value

*Par value* is the minimum amount of consideration that a corporation can legally accept from an investor for a share of its common or preferred stock. For example, if the par value of a share of a company's common stock is $1.00, then a potential investor must pay at least $1.00 per share for the stock he buys. Consideration paid by that investor equal to the aggregate par value of the shares he purchases will be included in the "capital stock" account on the company's balance sheet. (If the company has both common stock and preferred stock outstanding, this account is bifurcated into a "common stock account" and a "preferred stock account"). Of course, companies try to sell their shares of stock at prices significantly higher than par value. Any consideration that an investor pays in excess of par value is included in the "additional paid-in-capital account" (APIC) on the company's balance sheet.

Legal capital rules based on par value state that, at a minimum, the dollar amount contained in a company's capital stock account represents legal capital. Thus, in theory, the concept of par value looms large. Today, however, par values for common stock are typically extremely small amounts, such as a dollar or less per share. Par values on preferred stock, by contrast, range from $20 to $100 per share, as they are chosen to mimic the face value of a debt security. Lower par values hurt creditors because they minimize the size of the capital cushion designed to protect creditors. Higher par values, by contrast, help protect creditors.

Companies can issue so-called "no par" stock. See, e.g., DGCL § 151(a) and NYBCL § 501(a). However, at least some of the consideration from the sale of this stock still flows into the capital stock account. Instead, no par stock allows a company's board of directors to determine how much of the consideration received for the stock will be allocated to the company's capital stock account and its APIC account each time the company sells stock. Thus, no par value stock really means *"no predetermined amount of par value per share."* See, e.g., DGCL § 154 and NYBCL § 504(d). The board makes this ad hoc allocation through board resolutions. A failure to make an allocation within the time period specified by statute results in all the consideration received for the stock being allocated to the company's capital stock account. This, in turn, works to the advantage of the company's creditors. See, e.g., DGCL § 154 and NYBCL § 506(b).

### (3) Traditional Statutes

Traditional legal capital statutes are based, at least in part, on the concept of "par value." For example, Delaware's legal capital rule (DGCL § 170(a)) states that a company's directors may declare and pay dividends upon the shares of its capital stock (*e.g.,* common or preferred stock) either (1) out of the company's "surplus" (as determined in accordance with DGCL § 154) or (2) if there is no surplus, out of the company's net profits for the current fiscal year and/or the preceding fiscal year.

Thus, the initial inquiry is whether any "surplus" exists. If some does, then the second part of Delaware's test is irrelevant. Pursuant to Section 154 of the DGCL, "surplus" is the excess, if any, of the company's "net assets" over the amount determined to be "capital." All the information needed to calculate "surplus" comes directly from the company's balance sheet.

Par value comes into play with respect to "capital." Capital is simply the amount in the company's capital stock account. That amount is equal to the number of outstanding shares of stock multiplied by that stock's par value or, if the stock is "no par" stock, an ad hoc amount determined by the board of directors. If the company in question has issued both common and preferred stock, the capital stock account is broken down into a "common stock" account and a "preferred stock" account. When this is the case, "capital" is simply the sum of the amounts contained in those two accounts.

"Net assets," according to Section 154, is the amount by which the company's total assets (TA) exceed its total liabilities (TL). Thus, the following is the formula for "surplus":

$$\text{Surplus} = (TA - TL) - \text{Capital}$$

Under Section 170(a) of the DGCL, if a company has no surplus, it can still pay a dividend so long as the company has net profits in the current fiscal year *and/or* the previous fiscal year. The aggregate dividend paid, however, cannot exceed these profits. The result is clearly pro-stockholder and anti-creditor. Even if the company has a history of losing money, it nevertheless can pay a dividend to its stockholders as long as it was fortuitous enough to have a net profit in the current fiscal year and/or the previous fiscal year.

For example, assume that SGH Corp., a Delaware corporation, has 100,000 shares of outstanding common stock, each of which has a $2 par value. Therefore, the amount in SGH's capital stock account is $200,000 [100,000 shares x $2 par value]. Further assume that SGH's total assets equal $3 million and its total liabilities equal $2.6 million. Finally, assume that in the current fiscal year SGH has incurred a *net loss* of $400,000, while last fiscal year it had a *net profit* of $100,000. Based on these facts, can SGH pay a dividend to its common stockholders? If so, up to what amount per share?

First, determine whether SGH has "surplus." As seen below, the answer is yes.

$$\text{Surplus} \; = \; (\text{TA} - \text{TL}) - \text{Capital}$$
$$= \; (\$3{,}000{,}000 - \$2{,}600{,}000) - \$200{,}000$$
$$= \; \$200{,}000$$

Because SGH in this example has surplus, the net profit prong of Delaware's legal capital rule is irrelevant. Thus, based on its surplus, SGH can pay up to $200,000 in the aggregate in dividends, or $2 per share [$200,000 surplus ÷ 100,000 shares].

Changing the facts slightly, if SGH's total liabilities were $2.9 million rather than $2.6 million, can SGH pay a dividend? If so, up to what amount per share?

First, determine whether SGH has "surplus." As seen below, the answer is no.

$$\text{Surplus} \; = \; (\text{TA} - \text{TL}) - \text{Capital}$$
$$= \; (\$3{,}000{,}000 - \$2{,}900{,}000) - \$200{,}000$$
$$= \; (\$100{,}000)$$

Second, because SGH has no surplus, look to see if it has net profits in the current fiscal year and/or the previous fiscal year. Based on the facts, SGH's current fiscal year does not help because SGH has incurred a $400,000 loss. Its previous fiscal year, however, showed a net profit of $100,000. If the two are added together, a net loss of $300,000 exists. However, there is *no need* to add them together.

The net profit test is an "and/or" test. Therefore, SGH can declare and pay a dividend based on its net profits from the previous fiscal year without considering the net effect of both years. Thus, it can pay up to $100,000 in the aggregate in dividends, or $1 per share [$100,000 net profit from previous fiscal year ÷ 100,000 shares].

Under Section 174(a) of the DGCL, directors generally are jointly and severally liable for approving a dividend that illegally reduces the corporation's capital cushion. They are liable to the corporation or, if the corporation is in dissolution, the corporation's creditors for the amount by which the aggregate dividend paid exceeds the amount legally available for the payment of dividends.

Two important exceptions exist. First, Section 174(a) states that only directors who willfully or negligently violate the legal capital rule are liable. Importantly, Section 172 of the DGCL allows directors to rely on the determinations of the corporation's accountants when deciding whether the legal capital rule is met. A corporation's accountants normally make all legal capital calculations. Second, under Section 174(c), any director held liable can, in turn, sue any stockholders who received the dividend with knowledge that it was illegal. This is particularly important in the context of a closely-held corporation, because its stockholders typically keep a close eye on it. Therefore, they might be aware of the illegality of a given dividend.

### (4) New Model Statutes

Modern legal capital rules place more focus on whether a given corporation is *insolvent* when it makes a distribution or becomes insolvent as a result of that distribution. A thumbnail definition of an insolvent corporation is one that is "unable to pay its debts as they become due" in the ordinary course of business. See, e.g., *John T. Callahan & Sons, Inc. v. Dykeman Elec. Co.*, 266 F.Supp.2d 208 (D.Mass.2003).

The *Equity Insolvency Test* prohibits a corporation from making a distribution when it is insolvent or would be rendered insolvent as a result of that distribution. While this test is seemingly analogous to state fraudulent conveyance statutes, the consequences stemming from its violation differ. The equity insolvency test, like other legal capital rules, imposes liability on directors who authorize and pay excessive dividends. State fraudulent conveyance statutes, by contrast, allow trustees and receivers to force third parties (usually creditors) to return monies or property received from an insolvent corporation back to that corporation. See Nutshell Section 38A.

The *Balance Sheet Test* prohibits distributions that would reduce a corporation's total assets to an amount less than the sum of its total liabilities and the liquidation preferences of its preferred stock. The RMBCA uses the Equity Insolvency Test and the Balance Sheet Test as an "either/or" legal capital rule. See RMBCA § 6.40(c).

The *Balance Sheet Surplus Test* restricts distributions to the amount by which a corporation's assets exceed the sum of its liabilities and "stated capital." (This is simply the "surplus" prong of Delaware's legal capital rule, with Delaware referring to "stated capital" simply as "capital"). Stated capital is the amount set forth in the capital stock account on the corporation's balance sheet. New York corporations must satisfy both the Equity Insolvency Test and the Balance Sheet Surplus Test before they can legally make a distribution. See NYBCL § 510(a) & (b). However, in a true "race to the bottom," New York amended its Balance Sheet Surplus Test in 2008 to embody both prongs of Delaware's legal capital rule. Thus, assuming the Equity Insolvency Test is also met, a New York corporation can make distributions out of its net income in the current fiscal year and/or previous fiscal year if it has no surplus. In situations where a New York corporation pays a distribution when it has no surplus (but did have net income in the current and/or previous fiscal years), the corporation must be very careful not to run afoul of New York's Equity Insolvency Test as a result.

The *Earned Surplus Test* allows a corporation to make a distribution solely from the corporation's earnings rather than its capital. Earned surplus represents the "retained earnings" of the corporation over its life until the distribution is made. Thus, the maximum aggregate dividend a corporation can pay is the amount set forth in its retained earnings account on its balance sheet. Dividends based on earned surplus represent a return *on* capital rather than a return *of* capital. The Model Business Corporation Act employed this test prior to its revision.

The *California Test* allows a California corporation to make a distribution out of retained earnings (the same as the Earned Surplus Test). However, if retained earnings are insufficient to make the desired distribution, that distribution may still be made if, after giving effect to the proposed distribution (a) the corporation's ratio of assets to liabilities exceeds 1.25 to 1 and (b) either (1) its current assets are equal to or more than its current liabilities or (2) in the event the average of the earnings of the corporation before taxes and interest expense for the two preceding fiscal years was less than the average of the interest expense of the corporation for those fiscal years, its current assets are at least equal to 1.25 times its current liabilities. See Cal. Corp. Code § 500. In any event, a California corporation cannot make a distribution if it is insolvent or the distribution would render it insolvent. See Cal. Corp. Code § 501.

## C.   Cash Dividends

### (1)  Overview

A cash dividend is simply a cash payment by a corporation to investors who own shares of that corporation's stock. A corporation can pay cash dividends on any class or series of its capital stock, whether common or preferred. Dividends represent actual and observable returns on a stockholder's investment in a corporation.

The management of each profitable corporation debates its dividend policy periodically. How much of a corporation's available cash should be allocated to stockholders and how much should be invested back into the corporation? The ratio between these two amounts is called the *dividend payout ratio*.

Companies in mature industries, such as utilities, often choose to pay a quarterly cash dividend and strive to increase the dollar amount of that dividend gradually over time. Consistent payment of dividends is used to compensate investors for the lower potential in earnings growth that is inherent in mature companies. Income-oriented investors, like retirees, favor dividend paying stocks because they are relatively safe, less volatile investments offering a steady flow of income. Other companies, like Warren Buffett's Berkshire Hathaway, never pay cash dividends and instead reinvest all earnings. Likewise, many technology companies are notorious *zero payout* companies, even though many hold huge sums of cash. However, these companies typically offer investors a higher potential for growth, and thus wealth, through a rising stock price.

When a company pays out dividends to its stockholders, that payment has a "signaling effect" on the market. An increase in dividend payout is a "bullish" or positive signal, generally indicating management's favorable outlook for the company's future profitability and growth. Conversely, a decrease gives the market a "bearish" or negative signal. Accordingly, most companies are extremely careful to raise their dividend payouts only to sustainable levels to avoid having to reduce them in future years.

### (2) Dividend Policy Theories

The three major theories on the "optimal" payout ratio for dividends are the Traditional Theory, the Irrelevance Theory and the Tax Preference Theory. Each is discussed below.

#### a. The Traditional Theory

Espoused by Graham and Dodd, the Traditional Theory of dividend policy holds that investors prefer a stable and generous dividend over time. Indeed, investors seek a return on their investment, and what would be better than cash as a return? The market understands that a stable and generous dividend reduces the variability of returns on stocks. Moreover, earnings that are retained in the firm remain at risk as management's plans for the money may not come to fruition. This risk is eliminated when the money is returned to the stockholders. Thus, the Traditional Theory is sometimes referred to as the "bird in the hand" theory, because $1 in hand is thought to be less risky than $1 remaining at risk through reinvestment in the company. Given the questionable accounting methods used by some corporations in the past, it is understandable that many investors skeptically view corporations that report only "paper earnings" on their profit and loss statement.

Under the Traditional Theory, companies with relatively high returns on equity (ROE) should retain a greater portion of earnings because they have solid opportunities to pursue with it. An investor with a strong preference for cash can generate cash by simply selling some of his shares and need not rely on dividend payments to satisfy that preference. By contrast, companies with relatively low ROEs should retain a smaller portion, as it makes sense to pay cash dividends when opportunities for profitable expansion or diversification are not present.

### b. The Irrelevance Theory

Modigliani and Miller have argued that once a company has made and disclosed its investment policy to investors, its dividend payout ratio makes no difference for purposes of share values. They contend that share value depends entirely on the earning power of a company's assets. This power, they argued, is unaffected by how operations are financed—whether out of retained earnings or through additional borrowings or stock offerings. In other words, the Traditional Theory implicitly assumes a fixed capital structure and a trade-off between paying dividends and reinvesting. But this assumption fails to recognize that it is possible to do both through reconfiguring the capital structure with borrowings or new equity issues. Moreover, Modigliani and Miller disposed of the Traditional Theory's "bird in the hand" preference by arguing that most investors would reinvest the $1 in cash in the same or similar firms anyway and that the risk of reinvestment in any firm arises from risk with respect to a company's cash flows and not risk with respect to the future payment of dividends.

### c.  The Tax Preference Theory

The Tax Preference Theory of dividend policy recognizes features of tax law that create incentives for earnings retention and accumulation over dividend payments that may lead investors to prefer smaller or even no dividends, all other things being equal. The first cornerstone of this theory was the more favorable tax rates imposed prior to 1987 on capital gains than on ordinary income. That differential led stockholders to prefer to realize gains on the sale of their stock rather than through dividends taxed as ordinary income. However, the Bush tax cuts of 2003 reduced the maximum individual tax rate on corporate dividends to 15 percent, rather than an investor's personal income tax rate.

For example, suppose GAH Corporation's earnings per share before taxes is $1.00. Assuming a corporate tax rate of 35 percent, that $1.00 is reduced to $0.65. If GAH declares a cash dividend of $0.65 per share, each individual stockholder must declare the aggregate dividend payment she receives on her personal income tax return. If the individual stockholder is subject to the maximum individual tax rate on corporate dividends of 15 percent, she will pay about $0.10 of the $0.65 dividend to the Federal government [$0.65 x 15%]. Thus, she is left with about $0.55 of the pre-tax $1.00 per share earned by GAH.

Without the reductions in dividend tax rates, an investor in the top Federal income tax bracket of 39.5 percent would net only about $0.39 from the $0.65 cash dividend, rather than about $0.55. Thus, the dividend tax reduction represents approximately a 41 percent increase in the personal after-tax dividend income for investors in the highest tax bracket.

As a result of the reduction in taxes on the receipt of dividends, most publicly-traded companies reexamined their dividend policy. In particular, Microsoft, which had never before paid a dividend to its stockholders, declared a $3 per share dividend which amounted to $32 billion in the aggregate. The payout, which personally netted founder and Chairman Bill Gates about $3 billion, remains far and away the largest single dividend payout in U.S. corporate history.

The second cornerstone to the Tax Preference Theory relates to a corporation's ability to invest earnings that would otherwise have been used to pay taxes at the shareholder level if distributed in the form of a dividend. If a shareholder receives $100 as a dividend, that shareholder can only invest the net after tax (and transaction cost) distribution. If the same earnings are not distributed, but instead are reinvested in the corporation, the full $100 is available for later distribution or to increase share prices through deployment of retained earnings. The avoidance of tax at the shareholder level led Congress to adopt the "accumulated earnings tax" on what it viewed were excessive retained earnings. The tax is imposed on what the Internal Revenue Code defines as "accumulated taxable income." See IRC § 535. A 28% tax is then applied to the accumulated taxable income of the corporation. See IRC § 531.

Two other tax incentives also favor the retention of earnings over payout. One is based on timing. While shareholders can control capital gains tax as it is owed only upon the disposition of the stock in question, they cannot control the timing of their receipt of a cash dividend. The other is that capital assets upon transfer at death are not subject to capital gains taxes at all, but rather the beneficiaries get a so-called stepped-up basis. That is, they take the current value of the stock on the grantor's death as the starting point for measuring capital gains or losses on the asset.

As mentioned, the new dividend tax rates caused most public companies to reexamine their dividend policy. In general, and with few exceptions (mutual funds, margin accounts, and more), the new dividend tax cut makes it more appealing for investors to own stocks that regularly pay cash dividends, and thus more beneficial for companies to declare dividends.

### (3) Dividend Payment Process

As a technical matter, the dividend payment process for cash dividends is based on four important dates: the declaration date, the record date, the payment date, and the ex-dividend date.

The *declaration date* is the date on which the company's board announces that the company will pay a dividend in the near future. On the declaration date, the company will also state the dividend's record date and the size of the dividend in the aggregate and on a per share basis.

On the *record date,* the company determines which stockholders will receive the dividend. Only stockholders "of record" (*i.e.,* on the books of the company or its transfer agent) will receive the dividend.

The next important date, the *payment date*, typically occurs about two weeks after the record date and is the date on which the company (or more likely its agent) actually issues dividend checks.

Finally, the *ex-dividend date* is situated two business days before the record date. Any investor that purchases stock on or after the ex-dividend date will not receive the dividend. The reasoning behind the ex-dividend date is that a normal purchase of common shares in the market takes three business days after the trade date ("T+3") to settle (*i.e.,* to appear in the company's records). (Studies are being conducted to determine if $T+3$ can be shortened to $T+1$).

Thus, an investor that buys shares two business days before the record date will not appear on the stockholder list until the day after the record date. Therefore, she does not receive the dividend. However, the seller of those shares, who is still listed in the company's records, does receive the dividend even though she no longer owns the shares. Moreover, the market factors the dividend into the trading price of the shares, as normally the price per share drops by an amount equal to the dividend per share. The buyer and seller, therefore, are not affected economically. Newspaper stock listings indicate stocks that have gone "ex-dividend" by placing an "x" next to their ticker symbols.

An example is in order. Assume that the board of directors for SGH Corporation issues a press release on December 1 stating that the company will be paying a dividend of $0.15 per share to each of its stockholders of record as of December 15, with payment occurring on December 29. Hence, December 1 is the declaration date, December 15 is the record date, and December 29 is the payment date. The ex-dividend date falls on December 13, two business days prior to the record date. Therefore, an investor who purchases shares on or after December 13 will not receive the dividend; however, the investor who sold those shares (but no longer owns them) will receive the dividend.

For non-cash dividends, such as stock dividends (see Nutshell Section 49D(2)), the sequence of the declaration, record and payment dates is the same as it is for cash dividends. The ex-dividend date, however, is called the *ex-distribution date* when non-cash dividends are involved. The ex-distribution date is positioned one day after the payment date, and all investors who buy shares of a company and receive delivery of those shares before the ex-distribution date (*i.e.*, on or before the payment date) are entitled to the non-cash dividend. Thus, using the previous example, if SGH Corporation paid a stock dividend rather than a cash dividend, the ex-distribution date falls on December 30 and the other three dates remain unchanged.

## D.   Non–Cash Dividends and Stock Splits

### (1)   Generally

While many investors may prefer to receive cash dividends, non-cash dividends and distributions are statutorily permissible and occur frequently. See DGCL § 173; NYBCL § 510(a). Companies can distribute shares of their own stock, shares of stock in other companies, debt securities and even other property. For example, one publicly-traded producer of whiskey (Park & Tilford, Inc.), in a successful attempt to inflate its stock trading price, issued a dividend of whiskey at cost during a severe shortage of whiskey during World War II. Later it attempted to sell to its stockholders up to six cases of whiskey for each share of stock they held. Unfortunately, the Office of Price Administration stepped in and limited the resale prices of both the whiskey purchase rights and the whiskey itself, thus causing the company's stock price to return back to Earth. See *In the Matter of Ira Haupt & Co.*, 23 S.E.C. 589 (1946).

### (2) Stock Dividends

Stock dividends are dividends that are paid to stockholders in the form of stock rather than cash. The stock a company distributes may be shares of its own stock. In this case, the dividend is usually expressed as a percentage of the shares held by stockholders. For example, a company that pays a 10% stock dividend issues one additional share of stock to its stockholders for every 10 shares of common stock they own.

The stock that a company distributes may also be shares in a wholly-owned subsidiary owned by that company. If the company distributes all the subsidiary's shares in the form of a stock dividend, the distribution is called a *spin-off*. The subsidiary, which was indirectly owned by the parent company's stockholders prior to the spin-off, is directly owned by those stockholders thereafter. See Nutshell Section 54G. If the company distributes only a portion of those shares, the distribution is called a *carve-out*. In this case, the parent company continues to own a large portion (typically 80%) of the subsidiary's shares.

There are several reasons why companies declare dividends in shares of their own stock. First, stock dividends conserve cash needed to run the business. Second, stock dividends give the investor the ability to sell the shares he receives and generate cash from the sale. Thus, a stock dividend provides the investor with the option of *timing* his cash income. Third, shares received as a dividend are taxed only when those shares are sold, whereas a cash dividend must be declared on an investor's tax return covering the year in which the cash dividend is received.

Finally, a corporation may declare a stock dividend for the purpose of lowering its stock price into a more desirable trading range in the secondary market. Because the issuance of a large number of shares reduces the percentage ownership that each outstanding share represents, the trading value of each share declines. Stockholders receiving the dividend, however, are not hurt because the price decline is offset by their receipt of additional shares. This concept unfolds more dramatically in the context of forward and reverse stock splits. See Nutshell Section 49D(3).

From an investor's standpoint, a stock dividend in shares of the company's own stock serves as a virtually costless method of reinvesting returns. If a company distributes a cash dividend, an investor seeking to reinvest in the company must use the dividend to buy additional shares in the open market. A stock dividend, by contrast, allows the investor to postpone recognition of tax liabilities, as well as avoid brokerage expenses and other transaction costs associated with a cash purchase of stock.

A company's issuance of a stock dividend in shares of its own stock is only an accounting transaction. The company does not transfer any physical assets to its stockholders (unlike in the case of a cash dividend). The stock dividend is charged to a company's retained earnings (earned surplus) account on its balance sheet. The dividend results in a transfer of the aggregate par value of the distributed shares (or, in the case of no par stock, an amount determined by the board) from the retained earnings (earned surplus) account to the common stock account on the balance sheet. As seen in Nutshell Section 49D(3), the accounting treatment for a stock dividend is one of the ways a stock dividend is distinguished from a stock split.

The DGCL requires a board resolution approving the issuance of any dividend, including a stock dividend. In the case of a stock dividend, the company must ensure that it has sufficient authorized, but unissued, shares to cover the dividend. If enough authorized shares exist, the board need not obtain stockholder approval for the stock dividend. If not, then the company must increase its authorized shares of capital stock by amending its charter. Stockholders must approve most charter amendments, including one that increases the number of authorized shares of capital stock.

### (3) Stock Splits

A company may declare either a forward stock split or a reverse stock split. However, it is not unusual to simply hear someone use the term "stock split." When the term "stock split" alone is used, the person is referring to a *forward stock split*.

### a.   Forward Stock Splits

Like a stock dividend, a forward stock split is also an accounting adjustment that does not result in the company transferring assets to its stockholders. A stock split simply *increases* the number of outstanding common shares, but on a much larger scale than a stock dividend. NYSE regulations stipulate that any "stock dividend" affecting 20% or more of a company's common stock must be referred to as a split rather than a dividend. Regardless, many involved in finance and investing use the terms interchangeably. An example will illustrate the effect of a stock split.

Suppose AIH Corporation's common stock is trading at $100 per share. As seen in Table 6, a 3–for–1 stock split would give stockholders three shares of common stock for each share they currently hold. Assuming that AIH had 5 million shares of common stock outstanding, the 3–for–1 stock split will raise the total number of outstanding shares to 15 million [5 million shares x 3]. However, it will also *lower* the per share trading price to $33.33 [$100 per share ÷ 3].

While the decrease in the stock's trading price appears alarming, it is not. Current stockholders are not harmed because they now own three times as many shares as before. The increase in shares held directly offsets the decline in the per share trading price. If, for example, a stockholder of AIH held 50 shares worth $100 each (a total of $5,000) before the split, he will own 150 shares worth $33.33 each (a total of $5,000) after the split.

### Table 6
### Calculating Forward Stock Splits

| Split | Outstanding Shares After Split | Stock Price After Split |
|-------|-------------------------------|-------------------------|
| 2–for–1 | Pre-split shares × 2 | Pre-split price ÷ 2 |
| 3–for–1 | Pre-split shares × 3 | Pre-split price ÷ 3 |
| 3–for–2 | Pre-split shares ÷ 2, then × 3 | Pre-split price × 2, then ÷ 3 |
| 5–for–4 | Pre-split shares ÷ 4, then × 5 | Pre-split price × 4, then ÷ 5 |

A company effects a stock split primarily to make its common stock more affordable on a per share basis to a broader range of investors. Investors prefer buying shares in "round lots," each of which is 100 shares. Many investors, particularly retail investors, cannot afford 100 shares at prices of $100 per share or more (an aggregate price of $10,000 or more). However, they are more likely to be able to afford 100 shares at $20 per share (an aggregate price of $2,000). Hence, a company will often split its stock when its share price is perceived by management as too high in order to bring that price back down into a more affordable trading range.

Importantly when a split is declared, the company's stock price often trades *slightly above* what Table 6 would indicate. Take the example where a company announces a 2–for–1 split of its shares currently trading at $50. When the split is effected, the price of the stock will likely trade at an initial price slightly higher than $25. The reason for this is twofold. First, the market generally views a stock split as a "bullish" or positive sign. The market perceives the split as a sign of managerial confidence that the company's stock price will continue rising in the immediate future. Therefore, management is seeking to bring the stock price back down into a more affordable trading range now. Second, the effect of a reduced trading price is often an increase in the demand for the stock because the stock is more affordable on a per share basis.

### b.  Reverse Stock Splits

As seen in Table 7, when a company declares a reverse stock split, the number of its outstanding shares decreases while the per share trading price increases. For example, suppose PNH Corporation had 100 million shares of common stock outstanding, and that its per share trading price was $1. If PNH declared a 1–for–20 reverse stock split, the number of outstanding shares would decline to 5 million [100 million shares ÷ 20], while the per share trading price of those shares would increase to $20 [$1 per share x 20].

## Table 7
## Calculating Reverse Stock Splits

| Split | Outstanding Shares After Split | Stock Price After Split |
|---|---|---|
| 1–for–2 | Pre-split shares ÷ 2 | Pre-split price × 2 |
| 1–for–3 | Pre-split shares ÷ 3 | Pre-split price × 3 |
| 2–for–3 | Pre-split shares ÷ 3, then × 2 | Pre-split price × 3, then ÷ 2 |
| 4–for–5 | Pre-split shares ÷ 5, then × 4 | Pre-split price × 5, then ÷ 4 |

A company conducts a reverse stock split primarily for one of two reasons. First, a reverse split is used to increase the per share trading price of the company's common stock. Second, it can be used to eliminate minority stockholders.

With respect to the first reason, a public company may find itself in danger of having its shares delisted when its per share trading price drops below the requisite stock exchange listing requirement (typically $1 per share). A low per share trading price is also unattractive to investors who may come to view the stock as a *penny stock* (*i.e.,* a stock trading below $1 per share). Many investors will not consider purchasing a penny stock.

The company, therefore, conducts a reverse stock split in order to lift its stock's per share trading price back into an acceptable trading range. The market, however, generally views a reverse stock split as a "bearish" or negative sign, because the company is increasing its stock price through a gimmick rather than through better performance. Thus, the market often punishes a company by valuing the company's shares below the price Table 7 would indicate. For example, when PNH conducts its 1–for–20 reverse stock split, its shares will likely trade *slightly below* $20 per share because the market views a reverse stock split as a negative event. Indeed, the market views the company's action as an attempt to raise its per share trading price through a "smoke and mirrors" gimmick rather than by increasing earnings and growing the company.

A reverse stock split can also be used to eliminate a company's minority stockholders. This is usually done at the urging of a controlling stockholder. Assume, for example, that NAH Corporation has 10,000 shares outstanding and that Mariam, the controlling stockholder, owns 5,100 of those shares. If NAH conducts a 1–for–5,100 reverse stock split, with fractional shares converted solely into cash, Mariam will end up owning the one and only share in NAH [5,100 shares ÷ 5,100]. All other stockholders end up owning a fraction of one share, and thus will receive cash compensation for their fractional share pursuant to the terms of the reverse stock split.

In *Leader v. Hycor Inc.*, 479 N.E.2d 173 (Mass. 1985), the defendant corporation conducted a 1–for–4,000 reverse stock split for the purposes of a recapitalization. All the major stockholders of the corporation were members of the board of directors and owned more than 4,000 shares each. After the recapitalization of Hycor, all fractional shares would be cashed out. The remaining shares of the company were owned by 331 minority stockholders, none of whom owned more than 4,000 shares.

The minority stockholders brought suit against the company for fraud and breach of fiduciary duty based on the declaration of an allegedly unfair reverse stock split. The Massachusetts Supreme Judicial Court ruled that the minority stockholders must establish that the board of directors could have achieved its desired results through an alternative course of action that was "less harmful to the minority's interests." While acknowledging that the reverse stock split "froze-out" minority stockholders, the Court entered judgment in favor of the majority stockholders because the plaintiffs had not met their burden of proof on this point.

The Delaware Supreme Court in *Applebaum v. Avaya*, 812 A.2d 880 (Del.2002), upheld a company's disparate treatment of stockholders in the context of a reverse stock split immediately followed by a forward stock split. Avaya's stockholder base was comprised of a large number of retail investors each holding a relatively small ownership stake in the company. Avaya incurred significant annual expenses on account of its large stockholder base, including $4 million to print and mail proxy statements to stockholders and another $3.5 million in administrative fees. The company's plan was to execute a reverse stock split which would effectively cash out all small investors. Indeed, after the split, small investors would hold only a fraction of one share and would be cashed out accordingly. Once this occurred, the company would execute a forward stock split to turn the fractional shares held by the remaining stockholders (all of whom, at that time, would also own at least one whole share) into whole shares.

Several stockholders who would be cashed out after the reverse stock split filed an action against the company under Section 155 of the DGCL based on the disparate treatment they were receiving. Section 155 allows a company, if it so desires, to issue fractional shares of its common stock. If the company chooses not to issue fractional shares, the DGCL requires the company to repurchase them through cash payments at fair value. Because Avaya was paying fair value for the fractional shares of stockholders being cashed out through the reverse split, the Court held that no violation of Section 155 occurred. In the context of that section, only fair treatment, rather than "equal" treatment, is required, according to the Court.

The Court also noted that Avaya was simply asking the stockholders who would be left with less than one whole share after the reverse split to affirmatively decide before the split whether they wished to remain stockholders of Avaya. If so, those stockholders simply could have purchased enough pre-reverse split shares to equal at least one full post-reverse split share.

### (4) Distinguishing Stock Dividends and Splits on the Balance Sheet

#### a. Stock Dividends

Section 173 of the DGCL makes a clear distinction between stock dividends, on the one hand, and forward and reverse stock splits, on the other. In reference to stock dividends, that Section provides:

> If the dividend is to be paid in shares of the corporation's theretofore unissued capital stock the board of directors shall, by resolution, direct that there be designated as capital in respect of such shares an amount which is not less than the aggregate par value of par value shares being declared as a dividend and, in the case of shares without par value being declared as a dividend, such amount as shall be determined by the board of directors.

From an accounting standpoint, the total amount of stockholders' equity will remain the same after the issuance of a stock dividend. However, a stock dividend requires journal entries to transfer the amount of the dividend from the retained earnings (earned surplus) account on the balance sheet to the additional paid-in-capital (capital surplus) account on the balance sheet. The amount transferred depends on whether the stock dividend is (1) a small stock dividend or (2) a large stock dividend.

*Example: "Small" common stock dividend.* A stock dividend is considered to be *small* if the new shares being issued are less than 20–25% of the total number of shares outstanding prior to the stock dividend. If that is the case, then the *market value* of the shares being issued will be transferred from the retained earnings account and divided between the additional paid-in-capital and common stock accounts of shareholders' equity, with the common stock account receiving the aggregate par value of the shares and the additional paid-in-capital account receiving the remainder.

Assume that GAH, Inc. has 5,000 shares of common stock outstanding when it declares a 5% stock dividend. This means that 250 new shares of stock (5,000 shares times 5%) will be issued to existing stockholders. Assuming the stock has a par value of $0.10 per share and a market value of $20 per share at that time, the net effect will be to decrease retained earnings by $5,000 (250 shares times $20 per share market value), and to increase the common stock account by $25 (250 shares times $0.10 par value per share) and the additional paid-in-capital account by the remaining $4,975.

*Example: "Large" common stock dividend.* A stock dividend is considered *large* if the new shares being issued represent more than 20–25% of the total number of shares outstanding prior to the stock dividend. If that is the case, then the par value of the shares being issued (and not their market value) will be transferred from retained earnings to the common stock account.

Assume that GAH, Inc. has 5,000 shares of common stock outstanding when it declares a 50% stock dividend. This means that 2,500 new shares of stock (5,000 shares times 50%) will be issued to existing stockholders. Assuming the stock has a par value of $0.10 per share, the net effect will be to decrease retained earnings by $250 (2,500 shares times $0.10 par value per share), and to increase the common stock account by that same amount ($250).

### b. Stock Splits

As for forward and reverse stock splits, Section 173 of the DGCL states that "[n]o such designation as capital shall be necessary if shares are being distributed by a corporation pursuant to a split-up or division of its stock rather than as payment of a dividend declared payable in stock of the corporation." The accounting for a forward or reverse stock split does not affect the additional paid-in-capital (capital surplus) account or the retained earnings (earned surplus) account of the corporation. Moreover, the dollar value in the capital stock account does not change; rather, the *parenthetical description* of the capital stock will differ after a forward or reverse split.

*Example: forward stock split.* Assume AIH Corp. has 10,000 shares of common stock authorized, 3,000 shares actually issued and outstanding, and that the par value of the common stock is $1.00 per share. The parenthetical description under its common stock account in the Stockholders' Equity portion of its balance sheet will read: "(par value $1.00 per share, 10,000 shares authorized, 3,000 shares issued and outstanding)." If AIH Corp. thereafter effects a 2–for–1 forward stock split, the dollar amounts in AIH's Stockholders' Equity section of its balance sheet will not change, but the parenthetical description under its common stock account will change and will read as follows: "(par value *$0.50* per share, 10,000 shares authorized, *6,000* shares issued and outstanding)." In other words, the par value of the common shares of AIH Corp. is decreased 50% to $0.50, while the number of outstanding shares are doubled to 6,000 accordingly.

## E.  Board's Discretion in Paying Dividends

Dividends are payable at the discretion of the board of directors, subject only to restrictions in the company's charter (if any), the legal capital rule of the state of formation and the board's fiduciary duties. With respect to those fiduciary duties, directors normally have wide latitude in declaring and paying dividends. This latitude stems from the presumptive protections of the business judgment rule. This rule protects directors in their decision to declare—or not declare—a dividend to their stockholders. See, e.g., *Sinclair Oil Corp. v. Levien*, 280 A.2d 717 (Del.1971).

Courts historically have taken a "hands-off" approach when it comes to second-guessing a board's decision not to declare a dividend. Because of the business judgment rule, plaintiffs must overcome the heavy burden of proving fraud or gross abuse of discretion on the part of directors before the courts will interfere in a board's dividend decisions. This is true even when the company has funds available that could be used to pay dividends. "The determination as to when and in what amounts a corporation may prudently distribute its assets by way of dividends rests in the honest discretion of the directors in the performance of their fiduciary duties." *Baron v. Allied Artists Pictures Corp.*, 337 A.2d 653 (Del.Ch.1975). See also *Moskowitz v. Bantrell*, 190 A.2d 749 (Del.1963); *Gabelli & Co., Inc. Profit Sharing Plan v. Liggett Group, Inc.*, 444 A.2d 261 (Del.Ch.1982).

Thus, the Delaware Supreme Court applied the business judgement rule to a dividend policy dispute in the case of *Sinclair Oil Corp. v. Levien*, 280 A.2d 717 (Del.1971). Plaintiffs were the minority stockholders in a subsidiary of which 97% was owned by the defendant, Sinclair. Instead of causing the subsidiary to pursue available business opportunities, the subsidiary's board began declaring and paying out massive dividends, 97% of which were going straight to Sinclair.

Plaintiffs charged that these huge dividend payments stunted the subsidiary's industrial development and constituted a form of "self-dealing." Therefore, the directors who approved them violated the fiduciary duty they owed to the minority stockholders. The Court, however, disagreed. It held that the actions taken by the directors were reasonable and were deserving of the protections of the business judgment rule. Moreover, the Court rejected the accusation that Sinclair had engaged in self-dealing, because every stockholder—including the plaintiffs—received their pro rata share of every dividend the board had declared.

Courts, however, do have the equitable power to compel a corporation to pay a dividend when warranted. In *Eshleman v. Keenan*, 194 A. 40 (Del.Ch. 1937), the Delaware Chancery Court stated:

> [C]ourts have the power in proper cases to compel the directors to declare a dividend.... But that they should do so on a mere showing that an asset exists from which a dividend may be declared, has never, I dare say, been asserted anywhere. In such a case a court acts only after a demonstration that the corporation's affairs are in a condition justifying the declaration of the dividend as a matter of prudent business management and that the withholding of it is explicable only on the theory of an oppressive or fraudulent abuse of discretion.

*Dodge v. Ford Motor Co.*, 170 N.W. 668 (Mich. 1919), is one of the rare instances when a court did step in to help stockholders in their pursuit of a dividend (or, in this case, more dividends). At the time of the case, Henry Ford owned almost 60 percent of Ford Motor Company's stock and the Dodge brothers owned 10 percent. The company had paid out regular dividends of about $1.2 million per year and "special dividends" of $10 million per year. Ford caused the company to stop paying special dividends to stockholders, and the Dodge brothers sued.

Ford claimed that the company's stockholders had made enough money and that he wanted to give some of that money back to the American people through lower car prices. He also wanted to expand the business so as to put more men to work.

The Michigan Supreme Court was not impressed with the "social benefit" explanation offered by Ford for canceling the special dividends. It then set forth a "bad faith" test for corporate dividend policy decisions by directors. Based on this test, a court will interfere only if the directors' action in paying or not paying dividends is such an abuse of discretion that it would constitute fraud or a breach of the good faith duty that the directors owe to stockholders.

## § 50.  DILUTION AND PREEMPTIVE RIGHTS

Dilution results whenever the number of outstanding shares of a company's common stock increases. Thus, dilution occurs when a company issues additional shares of common stock. It also occurs when holders of the company's convertible securities convert those securities into shares of common stock or when employees exercise their stock options. Two types of dilution may occur when these events transpire: value dilution and voting dilution.

## A.  Value Dilution

Any difference between what a new investor pays on a per share basis for newly-issued shares and what existing investors as a whole paid on a per share basis for their shares results in *value dilution*. If, on the one hand, a new investor pays *more* than what existing investors paid on average, he suffers value dilution. If, on the other hand, the investor pays less than what existing investors paid on average, existing investors suffer value dilution. An example using the dynamics of fluids illustrates this point.

Assume GAH Corporation raised capital through the sale of 50,000 shares of common stock on two different occasions one year apart. Further assume that the consideration GAH received could be visualized as water deposited into a tank with two chambers separated by a vertical partition. Chamber One is filled with the consideration paid by stockholders who bought shares in the first stock offering; Chamber Two is filled with the consideration paid by new stockholders who invested one year later. Finally, assume that the first group of stockholders paid $1.50 per share while the second group paid $2.50 per share.

Based on the foregoing, the water level is much lower in Chamber One than in Chamber Two, because the second group of investors paid much more for its shares. If the partition between the two chambers is removed, the water in the two chambers will commingle and achieve a level somewhere in between the previous water levels of the two chambers. The first group of investors receives a benefit from the investment made by the second group, because the water level is now higher than the level at which they invested. By contrast, the second group suffers because the water level has now declined below the level at which they invested. The second group has suffered value dilution.

Companies going public (and in certain instances companies that are already reporting companies under the Exchange Act) are required to set forth the effect of value dilution in their prospectuses. See Item 506 of SEC Regulation S–K. Specifically, the disparity in the price at which common shares are being offered to the public and the effective cash cost to the issuer's officers, directors, promoters and affiliated persons of common shares acquired by them in transactions during the last five years must be highlighted. Under SEC regulations, dilution is determined by comparing a company's net tangible book value per share before and after the stock issuance. Net tangible book value per share is determined by (a) subtracting a company's intangible assets from its total assets to determine tangible assets, (b) subtracting total liabilities from tangible assets to determine net tangible assets, and (c) dividing net tangible assets by the number of shares of common stock outstanding. Dilution in net tangible book value per share represents the difference between the amount per share to be paid by those purchasing common shares in the offering in question and that paid by those who purchased before (*e.g.*, the issuer's officers, directors, promoters and affiliated persons).

Table 8 is the dilution table set forth in the prospectus used by Google Inc. when it went public during the Summer of 2004:

## Table 8
## Dilution Table Contained in Google Inc's 2004 IPO Prospectus

| | | | |
|---|---|---|---|
| Assumed initial offering price per share of Class A common stock | | | $85.00 |
| | Pro forma net tangible book value per share at June 30, 2004 | $3.55 | |
| | Increase in pro forma net tangible book value per share attributable to this offering | 4.11 | |
| Pro forma as adjusted net tangible book value per share after the offering | | | 7.66 |
| Dilution per share to new investors | | | $77.34 |

Item 506 of SEC Regulation S–K also requires a company going public to include another dilution-related table in its prospectus when there is a substantial disparity between the public offering price and the effective cash cost of shares to existing stockholders. The table must set forth (a) the number of shares owned or purchased by existing stockholders and new investors, (b) the percentage ownership of each group, (c) the total consideration paid by each group, (d) the percentage of total consideration paid by each group and (e) the average price per share paid by each group.

Table 9 sets forth this information for Google Inc. The table highlights that while new investors in the company's IPO paid 93.1% of the total consideration received by Google Inc. through stock issuances, those investors received only 5.2% of Google Inc.'s shares. For those seeking to get in on IPOs, this result is simply part of the price of admission.

## Table 9
## Additional Dilution Information Contained in Google Inc.'s 2004 IPO Prospectus

| | SHARES PURCHASED | | TOTAL CONSIDERATION | | |
|---|---|---|---|---|---|
| | Number | Percent % | Amount | Percent % | Average Price Per Share |
| Existing Stockholders | 257,077,508 | 94.8 | $89,523,000 | 6.9 | $0.35 |
| New Investors | 14,142,135 | 5.2 | 1,202,081,000 | 93.1 | 85.00 |
| Total | 271,219,643 | 100.0% | $1,291,604,000 | 100.0% | |

## B.  Voting Dilution and Preemptive Rights

The second type of dilution is voting dilution. *Voting dilution* is the reduction in a given stockholder's voting power that results from an increase in the corporation's number of outstanding shares. Such an increase occurs whenever the corporation issues additional shares of common stock, holders of stock options and warrants exercise their options and warrants and receive shares of common stock, and convertible security holders convert their convertible securities into shares of common stock. As the total number of shares outstanding increases, the voting power that each share represents in the company decreases. An example will clarify this concept.

Suppose you own 10,500 shares of common stock of a company with 20,000 shares outstanding. If each share of common stock entitles its holder to one vote, your shares represent 52.5% of the total voting power of the common stock. If the company issues 1,500 new shares to a third party (and thus 21,500 shares are now outstanding), your voting power would decline from 52.5% to only 48.4%. You have suffered voting dilution, and as a result you are no longer the majority stockholder.

One way a stockholder can protect against voting dilution is by purchasing the same percentage of the shares being sold as she currently owns. In the above example, therefore, you would purchase 52.5% of the 1,500 newly-issued shares, thereby preserving your 52.5% majority stake. The problem, however, is ensuring that you have a *legal right* to do so. One way is through the exercise of preemptive rights.

*Preemptive rights* refers to a stockholder's right to subscribe to new stock issuances in preference to persons who are not stockholders. When a stockholder has preemptive rights, the corporation must first offer her a fair and reasonable opportunity to purchase the portion of the newly-issued shares necessary to maintain and preserve her current ownership interest in percentage terms. Preemptive rights, when available, may only be exercised by common stockholders, although technically preferred stockholders, as contract claimants, could negotiate for these rights.

The common law historically recognized preemptive rights as an important protection for existing stockholders. Over time these rights became codified in many of the corporation statutes adopted by the states. Today, these statutory provisions generally provide stockholders with preemptive rights on a permissive rather than mandatory basis. When corporate charters are silent on the issue, no preemptive rights exist under the statute. Accordingly, corporations have the option to limit or deny preemptive rights through their charters.

For example, Section 157 of the DGCL includes a general presumption *against* granting preemptive rights to stockholders. Therefore, stockholders of a Delaware corporation do not receive preemptive rights *unless* those rights are set forth in their corporation's certificate of incorporation. The RMBCA (Section 6.30(a)) and the NYBCL (Section 622(b)(2)) are in accord.

Preemptive rights, if provided in a corporation's charter, typically are subject to a number of exceptions. These include:

- *An issuance of shares in connection with the exercise of stock options, warrants and convertible securities.* Granting preemptive rights in these situations would frustrate the

contractual rights of option holders, warrantholders and convertible security holders.

- *An issuance of shares that were originally
  authorized in the charter but have not been
  issued.* The rationale is that there is an implied understanding between the corporation
  and the original investors that the sale of the
  remaining authorized shares may be completed.

- *An issuance of treasury shares.* Stockholders
  are not injured because shares held in treasury were previously issued; therefore, their
  reissuance simply restores a dilution that
  previously existed.

- *An issuance of shares for property or services
  rather than for cash, or shares issued in
  connection with a merger.* Granting preemptive rights in these situations could frustrate
  or render impractical desirable transactions
  between the corporation and third parties.

- *An issuance of shares pursuant to a plan of
  reorganization or recapitalization under court
  supervision.* Granting preemptive rights in
  these situations could frustrate or render impractical the court supervised reorganization
  or recapitalization.

While preemptive rights protect existing stockholders, corporate managers typically dislike them
because they can delay or even scuttle capital raising activities. Indeed, a corporation must offer existing stockholders the opportunity to invest before

outside investors. This, of course, takes time. It also acts as a disincentive to new investors who could spend significant time and energy analyzing an investment opportunity only to have it fully or partially taken away by existing stockholders.

## § 51.   STOCK REPURCHASES AND REDEMPTIONS

### A.   Overview

Common stock repurchases and redemptions are, in many ways, similar to dividend payments. Both put the company's cash into the hands of its stockholders. Technically speaking, a *stock repurchase* primarily refers to a company's repurchase of its stock pursuant to its statutory right to do so. A *stock redemption*, by contrast, primarily refers to a contractual right that a company may have to redeem shares of its stock (usually preferred stock) at specified redemption prices. A stock repurchase generally benefits stockholders by putting cash in the hands of stockholders while reducing the number of shares outstanding. Stock redemptions generally benefit the company as it refinances more expensive (*i.e.,* higher yielding) preferred stock with less expensive preferred stock or debt financing.

## B.  Stock Repurchases

### (1) Generally

Like dividends, stock repurchases are another way in which stockholders can participate financially in a corporation's success. From a tax point of view, stock repurchases are appealing to stockholders, especially during periods when capital gains enjoy favorable tax treatment. Stockholders are taxed only on proceeds in excess of the price they paid for their stock.

A given state's corporate code provides the statutory authority for a corporation incorporated in that state to acquire its own shares. Repurchases, however, are subject to the legal capital rule of that state because of the adverse effect they may have on the corporation's creditors. See Nutshell Section 49B(1). For example, Section 160 of the DGCL allows a Delaware corporation to repurchase its own shares at any time unless the capital of the company is impaired or will be rendered impaired as a result of the repurchase. Section 513 of the NYBCL states that a New York corporation may repurchase its own shares only out of "surplus," and so long as the corporation is solvent and remains so after the repurchase.

Directors may be held jointly and severally liable for improper share repurchases if they acted either willfully or negligently. Such directors are liable to the corporation or, if the corporation is insolvent or has been dissolved, to the corporation's creditors for the amount unlawfully paid in connection with a share repurchase. See DGCL § 174(a).

A privately-held company may have different motivations in repurchasing its stock than a publicly-traded company. These are examined below.

### (2) Repurchases by Privately–Held Companies

A privately-held company primarily repurchases shares of its stock to facilitate a stockholder's exit from the company. For example, a company may choose to buy shares from a stockholder who is retiring, the estate of a deceased stockholder, or a stockholder with whom management is feuding. Often, the company is contractually required to repurchase shares upon the occurrence of certain events (such as the retirement of a stockholder-manager) pursuant to the terms of a shareholders' agreement. See Nutshell Section 2B(3)a.

When repurchases are not contractually required, the potential for abuse is considerable. This stems from the fact that shares of privately-held companies are not readily saleable. Thus, the two most likely purchasers of shares held by a stockholder are the company itself and the remaining stockholders. Therefore, the opportunity to sell shares back to the company is one in which many stockholders wish to participate.

In this regard, courts have held that a repurchase is valid so long as the board of directors had a valid business reason for making the repurchase and its decision was made in the utmost good faith. See, e.g., *Toner v. Baltimore Envelope Co.*, 498 A.2d 642 (Md.1985). When a company offers to repurchase shares from a controlling stockholder, it must offer to repurchase a similar proportion of shares from the minority stockholders as well. See, e.g., *Donahue v. Rodd Electrotype Co.*, 328 N.E.2d 505 (Mass. 1975).

### (3) Repurchases by Publicly–Traded Companies

A publicly-traded company typically decides to repurchase its own shares when its board of directors views the company's shares as undervalued in the market. In other words, the board decides that the best investment for the company's surplus funds is the company's own stock. Because of the "bullish" or positive signal this conveys, the company's stock price typically rises when the company announces a stock repurchase program. The repurchase also has the effect of reducing the supply of shares in the market, thus further bolstering the market price of the company's stock. Ordinary stock repurchase programs that public companies conduct must comply with Exchange Act Rule 10b–18, as such programs have a manipulative effect on stock prices.

A company may also repurchase stock for use in connection with an incentive stock option plan. When employees exercise options, the repurchased shares are delivered to the optionees. Using repurchased shares rather than authorized but unissued shares prevents further dilution. See Nutshell Section 50.

A corporation may also make a *tender offer* for its own shares (a so-called "issuer tender offer" or "self-tender"). The Williams Act (embedded in the Exchange Act) and SEC rules govern disclosure and procedures involved in self-tenders. See Nutshell Section 57G.

Stock repurchases by publicly-traded companies have the potential for abuse. During the 1980s, many public companies repurchased shares from hostile bidders or potential hostile bidders in order to induce these bidders to leave them alone. These repurchases were typically made at premium prices, and thus were referred to as *greenmail*. However, in the late 1980s, provisions were added to the Internal Revenue Code that discourage greenmail payments. See IRC §§ 162(k) (denying deductibility of greenmail payments) and 5881 (imposing excise tax on recipients of greenmail payments). Since then, several states have adopted statutes that discourage it as well. For example, Section 513(c) of the NYBCL prohibits a New York corporation from purchasing more than 10% of its own stock from a stockholder for more than its market value, unless the purchase is approved by a majority vote of the corporation's board and stockholders.

## C. Stock Redemptions

A company's certificate of incorporation may provide the company with the option to redeem shares of a given series of preferred stock and, in some cases, common stock. For example, a typical provision may specify that after a certain period of time, the company will have the right to redeem shares of a given series of preferred stock at a redemption price per share equal to the par value of that series plus a small premium. See Nutshell Section 43C(5)a.

A company generally cannot issue redeemable common stock unless another class of common stock is outstanding that cannot be redeemed. See, e.g, NYCBL § 512(b). Accordingly, most redemptions involve preferred stock, unless the company in question has shares of two or more classes of common stock outstanding.

The certificate of incorporation will set forth the redemption date or dates and the redemption prices for a given series of redeemable stock. Importantly, a corporation cannot redeem its stock at a price in excess of the redemption price set forth in its charter. See, e.g., DGCL § 160(a)(2) and NYBCL § 513(b). In some states, including New York, the redemption price may be increased to include an arrearage of dividends even if the certificate of incorporation does not provide for such an adjustment.

A corporation's statutory authority to redeem their redeemable shares of stock is similar to that for stock repurchases. See, e.g., DGCL § 160 and NYBCL § 513. See also Nutshell Section 51B.

## § 52. RECAPITALIZATIONS AND RESTRUCTURINGS

Please refer to Nutshell Sections 54F and G.

# PART IV

# MERGERS AND ACQUISITIONS

## CHAPTER 15

## FUNDAMENTAL CONCEPTS

### § 53. OPERATING IN A LEGAL AND REGULATORY MINE FIELD

Companies active in mergers, acquisitions and divestitures operate within a legal and regulatory mine field. Sales of whole companies, separate businesses operating within companies, and major assets owned by companies often implicate a whole host of substantive bodies of law.

Tax law is often a main consideration in structuring a merger or acquisition. Tax lawyers work closely with mergers and acquisitions (M&A) lawyers in order to structure a given transaction in a way that minimizes the tax consequences to the companies involved and their stockholders.

M&A lawyers must consult state corporate law to determine if stockholders of the constituent companies receive voting rights with respect to a given transaction and whether stockholders who dissent from the transaction receive appraisal rights. State corporate law also controls the mechanics of a merger as well as the stockholder voting process. Finally, state corporate law influences successor liability for target company obligations (such as products liability).

If the constituent corporations to a transaction are publicly-traded, the Federal securities laws significantly influence the transaction. For example, the Exchange Act governs the ability of an acquiror to make a tender offer for the shares of a publicly-traded company. It also controls how companies solicit proxies from their public stockholders when the transaction must be approved by a stockholder vote. The Securities Act, by contrast, governs an acquiror's public offering of equity or debt securities as merger or acquisition consideration.

Antitrust laws, particularly the Clayton Act of 1914 and the Hart–Scott–Rodino Antitrust Improvements Act of 1976, regulate all business combinations that may threaten competition in the relevant product and service markets. Parties planning significant transactions must consult the antitrust laws to see if advanced filings with the Federal Trade Commission and the Premerger Notification Office of the Department of Justice are required.

Depending on the constituents to a transaction, several additional bodies of law may be implicated. If the target company has a unionized workforce, Federal labor law will impact that transaction. The Employee Retirement Income Security Act of 1974

(ERISA) also may be implicated whenever the target company has a pension plan for its employees. Environmental law, particularly the Comprehensive Environmental Response, Compensation, and Liability Act (CERCLA) (commonly referred to as the "superfund"), impacts a given transaction whenever the target company has actual or potential exposure to environmental liabilities, as typically would be the case when the target is a manufacturer. In that event, products liability law also is likely implicated.

Some acquisitions are of companies or their significant assets in bankruptcy. In such event, an acquiror must consult legal counsel about the intricacies of Federal bankruptcy law. Other targets operate within specific regulated industries, such as banking, utilities, insurance or gaming. Thus, the laws affecting those industries will naturally impact the acquisitions of target companies operating within them.

## § 54.   M&A DEAL STRUCTURES

### A.   Overview

Five basic M&A transactions exist:

(1) *Acquisition or Purchase.* The first type of transaction is an acquisition or purchase transaction. An acquiror can choose to acquire or purchase a target company in one of two ways. The first is through a stock acquisition. Here, the acquiror pur-

chases the stock of the target company from the target's stockholders. The second is through an asset acquisition. In this situation, the acquiror purchases specified assets of the target company (*e.g.,* all assets associated with a particular line of business of the target company) and may also assume specified liabilities of the target company (typically those naturally associated with the purchased assets). See Nutshell Section 54B.

(2) *Merger, Consolidation or Conversion.* The second type of transaction is a merger, consolidation or conversion. In a classic "merger" transaction, one company is merged "with and into" another company, which is known as the "surviving company." The stockholders of the company being merged out of existence receive either cash, securities in the surviving company, or a mix of the two as merger consideration. By operation of law, the surviving company assumes the assets and liabilities of the company merged out of existence. Thus, after the merger, shares of stock in the surviving company represent an interest in the two combined companies. See Nutshell Section 54C.

A "consolidation" is essentially a merger between more than two companies. The typical transaction involves two existing operating companies that merge with and into a newly-formed third corporation.

A "conversion" is a transaction where an existing corporation converts into another form of business entity (such as a partnership or limited liability company), or a non-corporate entity converts into a corporation. For example, a business that is not a corporation needs to convert into a corporation before that business can "go public" by engaging in an IPO. See Nutshell Section 54D.

(3) *Leveraged Buy–Out (LBO)*. The third type of transaction is a leveraged buy-out. In the typical LBO, a private group of investors borrows substantially all the money needed to acquire a controlling interest in a target company. Indebtedness (either in the form of loans and/or debt securities) is secured by the assets of the target company, and the indebtedness is serviced (*i.e.,* paid down) with the cash flow that the target company generates going forward. A special variant of the LBO is the management buy-out (MBO). An MBO is simply an LBO led by one or more senior managers of the target company rather than a group of outside investors. By engaging in an MBO, those managers seek to take a publicly-traded company "private." See Nutshell Section 54E.

(4) *Recapitalization*. The fourth type of transaction is a recapitalization. In the typical "recap," a given company will replace (or swap out) certain existing securities (mostly debt or debt equivalents) with new equity securities. Thus, the company shuffles its existing capital structure in order to make the company more viable from a financial point of view going forward. See Nutshell Section 54F.

(5) *Restructuring*. The fifth type of transaction is a restructuring. A typical restructuring will have

the company in question divesting (*i.e.,* selling) certain businesses or divisions in an effort to refocus its business strategy on "core" operations. A good example of one type of restructuring is the "spin-off." Here, a parent company distributes some or all of the shares it holds in a subsidiary to the parent's stockholders in the form of a stock dividend. Thus, after the spin-off, parent company stockholders continue to hold shares in the parent (sans the subsidiary) and now also hold shares in the newly spun-off subsidiary. See Nutshell Section 54G.

## B.   Acquisition or Purchase Transactions

Those seeking to acquire a business do so either by purchasing the assets (an *asset acquisition*) necessary to operate that business or by purchasing the equity of the company that operates that business (a *stock acquisition*). Each of these is explored below.

### (1) Asset Acquisitions

When acquiring assets of a target company, the acquiror can use cash consideration (a *cash-for-assets* acquisition), stock consideration (a *stock-for-assets* acquisition), or a mix of both.

#### a.   Cash-for-Assets Acquisition

##### i.   *Generally*

In a cash-for-assets acquisition, Buyer Corp pays Seller Corp cash consideration for the assets of

Seller Corp that Buyer Corp is seeking to purchase. Buyer Corp may also negotiate to assume some of Seller Corp's liabilities (typically those directly related to the purchased assets), but is not legally required to do so except in certain instances. See Nutshell Section 54B(1)d. If Buyer Corp agrees to assume liabilities, then the purchase price Buyer Corp pays Seller Corp should be reduced, because Buyer Corp is required to pay those liabilities after the acquisition.

If Seller Corp has sold all or substantially all of its assets, it may choose to dissolve thereafter. To do so, Seller Corp must pay its remaining creditors in full and then distribute any remaining proceeds to stockholders of Seller Corp in the form of a *"liquidating distribution."* Thereafter, Seller Corp's certificate of incorporation is cancelled, its shares are extinguished and its corporate existence is dissolved.

Under Delaware law, holders of a majority of the outstanding shares of Seller Corp must approve both the asset sale (if the sale is of "all or substantially all" the assets of Seller Corp (DGCL § 271)) and any subsequent dissolution (DGCL § 275). Importantly, stockholders of Buyer Corp are not legally entitled to vote on the cash-for-assets acquisition.

From a tax perspective, a cash-for-assets deal followed by a dissolution by Seller Corp is taxed at two levels. First, Seller Corp itself is taxed on any gain from the sale of its assets. Second, Seller Corp stockholders are taxed on any gain they receive relating to Seller Corp's dissolution. There are generally no tax consequences for either Buyer Corp or its stockholders as a result of the transaction.

### ii. "All or Substantially All" Standard

A key question in any asset sale is whether the assets being sold constitute "all or substantially all" the assets of Seller Corp. If so, Seller Corp stockholders are legally entitled to vote on the sale under Section 271 of the DGCL. In the seminal case of *Gimbel v. Signal Companies*, 316 A.2d 599 (Del.Ch. 1974), the Delaware Chancery Court held that the resolution of the issue depends on whether "the sale of assets is *quantitatively vital* to the operation of the corporation and is out of the ordinary and substantially affects the existence and purpose of the corporation." The Delaware courts answer the question of "quantitative vitality" by examining two sub-issues. First, what percentage of the corporation's total assets do the assets being sold comprise? Second, what percentage of the corporation's total income do the assets being sold generate?

While sales of assets "out of the ordinary" course of business would appear to be a useful metric in deciding whether shareholder approval is necessary, the Delaware Chancery Court, in a partnership related case entitled *In re Nantucket Island Assoc. Ltd. Partnership Unitholders Litigation*, 810 A.2d 351 (Del.Ch.2002), indicated otherwise. According to the Court:

[T]he only one of the *Gimbel* factors that can
be confidently determined is the one that will
rarely help decide a case: whether the transaction is "out of the ordinary." That factor is
easily satisfied here. But that, of course, would
also be true if the partnership sold a quarter of
its productive assets. Such a sale would not
involve substantially all of a partnership's assets in any common sense way but would also
not be an ordinary, run-of-the-mill transaction.
Put another way, this aspect of the *Gimbel* test
will rarely be of much utility in resolving any
close case.

Thus, at best, a proposed "out of the ordinary" sale
of assets should trigger an analysis to see if *other
factors* indicate that shareholder approval is necessary under Section 271.

If the assets being sold generate a significant
portion of the corporation's income, then Section
271 of the DGCL will require stockholder approval
of that sale even if the assets being sold do not
quantitatively represent a large fraction of the corporation's total assets. For example, in *Katz v.
Bregman*, 431 A.2d 1274 (Del.Ch.1981), the Delaware Chancery Court held that a proposed sale of
assets which constituted 51% of the corporation's
total assets, and which generated approximately
45% of the corporation's 1980 net sales, would
constitute a sale of "all or substantially all" the
assets of the corporation. Similarly, in *Winston v.
Mandor*, 710 A.2d 835 (Del.Ch.1997), stockholder

approval was required in connection with a corporation's sale of assets representing 60% of its net assets and which generated *all* of its income over a recent six-month period.

The case of *Hollinger Inc. v. Hollinger Int'l Inc.*, 858 A.2d 342 (Del.Ch.2004), addressed the thorny issue of whether an asset sale conducted by a wholly-owned, indirect subsidiary of a parent company can trigger a vote of the parent's shareholders under Section 271. The assets being sold were those of the "Telegraph Group" which were held by an indirect, wholly-owned subsidiary of Hollinger International, Inc., a Delaware corporation ("International"). They were being sold to an entity controlled by Frederick and David Barclay. Shareholders of International sought a preliminary injunction preventing International from consummating the sale.

The Telegraph Group assets were held in a sixth-tier U.K. subsidiary of International and not by International itself. Thus, International argued that since it was not selling assets, Section 271 was inapplicable. The Delaware Chancery Court was able to avoid answering this difficult policy question, because it determined that the Telegraph Group did not constitute all or substantially all of International's assets in any event. Nonetheless, the Court indicated that if Section 271 was not triggered in situations where the assets did constitute all or substantially all of the assets of the parent company, then Section 271's voting requirement could easily be evaded through the use of a multiple subsidiary structure.

Contrasting with Section 271 is the bright line test found in Section 12.02(a) of the RMBCA. That section states that "a sale, lease, exchange, or other disposition of assets, other than [one done in the usual and regular course of business], requires approval of the corporation's shareholders if the disposition would leave the corporation without a significant continuing business activity." Importantly, that section contains a "significant continuing business activity" *safe harbor*. A "significant continuing business activity" will be found if the continuing business activity represents at least 25% of the corporation's total assets at the end of the most recently completed fiscal year, and 25% of either (1) income from continuing operations before income taxes or (2) revenues from continuing operations from that fiscal year, in each case of the corporation and its subsidiaries on a consolidated basis.

### b.   Stock-for-Assets Acquisition

Typically, a stock-for-assets acquisition requires two steps. In step one, Buyer Corp uses its own stock as acquisition consideration to purchase Seller Corp's assets. In step two, Seller Corp dissolves and the former Seller Corp stockholders receive shares of Buyer Corp in the form of a liquidating dividend. A stock-for-assets deal is a tax-free transaction under Section 338(a)(1)(C) of the IRC (referred to as a "C" reorganization by tax professionals).

If, in the first step, Buyer Corp assumes all of Seller Corp's liabilities (which is optional), the result is the same as a stock swap statutory merger. See Nutshell Section 54C(1). Thus, the assets and liabilities of both companies are combined within Buyer Corp, leaving only Buyer Corp stock outstanding.

In order to avoid or minimize the need for shareholder approval at the Buyer Corp level, sometimes a stock-for-assets acquisition is structured so that the big fish is swallowed by the little fish. This is known as a *"reverse asset sale."* However, due to the disparity in size, Buyer Corp (the smaller fish) is required to issue shares of Buyer Corp stock to Seller Corp (the big fish) in excess of the number of currently outstanding shares in Buyer Corp. Thus, once Seller Corp dissolves and distributes the shares of Buyer Corp to Seller Corp's former shareholders, those shareholders collectively own a larger percentage of Buyer Corp's equity than the one collectively owned by Buyer Corp's existing shareholders. This type of structure may be useful when the state corporate law in question (or a corporation's charter) requires supermajority shareholder approval for a merger but only majority shareholder approval for an asset sale.

Assuming that both Buyer Corp and Seller Corp are Delaware corporations, shareholder voting rights in a stock-for-assets acquisition are different from those associated with a stock swap statutory merger. Because Seller Corp is selling all its assets and thereafter dissolving, Seller Corp stockholders must approve both the asset sale (DGCL § 271) and the dissolution (DGCL § 275). However, unlike a stock swap statutory merger where Buyer Corp stockholders normally have voting rights, Buyer Corp stockholders have no voting rights under Delaware law in the context of an asset purchase. Nor, as discussed in Nutshell Section 23B, do they receive appraisal rights in connection with the transaction.

If Buyer Corp is a publicly-traded company, Buyer Corp stockholders *may* be entitled to voting rights under applicable stock exchange listing requirements. These voting rights arise if Buyer Corp stockholders are being significantly diluted as a result of the issuance of additional Buyer Corp shares. See Nutshell Section 50B. For example, if shares of Buyer Corp are listed for trading on the NYSE, Buyer Corp's stockholders are entitled to vote on the issuance of the additional shares— regardless of applicable state corporate law—if the voting power conferred on Seller Corp stockholders equals or exceeds 20% of the voting power outstanding before the issuance. See NYSE Company Manual ¶ 312.03(C)(1). Under this provision, at least a majority of all votes cast must be cast in favor of the proposal. In addition, all votes cast (favorable or otherwise) must constitute at least a majority of all the outstanding shares entitled to vote. See NYSE Company Manual ¶ 312.07.

Because a stock-for-assets acquisition can achieve the same result as a stock swap statutory merger, stockholders involved in the former transaction have complained that they should receive the same rights as those involved in the latter. In particular, they have argued that they deserve voting rights and/or appraisal rights.

In *Heilbrunn v. Sun Chem. Corp.*, 150 A.2d 755 (Del.1959), Sun, a NYSE listed company, sought to acquire Ansbacher–Siegle Corp. by purchasing Ansbacher's assets and assuming its liabilities. As acquisition consideration, Sun issued 225,000 shares of its common stock to Ansbacher. Thereafter, Ansbacher dissolved and distributed the Sun shares to its stockholders in the form of a liquidating dividend.

Ansbacher's stockholders had to affirmatively vote in favor of the asset sale and the dissolution. Sun's stockholders voted on the transaction as well, but not because of Delaware corporate law. Rather, their voting rights stemmed from NYSE listing requirements relating to acquisitions involving conflicts of interest. Here, the president of Sun was also a major stockholder of Ansbacher. Thus, a conflict of interest existed.

Certain stockholders of Sun complained, because they did not receive appraisal rights under the stock-for-assets acquisition structure. Had this transaction been consummated as a merger, they argued, they would have been entitled to appraisal rights. Because the result of a stock-for-assets deal where the buyer is assuming all of the seller's liabilities is the same as a stock swap statutory merger, they argued that the transaction was a "*de facto merger.*" Therefore, they deserved appraisal rights. Apparently these stockholders believed that the judicially-determined fair value of their shares—determined without giving effect to the merger—would be greater than the value of their shares in Sun post-merger.

The Delaware Supreme Court, however, disagreed with the disgruntled Sun stockholders. It noted that Sun's asset acquisition is governed by a provision of the DGCL that was separate and distinct from the merger provision. According to the Court, the fact that the asset acquisition provision and the merger provision overlapped was not important. Indeed, Delaware embraces the doctrine of "independent legal significance" rather than the "de facto merger" doctrine.

In *Hariton v. Arco Electronics, Inc.*, 188 A.2d 123 (Del.1963), another case involving a stock-for-assets acquisition substantially similar to the one involved in *Heilbrunn*, the Delaware Supreme Court reached the same conclusion. An Arco stockholder who did not vote on Arco's asset sale complained about not receiving appraisal rights. Like the plaintiffs in *Heilbrunn,* he argued that he deserved those rights based on the "de facto merger" doctrine. The Court, however, disagreed. According to the Court, an asset sale under Section 271 of the DGCL was "legally distinct" from a merger under Section 253 of the DGCL. Both sections deserve equal dignity, and an acquiror can use either type of corporate mechanic to achieve the desired result.

Like the Delaware courts, the courts of most states have refused to embrace the de facto merger doctrine. A few, including those in New York, appear open to the argument under the right circumstances. See *Irving Bank Corp. v. Bank of New York Co., Inc.*, 530 N.Y.S.2d 757 (N.Y.Sup.Ct.1988) (discussed in Nutshell Section 54C(2)). However, one state—New Jersey—not only has embraced this doctrine, but has codified it as well. See N.J. Stat. Ann. § 14A:10–12.

### c. Drawbacks to Asset Acquisitions

Those considering asset acquisitions should be aware that these transactions may not provide the desired benefits. A purchaser normally "cherry picks" the assets of the seller it wishes to buy. It also seeks to limit its exposure to the seller's liabilities. What assets the purchaser actually acquires, and which liabilities it assumes (if any), is of course subject to negotiations with the seller. Moreover, under the successorship doctrine (see Nutshell Section 54B(1)d), in some cases a purchaser may not legally escape from certain liabilities of the seller (*e.g.,* those relating to tort claims) even when the asset purchase agreement provides otherwise.

In addition, asset acquisitions tend to be very complex and time consuming for four reasons. First, the specific assets a purchaser is buying and any liabilities it is assuming must be identified. To simplify this process, an asset purchase agreement will normally list categories of assets rather than specific assets. For example, rather than listing each piece of office furniture in the seller's headquarters, the asset purchase agreement (or more likely a schedule to that agreement) will specify that the purchaser is acquiring "all office furniture in the seller's headquarters."

Second, the transfer of assets must be documented. While a generalized "bill of sale" can cover most of the assets the purchaser is buying, more formalized procedures must be followed for other assets. For example, real estate, automobiles and intellectual property cannot be transferred by a simple "bill of sale." In the context of real estate, the seller must formally transfer the deed for each parcel of land the purchaser is buying.

Third, if some of the assets the purchaser is acquiring consist of contracts between the seller and third parties, the purchaser's attorney must look through each of the contracts to determine if they contain non-assignability provisions. If these provisions are included, the purchaser may need the prior written consent of the third parties to effect the transfer of those contracts. Some of these third parties may not give their consent unless they receive an incentive payment.

Finally, where governmental licenses and permits are involved, the purchaser must ascertain whether they can be legally transferred. Many may not be purchased, but may be reissued in the purchaser's name. Reissuance is often a time-consuming process. Other licenses and permits, such as casino or liquor licenses, may not be transferable or reissued under any circumstance.

In recognition of the complexities of asset acquisitions, a proposed asset acquisition may be restructured as a stock acquisition to simplify the process. To accomplish this, the seller will "drop down" (*i.e.*, transfer) the assets the purchaser seeks to purchase, together with certain negotiated liabilities, into a newly-formed subsidiary. Once the assets and liabilities are contained in the new subsidiary, the seller will sell all the equity it has in the subsidiary to the purchaser. A "drop down" followed by the sale of the subsidiary's stock is often a much cleaner, simpler way to acquire the assets. Indeed, transfers to affiliates of the seller, such as a wholly-owned subsidiary, may be specifically carved-out from anti-assignment clauses in contracts that the seller decides to transfer.

### d. Successorship Issues in Asset Acquisitions

As a general rule, which seller liabilities (if any) the purchaser of assets will assume is the subject of negotiations between the purchaser and the seller. This generalization, however, is subject to a number of common law exceptions, most of which are followed to various degrees by all states. These exceptions reflect creditor complaints of the unfairness that results when certain liabilities, naturally related to purchased assets, are uncoupled from those assets. Thus, the exceptions are grounded in equity or fairness.

Most states follow the lead of Illinois which has four common law exceptions to the general rule on successor liability. Other states—such as California, Michigan and New Jersey—take a stance less favorable to an asset purchaser and more favorable to the seller's creditors.

Illinois law on successorship embraces the general rule that a corporation that purchases the principal assets of another corporation *does not* assume the seller's liabilities. However, the purchaser would assume those liabilities in the following four instances: (1) when the purchaser expressly agrees to assume the liabilities in question; (2) when the transaction amounts to a "de facto merger" (such a merger being found where an asset sale is conducted by two corporations that have substantially the same ownership (*i.e.*, an "identity of ownership")); (3) when the purchaser of assets is a "mere continuation" of the seller (because the "mere continuation" exception and the "de facto merger" exception both depend on an identity of ownership, some courts believe they are essentially identical); and (4) when the sale is for the fraudulent purpose of escaping liability for the seller's obligations. See *Ruiz v. Blentech Corp.*, 89 F.3d 320 (7th Cir.1996).

California's law on successorship is substantially the same as that of Illinois. It also has the same general rule and the four exceptions previously discussed. California, however, has a fifth exception to the general rule. The fifth exception—known as the "products line" exception—states that a corporation that purchases a *manufacturing business* and continues to produce the seller's line of products assumes strict liability in tort for defects in units of the same product line *previously* manufactured and distributed by the seller. According to the Seventh Circuit in *Ruiz*, the "products line" exception applies when (1) the plaintiff lacks an adequate remedy against the seller/manufacturer, (2) the purchaser knows about product risks associated with the line of products that it continues to manufacture, and (3) the seller transfers the goodwill associated with the product line to the purchaser.

Illinois courts have refused to adopt the "products line" exception. According to the Appellate Court of Illinois in *Domine v. Fulton Iron Works*, 395 N.E.2d 19 (Ill.Ct.App.1979), a "corporate successor to the manufacturer of an allegedly defective product, who takes succession after the product has left the manufacturer's control, is clearly outside of the original producing and marketing chain. Such a corporate successor cannot fairly be said to have participated in placing the product into the stream of commerce.... " The Court also pointed out that the main purpose of strict products liability is to place the loss caused by a defective product on the shoulders of those who created the risk and reaped the profit from placing the defective product into commerce.

### (2) Stock Acquisitions

When purchasing stock of a target company, the acquiror can use cash consideration (a *cash-for-stock* acquisition), stock consideration (a *stock-for-stock* acquisition), or a combination of both. Acquirors seek to purchase stock of another company either for investment purposes or for control. In the former situation, an acquiror will purchase an equity stake in a target company that does not confer any substantial control. In the latter situation, control of the target company is the central purpose.

#### a.   Cash-for-Stock Acquisition

In a cash-for-stock acquisition, Buyer Corp purchases, for cash, the stock of Seller Corp directly from the stockholders of Seller Corp. Once Buyer Corp owns the stock of Seller Corp, Seller Corp becomes a subsidiary of Buyer Corp. The cash-for-stock transaction is a taxable event for Seller Corp's stockholders. They must recognize any gain on the sale of their shares to Buyer Corp.

Most acquirors wish to purchase all the stock of their targets, thus turning those targets into wholly-owned subsidiaries. Indeed, an acquiror typically makes a sizeable investment in a target. If less than all the shares of the target are purchased, the acquiror owes fiduciary duties to minority stockholders of that target going forward. Accordingly, acquirors typically make a cash-for-stock acquisition the first step in a two-step acquisition strategy that ultimately eliminates minority stockholders.

In the first step, the acquiror attempts to purchase as many target shares as possible from target stockholders, but at least a majority of all outstanding shares. In the second step, the acquiror effects a cash-out statutory merger under either Section 251 or Section 253 of the DGCL if Delaware corporations are involved. (This merger is often referred to as a *"second step"* or *"back end"* merger.) Under Section 251, stockholders of the target must approve the cash-out merger. If the acquiror was successful in acquiring at least a majority stake in the target in the first step, the acquiror itself will have the votes necessary to approve the merger. Under Section 253 (the "short-form" merger provision), no approval of the target's stockholders is necessary if the acquiror purchased 90% or more of the target's stock during the first step.

A cash-for-stock acquisition does not have to be approved by the stockholders of either Buyer Corp or Seller Corp. Buyer Corp has the statutory authority to own subsidiaries, and it is not issuing stock as acquisition consideration. Seller Corp stockholders do not need the protection of a stockholder vote, because each individual Seller Corp stockholder can choose whether to accept Buyer Corp's offer to buy his shares.

If Seller Corp is a publicly-traded company, Buyer Corp will make its offer to Seller Corp stockholders through a *"tender offer"* governed by the Federal securities laws. Through the tender offer process, Buyer Corp will publicly invite Seller Corp's stockholders to "tender" their shares into Buyer Corp's tender offer in return for the acquisition consideration Buyer Corp is offering.

If that tender offer is being made with the approval of the board of directors of Seller Corp, the tender offer is considered "*friendly*." The terms of the first step tender offer and second step merger will have been fully negotiated between Buyer Corp and Seller Corp. If the tender offer is effected without the approval of Seller Corp's board, then the tender offer is considered "*hostile*" and its terms will have been set solely by Buyer Corp.

### b. Stock-for-Stock Acquisition

A stock-for-stock acquisition is similar to a cash-for-stock acquisition. Instead of Buyer Corp paying cash to Seller Corp stockholders in exchange for their stock, Buyer Corp issues shares of its own stock as acquisition consideration. Therefore, Seller Corp stockholders become Buyer Corp stockholders after the parties consummate the transaction. Seller Corp becomes a subsidiary of Buyer Corp, because Buyer Corp now owns shares of Seller Corp. If Buyer Corp purchases all the outstanding shares of Seller Corp, then Seller Corp becomes a wholly-owned subsidiary of Buyer Corp. A stock-for-stock acquisition is a tax-free transaction under Section 338(a)(1)(B) of the IRC (referred to as a "B" reorganization by tax professionals).

The result of a stock-for-stock acquisition is similar to a stock swap statutory merger in that Seller

Corp's former stockholders end up holding Buyer Corp stock. However, unlike a merger, Seller Corp's assets and liabilities remain within Seller Corp. Through a stock-for-stock acquisition, Buyer Corp assures itself that the creditors of Seller Corp will not be able to go after the assets of Buyer Corp in the event Seller Corp is unable to fully pay them. If Buyer Corp wants to achieve the exact same effect as a stock swap statutory merger at a later date, Seller Corp can be merged with and into Buyer Corp pursuant to the short-form merger provision of Section 253 of the DGCL, so long as Buyer Corp holds 90% or more of Seller Corp's shares.

If both corporations are Delaware corporations, their stockholders are not entitled to vote on the transaction. Seller Corp's stockholders, however, implicitly can veto the transaction if enough of them choose not to accept Buyer Corp's offer to exchange shares. If Buyer Corp is incorporated in certain states like California or New Jersey, rather than in Delaware, the corporate laws of those states would require Buyer Corp stockholders to approve a stock-for-stock acquisition if the number of new Buyer Corp shares that Buyer Corp will issue would significantly dilute the voting power existing Buyer Corp stockholders.

If Buyer Corp is a publicly-traded company, Buyer Corp stockholders *may* be entitled to voting rights under applicable stock exchange listing requirements. Voting rights arise if Buyer Corp stockholders are being significantly diluted as a result of the issuance of additional Buyer Corp shares. For example, assume shares of Buyer Corp are listed for trading on the New York Stock Exchange. Buyer Corp's stockholders would be entitled to vote on the issuance of the additional shares, regardless of applicable state corporate law, if the voting power conferred on Seller Corp stockholders equals or exceeds 20% of the voting power outstanding before the issuance of the additional shares. See NYSE Company Manual ¶ 312.03(C)(1). Under this provision, at least a majority of all votes cast must be cast in favor of the proposal. In addition, all votes cast (favorable or otherwise) must constitute at least a majority of all the outstanding shares entitled to vote. See NYSE Company Manual ¶ 312.07.

## C. Mergers, Consolidations and Statutory Exchanges

The two basic types of mergers are "stock swap" (stock-for-stock) statutory mergers and "cash-out" (cash-for-stock) statutory mergers. "Consolidations" are simply mergers effected among more than two companies (*e.g.,* two existing companies merge with and into a newly-formed third company). Therefore, the discussions below relating to stock swap and cash-out statutory mergers apply equally to consolidations. Statutory exchanges, where permitted, allow target company stockholders to vote on whether to exchange their stock for the consideration that an acquiring company is offering. These also are discussed below.

(1) Stock Swap (Stock-for-Stock) Statutory
    Mergers

In a "stock swap" or "stock-for-stock" statutory
merger, two corporations (Surviving Corp and
Merging Corp), each with different sets of stockholders, merge together. Merging Corp merges *with
and into* Surviving Corp. Thus, Surviving Corp survives the merger. Merging Corp's stockholders swap
their existing shares of Merging Corp stock for
shares of Surviving Corp stock (hence the term
"stock swap" or "stock-for-stock" merger).

As a result of this transaction, Merging Corp's
assets and liabilities are *combined* with those of
Surviving Corp by operation of law. Merging Corp's
existence is extinguished, leaving Surviving Corp as
the only surviving company after the merger is
consummated. Merging Corp's stockholders swap
their Merging Corp shares for shares in Surviving
Corp. Merging Corp stockholders thereafter are
Surviving Corp stockholders. Shares in Merging
Corp are then *cancelled*.

Stock swap statutory mergers under Delaware
law are governed by either Section 251 of the
DGCL, if the constituent corporations are both Delaware corporations, or Section 252 of the DGCL, if
the merger is between a Delaware corporation and a
non-Delaware corporation.

The merger must be approved by the boards of
directors of the constituent corporations. When two
Delaware corporations are involved, Section 251(b)
of the DGCL requires both boards to pass a resolu-

tion approving the merger and containing a statement declaring its advisability to their stockholders. Under Section 251(e), the agreement of merger can set forth amendments to the surviving corporation's certificate of incorporation. Once that agreement, or a summary of it called a "certificate of merger," is filed with the Secretary of State of Delaware, those amendments take effect automatically. Thus, a merger provides an alternative way to amend a corporation's charter.

With few exceptions, the stockholders of the constituent corporations must also approve the merger. In the case of a Delaware corporation with more than one class of stockholders, only those stockholders with general voting rights (*i.e.,* the right to vote in the election of directors in the ordinary course) typically have the right to vote on a merger. Thus, holders of common stock will vote on a merger, while holders of preferred stock ordinarily will not unless a merger voting provision is set forth in their contract. See Nutshell Section 43C(4).

Absent a higher threshold in the charter, holders of a majority of the outstanding shares must vote in favor of the merger for it to be approved. Importantly, in Delaware the standard is *not* a majority vote at a meeting at which a quorum is present. Rather, it is a true majority vote, *i.e.,* holders of over 50% of all outstanding shares (not just those represented at the stockholders' meeting) must vote to approve the merger; thus, a successful merger vote is more difficult to obtain with respect to a Delaware corporation.

Three significant exceptions to the stockholder voting requirement exist in Delaware. First, a *"small scale"* merger exception exists under Section 251(f) of the DGCL. Stockholders of Surviving Corp are not entitled to vote on a merger when (1) the rights associated with the stock they hold are not changed by virtue of the merger, (2) the agreement of merger does not amend Surviving Corp's certificate of incorporation in any respect and (3) their ownership is not diluted by more than 20% by the issuance of new Surviving Corp shares to Merging Corp stockholders. Thus, this exception typically is available when Merging Corp is not large in comparison to Surviving Corp.

The second exception is the *"short-form"* merger exception under Section 253 of the DGCL. Section 253 allows the merger of a subsidiary with and into its parent corporation (an "upstream" merger), but *not* the other way around, without the affirmative vote of the parent's stockholders when two conditions are satisfied. First, the parent's board of directors must pass a resolution approving the merger. Second, the parent must own at least 90% of all classes of the subsidiary's outstanding shares.

The third exception is the *"holding company"* exception under Section 251(g) of the DGCL. No stockholder vote is required when the merger is effected to establish a holding company structure. For example, assume X Corp, an operating company, wants to create a holding company structure that would result in X Corp's stockholders owning shares in the holding company and X Corp itself becoming a wholly-owned subsidiary of that holding company. To accomplish this, X Corp first would form a wholly-owned Delaware subsidiary called Holding Corp. Holding Corp, in turn, would form a wholly-owned subsidiary called Y Corp. X Corp would then merge with and into Y Corp. X Corp's stockholders would receive shares of Holding Corp as merger consideration. In the end, Holding Corp holds all the shares of Y Corp. Y Corp consists of all the assets and liabilities of the former X Corp. Former X Corp stockholders own all the stock of Holding Corp. In this context, X Corp stockholders are not entitled to vote on any of these transactions.

The holding company exception has a number of stringent requirements, including the following three. First, Holding Corp must have a certificate of incorporation and by-laws largely identical to those of the former X Corp. Second, the directors on the Holding Corp board must be those (and only those) that sat on the board of the former X Corp. Finally, the rights associated with the equity of Holding Corp must be identical to those associated with the equity of the former X Corp.

A stock swap statutory merger is a tax free transaction under Section 338(a)(1)(A) of the IRC (referred to as an "A" reorganization by tax professionals). The IRC makes a distinction between a sale transaction and a merger transaction, with the former usually taxable and the latter usually not taxable. In the case of a stock swap statutory merger, holders of Merging Corp shares that receive Surviving Corp shares continue as investors in the combined entity. Thus, there is no "sale" and, therefore, no recognizable gain or loss for tax purposes.

When two companies of approximately equal size decide to merge in a stock swap statutory merger, the parties typically refer to the transaction as a *"merger of equals."* Stockholders of each constituent company will own approximately 50% of the shares of the combined entities (hence, the "merger of equals"). Often, there is a power struggle between the CEO of the surviving company and the CEO of the company merged out of existence. To resolve this problem, the merger agreement sometimes requires the CEOs of the constituent corporations to share the top leadership position. In true Orwellian fashion, however, one need only look to see who is in charge a year after the merger to determine which of the two entities was "more equal" than the other.

### (2) Cash–Out (Cash-for-Stock) Statutory Mergers

A cash-out (cash-for-stock) statutory merger is substantially similar to a stock swap statutory merger, except that Surviving Corp uses cash to acquire Merging Corp shares rather than shares of Surviving Corp stock. Merging Corp stockholders are cashed out and thus do not become stockholders of Surviving Corp. Surviving Corp assumes all the assets and liabilities of Merging Corp by operation of law. Therefore, unlike a cash-for-stock acquisition, a cash-out merger does not result in Merging Corp becoming a subsidiary of Surviving Corp. A cash-out merger is a taxable transaction to Merging Corp stockholders.

While pure cash-out statutory mergers are possible, most are usually effected as the second step (or "back end") of a two-step acquisition. The first step consists of the acquiror purchasing a majority equity stake in the target company, typically through a wholly-owned subsidiary formed for that purpose. If the target company is a publicly-traded company, then the subsidiary will purchase that stake through an all-cash tender offer financed by the acquiror (known now as the parent company). See Nutshell Section 54B(2)a. The second step consists of the cash-out statutory merger through which any remaining minority stockholders of the target company receive cash for their shares as part of a squeeze out.

If the parent and subsidiary commence the tender offer with the approval of the board of directors of the target, the tender offer is considered *friendly*. The terms of the first step tender offer and second step merger will be fully negotiated between the parent company and target company before the tender offer is launched. If the tender offer is commenced without the target board's approval, then the tender offer is a *"hostile"* tender offer and the terms are set solely by the parent company.

Because a target company's stockholders are entitled to vote on most statutory mergers, acquiring companies seek to acquire at least a majority equity interest in the target before seeking a vote on the merger. If successful, a vote in favor of the merger is assured, because the acquiror will hold a majority stake in the target and will vote its shares in favor of the merger. Mechanics of the merger follow the same process discussed in Nutshell Section 54C(1). If the acquiror is successful in purchasing 90% or more of the target's stock through the first step tender offer, then it can effect the second step merger without target stockholder approval by following the "short-form" merger provision contained in Section 253 of the DGCL.

"Cashed out" stockholders sometimes complain about this result, as seen in *Rauch v. RCA Corp.*, 861 F.2d 29 (2d Cir.1988). In this case, RCA entered into a merger arrangement with General Electric and a wholly-owned subsidiary of GE called Gesub. Gesub merged with and into RCA (a reverse triangular merger), which caused RCA after the merger to become a wholly-owned subsidiary of GE. As part of the merger, stockholders of both RCA common and preferred stock were cashed out.

The plaintiff RCA preferred stockholder was entitled to receive $40 per share for each share of RCA preferred stock she held. If RCA had chosen to redeem the plaintiff's preferred stock, she would have received $100 per share, plus accrued and unpaid dividends. Therefore, she brought suit against RCA seeking $100 per share in damages. (The plaintiff did not seek the appraisal remedy to which she was entitled because presumably the $40 per share price offered in the merger was "fair.") She alleged that RCA was effectively "redeeming" her preferred stock by pursuing the merger with GE. Because the merger agreement compelled her to sell her preferred stock, the plaintiff argued that this constituted a redemption because the merger was a volitional act undertaken by RCA.

The Second Circuit, however, disagreed. Applying Delaware law, the Court noted that a "conversion of shares to cash that is carried out in order to accomplish a merger is legally distinct from a redemption of shares by a corporation." Mergers and redemptions are governed by separate provisions in the DGCL. These provisions are legally independent and are deserving of equal dignity.

The case of *Irving Bank Corp. v. Bank of New York*, 530 N.Y.S.2d 757 (N.Y.Sup.Ct.1988), involved a proposed two-step acquisition. Bank of New York (BONY) approached Irving Bank Corp. about a possible acquisition, but was rebuffed by Irving's board of directors. Thereafter, BONY launched a hostile takeover against Irving that involved two steps. First, BONY made a tender offer for all or a majority of Irving's shares. BONY proposed to pay for the Irving shares with a combination of cash and shares of BONY stock. Second, BONY planned on consummating a merger between Irving and either BONY itself or an affiliate of BONY (*i.e.,* a newly-formed subsidiary).

Irving brought suit complaining that BONY's plan, when viewed in its entirety, was a "de facto merger." Therefore, pursuant to Section 903 of the NYBCL, BONY needed the approval of holders of two-thirds of its outstanding shares. (Note: New York has since reduced the necessary vote to a majority vote.) BONY did hold a stockholder vote, but that vote was mandated by NYSE listing requirements and only required majority approval rather than supermajority approval.

The New York Supreme Court noted that the de facto merger doctrine is recognized in New York when two factors exist. First, the second step merger must take place soon after the initial transaction. Second, the acquired company must quickly cease to exist. The Court then ruled that BONY's two-step transaction did not constitute a de facto merger under New York law. In so ruling, it highlighted BONY's statement that the second step merger "may occur in the future." According to the Court, this implied that the merger might not have happened quickly enough to satisfy the second part of the New York test. The Court held that BONY was simply purchasing a new subsidiary (Irving) and not engaging in a de facto merger.

### (3) Triangular Mergers

As seen in Nutshell Sections 54C(1) and (2), the consummation of a merger generally requires a favorable vote of the stockholders of each constituent corporation. A favorable vote of the stockholders of the corporation merging out of existence is generally assured if the consideration—cash, stock or a mix of both—is alluring to those stockholders. A favorable vote of the surviving corporation's stockholders, however, is not always as certain. They may simply dislike the deal and vote no. Or many stockholders may fail to vote simply due to apathy. Thus, it may take time to secure that vote, and the services of a proxy solicitation firm are typically used. The surviving corporation can avoid the risks associated with a stockholder vote required by state corporate law by effecting a triangular merger.

Take the situation where two corporations (X Corp and Y Corp) decide to merge, with X Corp being the surviving corporation. X Corp can avoid the need for a vote of X Corp stockholders by forming ("dropping down") a new, wholly-owned subsidiary and having it, rather than X Corp itself, consummate the merger with Y Corp. The new subsidiary is capitalized with either cash or shares of X Corp stock, which Y Corp stockholders will receive as merger consideration.

By "dropping down" a subsidiary and having it, rather than X Corp, participate as a constituent to the merger, X Corp stockholders are not entitled to vote on the merger under applicable state corporate law. However, stockholders of the new subsidiary are entitled to vote, because that subsidiary is a party to the merger. Because X Corp owns all the shares in the subsidiary, the favorable vote of the subsidiary's stockholder (*i.e.,* X Corp) is never in question.

Because of the existence of three companies—X Corp, its merger subsidiary and Y Corp—the merger is called a *triangular merger*. There are two types of triangular mergers: forward and reverse. If Y Corp merges with and into the subsidiary (and thus the subsidiary survives), the merger is referred to as a *forward triangular merger*. If the subsidiary merges with and into Y Corp (and thus Y Corp survives), the merger is referred to as a *reverse triangular merger*.

Occasionally, stockholders of the parent corporation in a triangular merger have complained about the lack of voting rights under applicable state corporate law. For example, the case of *Equity Group Holdings v. DMG, Inc.,* 576 F.Supp. 1197 (S.D.Fla.1983), involved a forward triangular merger between DMI (the subsidiary of the parent DMG) and Carlsberg. Pursuant to the transaction, Carlsberg would merge with and into the subsidiary, DMI, and Carlsberg's stockholders would receive DMG stock as merger consideration. Importantly, the DMG stock issued to Carlsberg's stockholders represented 64% of the voting power of DMG.

DMG stockholders complained that they did not receive voting rights under Florida corporate law. NYSE listing requirements mandated a stockholder vote, but the approval threshold was lower than that required to approve mergers under Florida corporate law. DMG stockholders alleged that the triangular merger constituted a de facto merger involving DMG itself. In support of their allegation, they pointed out that Carlsberg was three times bigger than DMG, Carlsberg's former stockholders would end up holding 64% of DMG's common stock, and Carlsberg's former executives were entitled to elect four out of seven directors to DMG's board. DMG and Carlsberg also had engaged in a stock swap immediately prior to the signing of the merger agreement, and that swap was an integral part of the overall transaction. Thus, while DMG itself was not a constituent corporation to the merger, it was not isolated from the transaction either.

The District Court, however, disagreed with the plaintiffs. According to the Court, the plaintiffs alleged no fraud or breach of fiduciary duty on the part of DMG's board of directors. The Court also found no reason to doubt the business judgment of the board. The economics of the deal made sense to the Court, as DMG's consolidated balance sheet was strengthened by adding Carlsberg. DMG's tax loss carry-forwards were better utilized. Finally, stockholder democracy at the DMG level was protected by the vote mandated by the NYSE listing requirement.

Parent company stockholders can ensure that they have the right to vote on a triangular merger involving a subsidiary by putting that right in the parent's charter. For example, in *Pasternak v. Glazer*, 1996 WL 549960 (Del.Ch.), a parent company (Zapata), a subsidiary of the parent (Zapata Acquisition Corp.) and Houlihan's entered into a merger agreement. The agreement called for Houlihan's to merge with and into the subsidiary (a forward triangular merger), with Houlihan's stockholders receiving shares of parent common stock as merger consideration.

Stockholders of the parent claimed that the parent's charter provided them with the right to vote on the merger. That provision stated: "[T]he affirmative vote or consent of the holders of 80% of all stock ... entitled to vote in elections of directors, considered ... as one class, shall be required ... for a merger or consolidation with or into any other corp...." Facially, the provision only applied to mergers or consolidations of which the parent was a constituent. The Delaware Chancery Court nevertheless held that the provision applied to the proposed triangular merger. The Court reasoned that the charter provision must cover mergers involving subsidiaries of the parent, or otherwise the supermajority voting provision could be easily sidestepped. The Court refused to believe that the drafters of the provision would be so careless. However, given the Delaware Supreme Court's subsequent order to vacate the Chancery Court's decision based on mootness, the precedential value of *Pasternak* is unclear. See *Glazer v. Pasternak*, 1996 WL 549960 (Del.), and Nutshell Section 43C(4)c.

### (4) Statutory Exchanges

Section 11.03 of the RMBCA allows a corporation to acquire all the shares of one or more classes or series of another corporation in exchange for shares, securities, interests, obligations or other rights pursuant to a plan of share exchange. The plan must include the name of the acquired company and the acquiring company, the terms and conditions of the share exchange, as well as the manner and basis of exchanging shares of a corporation or interests. Share exchanges are not mergers, but are similar in the sense that shareholders are normally entitled to vote on the share exchange. If the share exchange is approved, *all* shareholders must go along with the share exchange, subject to their right of appraisal under Section 13.02 of the RMBCA.

### (5) Appraisal Rights

Please refer to Nutshell Section 23 for a discussion of appraisal rights in connection with mergers and consolidations.

## D.  Conversions and Reincorporations

A *conversion* is a transaction whereby an existing corporation converts into another form of business entity (such as a partnership or limited liability company), or a non-corporate entity converts into a corporation. Section 265 of the DGCL allows any Delaware limited liability company, partnership (whether general or limited), or statutory trust (typically a "business" trust) to convert into a Delaware corporation. Section 266 of the DGCL allows any Delaware corporation to convert into a Delaware limited liability company, partnership (whether general or limited), or statutory trust.

The typical conversion is of a non-corporate entity converting into a corporation. For example, a particular business may have operated for many years as a partnership. Now it needs access to the public capital markets to fund its continued expansion. Except in certain limited situations, only a corporation can "go public" by selling its stock in an initial public offering. Therefore, the non-corporate entity must first "convert" to the corporate form.

Similar to a conversion is a *reincorporation*. Here, a corporation incorporated under the laws of one state seeks to reincorporate under the laws of another state. Non–Delaware corporations seeking to go public often effect a reincorporation in Delaware immediately before going public. They do so in order to reap the perceived management-friendly benefits associated with being a publicly-traded Delaware corporation. A reincorporation is effected by having the non-Delaware corporation form a wholly-owned Delaware subsidiary, and then having the non-Delaware corporation merge with and into that subsidiary.

# E. Leveraged Buy–Outs

The term *leveraged buy-out* (LBO) relates more to how a particular acquisition is financed than the structure of the acquisition itself. Most LBOs are cash-for-stock acquisitions, whereby a group of investors purchases for cash all the stock of a target company from the target's existing stockholders (typically through a tender offer followed by a second step merger). However, the vast majority of the financing needed to consummate a given acquisition comes from debt financing (*a.k.a.* "leverage") provided by banks, other lenders, and purchasers of debt securities. Very little equity is provided by the investor group itself.

Post–LBO, the target is heavily laden with both senior and subordinated debt. To the extent some or all of the debt financing is secured, it is secured by the assets of the target company. The debt itself is serviced (*i.e.,* paid down) with the cash flow of the target company and, in "breakup" or "bust-up" LBOs, with the proceeds from the sale of certain assets or businesses of the target.

Today's LBOs are more strategic than past LBOs. An LBO firm or private equity firm may seek to purchase a specific business being operated within a conglomerate. The conglomerate seeks to sell the business because it no longer believes that business is essential to its success. The LBO firm or private equity firm seeks to buy it under the belief that the business' profitability can be enhanced once the bureaucratic inefficiencies of the conglomerate are removed and the business receives the managerial attention it deserves. Once the LBO firm or private equity firm improves the business' strategic plan and eliminates inefficiencies over the course of several years, it takes the business public through an IPO.

The LBO firm or private equity firm will raise acquisition proceeds from the issuance of debt. The cash flows of the acquisition target are used to make interest and principal payments on that debt. The debt is usually non-recourse to the LBO firm or private equity firm and debt holders have no claim on other investments managed by the LBO firm or private equity firm. An LBO transaction's financial structure is particularly attractive to an LBO firm's or private equity fund's limited partners, providing them with the benefits of leverage but greatly limiting the degree of recourse associated with that leverage.

A special variant of the LBO is the management buy-out (MBO). An MBO is simply an LBO led by one or more senior managers of the target company rather than a group of outside investors. When the target is a publicly-traded company, those engaging in an MBO seek to take the company "private." A conflict of interest arises, however, as the managers of the target (i.e., the agents of the target stockholders) offer to purchase shares from the hands of those stockholders.

Creditors of companies purchased through LBOs have sometimes brought suit against those companies or their acquirors due to the ill-effects that the extra leverage has on those companies. In *Metropolitan Life Insurance Co. v. RJR Nabisco, Inc.*, 716 F.Supp. 1504 (S.D.N.Y.1989), several of RJR Nabisco's public bondholders sued over the LBO of RJR Nabisco by Kohlberg Kravis Roberts & Co. They argued, unsuccessfully, that RJR Nabisco breached its implied covenant of good faith and fair dealing in its debt indentures by voluntarily becoming highly-leveraged through the LBO. This resulted in the plaintiffs' bonds losing substantial value, as those bonds were downgraded from "investment grade" to "speculative." See Nutshell Section 37B.

Somewhat more successful are creditors who allege that the incurrence of LBO debt constitutes a fraudulent conveyance under Federal bankruptcy law and state law. See Nutshell Section 38A. In this situation, the debt proceeds are not used to grow the business of the acquired company, nor to pay off its creditors, but rather flow directly to its stockholders. See, e.g., *United States v. Tabor Court Realty Corp.*, 803 F.2d 1288 (3d Cir.1986); *Protocomm Corp. v. Novell Advanced Serv., Inc.*, 171 F.Supp.2d 459 (E.D.Pa.2001); *Official Comm. of Unsecured Creditors v. Fleet Retail Fin. Group (In re Hechinger Invest. Co. of Del., Inc.)*, 274 B.R. 71 (D. Del.2002). In *Pay 'N Pak Stores, Inc. v. Court Square Capital, Ltd.*, 141 F.3d 1178 (9th Cir.1998), however, plaintiff creditors of Pay 'N Pak argued unsuccessfully that Citicorp's LBO of Pay 'N Pak rendered Pay 'N Pak insolvent and therefore unable to pay off its creditors. Pay 'N Pak did not file for bankruptcy until four and a half years *after* the LBO. The fact that Pay 'N Pak had paid its trade creditors during the first three years of that period undermined plaintiffs' "insolvency" argument.

## F. Recapitalizations

There are two main types of recapitalizations: strategic and leveraged. A discussion of each follows.

### (1) Strategic Recapitalizations

The typical *recapitalization* or "recap" is strategic. A company typically attempts to create a better balance sheet or create financial flexibility going forward. This may involve the company replacing (or "swapping out") certain existing securities (mostly debt or debt equivalents like preferred stock) with new equity securities. It may also involve the company amending its charter to change, modify or even eliminate existing outstanding securities, most notably preferred stock.

With respect to a Delaware corporation, Section 242(b)(1) of the DGCL requires an authorizing board amendment followed by a ratifying stockholder vote to amend the charter. Importantly, if the amendment will adversely affect the rights, privileges, etc. of a particular class of stock, then holders of that class of stock, voting as a separate class, must also approve the amendment. See DGCL § 242(b)(2).

It is difficult to convince a class of security holders voting as a separate class to approve a charter amendment that affects their rights adversely. Therefore, most companies use statutory mergers to sidestep the separate class voting requirement. Suppose, for example, that a company has both common and preferred stock outstanding, but would like to eliminate the preferred stock. It could do so by amending its charter, but the preferred stockholders voting as a separate class are likely to veto the amendment.

To solve this problem, a company will "drop down" (*i.e.*, form) a new, wholly-owned subsidiary. It will then merge itself with and into that subsidiary. As part of the merger, the parent stockholders (both common and preferred) will receive common stock of the subsidiary as merger consideration in exchange for their shares. Thus, the preferred stock of the parent is eliminated (along with any dividend arrearage) and replaced with common stock of the subsidiary. The subsidiary will then change its name to that of the parent.

This has not sat well with preferred stockholders over the years, and many have sued—unsuccessfully. In the early case of *Federal United Corp. v. Havender*, 11 A.2d 331 (Del.1940), the cumulative preferred stock of a parent company was eliminated through the use of a statutory merger. At the time of the merger, the parent owed the preferred stockholders a substantial dividend arrearage. While the preferred stockholders did receive merger consideration, that consideration did not reflect the dividend arrearage.

When the preferred stockholders complained, the Delaware Supreme Court showed no mercy. The Court underscored that the preferred stockholders bought their shares knowing that mergers were a possibility and could deleteriously affect their rights. According to the Court, they should have protected their right to the dividend arrearage by adding a provision in their contract with the parent company that covered that contingency. The Court also pointed out that those preferred stockholders who believed the merger consideration they received was unfair could have perfected their appraisal rights under Delaware law.

*Warner Communications, Inc. v. Chris–Craft Indus.*, 583 A.2d 962 (Del.Ch.1989), involved the same issue. This case involved the heated battle over Warner Communications waged by Time, Inc. and Paramount Communications. After Time won the battle, its deal with Warner required Time to drop down a subsidiary and have that subsidiary merge with and into Warner (a reverse triangular merger). As part of the merger, Warner's existing Series B preferred stock (held by a subsidiary of Chris–Craft) would be exchanged for a new series of Time preferred stock. Both parties stipulated that the Time preferred stock was less desirable than the Warner preferred stock.

Chris–Craft sought a separate class vote of the Warner preferred stockholders with respect to the merger, pointing to the preferred stock contract for support. Chris–Craft argued that the merger triggered the provision that gave preferred stockholders a separate class vote on any action that adversely "alters or changes" the rights, preferences, etc. of the preferred stock.

Warner countered by pointing to another provision of the contract. That provision stated that preferred stockholders would receive a separate class vote whenever there is a merger and, as a result, the preferred stockholders fail to receive the most senior equity security in the surviving entity. Warner pointed out that the Time preferred stock that Chris–Craft was to receive as merger consideration would be Time's most senior equity security.

The Delaware Chancery Court ruled in favor of Warner and its interpretation of the preferred stockholder contract. Additionally, the Court stated that the "alter or change" language highlighted by Chris–Craft was extremely similar to Section 242(b) of the DGCL, the charter amendment provision. Because a merger is separate and distinct from a charter amendment, the provision to which Chris–Craft pointed was not triggered.

In another case, *Elliott Associates, L.P. v. Avatex*, 715 A.2d 843 (Del.1998), the certificate of incorporation for Avatex stated that a two-thirds vote of the holders of its First Series Preferred Stock was necessary to amend, "whether by merger, consolidation or otherwise," any provision in Avatex's certificate of incorporation that would materially and adversely affect any right, preference or privilege or voting power of the First Series Preferred Stock or its holders. The Delaware Supreme Court held that the phrase "by merger, consolidation or otherwise" was sufficient to distinguish the case from *Chris–Craft Indus.*, and thus a separate class vote of the First Series Preferred stockholders was required before any merger with Avatex could be approved. See Nutshell Section 43C(4)c.

### (2) Leveraged Recapitalizations

Another type of recap transaction is the *leveraged recap*. As its name implies, a leveraged recap involves a company's incurrence of a large amount of debt. The goal of the leveraged recap is to put a substantial amount of cash into the hands of a company's common stockholders by leveraging the company's assets. To achieve this goal, the company will borrow large amounts of debt and then distribute the proceeds to its stockholders in the form of an extraordinary dividend. A stockholder vote is not required to effect a leveraged recap. However, contracts between the company and its existing creditors may contractually preclude the company from incurring the large amount of additional debt.

After engaging in a leveraged recap, the company becomes highly-leveraged, its assets are used to secure the new debt, and its cash flow going forward services the new debt. Stockholders receive a large amount of cash, but their shares of stock become significantly less valuable as a result. They now own shares in a company weighted down with debt. In reality, the holders of the new debt rather than the company's common stockholders have the greatest interest in the company going forward.

A leveraged recap is a strategy implemented by company management in an attempt to enhance stockholder value. And what better way to enhance stockholder value than by sending the stockholders a big dividend check in the mail! This strategy is often employed by the management of a company confronting a hostile takeover bid, as that management scurries around looking for ways to put more value in the hands of the company's stockholders than that being offered by a hostile party.

Sometimes stockholders, rather than management, propose that the company engage in a leveraged recap. Management typically resists the idea, as it does most stockholder initiatives. Such was the situation in *Blasius Industries, Inc. v. Atlas Corp.*, 564 A.2d 651 (Del.Ch.1988), a case where the Delaware Chancery Court adopted the *"compelling justification"* standard of review. Blasius Industries acquired approximately 9.1% of Atlas Corp.'s outstanding common stock, making Blasius the largest stockholder of Atlas. Blasius believed that Atlas was poorly managed and encouraged Atlas' management to consider implementing a leveraged recapitalization or restructuring to enhance stockholder value.

Blasius' specific proposal required Atlas to pay its common stockholders an initial special cash dividend equal to $35 million (which would be borrowed) plus the proceeds from the exercise of stock options and the sale of Atlas' operations not related to its continuing minerals operations. Atlas would thereafter pay its common stockholders a special non-cash dividend in the form of 7% secured subordinated gold-indexed debentures worth $125 million in the aggregate.

Atlas' management reacted negatively to Blasuis' proposal, because its implementation would leave Atlas as a highly-leveraged company going forward. Additionally, management of most companies react negatively whenever stockholders meddle or are perceived to meddle in the business affairs of their companies. In turn, Blasius decided to take stockholder action through written consent as permitted by Section 228 of the DGCL. Among other things, Blasius sought to have stockholders consent to (1) an amendment to Atlas' by-laws which would expand the size of Atlas' board of directors from seven to 15 members (the maximum size allowed under the by-laws) and (2) the election of eight persons (specified by Blasius) to fill the eight new director seats.

Atlas' board responded by voting to amend the by-laws to increase the size of the board from seven to nine members. It then appointed two management-friendly individuals to fill the two additional director seats. These actions effectively precluded the holders of a majority of Atlas' shares from placing a majority of new directors on the board through Blasius' consent solicitation (assuming that the majority wanted to do so).

Upon review, the Court analyzed the directors' actions in terms of the delegation of authority as between the board of directors and its stockholders (*i.e.,* as between the fiduciary and the beneficiaries). The issue, according to the Court, was whether a board may validly act for the principal purpose of preventing a company's stockholders from electing a majority of new directors. The Court held that the board must have a *compelling justification* for taking unilateral action, the primary purpose of which is to interfere with or impede the exercise of the stockholders' voting franchise. If the board takes such action without a compelling justification, then it breaches its duty of loyalty to stockholders. In this case, Atlas' directors could not demonstrate a compelling justification for their actions. *Blasius'* "compelling justification" standard was later embraced by the Delaware Supreme Court in *Stroud v. Grace*, 606 A.2d 75 (Del.1992).

In *Mercier v. Inter–Tel (Delaware), Inc.*, 929 A.2d 786 (Del.Ch.2007), the Delaware Chancery Court found that a special committee had a "compelling justification" to postpone a stockholders' meeting so as to avoid the defeat of an advantageous merger proposal. The directors delayed the vote to gain greater support for the merger, in fear that the shareholders would lose the advantages that an attractive merger would provide. None of the defendant directors were offered a board seat subsequent to the merger, and there was no evidence that raised any doubt of the independence of the majority of the directors. Moreover, the directors' actions neither caused any loss of free will on the part of the shareholders nor precluded shareholders from choosing to reject the merger when the vote ultimately took place. The Court held that the directors had acted to protect the best interests of the shareholders.

Despite the *Mercier* decision, the Delaware Chancery Court has been reluctant to apply the *Blasius* compelling justification standard. It has noted that the burden of demonstrating a "compelling justification" is quite onerous. See *Portnoy v. Cryo–Cell Int'l, Inc.*, 940 A.2d 43 (Del.Ch.2008). Before applying the *Blasius* test, therefore, the Court has taken the approach of first applying the test found in *Schnell v. Chris–Craft Indus., Inc.*, 285 A.2d 437 (Del. 1971). In *Schnell*, the Delaware Supreme Court examined the *subjective motivations* of the defendant directors (who had moved up the date of the company's annual meeting to make it more difficult for dissident shareholders to mount a hostile proxy fight). The Court believed doing so helped safeguard the voting rights of stockholders. Although the bylaws allowed the defendant directors to bump up the annual meeting date, the Delaware Supreme Court held that such action was, nonetheless, inequitable and a breach of the defendant directors' duty of loyalty.

## G. Restructurings

In a typical restructuring transaction, the company will divest (*i.e.,* sell) certain businesses or divisions in an effort to refocus its business strategy on "core" operations. The primary goal of a restructuring is to provide value enhancement to stockholders.

One particular type of restructuring is the *spin-off*. As seen in Diagram 1 on the following page, a spin-off involves a parent company distributing ownership of a business or division to its stockholders through a stock dividend. Typically, that business or division is contained within a subsidiary of the parent company, and thus the parent merely distributes shares it owns in the subsidiary to parent stockholders. If the business or division is not a separate subsidiary, then the parent will "drop down" the assets and associated liabilities of that business or division into a newly-formed subsidiary, and then distribute the subsidiary's shares.

After a spin-off, parent stockholders continue to hold shares in the parent (sans the subsidiary) and also hold shares in the newly spun-off subsidiary. If those stockholders continue to hold shares in both the parent and the spun-off subsidiary, what the stockholders own has not changed. Only the form of ownership has changed. However, those stockholders can choose to sell the shares they receive in the newly spun-off subsidiary (now a stand-alone company), monetizing a portion of their investment.

The case of *HB Korenvaes Investments v. Marriott Corp.*, 1993 WL 257422 (Del.Ch.), involved a value enhancing spin-off. Marriott Corp. proposed a corporate restructuring that called for the separation of its growth businesses from its capital-intensive businesses. Marriott would drop down all of its growth businesses into a new, wholly-owned subsidiary of Marriott called Marriott International. Marriott would then spin-off Marriott International by distributing shares of Marriott International to Marriott's common stockholders through a stock dividend. Marriott would retain all the other businesses (*i.e.,* the capital-intensive businesses) and change its name to "Host Marriott." Diagram 1 illustrates this spin-off using *hypothetical* stock prices.

---

**Diagram 1**

**Marriott Spin-Off Using Hypothetical Stock Prices**

| *Pre-Spin-Off:* | *Step 1: Drop Down* | *Step 2: Spin-Off of Sub. Shares* | |
|---|---|---|---|
| stockholder | stockholder | stockholder | |
| \| ($40/sh) | \| ($40/sh) | ($35/sh.) / | \ ($10/sh.) = $45/sh. |
| **MARRIOTT** | **HOST MARRIOTT** | **INT'L** | **HOST MARRIOTT** |
| (all businesses) | (capital intensive bus.) | (growth) | (capital intensive) |
| | \| | | |
| | **INTERNATIONAL** | | |
| | (growth bus.) | | |

---

Why might Marriott have engaged in the spin-off? Marriott likely believed that stockholder value would be enhanced if its capital-intensive businesses were separated from its growth businesses. It may have felt that its common stock price (hypothetically trading at the pre-spin-off price of $40 per share in Diagram 1) was dragged down by the capital-intensive businesses it owned and operated. It therefore sought to "uncouple" the growth businesses from the capital-intensive businesses through the spin-off.

In Diagram 1, shares of Marriott pre-spin-off were hypothetically trading at $40 per share. However, if the capital-intensive businesses comprised a separate stand-alone company, its shares would have hypothetically traded at $10 per share. If the growth businesses comprised a separate stand-alone company, its shares would have hypothetically traded at $35 per share. By separating the growth businesses from the capital-intensive businesses through a spin-off, Marriott has replaced its single stock worth $40 per share with two stocks collectively worth $45 per share ($10 per share for the capital-intensive "Host Marriott" and $35 per share for the growth-oriented "Marriott International"). Thus, the "uncoupling" that results from a spin-off was worth an extra $5 per share in value to Marriott stockholders. Cf. *Isquith v. Caremark International, Inc.*, 136 F.3d 531 (7th Cir.1998) (noting the "value enhancement" motivation behind Baxter International's spin-off of its subsidiary Caremark International, Inc.).

Of course, there is no guarantee that a spin-off will actually enhance existing stockholder value. Statistics show that spun-off subsidiaries often outperform the stock market as a whole and thus often make good investments. Some of this stems from the former subsidiary being freed from the bureaucratic meddling of the parent. Another part, however, stems from the former subsidiary becoming vulnerable to takeovers now that it is separated from the parent.

In *Anadarko Petroleum Co. v. Panhandle Eastern Corp.*, 545 A.2d 1171 (Del.1988), a spun-off subsidiary brought an action against the parent corporation and the parent's directors for an alleged breach of fiduciary duty in modifying certain contracts prior to the distribution of a spin-off dividend by the parent corporation. The Delaware Supreme Court held that fiduciary duties were not owed until the stock in the subsidiary was actually received by the parent's stockholders. In general, the vesting of cash dividends is considered a contractual right of the stockholder to the dividend, which becomes fixed upon the declaration of a dividend. See Nutshell Section 49C(3). Stock dividends, according to the Court, are different. Because of the possibility of a change in the equity value between the date of the dividend declaration and the actual issuance of the stock dividend, the stock interest held by Anadarko's prospective shareholders does not support the conclusion that a separate class of beneficial shareholders had been created by the mere declaration of a stock dividend to effect a spin-off.

# CHAPTER 16

# FEDERAL LAW ASPECTS

## § 55. INTRODUCTION

The Federal securities laws apply to merger and acquisition activity involving one or more publicly-traded companies. Of particular importance is the Williams Act, which added additional sections to the Exchange Act, as it regulates tender offers. The Federal proxy rules and regulations, which are also found within the Exchange Act, are important too because they regulate the disclosure given to stockholders of publicly-traded companies who are being asked to vote on a given transaction. Lastly, the Securities Act is implicated whenever an acquiror must register shares of its stock or other securities for use as acquisition consideration.

## § 56. PROXY REGULATION

### A. Dual Federal and State Regulation

Both state and Federal law govern proxy regulation. State corporate law is always implicated whenever stockholders of a given company, whether public or private, are asked to vote on a matter requiring their attention. These matters include electing corporate directors and approving a merger, a sale of all or substantially all the assets of their company, and a dissolution of their company. Federal law, by contrast, is only implicated when the stockholders being asked to vote on a given matter are stockholders of a public company.

Stockholders may vote either in person at a stockholders' meeting or by proxy. A proxy represents a given stockholder's delegation of voting power over her shares to an agent (typically a corporate officer) who is referred to as the *proxy holder*. The proxy itself typically takes the form of a card called the *proxy card*. The stockholder will indicate on the proxy card how she desires her agent to vote her shares at the stockholders' meeting. The agent will then carry out those voting instructions on the stockholder's behalf. That way, the stockholder does not have to attend the meeting in person.

State corporate law governing proxies primarily focuses on mechanics rather than disclosure. Mechanics include such things as the timing of notices for stockholders' meetings, required quorums and voting thresholds. For example, Section 222(b) of the DGCL specifies that a Delaware corporation must mail notice to its stockholders before any annual or special meeting not less than 10 days nor more than 60 days prior to the meeting. In terms of disclosure, Section 251(c) of the DGCL only requires directors of a Delaware corporation to send stockholders a notice containing a copy of the merger agreement or a "brief summary" thereof.

The Federal proxy rules, by contrast, are primarily focused on disclosure. Federal regulation of proxies is found in Section 14(a) of the Exchange Act and the seventeen "14a" and two "14b" rules (collectively known as *Regulation 14A*) promulgated by the SEC. Regulation 14A is implicated whenever anyone (either the company itself (*i.e.,* management) or a third party) solicits proxies from the stockholders of a public company. It requires a party soliciting proxies to provide stockholders with a disclosure statement, called the *proxy statement,* containing detailed information.

## B. Federal Proxy Regulation

### (1) Applicability and Filing Requirements

Federal proxy rules broadly state that no "solicitation" (defined expansively in Exchange Act Rule 14a–1(*l* )) of a stockholder's vote in connection with an acquisition may be made unless each stockholder solicited is concurrently furnished or has previously been furnished with a written proxy statement containing the information specified in a Schedule 14A disclosure schedule. See Exchange Act § 14(a) and Exchange Act Rule 14a–3(a). Thus, those seeking to solicit proxies from stockholders must first file preliminary proxy materials (including a preliminary proxy statement) under the cover of Schedule 14A with the SEC. The filing must be made at least 10 days before the filer sends definitive proxy materials to stockholders. See Exchange Act Rule 14a–6(a).

Exchange Act Rule 14a–6(e)(2) permits issuers to file preliminary proxy materials confidentially with the SEC so long as (1) the transaction to which they relate is not a "going private" transaction governed by Exchange Act Rule 13e–3, (2) the parties to the transaction do not make any public communications about that transaction other than those allowed under Securities Act Rule 135 and (3) the materials are filed in paper and marked "Confidential–For Use of the Commission Only." Rule 135 is only implicated when an acquiror is registering securities under the Securities Act for use as acquisition consideration. In such event, Rule 135(a)(2)(viii)(D) allows an issuer to set forth in a press release the names of the parties to a given transaction, a brief description of the transaction, the transaction's basic terms and the businesses of the constituents, as well as the date, time and place of the stockholders' meeting.

If the SEC decides to review a filer's preliminary proxy materials, the filer must resolve any SEC comments on those materials prior to the time it sends out definitive materials to stockholders. The filer must send definitive proxy materials, when available, to the SEC and to each stock exchange on which any security of the issuer is listed concurrently with their distribution to stockholders. See Exchange Act Rule 14a–6(b).

(2) Proxy Statement Disclosure

The two most important documents filed under the cover of Schedule 14A (technically Exchange Act Rule 14a–101) are the proxy statement and the proxy card. The proxy statement discloses information to stockholders about the issues on which their votes are being solicited. The proxy card is used by a stockholder to vote her shares.

Schedule 14A requires that certain information appear in every proxy statement regardless of the type of action proposed to be taken at the stockholders' meeting. Among other things, this information includes the date, time and place of the meeting, any dissenters' appraisal rights, and the identity of the party soliciting the proxy.

Schedule 14A also requires that certain information appear in a given proxy statement based on the particular type of action proposed to be taken at the stockholders' meeting. M&A specific items include Items 11 (Authorization or Issuance of Securities Otherwise Than For Exchange), 12 (Modification or Exchange of Securities), and 14 (Mergers, Consolidations, Acquisitions and Similar Matters) of Schedule 14A.

Items 11 and 12 relate to recapitalizations. If stockholders are to vote on the authorization or issuance of any securities (other than those issued in exchange for currently outstanding securities of the company), Item 11 requires the company to describe the securities to be issued and the transaction in which they are to be issued.

If, by contrast, stockholders are to vote on the modification of any class of securities, or on the issuance or authorization of securities to be issued in exchange for currently outstanding securities, then Item 12 disclosure is applicable. Among other things, Item 12 requires:

- A description of the title and amount of the outstanding securities to be modified or exchanged and, in the case of an exchange, the exchange ratio (*e.g.*, one for one);

- A description of the differences between the outstanding securities and those for which they will be exchanged;

- A statement of the reasons for the modification or exchange; and

- A brief statement as to arrears in dividends or as to defaults in principal or interest in respect of the outstanding securities.

Item 14 requires specified information when stockholders are to vote on: (a) a merger or consolidation involving their company; (b) the acquisition by their company of securities of any other company; (c) the acquisition by their company of any other going business or the assets of a going business; (d) a sale or other transfer by their company of all or any substantial part of the company's assets; or (e) the liquidation or dissolution of their company. Among other things, Item 14 requires:

- A brief description of the business conducted by each party to the transaction;

- A description of the specific terms of the transaction;

- A statement of any required Federal and state regulatory approvals needed to effect the transaction;

- A description of any report or opinion received in connection with the transaction (*e.g.*, an investment banking "fairness" opinion);

- A description of past contacts, negotiations or transactions between the parties that have occurred during the periods for which financial statements are presented or incorporated by reference; and

- Certain specified financial information. This includes (a) pro forma selected financial data for the acquiror showing the pro forma effect of the transaction and (b) per share data in a table designed to facilitate comparison on a historical and pro forma basis.

Finally, if the transaction in question involves a cash-for-stock merger, Item 14(b)(1) requires that target company stockholders receive a *summary term sheet*. This reflects the SEC's realization that, in the context of an all cash deal, the eyes of the recipients rarely get beyond the dollar amount being offered.

### (3) Interaction with the Securities Act

If the acquiror is issuing securities in connection with a stock-for-stock merger with a publicly-traded target company, the acquiror must register those securities under the Securities Act on Form S–4. Like other Securities Act registration forms, the main part of Form S–4 is the prospectus. The prospectus is the primary disclosure document that the acquiror must distribute to the target company's stockholders.

In a stock-for-stock merger, the prospectus of the acquiror will double as the proxy statement used in connection with the required vote of target company stockholders. This avoids producing two separate documents (a prospectus and a proxy statement) which overlap substantially in content. Thus, target stockholders receive a disclosure document called a "proxy statement/prospectus" that embodies all the information contained in both types of disclosure documents.

In a stock-for-stock merger, stockholder approval of both companies is often required. Target company stockholders must approve the merger. The acquiror's stockholders may have to approve the issuance of shares pursuant to stock exchange listing requirements if that issuance is significantly dilutive. See Nutshell Section 54B(1)(b) & (2)(b). In addition, they may need to approve a charter amendment that increases the acquiror's authorized shares to provide the additional shares needed to effect the merger. The acquiror's stockholders typically do not need to approve the merger under state corporate law, because the acquiror normally "drops down" a subsidiary to effect a triangular merger and thus the acquiror technically is not a constituent corporation to the merger. See Nutshell Section 54C(3).

When stockholders of both the acquiror and target company must approve the merger, both companies work together to create a joint proxy statement that each sends to their respective stockholders. Moreover, because the transaction is a stock-for-stock merger, that joint proxy statement will double as a prospectus as well for purposes of the target company's stockholders. Thus, the disclosure document is referred to as a "joint proxy statement/prospectus."

### (4) Liability Under Federal Proxy Rules

Exchange Act Rule 14a–9 is the general antifraud provision relating to the solicitation of proxies. Those soliciting proxies may be held liable for false and misleading statements of material fact or for material omissions in written proxy materials and oral solicitations. The fact that the proxy materials were filed with, or even reviewed by, the SEC does not alter this. Importantly, the failure to include material information in a given proxy statement, even if Schedule 14A does not specifically require that information, is actionable under Rule 14a–9.

The U.S. Supreme Court has recognized a private cause of action for violations of Rule 14a–9. See, e.g., *TSC Indus., Inc. v. Northway, Inc.*, 426 U.S. 438 (1976). The rule supports both an action for damages (in the case of an injured stockholder) and an action for injunctive relief brought by either a stockholder or the SEC. Injunctive relief could entail either a postponement of the stockholders' meeting in question until corrective disclosure is made or, if the meeting has already been held, a new meeting.

## § 57.  FEDERAL TENDER OFFER REGULATION—THE WILLIAMS ACT

### A.  Overview

Congress passed the Williams Act—named after Senator Harrison Williams of N.J.—in 1968. The Williams Act added additional statutory provisions to the Exchange Act. These include:

- *Section 13(d),* which generally requires any person who directly or indirectly acquires beneficial ownership of *more than five percent* of the shares of any class of equity security registered under the Exchange Act to file prescribed disclosure with the SEC under cover of Schedule 13D;

- *Section 13(e),* which governs both issuer tender offers and "going private" transactions;

- *Section 14(d),* which governs third party tender offers (and thus covers all *"hostile"* tender offers) for more than five percent of a class of registered equity securities;

- *Section 14(e),* which prohibits fraudulent tender offer practices; and

- *Section 14(f),* which requires an acquiror after the completion of a successful tender offer for a target company's shares to send an "information statement" to the target company's remaining stockholders whenever the acquiror seeks to appoint directors to a target's board of directors without holding a stockholders' meeting.

Congress passed the Williams Act in response to perceived problems with tender offer practices. At that time, prospective acquirors disclosed little about why they were making tender offers and what they intended to do with target company shares once they acquired them. The disclosure requirements of the Williams Act mandate that those commencing tender offers (*bidders*) provide target company stockholders with prescribed information sufficient to evaluate the merits (or demerits) of a tender offer. Moreover, its mandatory temporal framework gives target stockholders more time to review that disclosure.

Another perceived abuse were the so-called "Saturday Night Special" tender offers. Held open for only a handful of days, they offered to buy only a limited amount of target company stock on a first come, first served basis at a substantial premium to the current stock price. Thus, target stockholders were forced to make their decision to tender not primarily on the merits of the tender offer, but rather out of the fear of being left behind. Many stampeded to tender their shares lest they be left holding minority (and thus typically illiquid) interests in the target company.

The Williams Act now provides for stockholder equality among target stockholders. A bidder cannot discriminate against certain target stockholders (*e.g.,* those that are not the first to tender). Moreover, its mandatory temporal framework provides additional time for target stockholders to decide whether to tender. Thus, they no longer feel stampeded into tendering their shares.

The Williams Act, however, is not without its critics, who level three primary criticisms against it. First, they claim the Williams Act tilts the balance of power between bidders and targets heavily towards targets. For example, the Act's temporal framework—which includes mandatory waiting periods—gives a target's management more time to establish takeover defenses. Second, they claim that by requiring a bidder to disclose what it is doing and why (including plans for the target if the bidder is successful), a bidder's interest in a given target could attract competing bidders who could "free ride" off the original bidder's work product. Third, they argue that the Williams Act's prohibition on price discrimination amongst target stockholders raises the cost to a bidder who seeks control of a target company.

## B. Terminology

Before analyzing the provisions of the Williams Act, an understanding of the following key terms is needed:

- *Tender offer* is a term not actually defined by the Williams Act, which is odd since the main purpose of the Williams Act is to regulate "tender offers." In general, a tender offer is a public announcement by an offeror to buy securities (most typically common stock) of a publicly-traded company at either a set cash price and/or in exchange for a set value of the offeror's securities. See Nutshell Section 57C.

- *Tender offer premium* is the excess over the current market price of a target company's security that the offeror is willing to pay for that security.

- *Partial tender offer* is a tender offer that specifies a maximum limit or "cap" on the number of securities the offeror is seeking.

- *Any and all tender offer* is a tender offer with no maximum limit or "cap" on the number of securities the offeror is seeking.

- *Bidder* is a third party offeror (*i.e.,* someone other than the target company itself) that launches a tender offer.

- *Target* or *issuer* is the publicly-traded company whose securities are the subject of a tender offer.

- *Self-tender offer* is a tender offer commenced by the issuer itself for its own securities. A self-tender offer can either be a *"going private"* transaction, if the issuer seeks to acquire 100% of its outstanding shares, or an *"issuer tender offer,"* if it seeks to acquire less than 100% of its outstanding shares.

## C. What Is a Tender Offer?

Congress purposefully did not define the term "tender offer" in the Williams Act. It feared enterprising parties would structure significant stock purchases so as to fall outside of any static statutory definition. Accordingly, Congress gave the SEC and the courts the flexibility necessary to fashion a definition broad enough to capture unorthodox transactions that carry with them the risks associated with conventional tender offers. Thus, whether a given stock acquisition is a "tender offer" depends on its substance rather than the label given to it by the party conducting it.

The SEC recognizes that not all significant stock acquisitions rise to the level of a "tender offer." Indeed, SEC rules clearly suggest this. For example, Exchange Act Rule 13e–4 regulates an issuer that repurchases its own shares through a "tender offer." By contrast, Exchange Act Rule 13e–1 regulates an issuer's purchases of its own stock—not through a tender offer—but during the pendency of a *third party's tender offer*. Moreover, the SEC recognizes that not all tender offers are worthy of regulation. For example, Exchange Act Section 14(d)(1) and Rule 14d–1 require a bidder to file a Schedule TO (which stands for "tender offer") only when it makes a tender offer for *more than five percent* of a class of equity securities of the target company.

The SEC has stated that the term "tender offer" goes beyond conventional tender offers to include acquisition programs that present the type of abuses that Congress intended to eliminate when it passed the Williams Act. The SEC has proffered an eight part "flexible factors" test in various amicus briefs. See, e.g., *Wellman v. Dickinson*, 475 F.Supp. 783 (S.D.N.Y.1979). Under the test, the issue of whether a given offer is a tender offer depends on the manner in which the offer is conducted and the overall pressure, if any, it has on the purported target's stockholders to sell their shares. The eight factors are:

(1) Active and widespread solicitation of public stockholders;

(2) Solicitation made for a substantial percentage of stock;

(3) The offer to purchase stock is made at a premium over the prevailing market price for that stock;

(4) Terms of the offer are firm rather than negotiable;

(5) The offer is contingent on the tender of a fixed minimum number of shares, and is

sometimes also subject to a fixed maximum number to be purchased;

(6) The offer is open for only a limited period of time;

(7) The offerees are subjected to pressure to sell their stock; and

(8) Public announcements of a purchasing program concerning the target's stock precede or accompany rapid accumulation of a large amount of the target's stock.

Unfortunately, the SEC has indicated that not all of the eight factors are deserving of equal weight. Moreover, it is of the view that not all factors need to be present in order to conclude that a particular stock acquisition is a tender offer.

A significantly different approach to determining what is a tender offer is found in *Hanson Trust PLC v. SCM Corp.*, 774 F.2d 47 (2d Cir.1985). Hanson had launched a hostile tender offer for shares of SCM Corp. SCM responded by adopting a number of anti-takeover devices, including agreeing to merge with Merrill Lynch. SCM also entered into a "crown jewel" lock-up agreement with Merrill. That agreement allowed Merrill to purchase SCM's two most profitable businesses at bargain basement prices if an unwanted third party was successful in acquiring more than one-third of SCM's outstanding shares.

Hanson concluded that its tender offer could not be successful given SCM's defensive strategy, and thus terminated it. Nevertheless, on the same day it terminated its tender offer, Hanson purchased close to one-third of SCM's outstanding shares through six separate transactions, five of which were privately-negotiated purchases and one of which was an open market purchase. Hanson apparently made these purchases in an attempt to scuttle the Merrill/SCM merger deal. At that time, SCM needed a two-thirds affirmative vote of its shares under New York law to effect the merger. (Note: New York has since reduced the necessary vote to a majority vote). It would be unlikely for SCM to achieve such a super-majority vote when Hanson owned close to one-third of SCM's outstanding shares. Therefore, the only logical party with whom SCM could negotiate thereafter was Hanson.

At issue was whether Hanson's six purchases of SCM stock in and of themselves constituted a de facto continuation of Hanson's previous tender offer. With respect to the five private purchases of stock, Hanson did not solicit them. The first purchase occurred after an SCM shareholder contacted Hanson unilaterally. Their deal was reported on the NYSE ticker pursuant to NYSE rules, but the identities of the parties were not listed. However, other professional investors surmised that Hanson was the buyer and contacted Hanson to make four other similar deals. In terms of the one open market purchase of stock, Hanson purchased the block of shares in the open market at the prevailing market price quoted at the time.

While the District Court believed Hanson was making "a deliberate attempt to do an 'end run' around the requirements of the Williams Act" and therefore issued a preliminary injunction against Hanson, the Second Circuit disagreed. It began its analysis of Hanson's actions by looking at how the typical tender offer was described in the congressional debates about the Williams Act:

> It consists of a general, publicized bid by an individual or group to buy shares of a publicly-owned company, the shares of which were traded on a national securities exchange, at a price substantially above the current market price. The offer was usually accompanied by newspaper and other publicity, a time limit for tender of shares in response to it, and a provision fixing a quantity limit on the total number of shares of the target company that would be purchased.

The Second Circuit, believing that the "elevation" of the *Wellman* test was both unwise and unnecessary, instead found guidance in the famous Supreme Court decision in *SEC v. Ralston Purina Co.*, 346 U.S. 119 (1953), a case which addressed the private placement transactional exemption of Section 4(2) of the Securities Act. The Second Circuit reasoned that the purpose of Section 14(d) of the Exchange Act is to protect the ill-informed solicitee, just as the registration requirements of Section 5 of the Securities Act are designed to protect those who, in the words of the Supreme Court in *Ralston*

*Purina*, "can't fend for themselves." Accordingly, the Second Circuit held that the issue of whether a solicitation constitutes a tender offer depends on whether, viewing the transaction in light of the totality of circumstances, it appears that, unless the pre-acquisition filing strictures of the Exchange Act are followed, there will be a substantial risk that solicitees will lack the information needed to make a carefully considered appraisal of the proposal put before them.

Based on this standard, the Second Circuit ruled that Hanson's purchases did not amount to a tender offer. The five private purchases that Hanson made reflected the parameters of the private placement transactional exemption (Section 4(2) of the Securities Act) and did not bear the hallmarks of a typical tender offer. Indeed, a "minuscule" number of sellers were involved and all were sophisticated private investors who could have either decided to sell to Hanson or wait for the SCM/Merrill merger (complete information about which had been disclosed) to be consummated. Perhaps oddly, the Second Circuit also pointed to several *Wellman*-type factors in reaching its conclusion. According to the Court, sellers were not pressured to sell their shares. They were motivated by market forces. Hanson did not engage in any active or widespread advance publicity or public solicitation. The price paid by Hanson was not the type of "premium" price typically paid in a real tender offer. Hanson's purchases were not contingent on the acquisition of a fixed minimum number of shares. Lastly, Hanson did not indicate a fixed time period within which it would make purchases of SCM stock.

The Second Circuit also addressed the fact that all of Hanson's purchases were made the *same day* it discontinued its real tender offer. Did that make Hanson's purchases a de facto continuation of its tender offer? In responding in the negative, the Court noted that Hanson's termination was clear and unequivocal. It had a valid reason to terminate the offer (SCM/Merrill's "crown jewel" lockup). There was no evidence that Hanson had *decided* (as distinguished from "considered"), before terminating the offer, to engage in cash purchases. Finally, Hanson had indicated in its tender offer filing papers that it *reserved the right* to purchase shares in the open market or through private negotiations if the tender offer was terminated.

## D.  Exchange Act Section 13(d) Trigger

Section 13(d) of the Exchange Act provides that any person or group which becomes the beneficial owner of *more than five percent* of a class of equity securities of a publicly-traded company must file a disclosure document under cover of Schedule 13D with the SEC, the publicly-traded company in question, and each stock exchange on which the securities in question are listed. Filings must be made within 10 days after the purchase that pushes beneficial ownership over the five percent threshold.

The policy behind Section 13(d) is twofold. First, its mandated disclosure alerts the market to the possibility that a given publicly-traded company may soon be the subject of a takeover. Critics, of course, point out that such an early warning system also gives the prospective target company advance warning so that it can install a panoply of takeover defenses. Second, Section 13(d) prevents creeping acquisitions of public companies. Without Section 13(d), a bidder could attempt to make periodic purchases of the target's stock through open market purchases that neither qualify as "tender offers" nor draw undue attention. Selling stockholders of the target, oblivious as to what was really happening, would sell their shares to the acquiror without receiving any control premium.

Disclosure in a Schedule 13D includes, among other information:

- The identity and background of the party or group making the filing;
- The source of funding used to purchase the shares;
- The number of shares of the security beneficially owned by the filer; and
- The purpose the purchase serves.

One of the most useful disclosures contained in a Schedule 13D is the acquiror's disclosure concerning its purpose for acquiring the shares in question. In addition, it must disclose any plans or proposals which relate to or would result in, among other things: (a) the acquisition or disposition of the target's securities by any person; (b) an extraordinary corporate transaction (such as a merger); and (c) any change in the present board of directors or management of the issuer.

Many who file Schedule 13D state that the purpose of their purchase is for "investment purposes only." Whether the market believes this statement has a lot to do with the person or entity making it. The market takes with a grain of salt such statements coming from well-known corporate raiders, many of whom make that disclosure only to change it later on through a well-timed amendment to their Schedule 13D. In fact, under Exchange Act Rule 13d–2(a), a filer must amend its Schedule 13D "promptly" if there is a material change to it (*e.g.,* a material increase or decrease in the percentage of the class of securities beneficially owned). "Promptly" is usually interpreted by the SEC to mean within two business days. Thus, if a filer changes its purpose in owning the shares in question, it must disclose this relatively quickly.

Section 13(d) focuses on *"beneficial ownership."* Under Exchange Act Rule 13d–3(a), a *"beneficial owner"* is any person who, directly or indirectly, through any contract, arrangement, understanding, relationship, or otherwise, has or shares either *"voting power"* over the shares in question and/or *"investment power"* over those shares. "Voting power" includes the power to vote, or to direct the voting of, the shares in question. "Investment power," by contrast, includes the power to dispose, or to direct the disposition, of those shares.

Section 13(d) applies to "groups" as well as individuals or separate entities. Exchange Act Rule 13d–5(b)(1) states that a "group" arises when two or more persons agree to act together for the purpose of acquiring, holding, voting, or disposing equity securities. The securities beneficially owned by each group member are aggregated at the time the group is formed and then measured against Section 13(d)'s "more than five percent" test to determine if the group must file a Schedule 13D.

A major criticism of Exchange Act Rule 13d–5 is its use of the term "voting." Section 13(d)(3) of the Exchange Act does not use that term, and thus some argue persuasively that the SEC overstepped its authority by including that term in Rule 13d–5. By including the term "voting," Rule 13d–5 dissuades some institutional investors from getting together to vote their shares on matters put forth to a stockholder vote. Indeed, if they did get together for that purpose, they would have the hassle of filing a Schedule 13D.

A Section 13(d) safety valve of sorts is provided in Section 13(g) of the Exchange Act. Section 13(g) allows certain institutional investors who cross the five percent ownership threshold to file a "short form" Schedule 13G instead of a full blown Schedule 13D. Such an investor, however, must have acquired the securities in question in the ordinary course of its business and not with the purpose of changing or influencing the control of the issuer. An institutional investor must file its Schedule 13G within 45 days after the end of the calendar year in which it became obligated to report its beneficial ownership, so long as it still owns more than five percent of the class of equity securities at the end of that calendar year. However, institutional investors whose ownership exceeds 10% of the class of equity securities in question must make an accelerated filing with the SEC. See Exchange Act Rule 13d–1(b)(2).

## E.   Applicability of Exchange Act Regulations 14D and 14E

As a general matter, Section 14(d) of the Exchange Act and the eleven rules promulgated by the SEC thereunder (known as *Regulation 14D*) only apply to bidder tender offers that would result in the bidder acquiring more than five percent of a class of voting equity securities of a publicly-traded company. The general antifraud provisions of Section 14(e) of the Exchange Act and the eight rules promulgated thereunder (known as *Regulation 14E*) apply to all offers that qualify as "tender offers," regardless of whether those offers are also governed by Section 14(d). See Exchange Act Rule 14d–1(a). Thus, tender offers for debt securities, while not subject to Section 14(d) and Regulation 14D, are subject to Section 14(e) and Regulation 14E.

### (1)  Minimum Time Period

Exchange Act Rule 14e–1(a) requires all tender offers to remain open for a minimum of 20 business days, but by necessity most tender offers are held open longer. Exchange Act Rule 14d–2(a) states that a bidder will have commenced its tender offer at 12:01 a.m. on the date the bidder has first published, sent or given the means to tender to the target's stockholders. The "means to tender" includes a transmittal form (commonly referred to as a *letter of transmittal*) or a statement regarding how the transmittal form may be obtained.

The prescribed minimum time period of 20 business days is subject to extension both mandatorily and at the option of the bidder. In terms of mandatory extensions, Exchange Act Rule 14e–1(b) requires at least a 10 business day extension from the time a bidder notifies target stockholders of any increase or decrease in either the consideration offered or in the percentage of the class of securities sought in the tender offer. In terms of the percentage of the class of securities sought, however, the rule specifically carves out increases of two percent or less. Finally, in the event there is a material change in the information that the bidder gives to the target stockholders, the SEC generally requires a bidder to add an additional five business days to its offering period, if information concerning the change is disseminated via press release, or 10 business days, if the information is disseminated via the mail.

Bidders can always extend their offers voluntarily for additional periods of time (typically one or more additional 20 business day periods). Voluntary extensions are common place in both friendly and hostile tender offers, as it is highly unlikely that all the conditions to a tender offer (especially a hostile one) will be met within a 20 business day time frame. Because a tender offer is open until midnight of the business day the offer expires, a tactic hostile bidders take is to postpone an announcement of an extension until just before the stock market opens on the next business day. This forces many target stockholders to tender their shares just in case the bidder does accept shares for payment rather than extend its offer. The hostile bidder will then extend its offer just before the opening of the stock market the next business day by issuing a press release announcing the extension. That release typically reports the number and percentage of target shares tendered the preceding business day. A high tender percentage puts heat on target management, because it indicates that target stockholders favor the hostile bidder's offer.

Under Exchange Act Rule 14d–7(a)(1), target stockholders who tender their shares into a tender offer have the legal right to withdraw those shares at any time during the pendency of the offer. The SEC, under Exchange Act Rule 14e–1(c), also requires a bidder to either pay for or return tendered securities "promptly" upon expiration of its tender offer.

Under Exchange Act Rule 14d–11, a bidder who had made a tender offer for all outstanding securities of a class may elect to provide target stockholders with a *"subsequent offer period"* of at least three business days after a tender offer ends. This period is essentially a clean up period during which target stockholders who failed to tender their shares during the tender offer have another chance to tender. By tendering during the subsequent offer period, these stockholders do not have to wait until a second step merger is completed to get paid for their shares. The period also helps bidders achieve the percentage of target shares necessary to complete a "short-form" merger (typically 90% or more), thus avoiding the need for a vote of target stockholders. See DGCL § 253 and Nutshell Section 54C(1). Under Exchange Act Rule 14d–7(a)(2), bidders need not offer withdrawal rights to target stockholders who tender their shares during a subsequent offer period; however, Rule 14d–11(e) requires bidders to immediately accept and promptly pay for all securities as they are tendered during the subsequent offering period.

### (2) Anti–Discrimination Rules

#### a. Pro Rata Treatment

The Williams Act prohibits discriminatory treatment of target stockholders. Exchange Act Rule 14d–8 requires a bidder to accept shares tendered by target stockholders on a pro rata basis in the event those stockholders have tendered more shares than the bidder is seeking to buy (*i.e.*, the tender offer is *oversubscribed*).

### b.　All Holders Rule

Exchange Act Rule 14d–10(a)(1) is the "all holders rule." It requires a bidder to accept tenders of shares from all holders of the class of equity securities that the bidder is seeking. This rule was adopted by the SEC to prohibit the actions taken by companies like Unocal Corp. towards a hostile party. In *Unocal Corp. v. Mesa Petroleum Co.*, 493 A.2d 946 (Del.1985), Unocal Corp. launched a "discriminatory" self-tender offer as a defensive response to Mesa Petroleum's hostile tender offer. The self-tender offer was open to all holders of Unocal stock *except* Mesa Petroleum (which held a sizable block of Unocal stock). While the Delaware Supreme Court upheld Unocal's discriminatory self-tender offer as a reasonable defensive response to Mesa's hostile actions, discriminatory tender offers are now prohibited by Federal law. For more on the *Unocal* decision, see Nutshell Section 60D(2).

### c.　Best Price Rule

Exchange Act Rule 14d–10(a)(2) is the "best price rule." It provides that each tendering stockholder must receive the highest price paid to any other target stockholder for securities "tendered in the tender offer." The SEC clarified the rule in 2006. Before then, the rule had related to the highest amount paid "*during*" the tender offer. The previous language gave rise to many cases in an attempt to determine whether transactions that occurred immediately before a tender offer commenced or just after it was completed violated Rule 14d–10. See, e.g., *Epstein v. MCA, Inc.*, 50 F.3d 644 (9th Cir.1995) (rev'd on other grounds); *Lerro v. Quaker Oats Co.*, 84 F.3d 239 (7th Cir.1996).

Rule 14d–10 also became quite problematic in the context of severance agreements, noncompete agreements and other employee-related agreements. See, e.g., *Katt v. Titan Acquisitions, Ltd.*, 133 F. Supp. 2d 632 (M.D.Tenn.2000); *Gerber v. Computer Assoc. Int'l Inc.*, 303 F.3d 126 (2d Cir.2002). Concerned that Rule 14d–10 was being used by the courts in an overly inclusive way in the context of employee-related agreements, the SEC modified the rule in 2006 to make it clear that employment compensation and severance payments *are not* considered under the best price rule so long as (a) the amount payable is being paid or granted as compensation for past services performed, future services to be performed, or future services to be refrained from performing, (b) the amount payable is not calculated based on the number of securities tendered or to be tendered in the tender offer by the security holder in question, and (c) the arrangement is approved as an employment compensation, severance or other employee benefit arrangement solely by independent directors of the company. See Exchange Act Rule 14d–10(d).

### d. Purchases Outside the Tender Offer

Exchange Act Rule 14e–5(a) prohibits bidders from buying equity securities of a target company outside the tender offer from the time of the public announcement of a tender offer until the tender offer expires. A "public announcement" of a tender offer could occur earlier than the actual "commencement" of that tender offer. Thus, a bidder cannot privately negotiate to buy a large block of stock from a major stockholder of a target once that bidder has announced its intention to launch a tender offer. The Rule contains a series of exceptions for transactions that do not implicate the policies behind the Rule, such as purchases made pursuant to a "subsequent offer period" and those made pursuant to an unconditional and binding contract entered into before the public announcement of the tender offer in question. See Exchange Act Rule 14e–5(a) & (b).

### (3) Prohibition on Market Manipulation

Exchange Act Rule 14e–8 is designed to prevent prospective bidders from manipulating the market for the target company's stock. The Rule makes it illegal for any person to announce a plan to make a tender offer if that person (a) does not have a bona fide intent to launch the offer within a reasonable time period and complete it, (b) intends for the announcement to manipulate the market price of the stock of the bidder or subject company, or

(c) lacks a reasonable belief that it will have the means to purchase the securities it is seeking to buy. This rule is important given the fact that news that a particular company is about to be put "in play" (*i.e.,* made the target of a hostile tender offer) typically drives up that company's stock price.

The SEC has indicated that the antifraud provisions of Regulation 14E apply to so-called "*mini-tender offers*." A mini-tender offer is a "first come, first served" tender offer for typically less than five percent of a target company's stock. Because of its small size, Exchange Act Section 14(d) and Regulation 14D do not apply. These tender offers typically offer to pay *less per share* than the current trading price of the target company's stock, and often omit withdrawal rights. Apparently, there are enough ignorant investors in the world who accept these tender offers that make it worth bidders' time and expense to launch them. Many who tender are simply unaware what the current market price of their stock is, or they receive a legal disclosure document in the mail and assume they must tender. In an attempt to crack down on mini-tender offers, the SEC has stated that they must comply with Regulation 14E. Thus, mini-tender offers cannot offer less than the market price. Nor can they offer a price at or above the current market price while also omitting withdrawal rights and indicating that the bidder intends to close on the offer only if the market price rises above the offer price.

## F. Tender Offer Disclosure Documents

The two main tender offer disclosure documents are Schedule TO (which stands for "tender offer") and Schedule 14D–9 (named after the Exchange Act rule that requires it). Schedule TO is the bidder's disclosure document which the bidder must file with the SEC and deliver to the target company and any other bidder with a tender offer pending. Schedule 14D–9 is the target's disclosure document which the target must file with the SEC and deliver to the bidder and target company stockholders. The SEC may review and comment upon both of these disclosure documents.

### (1) Bidder's Disclosure

A bidder's Schedule TO must disclose, among other information, the terms and conditions of the tender offer itself, the purpose of the offer (*e.g.,* to take control of the target or otherwise), plans for the target after the tender offer, financing arrangements needed to purchase the target's shares, contacts between management of the constituent companies and, in the case of a cash tender offer or cash-for-stock merger, a plain English "term sheet" summarizing the terms of the offer. Most of this information is set forth in an exhibit to Schedule TO called the *Offer to Purchase* and incorporated by reference into the Schedule itself.

The bidder only sends certain exhibits to Schedule TO to stockholders of the target company. The two most important exhibits are the *Offer to Purchase* and the *Letter of Transmittal*. As indicated in the preceding paragraph, the Offer to Purchase contains detailed disclosure about the tender offer. The Letter of Transmittal is a lengthy form that each target stockholder must complete in order to tender her shares to the bidder.

Procedurally speaking, a bidder can choose how to announce its tender offer to target stockholders. It can choose between "long form" publication and "summary" publication. Under Exchange Act Rule 14d–6(a)(1), "long-form" publication involves the bidder publishing a slightly scaled down version of the offer set forth in its Schedule TO. That version must be published in a newspaper of national circulation, metropolitan or regional circulation, or a combination thereof depending on the facts and circumstances. See Exchange Act Rule 14d–4(c). Bidders rarely announce their tender offers in this way.

Virtually all bidders announce their tender offers through "summary" publication. Under Exchange Act Rule 14d–6(a)(2), "summary" publication involves the publication of a shorter newspaper advertisement referred to as the *summary ad*. Summary ads usually form a vertical rectangle flowing from the top to the bottom of the right third of a page of a newspaper. A summary ad describes the basic terms of the offer and invites target stockholders to request formal offering materials from the bidder's "information agent." Summary ads are typically published in Section C ("Money & Investing") of the *Wall Street Journal*, although they appear in the *New York Times* and *Los Angeles Times* occasionally. They *cannot* include a transmittal letter enabling stockholders to tender their securities. See Exchange Act Rule 14d–6(d)(3).

While a summary ad is required to invite target stockholders to request formal offering materials, a bidder actively seeks (and is also legally required) to send those materials to those stockholders. See Exchange Act Rule 14d–4(a)(2)(ii). In this regard, the target company can choose either to send the bidder's offering materials to the target's stockholders (at the bidder's cost and expense) or provide a list of stockholders to the bidder so that the bidder can send its materials out directly. See Exchange Act Rule 14d–5(a)(3).

### (2) Target's Disclosure

Any person who makes a solicitation or recommendation to the target company's stockholders with respect to a tender offer must file a Schedule 14D–9 with the SEC. Because Exchange Act Rule 14e–2(a) requires the target company to notify its stockholders of management's position on a pending tender offer not later than 10 business days from the commencement of that offer, the target must naturally set forth that position on Schedule 14D–9. The target company must file its Schedule 14D–9 with the SEC and send a copy of the completed schedule to each of its stockholders.

Although a Schedule 14D–9 sets forth much information, two pieces stand out. First, target management must provide its position on the pending tender offer. Does management recommend that stockholders tender their shares? Does it recommend that stockholders reject the bidder's offer? Is management expressing no opinion and thus remaining neutral toward the bidder's offer? Is management unable to take a position at this time based on limited information? Management must give a reason for its position.

When the bidder's tender offer is part of a friendly acquisition of the target company, the target's management will recommend the offer to the target's stockholders. In the case of a hostile tender offer, however, the recommendation of the target's management is just the opposite. One of its reasons for recommending to target stockholders that they not tender is almost always that the consideration being offered by the bidder is "inadequate from a financial point of view." That is a fancy way of saying the bidder is not offering enough money for the target's shares.

A second important piece of disclosure in a Schedule 14D–9 is any negotiations target management has had with third parties (*e.g.,* a "white knight") that wish to purchase the target company as a whole or a material portion of the target's assets. If the negotiations are merely preliminary, the target may disclose only the existence of the negotiations without naming the third party. If, however, an agreement in principle is reached, the name of the third party must be disclosed. Given that defensive strategies involving "white knights" and "white squires" can be highly effective (see Nutshell Section 60D(1)(c)), disclosure in this regard is not unusual.

If the bidder believes the target's Schedule 14D–9 is incorrect or misleading, the bidder can sue for injunctive relief against the target under Exchange Act Section 14(e) seeking corrective disclosure. The bidder, however, cannot sue for damages. A target's stockholders may sue for damages if they can show that, but for a fraudulent statement or omission in the target's Schedule 14D–9, they would or would not have tendered their shares to the bidder, as the case may be.

## G.  Issuer Tender Offers and "Going Private" Transactions

Hostile third parties are not the only ones launching tender offers. The original issuer of the securities in question can launch a tender offer for its own securities. These tender offers are referred to as *self-tender offers* or simply *self-tenders*. Self-tenders, in turn, can be broken down into *issuer tender offers* and *going private* transactions.

### (1)  Issuer Tender Offers

An issuer tender offer is any self-tender other than a going private transaction. Thus, an issuer tender offer is a *partial tender offer* in which the issuer seeks to repurchase less than all the outstanding shares of a class of its equity securities held by the public. After an issuer tender offer, the issuer has fewer shares outstanding yet typically remains a publicly-traded company.

An issuer tender offer is governed by Exchange Act Rule 13e–4. Importantly, that Rule essentially requires issuers to follow the same disclosure and timing requirements applicable to third party bidders. Thus, an issuer will file a Schedule TO with the SEC, publish a summary ad in a newspaper and send its Offer to Purchase and Letter of Transmittal to its stockholders. In addition, like third party bidders, an issuer engaging in an issuer tender offer must comply with the antifraud requirements of Section 14(e) of the Exchange Act and Regulation 14E promulgated thereunder.

An issuer engages in an issuer tender offer typically when its management believes the trading price of its shares is cheap. Management of the issuer thinks the best use of the issuer's surplus cash is to invest it in the issuer's own stock by buying some of it back. Accordingly, the market typically views an issuer tender offer as a "bullish" or positive sign from the issuer's management that indicates that management views the issuer's stock price as undervalued.

An issuer tender offer should be contrasted with issuer repurchases of its own equity securities *during the pendency of a third party tender offer*. Under

Exchange Act Rule 13e–1, an issuer that has received notice of a third party tender offer for the issuer's shares cannot buy back any of its own shares unless it files a "13e–1 statement" with the SEC. Within that statement, an issuer must disclose, among other things, the purpose of its stock purchases, its plans for the repurchased securities (*e.g.,* retire them, hold them in treasury, resell them at a later date), and the source and amount of funds used to make the purchases.

## (2) "Going Private" Transactions

A *going private* transaction is a self-tender by an issuer, the purpose of which is to convert a publicly-traded company back into a privately-held company. This is accomplished by the issuer repurchasing the company's outstanding stock held by the public. Once all the stock has been repurchased from public stockholders, the issuer no longer qualifies as a reporting company under the Exchange Act and, therefore, is considered a privately-held company.

Going private transactions are led by management of the issuer either alone or in connection with a handful of outside investors. The consideration used to buy out public stockholders is usually cash, debt securities of the issuer (thus turning the former stockholders into creditors) or a combination of the two. Cash consideration is sometimes raised through the issuance of debt securities by or through a leveraged buy-out firm.

Going private transactions involve tremendous conflicts of interest. When current management offers to buy out public stockholders and establishes the price at which to do so, the interests of management and stockholders diverge. Accordingly, the SEC promulgated Exchange Act Rule 13e–3 and Schedule 13E–3 to address going private transactions.

Two major differences exist between Schedule 13E–3 and Schedule TO disclosures that reflect these conflicts. First, Schedule 13E–3 requires an elaborate statement of the fairness of a going private transaction with supporting rationale. All material factors behind the statement must be itemized and disclosed. The issuer, therefore, is liable under the antifraud provisions for any false and misleading statements in this regard.

Second, Schedule 13E–3 requires disclosure of all reports and appraisals that the issuer received from outside parties (*e.g.,* an investment bank) "materially relating" to the fairness of the offer. Thus, the issuer must disclose all valuation information it has received. It simply cannot cherry pick the best valuation opinion (in this case the one giving the lowest possible valuation) of several it may have received.

If the going private transaction is by means of a tender offer, the issuer may file a combined Schedule TO and Schedule 13E–3 under cover of Schedule TO. However, the issuer must provide all information called for by both schedules (taking into consideration redundancies).

## H. Interaction with the Securities Act

The Securities Act governs the issuance of securities in primary offerings, especially those made to the public. See Nutshell Section 1A. When an acquiror issues securities as acquisition or merger consideration in a manner that constitutes a public offering, the Securities Act registration requirements apply to that issuance. Those requirements, however, have no application when the acquiror uses cash as acquisition or merger consideration or issues securities in a transaction exempt from registration under the Securities Act (*e.g.*, a private placement).

### (1) Exchange Tender Offers

#### a. Generally

In an *exchange tender offer,* the bidder uses its own stock or debt securities to purchase shares of stock held by the target company's stockholders. In this situation, the bidder must file both a Schedule TO under the Williams Act and a registration statement under the Securities Act.

A bidder will register its securities on Securities Act Form S–4. In addition to requiring standard Securities Act disclosure (*e.g.*, a description of the securities), Form S–4 also requires information about the target company and the terms of the transaction. Importantly, Form S–4 can double for the bidder's Schedule TO and the target's Schedule 14D–9 (assuming a friendly deal) if the parties are careful to integrate any additional information required by those schedules into the Form S–4.

A bidder engaged in an exchange tender offer enjoys relaxed "gun jumping" restrictions under the Securities Act. Unlike most other issuers of securities, a bidder can freely communicate with target stockholders about an anticipated exchange offer both before and after it files its Form S–4 with the SEC. If, however, it communicates in writing, a bidder must file all written materials with the SEC under Securities Act Rules 165, 424 and 425.

### b.   Hostile Exchange Offers

Prior to 2000, a bidder could not commence an exchange offer (*i.e.,* send tender offer materials to target stockholders) until the SEC declared its Securities Act registration statement effective. This meant that a bidder was effectively prevented from launching a *hostile* exchange offer because of the time delays generally associated with Securities Act registration. Indeed, because a Securities Act registration statement is a public document, a bidder had no way to surprise or sneak up on the target company. Thus, virtually all hostile offers were all cash tender offers to which the Securities Act did not apply.

In order to level the playing field between cash tender offers and exchange tender offers, the SEC now allows a bidder to commence its exchange tender offer upon the filing of, and prior to the effectiveness of, its Securities Act registration statement. However, Securities Act Rule 162(a) requires a bidder to file with the SEC a Securities Act registration statement that includes a preliminary prospectus containing all information, including pricing information, necessary for a target stockholder to make an informed investment decision. The SEC has promised expedited review of exchange tender offer filings.

A bidder must disseminate its preliminary prospectus to all target stockholders and file a tender offer statement with the SEC. It must also deliver any supplements containing material changes to the preliminary prospectus to all target stockholders. Once the bidder has complied with these requirements, it need not send a final prospectus to target stockholders. Target stockholders may tender their shares prior to the effectiveness of the bidder's registration statement. However, under Securities Act Rule 162(a), the bidder cannot accept any tendered shares for payment until the SEC declares its registration statement effective and the tender offer has expired in accordance with the tender offer rules.

### (2) Statutory Mergers and Asset Acquisitions

Most mergers and many asset acquisitions trigger stockholder voting requirements. If an acquiror uses its securities in a stock swap statutory merger or as acquisition consideration when purchasing assets, the issue arises as to whether the acquiror is engaged in a public offering of securities that needs to be registered under the Securities Act.

An argument certainly can be made that target stockholders in such a merger or asset sale technically are not "selling" their shares. Rather, what they are doing is simply voting on whether to approve a merger or an asset sale. This is particularly true in a stock-for-assets acquisition, because the recipient of the stock consideration is (at least initially) the target company, not its stockholders.

As seen in Securities Act Rule 145(a), however, the SEC has taken the position that a sale of securities has in fact occurred in the context of a stock swap statutory merger and a stock-for-assets acquisition. Accordingly, the acquiror must register the shares it is issuing under the Securities Act. The SEC's position is that target stockholders are being asked to vote on whether to accept a new or different security for their existing securities. In substance, therefore, they are making a *new investment decision*. The SEC believes this triggers the Securities Act disclosure requirements.

The acquiror in a stock swap statutory merger or stock-for-assets acquisition must file a Securities Act registration statement with the SEC. Moreover, one or both parties to the transaction must file an Exchange Act proxy statement depending on the identity of stockholders entitled to vote on the transaction. If a stockholder vote of both parties is required, the parties typically prepare a joint proxy statement/prospectus for this purpose. It is then filed under the cover of Securities Act Form S–4 with the SEC. Once the SEC has declared the Form S–4 effective, the acquiror and target company may mail the final form of joint proxy statement/prospectus to their respective stockholders.

The SEC allows an acquiror in a stock swap statutory merger or stock-for-assets acquisition to communicate freely with target stockholders about potential deals both before and after it files its Form S–4 registration statement. However, an acquiror must file all written communications with the SEC under Securities Act Rules 165, 424 and 425.

### (3) Resales of Securities

Securities lawyers are frequently asked by former target stockholders who received securities of the acquiror about *when* they can resell those securities. This issue is particularly important to a founder of a small company who sells her company to an acquiror in return for securities of the acquiror. Because a large portion of the founder's assets is likely to be tied up in securities of the acquiror, the founder understandably wants to know when she can sell in order to diversify her investments.

The answer to this question depends on whether the securities received from the acquiror were registered under the Securities Act. If the securities *were not registered* (suppose they were issued as part of a valid private placement), then any person who receives those securities receives *restricted securities* as defined in Securities Act Rule 144(a)(3). Accordingly, those who wish to resell those securities must either register them under the Securities Act for resale (unlikely, as it depends on the willingness of the issuer) or, more likely, comply with the resale restrictions applicable to restricted securities set forth in Rule 144. Of particular importance is the rule's requirement that the securities be held for at least six months (in the case where the issuer is a reporting company under the Exchange Act) before any resale can occur (a requirement that no doubt will grab the attention of the founder). See Securities Act Rule 144(d)(1).

If the securities issued as part of the business combination *were registered* by the issuer, then the answer to the resale question lies in Securities Act Rule 145. This Rule governs the ability of a target stockholder to resell registered securities of the acquiror received as part of a merger, consolidation or acquisition of assets. In the context of a resale, these securities are referred to as "Rule 145 securities." Until 2007, Rule 145 placed the "presumptive underwriter" label on two types of persons. First, any "affiliate" of an acquired company who received securities of an acquiror as part of a business combination was deemed an "underwriter" under Section 2(a)(11) of the Securities Act if she resold those securities to the public. An "affiliate" is generally a person with the power (whether exercised or not) to control or direct the affairs of a company. Second, in the context of a stock-for-assets transaction in which the company selling assets receives acquiror stock and then either dissolves or otherwise distributes that stock pro rata to its stockholders, the company selling assets was also deemed an "underwriter" under Rule 145(c) if it publicly offered or sold the securities it received.

In 2007 the SEC greatly liberalized the "presumptive underwriter" concept found in Rule 145(c) as it applies to registered securities. Today, only reporting and non-reporting *shell companies* (other than business combination related shell companies) and their affiliates and promoters are deemed "presumptive underwriters." Even so, shell companies can resell their Rule 145 securities under Rule 145(d), which requires that certain provisions of Securities Act Rule 144 are met. Importantly, all others are free to resell their registered Rule 145 securities at any time.

# CHAPTER 17

# STATE LAW ASPECTS

## § 58.  INTRODUCTION

All merger and acquisition transactions are negotiated and consummated against a backdrop of the corporate laws of the states in which the constituent corporations were formed. Delaware corporate law plays a particularly important role in this regard, as the majority of publicly-traded corporations are Delaware corporations. Moreover, the courts of other states often look to the Delaware courts for guidance on how to resolve disputes relating to actual or proposed business combinations.

The Delaware Supreme Court has fashioned four basic tests for determining whether a board of directors has satisfied its fiduciary duties of care and loyalty in the context of a business combination. The first and most basic is the business judgment rule as espoused in *Smith v. Van Gorkom*, 488 A.2d 858 (Del.1985), and many other cases. See Nutshell Section 59.

The second test is the enhanced scrutiny test found in *Unocal v. Mesa Petroleum Co.*, 493 A.2d 946 (Del.1985), and *Revlon v. MacAndrews & Forbes Holdings, Inc.*, 506 A.2d 173 (Del.1986). It applies whenever a board adopts a takeover defense or puts the company up for sale. The enhanced scrutiny test must be satisfied before the business judgment rule will attach to those directorial decisions. See Nutshell Sections 60C & D(2).

The third test is the entire or intrinsic fairness test discussed in *Weinberger v. UOP, Inc.*, 457 A.2d 701 (Del.1983), and many other cases. This test applies to directorial action taken at a time when a conflict of interest exists. When applicable, it requires directors to demonstrate how the transaction in question was intrinsically fair to the corporation and its stockholders. See Nutshell Section 60A(1).

The last test is the "compelling justification" test espoused in *Blasius Industries, Inc. v. Atlas Corp.*, 564 A.2d 651 (Del.Ch.1988). If directors take unilateral defensive action that impinges on the stockholders' voting franchise, then they must demonstrate a compelling justification for doing so. Such would be the case when directors, faced with a hostile proxy fight over board membership, take action making it more difficult for stockholders to elect a competing slate of nominees to the board. For more on the "compelling justification" test, see Nutshell Section 54F(2).

## § 59. THE DUTY OF CARE AND THE BUSINESS JUDGMENT RULE

### A. A Board's Decision to Sell the Company

One of the most important decisions a board of directors can make is an affirmative decision to sell the company. After all, the board can only sell the company once and collect a control premium for its stockholders. In deciding whether to sell the company, the board must comply with its duty of care. The seminal Delaware case on point is *Smith v. Van Gorkom*, 488 A.2d 858 (Del.1985). In this case, plaintiff stockholders of Trans Union alleged that the Trans Union directors had acted with gross negligence by not making an informed business decision to sell Trans Union.

According to the Delaware Supreme Court, a director must inform herself prior to making a business decision of all material facts reasonably available to her. In the specific context of a merger, a director has a duty to act in an informed and deliberate manner in determining whether to approve an agreement of merger before submitting the proposal to the stockholders. A director may not abdicate that duty by leaving the decision to the stockholders alone.

The Court determined that the Trans Union directors did not satisfy their duty to make an informed business decision and had acted with gross negligence. The directors did not adequately inform themselves as to the role that Van Gorkom (Trans Union's CEO) played in forcing the sale of the company and in establishing the per share purchase price offered by the buyer. They also were uninformed as to the intrinsic value of Trans Union and thus could not determine whether the price the buyer offered was fair. Their approval was obtained at a meeting the purpose of which was not previously disclosed to them. They gave their approval without examining any of the transaction documentation and after deliberating for only two hours. Although the transaction allowed for a "market test period," a period of time during which third parties could make better offers, that prophylactic device proved mostly illusory due to Van Gorkom's hostility towards third party bidders and his favoritism shown towards the buyer. (Note: today, it is not unusual for a selling company to ask for a *"go shop"* provision, whereby the seller can actively seek out other buyers for the company for a specified period of time after an agreement is signed.)

On the valuation point, the Court stopped short of saying a board needs a "fairness opinion" from an investment bank. Such an opinion tells directors that the price being offered by a third party "is fair from a financial point of view." Nevertheless, the Court stated that a valuation is needed in order to determine whether the price being offered makes sense. That valuation could be generated by financial employees working inside the company as well as an investment banking firm. Importantly, under Section 141(e) of the DGCL, directors are entitled to rely on the valuation reports of management and others if they do so in good faith.

In later decisions, the Delaware courts have expanded on this valuation issue. In *Barkan v. Amsted Indus., Inc.*, 567 A.2d 1279 (Del.1989), the Delaware Supreme Court stated that "[w]hen ... directors possess a body of reliable evidence with which to evaluate the fairness of a transaction, they may approve that transaction without conducting an active survey of the market." Conversely, the Delaware Chancery Court in *In re Netsmart Technologies, Inc. Shareholders Litigation*, 924 A.2d 171 (Del.Ch.2007), held that "when [directors] do not possess reliable evidence of the market value of the *entity* as a whole, the lack of an active sales effort is strongly suggestive of a ... [fiduciary] breach."

A breach of the duty of care, as happened in *Van Gorkom*, rebuts the business judgment rule's presumption in favor of directors. The burden of proof then shifts to the directors to prove, under the entire or intrinsic fairness test, that the transaction they approved was entirely fair. See Nutshell Section 60A(1). Importantly, the shift by itself *does not* create substantive liability. See *Cinerama, Inc. v. Technicolor, Inc.*, 663 A.2d 1156 (Del.1995).

In this context, it is not necessary for the plaintiffs to prove they suffered damages, although they could. This is because the entire fairness standard of review is not necessarily limited to the difference between the price offered by the acquiror and the "true" or "intrinsic" value of the company. The Delaware Chancery Court is entitled to fashion any form of equitable and monetary relief as may be appropriate, including rescissory damages. See *Cede & Co. v. Technicolor*, 634 A.2d 345 (Del.1993).

The *Van Gorkom* decision caused a panic among many directors of publicly-traded companies. Indeed, they likely thought it was virtually impossible to incur liability because of Delaware's gross negligence standard. *Van Gorkom*, however, changed their viewpoint. Many directors resigned as a result, and the cost of directors' and officers' (D&O) insurance increased twelve-fold the year *Van Gorkom* was decided, as insurance companies realized they may have to pay out claims in this regard.

The Delaware legislature, seeking to maintain Delaware's preeminence in corporate law, passed Section 102(b)(7) of the DGCL as a result of *Van Gorkom*. This section allows a Delaware corporation to adopt an exculpatory charter provision that essentially relieves directors from personal liability for any breach of the duty of care except in the case of illegal dividend payments. Many Delaware corporations did just that. In *Malpiede v. Townson*, 780 A.2d 1075 (Del.2001), the Delaware Supreme Court held that an exculpatory charter provision provides an adequate independent ground for dismissing a due care claim. However, the Court held that the defendant directors have the burden of *affirmatively raising* the exculpation afforded by Section 102(b)(7). Proving the existence of a valid exculpatory provision in the corporate charter entitles directors to dismissal of any claims for money damages against them that are based *solely* on alleged breaches of the Board's duty of care. Exculpatory charter provisions do not prevent stockholders from seeking *injunctive relief* with respect to directorial breaches of the duty of care.

## B. A Board's Decision to Purchase a Company

Another important decision a corporate director can make is a decision to acquire another company. The case of *Ash v. McCall*, 2000 WL 1370341 (Del. Ch.), involved a stockholder challenge to such a decision based on, among other grounds, a failure to make an informed decision and the failure to conduct appropriate due diligence with respect to the target company.

In *McCall*, two companies—McKesson and HBOC—merged as part of a stock swap statutory merger. Pursuant to it, McKesson exchanged approximately $14 billion of its stock for all of HBOC's outstanding stock. As a result, former HBOC stockholders owned shares representing the combined entity—McKesson HBOC. Shares of McKesson owned by McKesson stockholders thereafter represented shares in the combined entity as well.

Soon after the merger, McKesson HBOC's auditors discovered major accounting irregularities. Importantly, all the irregularities were attributable to the operations of HBOC both before and after the merger. As a result, McKesson HBOC's stock price plunged 50% in value and the McKesson HBOC board, which was comprised of six former directors of HBOC and six former directors of McKesson, fired several senior officers and otherwise shook up the management team.

The plaintiff stockholders of McKesson HBOC alleged that McKesson directors had wasted McKesson's assets by exchanging fairly valued McKesson stock for overvalued shares of HBOC stock and had breached their duty of care by failing to catch HBOC's accounting irregularities during the due diligence process associated with the merger. They also alleged that the McKesson HBOC directors breached their duty of care by failing to monitor adequately the company's financial reporting during the three and one-half month period following the merger.

The Delaware Chancery Court dismissed the plaintiffs' waste claim after reviewing the *process* the McKesson board followed in approving the exchange rather than the substance of the board's decision. While HBOC's stock was overvalued at the time the McKesson board granted its approval, the board was reasonably well-informed of all material information reasonably available at the time it made its decision. According to the Court, the fact that 20/20 hindsight proved that the decision was ill-advised was not important.

The Court also dismissed the plaintiffs' breach of the duty of care claim relating to the due diligence performed by McKesson in connection with the merger. Because the plaintiffs did not allege that McKesson's directors actually knew about the problems at HBOC, their claim was really one of negligence. These directors, however, did not perform the actual due diligence. As is standard operating procedure, financial due diligence was performed by McKesson's accounting firm, its investment bankers and internal McKesson management. Under Section 141(e) of the DGCL, directors are protected by the business judgment rule when they rely in good faith on the reports of qualified experts. Additionally, the Court pointed to the exculpatory charter provision in McKesson's charter as adequate independent grounds for dismissing the due care claim.

The Court also dismissed the plaintiffs' final claim relating to the McKesson HBOC board's alleged failure to exercise oversight after the merger. Plaintiffs claimed that the failure of the board to detect and cure the accounting irregularities during the three and one-half month period following the merger indicated a lack of oversight. While a failure of oversight is essentially a duty of care violation, the Court found none here. Indeed, it noted that the board responded quickly to the information provided by its accountants by conducting an internal investigation that culminated in sweeping earnings restatements and a major shake up in management. Moreover, it found that the directors easily met Delaware's oversight standard espoused in *In re Caremark Int'l Inc. Derivative Litigation*, 698 A.2d 959 (Del.Ch.1996). Under that standard, directors must be found to have "utterly failed to attempt to assure [that] a reasonable reporting system exists" or exhibited a "sustained and systematic failure to exercise reasonable oversight."

## § 60.  THE DUTY OF LOYALTY

### A.  Transactions with Controlling Stockholders

#### (1)  Entire Fairness Test—Generally

When directors approve a transaction that involves a conflict of interest, Delaware law shifts the burden to the directors to prove that the transaction was intrinsically or entirely fair to the corporation and its stockholders. The seminal case of *Weinberger v. UOP, Inc.*, 457 A.2d 701 (Del.1983), which involved a complaining minority stockholder who was squeezed out through a merger, illustrates this point.

The case involved a so-called "interested merger" because the constituents were Signal (a corporate controlling stockholder) and its partially-owned subsidiary, UOP. Signal and UOP had an *"interlocking directorate,"* because their boards had two common directors. These two individuals were also senior officers of Signal. They used UOP information garnered in their capacity as UOP directors to generate a report concerning the amount Signal should pay to the UOP minority stockholders as part of a squeeze out merger. This report was never given to any of the other UOP directors nor was it disclosed to the minority stockholders prior to the merger vote.

The *Weinberger* decision is well known for the guidance it provides in valuing shares in an appraisal proceeding. See Nutshell Section 23D(3). However, it also carefully lays out the burdens the parties must meet in a general action for directorial misconduct in connection with a squeeze out merger. Initially, the plaintiff seeking to attack a merger must overcome the presumptive protections of the business judgment rule by demonstrating some basis for invoking the entire fairness test. To do so, the plaintiff must proffer particularized facts that the directors either acted grossly negligent or with self-interest. If the plaintiff is successful, the directors then have the burden of showing that the transaction was entirely or intrinsically fair to the minority stockholders.

Here, the plaintiff was successful in shifting the burden to the UOP directors because of the existence of the interlocking directorate. Accordingly, the UOP directors were required to demonstrate their utmost good faith and the most scrupulous inherent fairness of the bargain.

The Delaware Supreme Court held that "entire fairness" meant two things: fair dealing and fair price. Fair dealing is a process-driven inquiry that looks at how the transaction was timed, structured, negotiated and disclosed to the directors and stockholders and how their approvals were obtained. Fair price is determined by looking at the price paid in light of the economic and financial considerations of the proposed merger, which would include: assets, market value, earnings, future prospects, and any other element that affects the intrinsic or inherent value of a company's stock. Although discussed as a two part test, the Delaware Supreme Court views an entire fairness review as "unbifurcated." See *Cinerama, Inc. v. Technicolor, Inc.*, 663 A.2d 1156 (Del.1995).

### (2) "Cleansing" an Acquisition of a Minority Interest in a Controlled Subsidiary

Controlling stockholder going-private transactions can be affected through one of two deal structures:

(1) A *"long-form"* merger requiring both director and stockholder approval. Assuming the merger is approved in accordance with applicable legal standards (including application of the entire or intrinsic fairness test), the minority shareholders are merged out of existence.

(2) A tender offer followed by a "short-form" merger. Here, the controller will acquire at least 90% of the outstanding shares through a *first step tender offer*, and then use DGCL Section 253's short-form merger provision to squeeze out the remaining stockholders. Importantly, no target board involvement or approval is needed under Delaware law.

While both deal structures lead to the *same conclusion*, as seen below the legal treatment of each is remarkably different under Delaware law.

### a. Long–Form Mergers

In terms of the *long-form merger*, the Delaware courts apply a stringent entire fairness review. This is true even if, following proper disclosure, the transaction is approved either by a properly functioning *special committee* of disinterested and independent directors or by a *majority of the minority stockholders*. This stems from the fact that the minority stockholders would always be fearful of retribution (*e.g.,* the cessation of future dividends) from the majority stockholder should the independent directors, a special committee, or the minority stockholders themselves vote against the merger. However, given that the aforementioned safety procedures do have some merit, when they are implemented the burden of proof shifts back to the plaintiff stockholder to prove that the transaction was unfair. See *Kahn v. Lynch Communication Systems*, 638 A.2d 1110 (Del.1994).

Given that the entire or intrinsic fairness test always applies in a *Lynch Communication* situation, attorneys for plaintiff stockholders have brought many unmeritorious lawsuits in order to exploit their nuisance value. Indeed, the test's application makes it impossible for a controlling stockholder to ever structure a transaction in a manner that will enable it to obtain dismissal of a complaint challenging the transaction. Therefore, each *Lynch Communication* case has settlement value, not necessarily because of its merits but because it cannot be dismissed. See *In re Cox Communications, Inc.*

*Shareholders Litigation*, 879 A.2d 604 (Del.Ch. 2005).

Accordingly, Vice Chancellor Strine in writing the *Cox Communications* opinion *suggested* what he believed would be an improvement in the law in this area. Specifically, he would allow defendant directors to invoke the business judgment rule standard of review when a going private merger with a controlling stockholder was effected using a process that mirrored *both* elements of an arms'-length merger: (1) approval by disinterested directors; and (2) approval by a majority of the minority stockholders. He noted that the two elements are "complementary"—and not substitutes. He viewed the first element as important because the directors have the capability to act as effective and active bargaining agents, which disaggregated stockholders do not. He viewed the second element as critical "because bargaining agents are not always effective or faithful." When these two elements are met, the business judgment standard of review should presumptively apply, and any plaintiff ought to have to plead particularized facts that, if true, support an inference that, despite the facially fair process, the merger was tainted because of fiduciary wrongdoing. He argues that this reform to *Lynch Communication* would not permit a controller to obtain business judgment rule protection merely by using a special committee *or* a majority of the minority vote; in that case, *Lynch Communication* in its current form would still govern. To invoke the business judgment rule standard of review, the controller would have to replicate fully both elements of the arms'-length merger process.

### b. Tender Offer/Short–Form Merger Combination

The second deal structure—*i.e.,* a tender offer followed by a "short-form" merger—is referred to as a *Siliconix* transaction, a structure examined in the case of *In re Siliconix Inc. Shareholders Litigation*, 2001 WL 716787 (Del.Ch.). The Delaware standard in the context of a Siliconix transaction, as seen below, has become quite jumbled, as different Vice Chancellors of the Delaware Chancery Court have had slightly different perspectives on that transaction.

In the *Siliconix* case, an 80% stockholder—Vishay—made a "stock for stock" exchange tender offer for the remaining shares of its subsidiary, Siliconix. A minority stockholder of Siliconix brought a lawsuit seeking to preliminarily enjoin the tender offer, arguing that the price Vishay was offering was unfair and that the tender offer could not satisfy the entire fairness test. However, Vice Chancellor Noble of the Delaware Chancery Court held that a controller is under no duty to offer a "fair price" in its tender offer, so long as it makes proper disclosure about the offer and does not "coerce" minority shareholders into accepting it. He believed that the free choice of the minority shareholders to reject the tender offer provided them with sufficient protection. Therefore, unless a plaintiff shareholder can show either coercion or a disclosure violation, no defendant has the duty to demonstrate the entire fairness of the proposed tender offer.

On the *disclosure* point, Vice Chancellor Noble held that a controlling stockholder owes a fiduciary duty to "disclose accurately all material facts surrounding the tender." In addition, when the target's directors communicate with their shareholders—through the Federally mandated Schedule 14D–9—they must, while complying with their ever-present fiduciary duties of care, good faith and loyalty, communicate honestly. On the *coercion* issue, he indicated that a tender offer is coercive when tendering shareholders are wrongfully induced by some act of the defendant to sell their shares for reasons unrelated to the economic merits of the offer. The wrongful acts must influence in some *material way* the shareholder's decision to tender.

Finally, Vice Chancellor Noble addressed the fact that different judicial approaches were applied to long-form mergers and tender offers:

The difference in judicial approach can be traced to two simple concepts. The first is that accepting or rejecting a tender is a decision to be made by the individual shareholder, and at least as to the tender itself, he will, if he rejects the tender, still own the stock of the target company following the tender. The second concept is that the acquired company in the merger context enters into a merger agreement, but the target company in the tender context does not confront a comparable corporate decision because the actual target of a tender is not the corporation (or its directors), but, instead, is its shareholders. Indeed, the board of the tender target is not asking its shareholders to approve any corporate action by the tender target.

Subsequently, the Vice Chancellor Strine expanded on the coercion discussion contained in the *Siliconix* decision in *In re Pure Resources, Inc. Shareholders Litigation*, 808 A.2d 421 (Del.Ch.2002). He was concerned that the distinction between long-form mergers and *Siliconix*-type transactions were more illusory than substantive. Therefore, he required that tender offers by controlling shareholders be structured in a manner that reduces the distorting effect of the tendering process on free stockholder choice, and that minority stockholders receive a candid and unfettered tendering recommendation from the independent directors of the target board. He held that an acquisition tender offer by a controlling stockholder will be deemed "non-coercive" *only when*:

(1) it is subject to a *non-waivable* "majority of the minority" tender condition;

(2) the controlling stockholder promises to consummate a prompt short-form merger under DGCL Section 253 at the same price as the tender offer price if it obtains more than 90% of the shares through the tender offer; and

(3) the controlling stockholder has made no retributive threats.

Vice Chancellor Strine also believed that the informational and timing advantages that controlling stockholders held required additional countervailing protection. Therefore, he required that the independent directors of the target be given free rein and adequate time to hire their own advisers, make a recommendation to the minority stockholders as to the advisability of the tender offer, and disclose all necessary information to the minority stockholders.

Later, Vice Chancellor Strine, in *In re Cox Communications, Inc. Shareholders Litigation*, 879 A.2d 604 (Del.Ch.2005), proposed a *suggested* gloss to the *Pure Resources* requirements in order to help them line up with his suggested changes to the *Lynch Communication* standard discussed above. See Nutshell Section 60A(2)a. Accordingly, he suggested supplementing the *Pure Resources* requirements by subjecting the controlling stockholder to the entire fairness standard if a special committee recommended that the minority *not* tender. Because *Pure Resources* already requires the equivalent of an informed, uncoerced majority of the minority vote condition for a controller to avoid entire fairness review, the additional step of triggering fairness review when a controller proceeded against the views of the special committee would, according to the Vice Chancellor, ''bring together both lines of [Delaware's] going-private jurisprudence in a sensible manner, providing stockholders with substantial procedural guarantees of fairness that work in tandem while minimizing the rote filing of makeweight [lawsuits]."

The subtleties of Delaware's law in this regard can be gleaned in the case of *Abrons v. Maree*, 911 A.2d 805 (Del.Ch.2006). *Abrons* involved an attempted *Siliconix* transaction with an important difference. Following the controlling shareholder's initial offer to the target company, the target company formed a special committee which, in turn, retained its own outside counsel and financial advisers. Importantly, between the time of the controlling stockholder's *initial proposal* and the commencement of its tender offer, the controlling stockholder *negotiated* with the special committee. The result of these negotiations was an increase in the purchase price the controlling stockholder offered in the *Siliconix*-styled transaction, which was ultimately approved by the special committee. A merger agreement was then signed by both the target company and the controlling stockholder.

Because the controlling stockholder had negotiated both the price and other terms of its offer with the special committee and signed a merger agreement, the Delaware Chancery Court applied the exacting standard of entire fairness to the transaction. This was done despite the fact that the *negotiated aspect* of the transaction, which was layered on top of a *Siliconix* structure, arguably afforded the minority stockholders *additional protections* not available in a standard *Siliconix* transaction.

### (3) Applicability to Short–Form Mergers

The "entire fairness" standard of review does not apply to short-form mergers effected by a parent company and its subsidiary if the parent holds at least 90% of the stock of the subsidiary. In such event, Section 253 of the DGCL allows the merger to be effected through the filing of a certificate of ownership and merger to which the resolutions of the parent's board approving the merger are attached. As seen in *Glassman v. Unocal Exploration*, 777 A.2d 242 (Del.2001), the exclusive remedy for minority stockholders in short-form mergers is the appraisal remedy. See Nutshell Section 23B.

### (4) Sale of a Controlled Subsidiary to a Third Party

Delaware's law applicable to the sale of a controlled subsidiary to an *unrelated third party* is only slightly less tortured than that applicable when the controller itself seeks to acquire the remaining interest in a controlled subsidiary (see Nutshell Section 60A(2)). In *McMullin v. Beran*, 765 A.2d 910 (Del.2000), ARCO, an 80% shareholder of ARCO Chemical ("Chemical"), negotiated a two-step sale of Chemical to a company called Lyondell. Lyondell would make a public tender offer for shares of Chemical. ARCO agreed in advance to tender its 80% block. Any Chemical shares that remained outstanding after the tender offer would be acquired by Lyondell through a cash-out merger.

A plaintiff minority stockholder brought suit, complaining that ARCO was causing Chemical to be sold at a cheap price because ARCO desperately needed cash for another deal it was pursuing. Normally, a controller like ARCO can sell its 80% interest in Chemical for whatever consideration it wants, and it has no duty to share any control premium it may receive with the minority stockholders. See, e.g., *Harris v. Carter*, 582 A.2d 222 (Del.Ch.1990); *Zetlin v. Hanson Holdings, Inc.*, 397 N.E.2d 387 (N.Y.1979). However, in this case ARCO was not just selling its shares, but rather it negotiated for, with the Chemical board's approval, the entire sale of Chemical to Lyondell.

According to the Delaware Supreme Court, when Chemical's board became involved, it had to act in accordance with its fiduciary duties. In particular, pursuant to Section 251 of the DGCL, the board must approve the transaction and recommend it to its stockholders. The Court indicated that the board's recommendation is so important in this context because stockholders need the board's input, particularly on the fairness of the price being offered, in order to make an informed decision about whether to tender their shares or seek their appraisal rights.

The Court noted that "[w]hen a board is presented with the majority shareholder's proposal to sell the entire corporation to a third party, the ultimate focus on value maximization is the same as if the board itself had decided to sell the corporation to a third party." Of course, ordinarily in this situation the board would have duties under *Revlon, Inc. v. MacAndrews & Forbes Holdings, Inc.*, 506 A.2d 173 (Del.1986), to seek out the highest price realistically obtainable. See Nutshell Section 60C. However, the Court noted that the imposition of *Revlon* duties would be futile in this context due to the existence of a controlling stockholder. Indeed, if the board had conducted an auction, the controlling stockholder—ARCO—could have undermined it simply by voting in favor of the transaction that it had proposed to the board.

Nevertheless, the Court held that Chemical's board must make an informed decision in good faith about whether the sale of the company to a third party that is being proposed by the majority stockholder will result in the *maximization of value* for the minority shareholders. In satisfying this obligation, the board must follow two steps. First, it must conduct a critical assessment of the proposed third party transaction that the majority stockholder is proposing. Second, it must make an independent determination on whether that transaction maximizes value for all stockholders.

In this case, taking the plaintiff stockholder's allegations as true, the Court noted problems with the board's deliberative process and composition. The board's deliberative process was flawed because it had relied upon ARCO and ARCO'S financial advisor to conduct the solicitation of interested buyers and all negotiations for the sale of Chemical.

Additionally, the board approved the transaction after only one meeting and based on the disclosures made to it by ARCO's financial advisor. In terms of the board's composition, the Court noted that a large conflict of interest existed. Six of the 12 Chemical directors were employees of ARCO, and two others had prior affiliations with ARCO. This was particularly problematic because the board did not establish a special committee of disinterested directors to review the transaction.

Of course, a different result would have occurred had ARCO simply sold itself rather than trying to sell Chemical. In that situation, Chemical's board would owe no fiduciary duties. While the identity of Chemical's majority stockholder would be changing, Chemical's minority stockholders would not be affected. See *In re Digex, Inc. Shareholders Litigation*, 789 A.2d 1176 (Del.Ch.2000).

## B. Which Directors Are "Conflicted"?

When are directors so conflicted that their decisionmaking is rightfully called into question? The case of *Orman v. Cullman*, 794 A.2d 5 (Del.Ch. 2002), is instructive on this issue. In *Orman*, plaintiff shareholders alleged facts suggesting that certain members of General Cigar's board were conflicted in connection with a merger between the acquiror Swedish Match and General Cigar. Specifically, the plaintiff shareholders alleged that these members were either interested in the transaction with Swedish Match or lacked independence in their decisionmaking.

According to the Delaware Chancery Court, a director is *"interested"* in a given transaction if she appears on *both sides* of the transaction or derives a *personal* financial benefit from the transaction which does not devolve upon the corporation or all stockholders generally. Additionally, self-interest can be demonstrated when the transaction in question would have a *materially detrimental impact* on a given director, but not on the corporation and the other stockholders, and thus the director wants to stop it.

The benefit or detriment, as the case may be, must be *"material."* Materiality means that the alleged benefit (or detriment) is significant enough in the context of the *director's* personal economic circumstances as to have made it improbable that the director could perform her fiduciary duties to the shareholders without being influenced by her overriding personal interest.

With respect to directorial *"independence,"* the Court stated that an *independent* director is one who bases her decision solely on the *merits* of the action to be taken. When a director is beholden to a controlling person or so under his influence that the director's discretion would be sterilized, the director *is not* acting independently.

Finally, the Court highlighted that, when determining whether a given director is interested in a transaction or lacks independence, the Delaware courts apply a *subjective*, "actual person" standard. Indeed, what is important to determine is whether the *director in question* had an interest that was *material and debilitating* or was *controlled* by another person.

In a more recent decision, the Delaware Chancery Court set forth what a plaintiff must do in this context to survive a motion to dismiss by defendant directors. According to the Court, "[a] plaintiff can survive a motion to dismiss ... by pleading facts from which a reasonable inference can be drawn that a *majority* of the board was interested or lacked independence with respect to the relevant decision." *In re Trados Inc. Shareholder Litigation*, 2009 WL 2225958 (Del.Ch.).

The Federal government and the stock exchanges have also gotten into the business of defining "independence" in the context of corporate directors. Section 301 of SOX requires all publicly-traded companies to have an audit committee comprised solely of "independent directors." Directors are "independent" if they have not accepted any consulting, advisory or other compensatory fee from the issuer. In terms of the stock exchanges, the NYSE requires that listed companies have boards of directors made up of a majority of independent directors. No director qualifies as "independent" unless the board of directors affirmatively determines that the director has *no material relationship* with the listed company (either directly or as a partner, shareholder or officer of an organization that has a relationship with the company). Additionally, those directors who were employed by the listed company within the last three years as an executive officer are not deemed "independent." See NYSE Corporate Governance Standards 303A.01 & 303A.02.

## C. A Board's Decision to Sell the Company— *Revlon* Duties

The seminal case involving a board's fiduciary duties in the context of a decision to sell its company is *Revlon, Inc. v. MacAndrews & Forbes Holdings, Inc.*, 506 A.2d 173 (Del.1986). Although its holding has been refined by the Delaware courts over the years, the case remains the starting point for understanding this vital area of the law.

*Revlon* involved the bitter hostile takeover battle waged by Pantry Pride against Revlon, Inc. Pantry Pride was owned by Ron Perelman's takeover vehicle—MacAndrews & Forbes Holdings, Inc. When it became apparent to Revlon's board that Revlon would not remain an independent company much longer, Revlon's board authorized management to negotiate a merger or buyout with a third party (*i.e.,* a "white knight"). According to the Delaware Supreme Court, this directorial action constituted putting the company "up for sale."

When a board puts its company up for sale, its duty changes from preserving the corporate enterprise to maximizing the company's value for the stockholders' benefit. Accordingly, defensive measures designed to protect the company from hostile bidders become moot, as the directors are now trying to sell the company rather than prevent the sale of the company. Indeed, the board's sole function is to act as an auctioneer charged with obtaining the best price for the stockholders. Leaving a company's strategic defenses in place during an auction is inconsistent with the board's duty as an auctioneer and thus constitutes a breach of the directors' duty of loyalty towards stockholders.

*Mills Acquisition Co. v. Macmillan, Inc.*, 559 A.2d 1261 (Del.1989), refined a board's *Revlon* duties by adding a gloss on a board's duty to accept the "best price" for its stockholders. The Delaware Supreme Court recognized that offers to purchase a company come in many shapes and sizes, and thus a company's board often has to compare apples and oranges. The Court, therefore, stated that the board must accept a bid offering the "highest price reasonably available for the company, provided that the price is offered by a reputable and responsible bidder." In fulfilling its duty in this regard, a board may consider, with respect to any given offer, the following:

- The adequacy and terms of the offer;

- The offer's fairness and feasibility;

- The proposed or actual financing of the offer and the consequences of the financing;

- Questions of illegality;

- The impact of both the bid and the potential acquisition on other constituencies, provided it bears some reasonable relationship to general stockholder interests;

- The risks of nonconsummation;
- The basic stockholder interests at stake;
- The bidder's identity, prior background and other business venture experiences; and
- The bidder's business plans for the corporation and their effects on stockholders' interests.

The Court also addressed lock up options and no shop provisions, both of which often foreclose bidding and thus end active auctions early. While refusing to rule that these devices are per se illegal, the Court held that these devices must confer a substantial benefit upon the stockholders of the company up for auction in order to withstand the exacting scrutiny of the courts.

The Court concluded by setting forth the process the Delaware Chancery Court must go through when confronted by a plaintiff stockholder's complaint about a *Revlon* auction. The plaintiff must first show that the directors of the target company treated one or more of the respective bidders on unequal terms. If the plaintiff is successful, the Delaware Chancery Court must apply a two part *Unocal*-styled test. First, did the directors properly perceive that stockholder interests were enhanced? Second, was the board's action reasonable in relation to the advantage sought to be achieved, or conversely, to the threat which a particular bid allegedly posed to stockholders' interests?

The Delaware Supreme Court has also provided guidance as to *when* a board has put its company up for sale. In *Arnold v. Society for Savings Bancorp*, 650 A.2d 1270 (Del.1994), the Court stated that *Revlon* duties apply in *at least* the following three scenarios:

(1) *Initiation of Active Bidding Process.* A company's board initiates an active bidding process seeking to sell the company or to effect a business reorganization involving a clear break-up of the company.

(2) *Responsive Break–Up.* In response to a bidder's offer, a target company's board abandons its long-term business strategy and seeks an alternative transaction involving the break-up of the company.

(3) *Change in Control.* A company's board approves a transaction resulting in a sale or change in control. Importantly, where a potential sale of control is not the consequence of actions taken by a company's board, the board is entitled to resist a third party's unsolicited acquisition proposal or offer. In other words, only the actions of the board itself—not those of a third party—can result in the company being put "up for sale." See *Paramount Communications, Inc. v. Time, Inc.*, 571 A.2d 1140 (Del.1989) (up-

holding the "just say no" defense that Time's board implemented).

The Delaware Supreme Court further discussed the *Revlon* standard in *Lyondell Chem. Co. v. Ryan*, 970 A.2d 235 (Del.2009). In *Lyondell*, shareholders alleged that the defendant directors breached their fiduciary duties, including the duty of good faith, in connection with the sale of their company. The Delaware Supreme Court clarified that *Revlon* did not create any new fiduciary duties. It simply requires that the board perform its fiduciary duties in the service of a specific objective: maximizing the sale price of the enterprise. The Court explained that no court can tell directors exactly how to accomplish that goal, because the directors will face a unique combination of circumstances, many of which will be outside their control. Thus, directors' failure to take any specific steps during a sale process cannot demonstrate a conscious disregard of their duties.

An example of a board of directors that failed to conduct a reasonable *Revlon* sale process is found in *In re Netsmart Technologies, Inc. Shareholders Litigation*, 924 A.2d 171 (Del.Ch.2007). The board of Netsmart had the company enter into a merger agreement with two private equity firms. It did not seek out any strategic buyers given its inability to attract the interest of strategic buyers from time-to-time over the past five years. Additionally, the company's financial advisor steered the company away from strategic buyers and towards private equity buyers. Unhappy with the deal that the board struck, shareholders of Netsmart sued for a preliminary injunction to stop the consummation of the merger.

The Delaware Chancery Court held that the plaintiff shareholders established that the board likely did not have a reasonable basis for failing to undertake any exploration of interest from strategic buyers. The Court underscored that once the board decided to sell the corporation for cash, it assumed the fiduciary duty to undertake reasonable efforts to secure the highest price realistically achievable given the market for the corporation. The board need not follow a judicially prescribed checklist of sales activities, but it must act reasonably by undertaking a logically sound process to get the best deal that is realistically attainable.

The Court noted that the mere fact that a board did not, for example, canvass all possible buyers before signing an acquisition agreement does not mean that it necessarily acted unreasonably. Here, however, the board's consideration of whether to seek out strategic buyers was cursory and poorly documented at best. The previous "sporadic chats" by the CEO and the corporation's financial advisor with potential strategic buyers over the past five years were, according to the Court, "hardly the stuff of a reliable market check." What was never done by the board, senior management or the corporation's financial advisor, the Court highlighted, "was a serious sifting of the strategic market to develop a core list of larger healthcare ... players for whom an acquisition of Netsmart might make sense. Perhaps such an effort might have yielded no names. But it might have.''

## D. Takeover Defenses and a Board's Ability to Adopt Them

### (1) Takeover Defenses

Over the years, the boards of potential target companies have adopted a great many takeover defenses. These are discussed below.

### a. Shark Repellent Charter Provisions

Many target companies add charter provisions that make it more difficult for a hostile bidder to acquire them. Some of these provisions make it difficult to remove existing directors. Others attempt to handicap a hostile bidder by reducing the voting rights of shares in the hands of that bidder, or by increasing the required vote needed to approve a merger. Because of the difficulty most targets would have in obtaining stockholder approval for such a provision after the company becomes publicly-traded, most add these provisions to their charters before they go public or, at a minimum, while they are not the subject of a hostile bid.

Charter provisions that make it difficult for a hostile bidder to replace existing directors with directors more receptive to the hostile bidder's offer include:

- Staggered or classified board of directors;

- Elimination of the stockholders' ability to take action through written consent;

- Limitations on the stockholders' ability to call a special meeting of stockholders;

- Prohibition on removing directors other than "for cause";

- Limitations on the ability to expand the size of the board of directors;

- Provision that only existing directors can choose a replacement for a director that resigns in mid-term;

- "Tenure" or "time phased" voting system, whereby each share receives multiple votes, but those multiple votes disappear when the share is transferred or sold. The multiple votes only reattach if a stockholder has held the share for a multiple year period. See *Williams v. Geier*, 671 A.2d 1368 (Del.1996) (upholding a tenure voting system);

- "Capped voting" plan, whereby a stockholder does not receive any additional voting power for any shares purchased in excess of a pre-established percentage of stock; and

- "Two-tier voting stock," whereby one class of shares (in the hands of insiders) receives more votes per share than another class of shares (in the hands of public stockholders).

Charter provisions that make it difficult for a hostile bidder to complete an acquisition of a target company after it has purchased a sizeable block of the target's shares include the following:

- Requirement of a supermajority vote on all business combinations with a controlling stockholder if that stockholder acquired its shares without the specific approval of the board that existed prior to that acquisition;

- Allowing non-tendering stockholders to "put" their shares back to the target company in exchange for an above-market price if a hostile bidder acquires more than a specified percentage of target stock; and

- Reduction of voting rights for any bidder who acquires a large block of the target's stock if a "fair price" was not paid or unless full voting rights are approved by stockholders who did not tender their shares into that bidder's tender offer.

### b. Poison Pills

*Shareholder rights plans*, better known as *poison pills,* remain the prime defensive strategy for most public companies, because they can be adopted quickly by a board of directors *without stockholder approval*. A shareholder rights plan consists of a company's distribution of stock, stock rights or other securities to its stockholders that have special redemption or conversion provisions. The conversion option is triggered by a number of events, but especially by a bidder's acquisition of more than a specified percentage (typically 15%) of a target company's stock *without* the prior approval of the target's board.

The typical poison pill is a "*call pill.*" When it is triggered by a bidder, the company's common stockholders, as rights holders, generally have the option to buy stock at half price in either the target or the bidder. If the bidder acquires more than the specified percentage of the target's stock, the rights holders (other than the bidder and its affiliates) can purchase half price stock in the target itself (a *flip-in*). This would significantly dilute the value of the target stock held by the bidder, as the bidder itself is prohibited by the rights plan from exercising the rights associated with the target's common stock it owns. If the target is made a party to a merger in which it is not the surviving corporation, or in which it is the survivor but its common stock is changed or exchanged, then the company's common stockholders, as rights holders, are entitled to purchase stock of the *bidder* at half price (a *flip-over*). This impairs the bidder's capital structure and drastically dilutes the interests of the bidder's existing stockholders. Either way, triggering the poison pill makes the target prohibitively expensive for the bidder to buy. Not surprisingly, a poison pill implemented to ward off a takeover has never been triggered by a hostile party since the debut of the first pill in the 1980s. (Poison pills designed to protect specific corporate assets, like net operating loss carryforwards, typically have a lower triggering threshold and have, on rare occasion, been triggered. See *Selectica, Inc. v. Versata Enterprises, Inc.*, 2010 WL 703062 (Del.Ch.)).

The benefit of a poison pill is the leverage it provides a target's board in its negotiations with a bidder. This leverage derives from the board's ability under the plan to redeem the rights at any time before they expire, on such conditions as the board in its sole discretion may establish. An effective pill often turns a hostile acquisition into a "friendly" (*i.e.*, "negotiated") acquisition on terms acceptable to the target's board. The board will only redeem the pill if it deems the transaction in question to be in the target stockholders' best interest.

Because of a target board's ability to redeem a poison pill, a hostile bidder often seeks to replace the board with new directors who are more receptive to the hostile party's bid. The hostile bidder does so through a hostile proxy fight. In order to counter a hostile bidder's hostile proxy fight over directors, some companies have adopted "*dead hand*" or "*no hand*" poison pills.

A *dead hand pill* is a regular poison pill that can only be redeemed by so-called "*continuing directors*." Continuing directors are those directors in office at the time the target's board approved the pill and their designated successors. Thus, director-nominees of the hostile party do not qualify. This effectively eliminates a hostile proxy contest as a weapon that a hostile party can use to gain control of the target. Even if the hostile party wins the proxy contest, its newly-elected director representatives cannot redeem the rights.

The Delaware Chancery Court refused to dismiss a complaint alleging that a dead hand pill was illegal in *Carmody v. Toll Brothers, Inc.*, 723 A.2d 1180 (Del.Ch.1998). The plaintiff attacked the pill on both statutory grounds and fiduciary duty grounds. The plaintiff alleged that the dead hand pill unlawfully restricted the powers of future boards of directors by creating different classes of directors—those who have the power to redeem the pill, and who that do not. While such a distinction seemingly could be set forth in a corporation's charter if approved by stockholders (see DGCL § 141(a) and (d)), it cannot be instituted through unilateral board action. Thus, its adoption is arguably *ultra vires* (beyond the power of the corporation), and the pill is consequently invalid on its face. The plaintiff also argued that the dead hand pill interfered with the stockholders' voting franchise without a compelling justification, in derogation of the directors' fiduciary duty of loyalty. In refusing to dismiss the plaintiff's complaint, the Delaware Chancery Court appeared extremely sympathetic to the plaintiff's arguments.

A *no hand pill* or *delayed redemption pill* is a regular poison pill that prohibits a target's directors, no matter who nominated or elected them, from redeeming the pill for a stated period of time (such as six months) if the purpose of the redemption would be to facilitate a transaction with a hostile party. Thus, even if the hostile party replaced all the directors on the target's board, the new directors would have to wait a specified period of time before they could redeem the pill. In *Quickturn Design Systems, Inc. v. Shapiro*, 721 A.2d 1281 (Del.1998), the Delaware Supreme Court struck down a no hand pill. It held that the pill impermissibly deprived any newly-elected board of its statutory authority to manage the corporation as provided in Section 141(a) of the DGCL. Indeed, the no hand pill would prevent a new board from redeeming the pill even under circumstances where the board's fiduciary duties so required.

Other variations on the poison pill include the "morning after" pill and the "chewable pill." The *"morning after" pill* is a shareholder rights plan that is ready to go at a moment's notice. If a threat to the company appears, the directors can approve the plan immediately because it has previously been prepared and is simply awaiting the directors' approval. Directors, however, do not approve the plan in advance in order not to alienate those shareholders who dislike poison pills.

A twist on target board redemption of a poison pill is contained in a so-called *chewable pill*. A chewable pill is a regular poison pill that is automatically redeemed upon the occurrence of one or more specified events. One event might be the existence of a "respectable offer" for the target, *i.e.*, an all cash offer made by a bidder that represents a substantial premium over the trading price of the target's stock. Another might be a favorable vote by the target's stockholders on the bidder's plan of acquisition. Similarly, a TIDE provision (three year independent director evaluation) contained in a pill can impact on the pill's redemption. This "sunset" provision requires a company's independent directors to reconsider the pill every three years.

### c.   Asset–Based Defensive Strategies

Many asset-based defensive strategies exist, including the following:

- *Lock Ups*. The most typical lock up is the "crown jewel" lock up, whereby the target grants a friendly prospective acquiror an option to purchase a prime asset or business of the target at a bargain basement price in the event its deal with that party is scuttled by the arrival of an unwanted, third party suitor.

- *Greenmail*. Greenmail involves the target using its own cash to buy back shares of its own stock from a hostile party, typically at a premium price. In the late 1980s, provisions were added to the IRC that discourage the payment of greenmail, and several states have statutes that also discourage the practice. See, e.g., NYBCL § 513(c).

- *Golden Parachutes*. Golden parachutes are very handsome severance payments that a target must make to senior managers upon the occurrence of a change in control of the target.

- *White Squire.* The target issues a large amount of newly-issued shares to a friendly third party company (the "white squire"). That company agrees in a "standstill agreement" not to sell those shares to any party considered "hostile" by the target's board and to vote them only in accordance with the board's recommendation.

- *White Knight.* When a target's board knows the target cannot sustain its defense against a hostile party's advances, the board will sometimes seek to sell the target to a friendly third party buyer (the "white knight"). While the target will not remain independent, at least it will not be bought by the hostile party.

- *Clayton Defense.* The target itself makes one or more acquisitions of smaller companies or significant assets that will create an antitrust problem under the Clayton Act of 1914 for the hostile party if that party were to buy the reconstituted target.

- *Pentagon Defense.* If the hostile party is a non-U.S. company, a U.S. target may make one or more acquisitions of smaller companies or significant assets involved in the U.S. defense industry. The hostile party may violate the Exon–Florio amendment to the Om-

nibus Trade and Competitiveness Act of 1988
if it goes through with its acquisition of the
reconstituted target.

- *Pac Man Defense*. In response to a hostile
takeover bid made for the target, the target
in turn launches a hostile takeover bid for
the hostile bidder. That is, the little fish
turns around and tries to swallow the bigger
fish before the bigger fish can swallow it.

### d.   Liability–Based Defensive Strategies

A target may also employ liability-based defensive
strategies to ward off a hostile bidder. The most
common is a leveraged recapitalization. This involves the target borrowing substantial sums of
money secured against its own assets. It uses the
money to pay a one-time, extraordinary dividend to
its common stockholders. See Nutshell Section
54F(2). This defense is particularly effective against
a hostile bidder that was planning on using the
target's assets to secure the loans necessary to buy
the target's shares in a hostile takeover. Once the
target has encumbered its own assets, the hostile
party will not be able to secure the financing necessary to effect the takeover.

### (2) A Board's Ability to Adopt Takeover De-
fenses

The directors' adoption of a takeover defense
implicates a conflict of interest. Are they adopting

the defense in order to protect stockholders from an actual or perceived threat? Or are they doing so in order to preserve their jobs as directors? The two leading cases on point are *Unocal v. Mesa Petroleum Co.*, 493 A.2d 946 (Del.1985), and *Unitrin, Inc. v. American General Corp.*, 651 A.2d 1361 (Del.1995).

In *Unocal,* the Delaware Supreme Court noted that while a decision by the board is normally afforded the presumptive protections of the business judgment rule, this is not the case when the decision involves the implementation of takeover defenses. Indeed, in the context of a takeover battle, a board has a conflict of interest because of the "omnipresent specter" that it may be acting primarily in its own best interests rather than in the best interests of the corporation and its stockholders. Thus, before the board's action is protected by the business judgment rule, the board must satisfy its own two-part burden:

- *First,* the board must demonstrate that it had reasonable grounds for believing that a danger to corporate policy and effectiveness existed (the *"Reasonable Grounds Test"*); and

- *Second,* the board must demonstrate that its defensive response was reasonable in relation to the threat posed (the *"Proportionality Test"*).

If the board satisfies both tests of *Unocal*, its action will receive the protections of the business judgment rule. Accordingly, a plaintiff stockholder will then have the burden of showing that the directors breached their fiduciary duties. To do so, the plaintiff stockholder must demonstrate by a preponderance of the evidence that the directors' decision was primarily based on perpetuating themselves in office, involved some other breach of fiduciary duty such as fraud, overreaching or lack of good faith, or was not an informed one. See *Unitrin, Inc. v. American General Corp.*, 651 A.2d 1361 (Del.1995).

In *Unitrin,* the Delaware Supreme Court expanded on the *Unocal* standard. To satisfy the Reasonable Grounds Test, the board must demonstrate that, after a reasonable investigation, it determined in good faith that a third party's actions presented a threat to the corporation that warranted a defensive response. If the conclusion that a threat exists is made by a majority of outside directors, this enhances the ability of the board to meet this test.

The Court highlighted three recognized threats posed by hostile tender offers:

(1) *Lost Opportunity.* A hostile tender offer may deprive the target's stockholders of the opportunity to select a superior alternative offered by target management or by another bidder;

(2) *Structural Coercion.* A hostile tender offer could be structured in a way where target stockholders tender their shares for reasons other than the merits of the tender offer (*e.g.,* for fear of the position in which non-

tendering stockholders would find themselves); and

(3) *Substantive Coercion.* A hostile tender offer
could result in target stockholders tendering into an underpriced offer that prevents
them from receiving the intrinsic value of
their shares. (This is an argument that
virtually all target companies make against
hostile parties. See *Chesapeake Corp. v.
Shore*, 771 A.2d 293 (Del.Ch.2000).)

In terms of the Proportionality Test, the Court
stated that a board does not have unlimited discretion to defeat a threat by any draconian means
available. The nature of the threat associated with a
particular hostile offer sets the parameters for the
range of permissible defensive tactics. If a particular defensive response falls within this range, then
it is not draconian. It would fall outside this range,
however, if it *precludes* under all circumstances the
hostile bidder from acquiring the target, or if it is
*coercive* to the target's own stockholders. If a
board's defensive response is not draconian and is
within the range of reasonableness, a court will not
substitute its judgment for that of the board.

In *Omnicare, Inc. v. NCS Healthcare, Inc.*, 818
A.2d 914 (Del.2003), the Delaware Supreme Court
struck down as both preclusive and coercive three
"deal protection measures" contained in multiple
agreements evidencing the proposed acquisition of
NCS Healthcare by Genesis. The first, which was
contained in the merger agreement between the two

companies, required NCS to submit the merger agreement to NCS stockholders for their approval regardless of whether the NCS board continued to recommend the merger. The second was the failure of the merger agreement to include a standard "fiduciary out" provision, whereby NCS would be allowed to walk away from the transaction if the NCS directors believed their fiduciary duties so required. The third was the agreement by NCS stockholders holding more than 50% of NCS' outstanding voting securities to vote their shares in favor of the NCS–Genesis merger. According to the Court, these "tripartite defensive measures," taken together, made the NCS–Genesis merger a "fait accompli." The success of any other competing transaction was mathematically doomed no matter how superior it was to the NCS–Genesis merger. According to the Court, the NCS directors breached their fiduciary duty in approving these three measures in combination.

A board's unilateral adoption of a takeover defense that also infringes on the stockholders' voting rights is measured against both the "compelling justification" standard of *Blasius Industries, Inc. v. Atlas Corp.*, 564 A.2d 651 (Del.Ch.1988), and, assuming the defense survives that heightened level of judicial scrutiny, the *Unocal/Unitrin* "proportionality" standard. See *MM Companies, Inc. v. Liquid Audio, Inc.*, 813 A.2d 1118 (Del.2003).

In *MM Companies*, the Delaware Supreme Court addressed the validity of the *Blasius* compelling justification standard in the context of MM Companies' advances against Liquid Audio. MM Companies, as part of a group, collectively held slightly more than 7% of Liquid Audio's common stock. MM Companies sought to acquire control of Liquid Audio, but its overtures to Liquid Audio's board of directors were refused. As part of its strategy to acquire Liquid Audio, MM Companies provided formal notice to Liquid Audio that it intended to nominate two dissident nominees to fill the two seats on Liquid Audio's board that were up for re-election. Those seats were currently held by management-friendly individuals. MM Companies' notice also stated its intention to put a proposal before Liquid Audio's shareholders that would amend the bylaws and increase the size of the board by four members, thus raising the number of board members to nine. MM Companies had four potential MM Companies-friendly nominees in mind to fill the four newly-created directorships.

In response, Liquid Audio took several specific actions, including entering into a merger agreement with Alliance Entertainment Corp. Liquid Audio also postponed its regularly scheduled annual meeting given its proposed merger with Alliance. Instead, a special meeting of stockholders would be held to vote upon the merger at some point in the future. However, once it became apparent that MM Companies' nominees would win the two board seats that were up for re-election, Liquid Audio's board amended the bylaws to increase the size of the board to seven members from five members. It then appointed two management-friendly individuals to fill the two newly-created seats.

MM Companies challenged the board expansion. The Delaware Supreme Court noted that this case was unusual in that the defendant directors' action impacted the shareholder voting franchise in connection with "defending" Liquid Audio from the alleged threat posed by MM Companies. Thus, both *Blasius'* compelling justification standard and *Unocal's* proportionality standard appeared to be triggered. The Court held that when the primary purpose of a board's defensive measures is to interfere with or impede the effective exercise of the shareholder voting franchise in a contested election of directors, the Board must first demonstrate a compelling justification for such action as a *condition precedent* to any judicial consideration of the reasonableness and proportionality of the defensive measure. Here, because the defendant directors had failed to demonstrate a compelling justification for their defensive action, the Delaware Supreme Court held that the bylaw amendment that expanded the size of the Liquid Audio board, and permitted the appointment of two new members on the eve of a contested election, should have been invalidated by the Delaware Chancery Court.

## § 61.   STATE ANTI–TAKEOVER LEGISLATION

At present, over 40 states have some form of anti-takeover statute in place. Most of these statutes resulted from a hostile threat to an "in state" corporation. State legislatures passed these statutes due to the perceived negative impact that hostile takeovers would have on local companies.

The initial form of state anti-takeover legislation that various states passed in the early 1980s was dealt a fatal blow when the U.S. Supreme Court struck down the Illinois Business Takeover Act on Commerce Clause grounds. See *Edgar v. MITE Corp.*, 457 U.S. 624 (1982). State legislatures then adopted new anti-takeover legislation that took the form of traditional corporate governance regulation. By doing so, legislatures hoped to avoid the Commerce Clause infirmities of the Illinois statute.

## A. Anti–Takeover Statutes

States typically have adopted one or even more of the following four forms of anti-takeover legislation:

(1) *Control Share Acquisition Statutes* (*e.g.,* Indiana, Missouri, Ohio). These prevent a bidder that has acquired over a certain specified percentage of a target's voting securities without the approval of the target's board from voting those securities without a favorable vote of the remaining stockholders.

(2) *Fair Price Provision Statutes* (*e.g.,* Maryland). These prevent a non-approved bidder from merging its firm into the target unless (a) the remaining target stockholders are

paid a "fair price" (*i.e.,* the price paid to any other stockholder during a specified period of time prior to the merger) or (b) a majority of them approve the merger.

(3) *Right of Redemption or "Appraisal" Statutes* (*e.g.,* Pennsylvania, Maine, Utah). These give target stockholders a "put right" for "fair value" contingent on a triggering stock acquisition.

(4) *Business Combination Statutes* (*e.g.,* Indiana, Kentucky, New York). These prohibit all second step (*i.e.* "back end") mergers for a period of years (usually three to five) following a triggering stock acquisition not approved by the target's board.

In 1987, the U.S. Supreme Court affirmed the constitutionality of Indiana's new anti-takeover statute in *CTS Corp. v. Dynamics Corp.*, 481 U.S. 69 (1987). The Indiana statute combined a control share statute with a business combination statute. Pursuant to it, a non-approved bidder that acquired more than a specified percentage of target shares would lose voting rights relating to those shares. That bidder's shares, however, would regain voting rights if a majority of shares held by those other than the bidder itself and target management voted to restore those rights at either (a) the next annual meeting or (b) a special meeting of stockholders held within 50 days of the bidder's request. The statute also prohibited a second step merger for a period of years after a triggering stock acquisition that was not approved by the target's board.

Delaware's business combination statute—Section 203 of the DGCL—withstood constitutional challenge on both Federal preemption and Commerce Clause grounds in *BNS, Inc. v. Koppers Company, Inc.*, 683 F.Supp. 458 (D.Del.1988). Section 203 essentially prohibits business combinations between an "interested stockholder" and the target for a three-year period unless one of a number of exceptions is available. An "interested stockholder" is any person (other than the target or the target's direct or indirect majority-owned subsidiaries) that owns 15% or more of the outstanding voting stock of the target.

Under Section 203(a), an "interested stockholder" can nevertheless complete a business combination with the target if one of the following conditions is satisfied:

(1) *Prior Board Approval*. The target's board approved the business combination before the "interested stockholder" became an interested stockholder. In other words, the combination in question is a friendly deal.

(2) *85% Purchase*. The transaction that turns a hostile party into an "interested stockholder" results in the hostile party owning at least 85% of the outstanding voting stock of the target. For calculation purposes, shares owned by the target's officers who are also directors and shares owned by Employee

> Stock Ownership Plans (ESOPs) in which the employees themselves cannot direct how the shares are to be voted are not considered outstanding.
>
> (3) *Board Approval Plus Disinterested Stockholder Approval.* The target's board approves the business combination after the hostile party becomes an "interested stockholder" and the proposed combination is approved by 66–2/3% of the outstanding voting stock not owned by the interested stockholder.

Section 203(b) provides six exceptions where Delaware's business combination statute has no application. For example, Section 203 does not apply when a stockholder becomes an "interested stockholder" by default (*e.g.,* through gift or inheritance). Nor does it apply to companies that are not listed on a national stock exchange or have fewer than 2,000 stockholders. Also, Section 203 will not apply to any competing bid that a third party makes for a company if that bid is made within 20 days following the company's announcement that its management has made a bid for the company or has approved a bid by another party.

## B.   Other State Statutes

Besides anti-takeover statutes, many states have passed other statutory provisions that have a deterrent effect on hostile takeovers. These include:

- *Anti–Greenmail Statutes*. These generally prohibit a target from purchasing 10% or more of its stock from a stockholder that has held the shares for less than two years if the repurchase price is above the stock's fair market value, unless the purchase is approved by a majority vote of the target's stockholders. See, e.g., NYBCL § 513(c).

- *Disgorgement Statutes*. These allow target corporations to recover profits from unsuccessful bidders who have sold their "toehold" positions in the target at a profit within a specified period of time (*e.g.*, 18 months under Pennsylvania corporate law) of disclosing an intent to acquire control of the target.

- *Exculpatory Charter Provisions*. After the decision in *Smith v. Van Gorkom*, 488 A.2d 858 (Del. 1985), many states (including, of course, Delaware) amended their corporate statutes to allow companies to adopt "exculpatory charter provisions." These provisions essentially relieve a company's board from almost all of its duty of care responsibilities, but not its duty of good faith and loyalty responsibilities. See, e.g., DGCL § 102(b)(7) and NYBCL § 402(b).

- *Constituency Statutes*. These allow target directors to consider interests other than stockholder interests when deciding whether to accept a takeover offer and, in certain states, when making any corporate decision. These constituencies could include creditors, suppliers, vendors, customers, employees, retired employees and local communities. See, e.g., NYBCL § 717(b). Importantly, Delaware does not have a constituency statute.

# EXHIBIT I

## FUTURE VALUE AND PRESENT VALUE FACTOR TABLES

*EXHIBIT I*     725

**Future Value of $1 at the End of "n" Periods**

| Periods | 1% | 2% | 3% | 4% | 5% | 6% | 7% | 8% | 9% | 10% | 12% | 14% | 16% | 18% | 20% |
|---|---|---|---|---|---|---|---|---|---|---|---|---|---|---|---|
| 1 | 1.0100 | 1.0200 | 1.0300 | 1.0400 | 1.0500 | 1.0600 | 1.0700 | 1.0800 | 1.0900 | 1.1000 | 1.1200 | 1.1400 | 1.1600 | 1.1800 | 1.2000 |
| 2 | 1.0201 | 1.0404 | 1.0609 | 1.0816 | 1.1025 | 1.1236 | 1.1449 | 1.1664 | 1.1881 | 1.2100 | 1.2544 | 1.2996 | 1.3456 | 1.3924 | 1.4400 |
| 3 | 1.0303 | 1.0612 | 1.0927 | 1.1249 | 1.1576 | 1.1910 | 1.2250 | 1.2597 | 1.2950 | 1.3310 | 1.4049 | 1.4815 | 1.5609 | 1.6430 | 1.7280 |
| 4 | 1.0406 | 1.0824 | 1.1255 | 1.1699 | 1.2155 | 1.2625 | 1.3108 | 1.3605 | 1.4116 | 1.4641 | 1.5735 | 1.6890 | 1.8106 | 1.9388 | 2.0736 |
| 5 | 1.0510 | 1.1041 | 1.1593 | 1.2167 | 1.2763 | 1.3382 | 1.4026 | 1.4693 | 1.5386 | 1.6105 | 1.7623 | 1.9254 | 2.1003 | 2.2878 | 2.4883 |
| 6 | 1.0615 | 1.1262 | 1.1941 | 1.2653 | 1.3401 | 1.4185 | 1.5007 | 1.5869 | 1.6771 | 1.7716 | 1.9738 | 2.1950 | 2.4364 | 2.6996 | 2.9860 |
| 7 | 1.0721 | 1.1487 | 1.2299 | 1.3159 | 1.4071 | 1.5036 | 1.6058 | 1.7138 | 1.8280 | 1.9487 | 2.2107 | 2.5023 | 2.8262 | 3.1855 | 3.5832 |
| 8 | 1.0829 | 1.1717 | 1.2668 | 1.3686 | 1.4775 | 1.5938 | 1.7182 | 1.8509 | 1.9926 | 2.1436 | 2.4760 | 2.8526 | 3.2784 | 3.7589 | 4.2998 |
| 9 | 1.0937 | 1.1951 | 1.3048 | 1.4233 | 1.5513 | 1.6895 | 1.8385 | 1.9990 | 2.1719 | 2.3579 | 2.7731 | 3.2519 | 3.8030 | 4.4355 | 5.1598 |
| 10 | 1.1046 | 1.2190 | 1.3439 | 1.4802 | 1.6289 | 1.7908 | 1.9672 | 2.1589 | 2.3674 | 2.5937 | 3.1058 | 3.7072 | 4.4114 | 5.2338 | 6.1917 |
| 11 | 1.1157 | 1.2434 | 1.3842 | 1.5395 | 1.7103 | 1.8983 | 2.1049 | 2.3316 | 2.5804 | 2.8531 | 3.4785 | 4.2262 | 5.1173 | 6.1759 | 7.4301 |
| 12 | 1.1268 | 1.2682 | 1.4258 | 1.6010 | 1.7959 | 2.0122 | 2.2522 | 2.5182 | 2.8127 | 3.1384 | 3.8960 | 4.8179 | 5.9360 | 7.2876 | 8.9161 |
| 13 | 1.1381 | 1.2936 | 1.4685 | 1.6651 | 1.8856 | 2.1329 | 2.4098 | 2.7196 | 3.0658 | 3.4523 | 4.3635 | 5.4924 | 6.8858 | 8.5994 | 10.6990 |
| 14 | 1.1495 | 1.3195 | 1.5126 | 1.7317 | 1.9799 | 2.2609 | 2.5785 | 2.9372 | 3.3417 | 3.7975 | 4.8871 | 6.2613 | 7.9875 | 10.1470 | 12.8390 |
| 15 | 1.1610 | 1.3459 | 1.5580 | 1.8009 | 2.0789 | 2.3966 | 2.7590 | 3.1722 | 3.6425 | 4.1772 | 5.4736 | 7.1379 | 9.2655 | 11.9740 | 15.4070 |
| 16 | 1.1726 | 1.3728 | 1.6047 | 1.8730 | 2.1829 | 2.5404 | 2.9522 | 3.4259 | 3.9703 | 4.5950 | 6.1304 | 8.1372 | 10.7480 | 14.1290 | 18.4880 |
| 17 | 1.1843 | 1.4002 | 1.6528 | 1.9479 | 2.2920 | 2.6928 | 3.1588 | 3.7000 | 4.3276 | 5.0545 | 6.8660 | 9.2765 | 12.4680 | 16.6720 | 22.1860 |
| 18 | 1.1961 | 1.4282 | 1.7024 | 2.0258 | 2.4066 | 2.8543 | 3.3799 | 3.9960 | 4.7171 | 5.5599 | 7.6900 | 10.5750 | 14.4630 | 19.6730 | 26.6230 |
| 19 | 1.2081 | 1.4568 | 1.7535 | 2.1068 | 2.5270 | 3.0256 | 3.6165 | 4.3157 | 5.1417 | 6.1159 | 8.6128 | 12.0560 | 16.7770 | 23.2140 | 31.9480 |
| 20 | 1.2202 | 1.4859 | 1.8061 | 2.1911 | 2.6533 | 3.2071 | 3.8697 | 4.6610 | 5.6044 | 6.7275 | 9.6463 | 13.7430 | 19.4610 | 27.3930 | 38.3380 |
| 21 | 1.2324 | 1.5157 | 1.8603 | 2.2788 | 2.7860 | 3.3996 | 4.1406 | 5.0338 | 6.1088 | 7.4002 | 10.8040 | 15.6680 | 22.5740 | 32.3240 | 46.0050 |
| 22 | 1.2447 | 1.5460 | 1.9161 | 2.3699 | 2.9253 | 3.6035 | 4.4304 | 5.4365 | 6.6586 | 8.1403 | 12.1000 | 17.8610 | 26.1860 | 38.1420 | 55.2060 |
| 23 | 1.2572 | 1.5769 | 1.9736 | 2.4647 | 3.0715 | 3.8197 | 4.7405 | 5.8715 | 7.2579 | 8.9543 | 13.5520 | 20.3620 | 30.3760 | 45.0080 | 66.2470 |
| 24 | 1.2697 | 1.6084 | 2.0328 | 2.5633 | 3.2251 | 4.0489 | 5.0724 | 6.3412 | 7.9111 | 9.8497 | 15.1790 | 23.2120 | 35.2360 | 53.1090 | 79.4970 |
| 25 | 1.2824 | 1.6406 | 2.0938 | 2.6658 | 3.3864 | 4.2919 | 5.4274 | 6.8485 | 8.6231 | 10.8350 | 17.0000 | 26.4620 | 40.8740 | 62.6690 | 95.3950 |

**Present Value of $1 at the End of "n" Periods**

| Periods | 1% | 2% | 3% | 4% | 5% | 6% | 7% | 8% | 9% | 10% | 12% | 14% | 16% | 18% | 20% |
|---|---|---|---|---|---|---|---|---|---|---|---|---|---|---|---|
| 1 | 0.9901 | 0.9804 | 0.9709 | 0.9615 | 0.9524 | 0.9434 | 0.9346 | 0.9259 | 0.9174 | 0.9091 | 0.8929 | 0.8772 | 0.8621 | 0.8475 | 0.8333 |
| 2 | 0.9803 | 0.9612 | 0.9426 | 0.9246 | 0.9070 | 0.8900 | 0.8734 | 0.8573 | 0.8417 | 0.8264 | 0.7972 | 0.7695 | 0.7432 | 0.7182 | 0.6944 |
| 3 | 0.9706 | 0.9423 | 0.9151 | 0.8890 | 0.8638 | 0.8396 | 0.8163 | 0.7938 | 0.7722 | 0.7513 | 0.7118 | 0.6750 | 0.6407 | 0.6086 | 0.5787 |
| 4 | 0.9610 | 0.9238 | 0.8885 | 0.8548 | 0.8227 | 0.7921 | 0.7629 | 0.7350 | 0.7084 | 0.6830 | 0.6355 | 0.5921 | 0.5523 | 0.5158 | 0.4823 |
| 5 | 0.9515 | 0.9057 | 0.8626 | 0.8219 | 0.7835 | 0.7473 | 0.7130 | 0.6806 | 0.6499 | 0.6209 | 0.5674 | 0.5194 | 0.4761 | 0.4371 | 0.4019 |
| 6 | 0.9420 | 0.8880 | 0.8375 | 0.7903 | 0.7462 | 0.7050 | 0.6663 | 0.6302 | 0.5963 | 0.5645 | 0.5066 | 0.4556 | 0.4104 | 0.3704 | 0.3349 |
| 7 | 0.9327 | 0.8706 | 0.8131 | 0.7599 | 0.7107 | 0.6651 | 0.6227 | 0.5835 | 0.5470 | 0.5132 | 0.4523 | 0.3996 | 0.3538 | 0.3139 | 0.2791 |
| 8 | 0.9235 | 0.8535 | 0.7894 | 0.7307 | 0.6768 | 0.6274 | 0.5820 | 0.5403 | 0.5019 | 0.4665 | 0.4039 | 0.3506 | 0.3050 | 0.2660 | 0.2326 |
| 9 | 0.9143 | 0.8368 | 0.7664 | 0.7026 | 0.6446 | 0.5919 | 0.5439 | 0.5002 | 0.4604 | 0.4241 | 0.3606 | 0.3075 | 0.2630 | 0.2255 | 0.1938 |
| 10 | 0.9053 | 0.8203 | 0.7441 | 0.6756 | 0.6139 | 0.5584 | 0.5083 | 0.4632 | 0.4224 | 0.3855 | 0.3220 | 0.2697 | 0.2267 | 0.1911 | 0.1615 |
| 11 | 0.8963 | 0.8043 | 0.7224 | 0.6496 | 0.5847 | 0.5268 | 0.4751 | 0.4289 | 0.3875 | 0.3505 | 0.2875 | 0.2366 | 0.1954 | 0.1619 | 0.1346 |
| 12 | 0.8874 | 0.7885 | 0.7014 | 0.6246 | 0.5568 | 0.4970 | 0.4440 | 0.3971 | 0.3555 | 0.3186 | 0.2567 | 0.2076 | 0.1685 | 0.1372 | 0.1122 |
| 13 | 0.8787 | 0.7730 | 0.6810 | 0.6006 | 0.5303 | 0.4688 | 0.4150 | 0.3677 | 0.3262 | 0.2897 | 0.2292 | 0.1821 | 0.1452 | 0.1163 | 0.0935 |
| 14 | 0.8700 | 0.7579 | 0.6611 | 0.5775 | 0.5051 | 0.4423 | 0.3878 | 0.3405 | 0.2992 | 0.2633 | 0.2046 | 0.1597 | 0.1252 | 0.0985 | 0.0779 |
| 15 | 0.8613 | 0.7430 | 0.6419 | 0.5553 | 0.4810 | 0.4173 | 0.3624 | 0.3152 | 0.2745 | 0.2394 | 0.1827 | 0.1401 | 0.1079 | 0.0835 | 0.0649 |
| 16 | 0.8528 | 0.7284 | 0.6232 | 0.5339 | 0.4581 | 0.3936 | 0.3387 | 0.2919 | 0.2519 | 0.2176 | 0.1631 | 0.1229 | 0.0930 | 0.0708 | 0.0541 |
| 17 | 0.8444 | 0.7142 | 0.6050 | 0.5134 | 0.4363 | 0.3714 | 0.3166 | 0.2703 | 0.2311 | 0.1978 | 0.1456 | 0.1078 | 0.0802 | 0.0600 | 0.0451 |
| 18 | 0.8360 | 0.7002 | 0.5874 | 0.4936 | 0.4155 | 0.3503 | 0.2959 | 0.2502 | 0.2120 | 0.1799 | 0.1300 | 0.0946 | 0.0691 | 0.0508 | 0.0376 |
| 19 | 0.8277 | 0.6864 | 0.5703 | 0.4746 | 0.3957 | 0.3305 | 0.2765 | 0.2317 | 0.1945 | 0.1635 | 0.1161 | 0.0829 | 0.0596 | 0.0431 | 0.0313 |
| 20 | 0.8195 | 0.6730 | 0.5537 | 0.4564 | 0.3769 | 0.3118 | 0.2584 | 0.2145 | 0.1784 | 0.1486 | 0.1037 | 0.0728 | 0.0514 | 0.0365 | 0.0261 |
| 21 | 0.8114 | 0.6598 | 0.5375 | 0.4388 | 0.3589 | 0.2942 | 0.2415 | 0.1987 | 0.1637 | 0.1351 | 0.0926 | 0.0638 | 0.0443 | 0.0309 | 0.0217 |
| 22 | 0.8034 | 0.6468 | 0.5219 | 0.4220 | 0.3418 | 0.2775 | 0.2257 | 0.1839 | 0.1502 | 0.1228 | 0.0826 | 0.0560 | 0.0382 | 0.0262 | 0.0181 |
| 23 | 0.7954 | 0.6342 | 0.5067 | 0.4057 | 0.3256 | 0.2618 | 0.2109 | 0.1703 | 0.1378 | 0.1117 | 0.0738 | 0.0491 | 0.0329 | 0.0222 | 0.0151 |
| 24 | 0.7876 | 0.6217 | 0.4919 | 0.3901 | 0.3101 | 0.2470 | 0.1971 | 0.1577 | 0.1264 | 0.1015 | 0.0659 | 0.0431 | 0.0284 | 0.0188 | 0.0126 |
| 25 | 0.7798 | 0.6095 | 0.4776 | 0.3751 | 0.2953 | 0.2330 | 0.1842 | 0.1460 | 0.1160 | 0.0923 | 0.0588 | 0.0378 | 0.0245 | 0.0160 | 0.0105 |

EXHIBIT I

727

Present Value of an Ordinary Annuity of $1 per Period for "n" Periods

| Periods | 1% | 2% | 3% | 4% | 5% | 6% | 7% | 8% | 9% | 10% | 12% | 14% | 16% | 18% | 20% |
|---|---|---|---|---|---|---|---|---|---|---|---|---|---|---|---|
| 1 | 0.9901 | 0.9804 | 0.9709 | 0.9615 | 0.9524 | 0.9434 | 0.9346 | 0.9259 | 0.9174 | 0.9091 | 0.8929 | 0.8772 | 0.8621 | 0.8475 | 0.8333 |
| 2 | 1.9704 | 1.9416 | 1.9135 | 1.8861 | 1.8594 | 1.8334 | 1.8080 | 1.7833 | 1.7591 | 1.7355 | 1.6901 | 1.6467 | 1.6052 | 1.5656 | 1.5278 |
| 3 | 2.9410 | 2.8839 | 2.8286 | 2.7751 | 2.7232 | 2.6730 | 2.6243 | 2.5771 | 2.5313 | 2.4869 | 2.4018 | 2.3216 | 2.2459 | 2.1743 | 2.1065 |
| 4 | 3.9020 | 3.8077 | 3.7171 | 3.6299 | 3.5460 | 3.4651 | 3.3872 | 3.3121 | 3.2397 | 3.1699 | 3.0373 | 2.9137 | 2.7982 | 2.6901 | 2.5887 |
| 5 | 4.8534 | 4.7135 | 4.5797 | 4.4518 | 4.3295 | 4.2124 | 4.1002 | 3.9927 | 3.8897 | 3.7908 | 3.6048 | 3.4331 | 3.2743 | 3.1272 | 2.9906 |
| 6 | 5.7955 | 5.6014 | 5.4172 | 5.2421 | 5.0757 | 4.9173 | 4.7665 | 4.6229 | 4.4859 | 4.3553 | 4.1114 | 3.8887 | 3.6847 | 3.4976 | 3.3255 |
| 7 | 6.7282 | 6.4720 | 6.2303 | 6.0021 | 5.7864 | 5.5824 | 5.3893 | 5.2064 | 5.0330 | 4.8684 | 4.5638 | 4.2883 | 4.0386 | 3.8115 | 3.6046 |
| 8 | 7.6517 | 7.3255 | 7.0197 | 6.7327 | 6.4632 | 6.2098 | 5.9713 | 5.7466 | 5.5348 | 5.3349 | 4.9676 | 4.6389 | 4.3436 | 4.0776 | 3.8372 |
| 9 | 8.5660 | 8.1622 | 7.7861 | 7.4353 | 7.1078 | 6.8017 | 6.5152 | 6.2469 | 5.9952 | 5.7590 | 5.3282 | 4.9464 | 4.6065 | 4.3030 | 4.0310 |
| 10 | 9.4713 | 8.9826 | 8.5302 | 8.1109 | 7.7217 | 7.3601 | 7.0236 | 6.7101 | 6.4177 | 6.1446 | 5.6502 | 5.2161 | 4.8332 | 4.4941 | 4.1925 |
| 11 | 10.3676 | 9.7868 | 9.2526 | 8.7605 | 8.3064 | 7.8869 | 7.4987 | 7.1390 | 6.8052 | 6.4951 | 5.9377 | 5.4527 | 5.0286 | 4.6560 | 4.3271 |
| 12 | 11.2551 | 10.5753 | 9.9540 | 9.3851 | 8.8633 | 8.3838 | 7.9427 | 7.5361 | 7.1607 | 6.8137 | 6.1944 | 5.6603 | 5.1971 | 4.7932 | 4.4392 |
| 13 | 12.1337 | 11.3484 | 10.6350 | 9.9856 | 9.3936 | 8.8527 | 8.3577 | 7.9038 | 7.4869 | 7.1034 | 6.4235 | 5.8424 | 5.3423 | 4.9095 | 4.5327 |
| 14 | 13.0037 | 12.1062 | 11.2961 | 10.5631 | 9.8986 | 9.2950 | 8.7455 | 8.2442 | 7.7862 | 7.3667 | 6.6282 | 6.0021 | 5.4675 | 5.0081 | 4.6106 |
| 15 | 13.8651 | 12.8493 | 11.9379 | 11.1184 | 10.3797 | 9.7122 | 9.1079 | 8.5595 | 8.0607 | 7.6061 | 6.8109 | 6.1422 | 5.5755 | 5.0916 | 4.6755 |
| 16 | 14.7179 | 13.5777 | 12.5611 | 11.6523 | 10.8378 | 10.1059 | 9.4466 | 8.8514 | 8.3126 | 7.8237 | 6.9740 | 6.2651 | 5.6685 | 5.1624 | 4.7296 |
| 17 | 15.5623 | 14.2919 | 13.1661 | 12.1657 | 11.2741 | 10.4773 | 9.7632 | 9.1216 | 8.5436 | 8.0216 | 7.1196 | 6.3729 | 5.7487 | 5.2223 | 4.7746 |
| 18 | 16.3983 | 14.9920 | 13.7535 | 12.6593 | 11.6896 | 10.8276 | 10.0591 | 9.3719 | 8.7556 | 8.2014 | 7.2497 | 6.4674 | 5.8178 | 5.2732 | 4.8122 |
| 19 | 17.2260 | 15.6785 | 14.3238 | 13.1339 | 12.0853 | 11.1581 | 10.3356 | 9.6036 | 8.9501 | 8.3649 | 7.3658 | 6.5504 | 5.8775 | 5.3162 | 4.8435 |
| 20 | 18.0456 | 16.3514 | 14.8775 | 13.5903 | 12.4622 | 11.4699 | 10.5940 | 9.8181 | 9.1285 | 8.5136 | 7.4694 | 6.6231 | 5.9288 | 5.3527 | 4.8696 |
| 21 | 18.8570 | 17.0112 | 15.4150 | 14.0292 | 12.8212 | 11.7641 | 10.8355 | 10.0168 | 9.2922 | 8.6487 | 7.5620 | 6.6870 | 5.9731 | 5.3837 | 4.8913 |
| 22 | 19.6604 | 17.6580 | 15.9369 | 14.4511 | 13.1630 | 12.0416 | 11.0612 | 10.2007 | 9.4424 | 8.7715 | 7.6446 | 6.7429 | 6.0113 | 5.4099 | 4.9094 |
| 23 | 20.4558 | 18.2922 | 16.4436 | 14.8568 | 13.4886 | 12.3034 | 11.2722 | 10.3741 | 9.5802 | 8.8832 | 7.7184 | 6.7921 | 6.0442 | 5.4321 | 4.9245 |
| 24 | 21.2434 | 18.9139 | 16.9355 | 15.2470 | 13.7986 | 12.5504 | 11.4693 | 10.5288 | 9.7066 | 8.9847 | 7.7843 | 6.8351 | 6.0726 | 5.4509 | 4.9371 |
| 25 | 22.0232 | 19.5235 | 17.4131 | 15.6221 | 14.0939 | 12.7834 | 11.6536 | 10.6748 | 9.8226 | 9.0770 | 7.8431 | 6.8729 | 6.0971 | 5.4669 | 4.9476 |

# EXHIBIT II

## PROBLEMS INVOLVING FUTURE AND PRESENT VALUE
### (With Answers and Explanations)

The following problems illustrate the concepts of present value and future value. All numbers (including present and future value factors) other than dollar amounts are rounded to the fourth decimal. Dollar amounts are rounded to the second decimal. *Refer to the tables in Exhibit I for all future and present value factors.* **Answers to these problems appear at the end of this exhibit.**

1. Exxon Mobil Corporation (ticker symbol: EXO) is engaged in the exploration, production, manufacture, transportation and sale of crude oil, natural gas, and petroleum products, as well as the manufacture of packaging films and specialty chemicals. This year, EXO paid a cash dividend of $1.00 per share. You believe that management will increase the cash dividend at 6% per year. Therefore, what amount do you expect EXO to pay out in cash dividends per share seven years from now?

2. Lisa's parents want to set up a trust fund for Lisa with $75,000. Assume that the principal value of the trust will appreciate at 8% annual-

728

*EXHIBIT II*     729

ly, compounded semi-annually. How much money will the trust fund have at the end of 10 years?

3. In 1803, the United States purchased Louisiana (which comprised not only Louisiana, but most of middle America) for $11,250,000 and assumed claims of its own citizens against France of up to $3,750,000, for a total purchase price of $15 million. Suppose that the annual inflation rate for the time period between 1803 and 2011 was 3%. How much would the $15 million purchase price be worth in 2011 based on annual compounding?

4. Ever since Sandra was a child, she wanted to drive a Porsche. After graduating from the University of Michigan in 2007, Sandra went to work for a hedge fund called Short Term Capital Management (STCM). After working for STCM for 4 years, Sandra had managed to save $100,000. She went shopping for Porsches and found a Porsche 911 for $110,000. Sandra estimated that the sticker price of a new Porsche 911 usually increases 6% annually after consulting several Porsche salespersons and reading various car magazines. Sandra cannot afford to purchase the Porsche 911 at this juncture, but wants to invest the $100,000 that she has saved in a security that will enable her to buy a new Porsche 911 in three years. What rate of return must Sandra obtain so that she can afford to purchase the car in three years?

5. Evan would like to buy a boat five years from now. He estimates that the boat will cost $450,000 at that time. Evan could earn 5% by investing in municipal bonds (assume there are no transaction costs associated with the purchase and sale of municipal bonds). How much money does Evan have to invest today in order to buy the boat in five years?

6. On November 23, 2011, Jet Blue Airways sold zero coupon debt securities to the public. Pursuant to the terms of the deal, Jet Blue Airways would pay each holder $2,000 per security on November 22, 2021, but nothing before that. Each security was originally sold for $1,000. What rate of return is Jet Blue Airways implicitly offering to its investors who bought these securities?

7. Katie is interested in rhinoplasty to enhance the appearance of her nose. Rhinoplasty costs $4,000 today and has consistently increased in price over the last 10 years at a 5% rate. How much money would Katie have to invest today in a security that yields 9% in order to obtain rhinoplasty in five years, assuming the price of rhinoplasty continues to increase 5% annually?

8. Rodney's mother-in-law offered Rodney $5,000,000 to quit smoking, drinking, gambling, excessively eating, and using foul language during a five-year period. Rodney's mother-in-law has located an investment in which she will earn 10% per annum, compounded semi-annual-

*EXHIBIT II* 731

ly. How much money should Rodney's mother-in-law put in this investment so that she can pay Rodney the $5,000,000 at the end of five years?

9. In 2011, Robert and Lisa gave birth to twins. Although the current annual rate of inflation is 1.5%, private college tuition is presently increasing at an average of 6% annually. If private college tuition continues to increase at the same rate, how much will Robert and Lisa need to put away in 2011 in order to pay the first year of a private college for both children in 2029? Assume Robert and Lisa can find an investment that will return 8% annually and the current cost of one year of private college tuition is $45,000 per student.

10. The New York Jets want to sign Quinn Stevens, a third round draft choice, as their quarterback of the future. The Jets offered Stevens $1,600,000 up front *or* $400,000 per year for the next 5 years. Assuming a discount rate of 9%, which payment schedule is economically more beneficial to Stevens?

11. Josh was a passenger in a taxi cab one night. The taxi driver negligently ran a red light and collided with a bus. Josh broke his arm and tore his rotator cuff. Josh sued the taxi company, and shortly thereafter the taxi company and Josh entered into settlement negotiations. The taxi company offered Josh either $125,000 in one lump sum payment *or* $15,000 a year

for the following 10 years. Assuming a discount rate of 3%, which payment method would benefit Josh from a purely financial perspective?

12. Warren owns a farm on the east end of Long Island. For the past 10 years Warren has leased the premises to a farmer and his family. Prices for real estate, however, have increased dramatically. Warren wants to realize his gains in real estate while the market remains at a relatively high level. A non-profit organization approached Warren about buying his farm. The non-profit organization offered Warren either $3,000,000 up front *or* $250,000 a year for the following 15 years. Which deal is more appealing to Warren from a financial perspective assuming a discount rate of 4%?

13. Chuck is the owner of Legend Inc., a company specializing in designing, manufacturing and marketing handbags and accessories. Chuck has been negotiating with K–Mart for several weeks with respect to the sale of 150,000 backpacks. Consummation of the deal has been held up over a dispute on how to structure the financing. K–Mart has offered to pay Legend $300,000 annually for seven years. Chuck, on the other hand, wants K–Mart to pay Legend $1,200,000 in one lump sum because he believes K–Mart may go back into bankruptcy. The current discount rate is 14%. What is the

*EXHIBIT II*     733

numeric difference in today's dollars between the two types of financing?

14. Assume the same facts as in question 13, and that Legend is not selling as many products as Chuck had thought. As a result, Chuck is desperate to make the sale to K–Mart regardless of the financing structure. Consequently, Chuck has accepted K–Mart's offer to pay $300,000 annually over seven years. However, K–Mart now wants to pay $300,000 annually with the interest compounded quarterly. What is the present value of $300,000 annual payments over seven years at a discount rate of 14% based on quarterly compounding?

15. Assume the same facts as in question 13, but assume further that Chuck has accepted K–Mart's offer to make $300,000 payments annually over seven years at a discount rate of 14% compounded annually. Payments, however, are to be made in the beginning of each year rather than at the end. What is the present value of this stream of payments (round to the second decimal throughout the question)?

16. General Electric (GE) would like to expand its numerous businesses with $5 billion raised through the issuance of debt securities. Specifically, GE will issue interest-only bonds to the public with 30 years to maturity, a 3.5% coupon rate, and a $1,000 face value in one week. David Dami is planning on purchasing some of the GE bonds. However, he also believes that

interest rates for high grade corporate debt will increase to 7% within five years. How much money would David Dami lose if he were to buy $10,000 worth of GE's 30–year bonds at issuance and sell them in five years in the secondary market if his assumption about interest rates comes true?

17. Martin Sloane Telecom Corp. (MSTC) must raise funds to finance its operations in the near term or it will experience a liquidity crises that may result in bankruptcy. MSTC is in the midst of a strong marketing campaign to sell junk-rated, interest-only corporate debentures with a 10% coupon, a $1,000 face value and 15 years until maturity. Brent Friedman is entertaining the thought of purchasing some of these bonds in the next couple of weeks because he believes that the market interest rate for telecom corporate debt will decrease to 6% in four years. If Friedman is accurate in his assumptions, what is the dollar amount of the premium he would make four years from now if he invests $3,000,000 in MSTC's debenture offering and sells his investment in four years in the secondary market?

18. Mark Wiener earns a living buying and selling bonds. Suppose Wiener located an interest-only, 20–year bond with a 93:19 bid price. The bond was issued by Pfizer 10 years ago with an

*EXHIBIT II*        735

8% coupon rate. What is the yield to maturity for this particular bond today?

19. Tribeca Capital Management, a private equity fund, has liabilities that require it to pay $15,000 at the end of 6 years from today, and $22,000 at the end of 7 years from today, leaving nothing in the account from which it is to pay off those liabilities. If Tribeca Capital Management can earn 5% per annum on that account, how much must it deposit today to satisfy the liabilities when they come due?

20. Ginny makes a deposit of $30,000 into a high yield savings account. The deposit is to earn interest at the rate of 8% per annum compounded quarterly for 4 years. How much will Ginny have in the account at the end of 4 years? How much less would she earn if interest was compounded only annually?

## Answers and Explanations

1. $FV_n$ = $x (1 + k)^n$
   = $\$1.00 (1.06)^7$
   = $\$1.00 (1.5036)$
   = <u>$\$1.50$ per share</u>

This question illustrates the future value of a lump sum compounded annually. It requires the student to calculate the future value of a $1.00 cash dividend in seven years assuming management increases the cash dividend 6% every year. Because seven years is the time period during which you expect management to increase the dividend annually, "n" equals 7. The rate of return "k" is 6% (or .06 expressed as a decimal), because you believe management is going to increase the dividend 6% annually. Based on the calculations above, EXO's cash dividend is expected to be $1.50 per share in seven years if EXO increases it 6% annually over the next seven years.

2. $FV_n$ = $x (1 + k/m)^{n \cdot m}$
      = $\$75,000 (1 + .08/2)^{10 \cdot 2}$
      = $75,000 (2.1911)
      = $164,332.50

This question requires the student to calculate the future value of $75,000 in 10 years at an 8% annual rate of return, compounded semi-annually. Because 10 years is the time period during which the trust fund is expected to appreciate, "n" equals 10 years. The rate of return "k" of the trust fund is 8% (or .08 expressed as a decimal). Because the trust fund's rate of return is compounded semi-annually, "m" is equal to 2. Based on the calculations above, the trust fund will have $164,332.50 at the end of 10 years.

3. $FV_n$ = $x (1 + k)^n$
      = $\$15,000,000 (1.03)^{208}$
      = $15,000,000 (467.8889)
      = $7,018,333,500 or $7.018 billion

This question illustrates the future value of a lump sum compounded annually. It requires the student to calculate the future value of $15 million

*EXHIBIT II* 737

over 208 years at a rate of return of 3%. Because 208 years is the time period, "n" equals 208. The rate of return "k" is the rate of inflation, which is 3% (or .03 when expressed as a decimal). You must use a financial calculator to make this calculation, because the table in Exhibit I only covers up to 25 time periods. Based on the calculations above, the future value of the Louisiana Purchase in 2011 is approximately $7.018 billion. Did the United States get a good deal? Consider that in 2008 the U.S. Government bailed out American International Group, Inc. (AIG) by creating an *$85 billion* credit facility to enable AIG to meet increased collateral obligations resulting from its credit rating down-grade!

4. This problem is solved in two steps.

*Step One:* Determine the future value of a Porsche 911 in three years.

$$
\begin{aligned}
FV_n &= x(1 + k)^n \\
&= \$110,000(1 + .06)^3 \\
&= \$110,000(1.1910) \\
&= \$131,010.00
\end{aligned}
$$

*Step Two:* Determine the rate of return required in order to purchase the Porsche 911 in three years.

$$
\begin{aligned}
FV_n &= x(1 + k)^n \\
131,010 &= \$100,000(1 + k)^3 \\
1.3101 &= (1 + k)^3 \\
1.3101^{.33} &= 1 + k \\
1.0932 &= 1 + k \\
\underline{.0932} \text{ or } \underline{9.32\%} &= k
\end{aligned}
$$

This question requires the student to perform two steps. First, the student must determine the future value of a new Porsche 911 three years from now. Because three years is the time period in which Sandra would like to purchase the Porsche 911, "n" equals 3 years. The present value of the car is $110,000, so "x" equals $110,000. The sticker price of a Porsche 911 increases 6% annually, so "k" equals 6% (.06 expressed as a decimal). Based on the calculations in step one above, the Porsche 911 will cost $131,010 in three years.

Second, once the future value of the Porsche 911 is calculated, the student must determine the rate of return required from a security that would enable Sandra to invest $100,000 today and have a future value of $131,010 in three years. (A financial calculator is needed for the calculations in step two above.) An understanding of the concepts of future value and present value is needed in order to calculate the rate of return necessary for a specific time period. The present value of $100,000 is given, and the future value of $131,010 was just calculated in step one. The time period "n" is also specified at 3 years. Accordingly, Sandra would need a security with a rate of return of 9.32% compounded annually to achieve her goal.

*EXHIBIT II*      739

5.    PV    =    $\dfrac{x_n}{(1 + k)^n}$

          =    $\dfrac{\$450,000}{(1 + .05)^5}$

          =    $\$450,000 \times .7835$

          =    $\underline{\$352,575.00}$

This question illustrates the present value of a lump sum compounded annually. It requires the student to calculate how much money Evan would need to invest today in order to have $450,000 in five years to buy a boat if he earns 5% per annum on his money. The time period "n" is 5 years. The rate of return per annum "k" is 5% (or .05 expressed as a decimal). Based on the calculations above, Evan must invest $352,575 for five years at 5% per annum in order to have $450,000 to buy the boat on that future date.

6.                  PV    =    $\dfrac{x_n}{(1 + k)^n}$

                $\$1,000$    =    $\dfrac{\$2,000}{(1 + k)^{10}}$

     $\$1,000\,(1 + k)^{10}$    =    $\$2,000$

         $(1 + k)^{10}$    =    $2$

            $1 + k$    =    $2^{.1}$

            $1 + k$    =    $1.0718$

                $k$    =    $\underline{.0718}$ or $\underline{7.18\%}$

This question illustrates the present value of a lump sum compounded annually. It requires the student to calculate the rate of return "k" inherent in a present value calculation when she is given the present value, future value and time period. Here, the student must be able to determine that $1,000 is the price paid by investors for each security, and thus represents its present value. $2,000 is the amount that the investor will receive for each security at the end of the time period, and thus represents its future value. The time period "n" is 10 years. Based on the calculations above, the rate of return is 7.18%. For an explanation of zero coupon debt securities, see Nutshell Section 16.

7.   This problem is solved in two steps.

*Step One:* Determine the future value of rhinoplasty in five years.

$$FV_n = x (1 + k)^n$$

$$= \$4,000 (1 + .05)^5$$

$$= \$4,000 (1.2763)$$

$$= \$5,105.20$$

*Step Two:* Determine the present value of $5,105.20 payable five years from today at a 9% discount rate.

*EXHIBIT II*                    741

$$PV = \frac{x_n}{(1 + k)^n}$$

$$= \frac{\$5,105.20}{(1 + .09)^5}$$

$$= \$5,105.20 \times .6499$$

$$= \underline{\$3,317.87}$$

This question requires the student to perform two steps. First, the student must calculate the future value of \$4,000 at an annual rate of appreciation of 5% for five years. Five percent is the rate of appreciation, and thus "k" equals 5% (.05 expressed as a decimal). The time period "n" is 5 years. The present value is \$4,000. Based on the calculations in step one above, the future value of \$4,000 at an annual rate of appreciation of 5% for five years is \$5,105.20.

The second step requires the student to determine the present value of the future sum of \$5,105.20 assuming Katie is able to locate an investment with a 9% annual yield. Nine percent is the discount rate, and thus "k" equals 9% (.09 expressed as a decimal). "n" is 5 since the life of the investment is five years. Based on the calculations in step two above, the present value of the future sum of \$5,105.20 assuming a 9% discount rate over five years is \$3,317.87.

8. $PV$ = $\dfrac{x_n}{(1 + k/m)^{n \cdot m}}$

= $\dfrac{\$5,000,000}{(1 + .10/2)^{5 \cdot 2}}$

= $\$5,000,000 \times .6139$

= $\underline{\$3,069,500.00}$

This question requires the student to determine the present value of a lump sum payment when given the future value, rate of return and time period. Here, the student should calculate the present value of $5,000,000 payable five years from now at a discount rate of 10% compounded semi-annually. "n" is 5 since the investment has a five year life. "k" is 10% (.10 expressed as a decimal) since the annual rate of return is 10%. "m" is 2 since the discount rate is compounded semi-annually. Based on the calculations above, Rodney's mother-in-law must set aside $3,069,500 if she is going to adhere to the contract assuming Rodney complies with his end of the bargain.

9. This problem is solved in three steps.

*Step One:* Determine the cost of tuition in 18 years.

$FV_n$ = $x (1 + k)^n$

= $\$45,000 (1.06)^{18}$

= $\$45,000 (2.8543)$

= $\$128,443.50$

*Step Two:* Multiply the number derived in step one by two because there are two children.

*EXHIBIT II*          743

$128,443.50 x 2 = $256,887.00

*Step Three:* Determine the amount to be invested today in order to have $256,887 in 18 years.

$$PV = \frac{x_n}{(1 + k)^n}$$

$$= \frac{\$256,887}{(1.08)^{18}}$$

$$= \$256,887 \times .2502$$

$$= \underline{\$64,273.13}$$

This question integrates the concepts of both future value and present value. Step one requires the student to calculate the future value of private college tuition for one child. The student is given the amount of tuition for the present time period, which is equal to $45,000. Private college tuition is increasing annually at an average rate ("k") of 6% (.06 expressed as a decimal). Finally, the time period "n" is 18 years. Based on the calculation in step one above, the future value of $45,000 increasing at an annual rate of 6% for 18 years is $128,443.50.

The second step requires the student to multiply $128,443.50 by two (a total cost of $256,877) because Robert and Lisa have twins.

The third step requires the student to calculate the amount that Robert and Lisa would need to put aside today in order to ensure that they can pay for the first year of tuition for their twins. The future value is equal to $256,877, which was calculated in the first two steps of the question. The time period "n" is 18 years. Since Robert and Lisa were able to locate an investment which yields 8%, "k" equals 8% (.08 expressed as a decimal). Based on the calculations in step three above, Robert and Lisa need to set aside $64,273.13 today in an investment yielding 8% annually for 18 years in order to pay for their twins first year of private college (a bill of $256,887). Perhaps Robert and Lisa should consider putting away money for years two, three and four as well!

10.   This problem is solved in two steps.

*Step One:* Calculate the present value of the ordinary annuity.

$$PV_a = \sum \frac{x_n}{(1+k)^n}$$

$$= \sum \frac{\$400,000}{(1.09)^5}$$

$$= \$400,000 \times 3.8897$$

$$= \$1,555,880.00$$

*Step Two:* Compare present values of the two alternative payments.

$$\underline{\$1,600,000} > \$1,555,880$$

Stevens should choose the lump sum payment.

This question requires the student to calculate the present value of an ordinary annuity over a five year period when the discount rate is 9%. The

*EXHIBIT II* 745

present value factor for an ordinary annuity when "n" is equal to five years and the discount rate is 9% compounded annually is 3.8897. Based on the comparison in step two, Stevens should take the $1.6 million unless tax consequences or other considerations dictate otherwise.

11.  This problem is solved in two steps.

*Step One:* Calculate the present value of the ordinary annuity.

$$PV_a = \sum \frac{x_n}{(1 + k)^n}$$

$$= \sum \frac{\$15,000}{(1.03)^{10}}$$

$$= \$15,000 \times 8.5302$$

$$= \$127,953.00$$

*Step Two:* Compare present values of the alternative payments.

$$\underline{\$127,953} > \$125,000$$

Josh should take the annuity.

This question requires the student to calculate the present value of an ordinary annuity over a 10–year period when the discount rate is 3%. The present value factor for an ordinary annuity when "n" is equal to 10 years and the discount rate is 3% compounded annually is 8.5302. Based on the comparison in step two, Josh should take the $15,000 a year annuity unless tax consequences or other considerations dictate otherwise.

12.   This problem is solved in two steps.

*Step One:* Calculate the present value of the ordinary annuity.

$$PV_a = \sum \frac{x_n}{(1 + k)^n}$$

$$= \sum \frac{\$250,000}{(1.04)^{15}}$$

$$= \$250,000 \times 11.1184$$

$$= \$2,779,600.00$$

*Step Two:* Compare present values of the alternative payments.

$$\underline{\$3,000,000} > \$2,779,600$$

Warren should take the lump sum payment.

This question requires the student to calculate the present value of an ordinary annuity over a 15–year period when the discount rate is 4%. The present value factor of an ordinary annuity when "n" is equal to 15 years and the discount rate is 4% compounded annually is 11.1184. Based on the comparison in step two, Warren should take the $3,000,000 today unless tax consequences or other considerations dictate otherwise.

13.   This problem is solved in two steps.

*EXHIBIT II* 747

*Step One:* Calculate the present value of the ordinary annuity.

$$PV_a \ = \ \sum \ \frac{x_n}{(1 + k)^n}$$

$$= \ \sum \ \frac{\$300,000}{(1.14)^7}$$

$$= \ \$300,000 \ \times \ 4.2883$$

$$= \ \$1,286,490.00$$

*Step Two:* Determine the difference between the annuity and the lump sum payment.

$$\$1,286,490 \ - \ \$1,200,000 \ = \ \underline{\$86,490}$$

This question requires the student to calculate the present value of an ordinary annuity over a seven year period when the discount rate is 14%. The present value of annual payments of \$300,000 when "n" is equal to 7 and the discount rate "k" is equal to 14% (.14 expressed as a decimal) is \$1,286,490. The numeric difference in dollars between the two types of financing is thus \$86,490, with the receipt of \$300,000 annually for seven years being the better deal.

14.  This problem is solved in two steps.

*Step One:* Determine the Effective Annual Interest Rate (EAIR).

$$\text{EAIR} = (1 + i/m)^m - 1$$

$$= (1 + .14/4)^4 - 1$$

$$= 1.1475 - 1$$

$$= .1475 \text{ or } 14.75\%$$

*Step Two:* Determine $PV_a$ using EAIR as the discount rate.

$$PV_a = \sum \frac{x_n}{(1 + k)^n}$$

$$= \sum \frac{\$300,000}{(1.1475)^7}$$

$$= \$300,000 \times 4.1918$$

$$= \underline{\$1,257,540.00}$$

This question illustrates that when interest is compounded more frequently than annually for ordinary annuities, the present value is less than when the interest is compounded annually. In order to calculate the present value when interest is compounded more frequently than annually, two steps are involved. First, the student must calculate the effective annual interest rate (EAIR). Here, the discount rate ("i") is 14% (.14 expressed as a decimal). Since interest is compounded on a quarterly basis, "m" is equal to 4. Based on the calculations in step one above, "EAIR" is equal to .1475. A financial calculator is helpful in making this calculation. The second step requires the student to

*EXHIBIT II* 749

perform the calculation for an ordinary annuity, except that "k" is replaced with EAIR. Students will need a financial calculator to make the calculation. Based on the calculations in step two above, the present value of this annuity is $1,257,540.

15. The formula for calculating an "annuity due" is:

$$PV_{ad} = \sum \frac{x_n}{(1 + k)^n} \cdot (1 + k)$$

An "annuity due" is calculated in two steps:

*Step One:* Calculate the present value of an ordinary annuity:

$$PV_a = \sum \frac{x_n}{(1 + k)^n}$$

$$= \sum \frac{\$300,000}{(1.14)^7}$$

$$= \$300,000 \times 4.2883$$

$$= \$1,286,490.00$$

*Step Two:* Multiply the present value of the ordinary annuity by 1 plus the discount rate:

$$PV_{ad} = \$1,286,490 \times (1 + .14)$$

$$= \$1,286,490 \times (1.14)$$

$$= \underline{\$1,466,598.60}$$

This question illustrates the difference between an ordinary annuity and an annuity due. In an ordinary annuity, payments are made at the end of each period or in *arrears*. By contrast, in an annuity due the payments are made in the beginning of each period. The calculation of an annuity due is the same as for an ordinary annuity except that the result must be multiplied by 1 plus the discount rate. First, the student must calculate the present value of an ordinary annuity over a seven year period when the discount rate is 14%. Based on the calculations in step one above, the present value of annual payments of $300,000 when "n" is equal to 7 years and the discount rate "k" is equal to 14% (.14 expressed as a decimal) is $1,286,490. Second, the student must multiply the present value of the ordinary annuity calculated in step one by 1 plus the discount rate (14%). Based on the calculation in step two above, the present value of the annuity due is $1,466,598.60.

16.  This problem is solved in five steps.

*Step One:* Calculate the present value of a bond's face value of $1,000 discounted at 7% for the remaining 25–year life of the bond:

*EXHIBIT II* 751

$$PV = \frac{x_n}{(1 + k)^n}$$

$$= \frac{\$1,000}{(1.07)^{25}}$$

$$= \$1,000 \text{ x } .1842$$

$$= \$184.20$$

*Step Two:* Calculate the present value of a bond's interest payments over the remaining 25 years using a discount rate of 7%. Recall that the bond pays \$35 [.035 x \$1,000] annually. Thus:

$$PV_a = \sum \frac{x_n}{(1 + k)^n}$$

$$= \sum \frac{\$35}{(1.07)^{25}}$$

$$= \$35 \text{ x } 11.6536$$

$$= \$407.88$$

*Step Three:* Add the two present values together:

$$PV_{bond} = \$184.20 + \$407.88$$

$$= \$592.08$$

*Step Four:* Because David Dami purchased ten GE bonds, multiply \$592.08 by 10 to determine the total value of his bonds five years from now:

$$\$592.08 \text{ x } 10 = \$5,920.80$$

*Step Five:* Subtract Dami's \$10,000 initial investment from his bonds' current value of \$5,920.80:

$$\$5,920.80 - \$10,000 = \underline{(\$4,079.20)} \ \ (\text{loss})$$

This question requires the student to perform a bond valuation on a GE bond after five years have passed and the interest rate on similar, newly-issued bonds has risen to 7%. In step one, the student must calculate the present value of the face value of a GE bond. The market interest rate "k" is 7% (.07 expressed as a decimal). The number of years to maturity "n" is 25. Based on the calculations in step one above, the face value of $1,000 when discounted by 7% over 25 years is $184.20.

Step two requires the student to calculate the present value of the interest payments on a GE bond. The coupon payment is $35 because GE agreed to pay a 3.5% coupon rate at issuance. The present value of an annuity factor when "n" is equal to 25 years and the discount rate is 7% (.07 expressed as a decimal) is 11.6536. Based on the calculations in step two above, the present value of the coupon payments is $407.88.

Step three requires the student to add the present value of the face value, $184.20, to the present value of the interest payments, $407.88, which equals $592.08.

In step four, the student must multiply $592.08 by 10 because David Dami is purchasing ten GE bonds at issuance.

In the final step, the student must subtract Dami's original investment of $10,000 from its current value of $5,920.80. Accordingly, David Dami

*EXHIBIT II* 753

will lose $4,079.20 if he buys $10,000 worth of the GE 30–year bonds at issuance and sells them in five years if his assumptions about interest rates turn out to be accurate.

17.   This problem is solved in five steps.

*Step One:* Calculate the present value of a MSTC debenture's face value of $1,000 discounted at 6% for the remaining 11–year life of the debenture:

$$PV = \frac{x_n}{(1 + k)^n}$$

$$= \frac{\$1,000}{(1.06)^{11}}$$

$$= \$1,000 \times .5268$$

$$= \$526.80$$

*Step Two:* Calculate the present value of a debenture's interest payments over the remaining 11 years using a discount rate of 6%. Recall that a MSTC debenture pays $100 [.10 x $1,000] annually. Thus:

$$PV_a = \sum \frac{x_n}{(1 + k)^n}$$

$$= \sum \frac{\$100}{(1.06)^{11}}$$

$$= \$100 \times 7.8869$$

$$= \$788.69$$

*Step Three:* Add the two present values together:

$$PV_{debenture} = \$526.80 + \$788.69$$

$$= \$1,315.49$$

*Step Four:* Because Brent Friedman purchased 3,000 MSTC debentures, multiply $1,315.49 by 3,000 to determine the total value of his debentures four years from now:

$$\$1,315.49 \times 3,000 = \$3,946,470.00$$

*Step Five:* Subtract Friedman's $3,000,000 initial investment from his debentures' current value of $3,946,470:

$$\$3,946,470 - \$3,000,000 = \underline{\$946,470} \text{ (profit)}$$

This question requires the student to perform a valuation on a 15–year debenture after four years have passed and the interest rate on similar, newly-issued debentures has decreased to 6%. In step one, the student must calculate the present value of the face value of a MSTC debenture. The market inter-

*EXHIBIT II* 755

est rate "r" is 6% (.06 expressed as a decimal). The number of years to maturity, "n," is 11. Based on the calculations in step one above, the face value of $1,000 when discounted by 6% over 11 years is $526.80.

The second step requires the student to calculate the present value of the interest payments on a MSTC debenture. The coupon payment is $100 because MSTC agreed to pay a 10% coupon rate at issuance. The present value of an annuity factor when "n" is equal to 11 years and the discount rate is 6% (.06 when expressed as a decimal) is 7.8869. Based on the calculations in step two above, the present value of the coupon payments is $788.69.

The third step requires the student to add the present value of the face value, $526.80, to the present value of the interest payments, $788.69, which equals $1,315.49.

The fourth step requires the student to multiply $1,315.49 by 3,000 because Brent Friedman is purchasing 3,000 MSTC debentures at issuance.

The fifth step requires the student to subtract Friedman's original investment of $3,000,000 from it current value of $3,946,470. Friedman will make a profit of $946,470 if he buys 3,000 MSTC 15–year debentures at issuance and sells them in four years in the secondary market if his assumptions about interest rates turn out to be accurate.

18.   This problem is solved in two steps.

*Step One:* Translate a 93:19 bid price into a dollar amount:

As seen in Nutshell Section 17, 93:19 means 93 19/32 or 93.59375. This means the price of the bond is 93.59375% of its $1,000 face value. Therefore, the bond's current price is $935.94 [$1,000 x .9359375] (rounded to the penny).

*Step Two:* Use a financial calculator to determine yield to maturity:

The answer is 8.99%.

Because the bond is trading at a discount to its $1,000 face value, its yield to maturity has to be greater than the bond's coupon rate of 8%. See Nutshell Section 14A. To calculate yield to maturity on a financial calculator, the usual method is: enter $80 as the coupon payment (PMT); 10 as the number of periods (n); $935.94 as the present value (PV); and $1,000 as the future value (FV). The final step is to solve for the interest rate (i). The answer is 8.99%.

19. This problem is solved in three steps.

*Step One:* Calculate the present value of the $15,000 payment due at the end of 6 years:

$$PV = \frac{x_n}{(1 + k)^n}$$

$$= \frac{\$15,000}{(1.05)^6}$$

$$= \$15,000 \text{ x } .7462$$

$$= \$11,193.00$$

*EXHIBIT II*     757

*Step Two:* Calculate the present value of the $22,000 payment due at the end of 7 years:

$$PV = \frac{x_n}{(1 + k)^n}$$

$$= \frac{\$22,000}{(1.05)^7}$$

$$= \$22,000 \times .7107$$

$$= \$15,635.40$$

*Step Three:* Add the two present values together:

$$PV_{both\ payments} = \$11,193.00 + \$15,635.40$$
$$= \underline{\$26,828.40}$$

This question requires the student to calculate the present values of two payments—one due 6 years from now and the other due 7 years from now. In step one, the student must calculate the present value of the $15,000 payment due 6 years from now assuming 5% interest per annum. Thus, the interest rate "k" is 5% (.05 expressed as a decimal). The number of years "n" is 6. Based on the calculations in step one above, the present value of the $15,000 payment when discounted by 5% over 6 years is $11,193.00.

In step two, the student must calculate the present value of the $22,000 payment due 7 years from now assuming 5% interest per annum. Thus, the interest rate "k" is 5% (.05 expressed as a decimal). The number of years "n" is 7. Based on the calculations in step two above, the present value of the $22,000 payment when discounted by 5% over 7 years is $15,635.40.

Step three requires the student to add the present value of the $15,000 payment ($11,193.00) to the present value of the $22,000 payment ($15,635.40), which equals $26,828.40.

20. This problem is solved in three steps.

*Step One:* Determine the future value of $30,000 in 4 years at an 8% annual rate of return, compounded *quarterly*:

$$\begin{aligned} FV_n &= x\,(1 + k/m)^{n \cdot m} \\ &= \$30,000\,(1 + .08/4)^{4 \cdot 4} \\ &= \$30,000\,(1.3728) \\ &= \$41,184.00 \end{aligned}$$

*Step Two:* Determine the future value of $30,000 in 4 years at an 8% annual rate of return, compounded *annually*:

$$\begin{aligned} FV_n &= x\,(1 + k)^{n} \\ &= \$30,000\,(1.08)^{4} \\ &= \$30,000\,(1.3605) \\ &= \$40,815.00 \end{aligned}$$

*Step Three:* Subtract the answer in Step Two from the answer in Step One:

$$\$41,184.00 - \$40,815.00 = \underline{\$369.00}$$

This question explores the mathematical difference between annual compounding and quarterly

*EXHIBIT II* 759

compounding. In step one, the student must calculate the future value of $30,000 in 4 years at an 8% annual rate of return, compounded *quarterly*. Thus, the interest rate "k" is 8% (.08 expressed as a decimal). The number of years "n" is 4. The frequency of compounding "m" is also 4 (*i.e.*, four quarterly periods). Based on the calculations in step one above, the future value of $30,000 in 4 years at an 8% annual rate of return, compounded quarterly, is $41,184.00.

In step two, the student must calculate the future value of $30,000 in 4 years at an 8% annual rate of return, compounded *annually*. Thus, the interest rate "k" is 8% (.08 expressed as a decimal). The number of years "n" is 4. The frequency of compounding "m" does not factor into the calculation, as the normal formula for calculating future value is used. Based on the calculations in step two above, the future value of $30,000 in 4 years at an 8% annual rate of return, compounded annually, is $40,815.00.

Step three requires the student to subtract the amount determined using annual compounding in Step Two ($40,815.00) from the amount determined using quarterly compounding in Step One ($41,184.00), which equals $369.00. This positive difference makes intuitive sense, because the more frequent the compounding is in a future value context, the higher your future value will be.

# INDEX

**References are to Pages**

# A

# B

# C

# E

# F

# M

# N

# O

# P

# R

# T

# U

# V

†